THE RISE OF ASIAN DESIGN 進んでるアジアのデザイン
떠오르는 아시아 디사인 亚洲设计新世代

HKDA Awards 05 香港設計師協會獎 05
Endorsed by ICOGRADA / 國際平面設計社團協會認可

Art Director : SK Lam
Editor : Editor/AllRightsReserved, Chloe Tang, Janet Lui
Associate Editor : Charles Ng, Eddy Yu, Cherry Yeung, Tony Mak
Copywriter : Cherise Fong
Senior Designer : Yan Ho
Designer : Lok Chan
Marketing : Portia So
Production Manager : Gary Lau and Ka Ming

Published by AllRightsReserved
w : www.allrights-reserved.com
e : info@allrights-reserved.com
t : 852 2712 0873
f : 852 2712 6701

Associate Publisher : Hong Kong Designers Association
a : GPO Box 9780 Hong Kong
w : www.hongkongda.com
e : info@hongkongda.com

First published in Hong Kong in 2005
Printed by Vision and Mission Co. Ltd.
ISBN 988-97054-7-8

Copyright ©2005 by "AllRightsReserved Ltd." All rights reserved.
No part of this publication may be reproduced, stored in a retrieval system
or transmitted in any form or by any means, electronic or mechanical,
including photocopying, recording or any information storage and retrieval
systems, without the written permission of the publisher.
While every effort has been made to ensure the accuracy of captions
and credits in this book, "AllRightsReserved Ltd." does not under any
circumstances accept any responsibility for errors or omissions.

Contents
目錄

Sponsors 鳴謝	004
Board of Advisors and Committee 顧問團及籌委會	005
Chairman's Message 主席致辭	006
About the Awards 關於本獎	010
Judges 評審委員	012
Judges' Commentary & Choices 評審委員會特選作品及評語	019
Gold Awards 金獎作品	045
Publication 出版物及刊物	068
Promotion 宣傳品	120
Poster 海報	176
Visual Identity 視覺形象系統	294
Illustration & Photography 插圖及攝影	352
Character Design 模型人偶及造像	370
Environmental Graphic 環境圖象	382
Product 產品設計	394
Spatial 空間設計	420
New Media 新媒體	450
Entries Statistics 入選者統計數據	466
Awardees' Statistics 得獎者統計數據	467
Entrants Appendix 入選者附錄	470
Members Appendix 會員附錄	476

Organizer:

HKDA

Co-organizers:

Hong Kong Productivity Council 香港生產力促進局

Leisure and Cultural Services Department 康樂及文化事務署

Gold Sponsors:

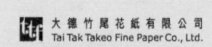

Adobe

DIGITAL MAGIC

Hong Kong Trade Development Council 香港貿易發展局

hinge architecture and design magazine

PACE

Polytrade Paper

Tai Tak Takeo Fine Paper Co., Ltd. 大橋竹尾花紙有限公司

Category Awards Sponsors:

Adobe   antalis

Media Partner:

Silver Sponors:

Art and Design Magazine
di Architectural & Design
Hong Kong Dragon Enterprises Ltd.
IdN Magazine
JET
Longyin Review Ltd.
Package and Design Magazine
Philips Electronics Hong Kong Ltd. - Philips Design
Sun Rise Printing Co.
Territory
XFUNS Creative & Design Magazine

Supporting Organizations:

Apparel Product Design and Development Centre
Australian Graphic Design Association
Beijing Industrial Design Promotion Organization
China Bridge International
91 Creation Association
Design Committee of China Package Technology Association
Designers Association Singapore
Graphic Arts Association of Hong Kong
Guangzhou University Industrial Design
Hong Kong Fashion Designers Association
Hong Kong Institute of Professional Photographers
Hong Kong Society of Illustrators
International Design Center NAGOYA Inc.
Interior Design Association (Hong Kong)
Japan Graphic Designers Association Inc.
Jiasu Graphic Designers Committee
Kaohsiung Creators Association, Taiwan
Macau Designers Association
Qingdao Industrial Design Association
Shanghai Graphic Designers Association
Shenzhen Graphic Design Association
Taiwan Graphic Design Association
Taiwan Poster Design Association
The Chartered Society of Designers (Hong Kong)
Zuhai Graphic Design Association

Board of Advisors & Committees
顧問委員會及委員

Board of Advisors 2004/06
2004 至 2006 年度顧問委員會

Mrs. Selina Chow GBS, OBE, JP 周梁淑怡
Mr. Timothy Fok GBS, JP 霍震霆
Dr. Christina Chu 朱錦鸞
Dr. Desmond Hui 許焯權
Dr. Stephen S F Lee 李錫勳
Prof. T P Leung 梁天培
Mr. Tom Ming 明基全
Mr. Alan Wong 黃錦輝
Prof. John Heskett
Mr. Alan Chan 陳幼堅
Mr. Max C L Cheung 張再厲
Mr. Alan Yip 葉智榮

The 2004/06 Executive Committee
2004 至 2006 年度執行委員會

Chairman 主席
Mr. Charles Ng 吳秋全

Vice-Chairman 副主席
Mr. Eddy Yu 余志光

Hon Secretary 榮譽秘書
Mr. Kelly Sze 施家禮

Hon Treasurer 榮譽司庫
Mr. Beam Leung 梁伯源

Executive Committee Members 執行委員
Mr. Eric Chan 陳超宏
Mr. Raymond Fung 馮永基
Mr. Joey Ho 何宗憲
Prof. Yanta Lam 林衍堂
Mr. Paul Lam 林席賢
Mr. Francis Lee 李躍華
Mr. Henry Lui 雷葆文
Ms. Prudence Mak 麥雅端
Mr. Winnif Pang 彭志江
Mr. Angus Wong 黃安
Mr. Stanley Wong 黃炳培
Mr. Clement Yick 易達華

HKDA Awards 05 Organizing Committee
香港設計師協會獎 05 籌委會

Head of Organizing Committee 籌委會主席
Mr. Kelly Sze 施家禮

Members 其他籌委會成員
Mr. Eric Chan 陳超宏
Mr. Joey Ho 何宗憲
Mr. Paul Lam 林席賢
Mr. Beam Leung 梁伯源
Mr. Henry Lui 雷葆文
Ms. Prudence Mak 麥雅端
Mr. Winnif Pang 彭志江
Mr. Angus Wong 黃安
Mr. Clement Yick 易達華
Mr. Eddy Yu 余志光

Chairman's Message

Charles Ng
Chairman, HKDA

It is always hard to judge a face-off among creative ideas.

Imagine 2,700 entries from all over Asia, lining up to be discerned, selected, graded and assigned the gold, silver, bronze and judges' choice awards. What a task? On the occasion of the 33rd Anniversary of the HKDA and the 20th HKDA Awards, 14 design masters from different parts of the world in various professional realms including graphics, products, interior and multi-media were invited to be the judges. Their mission was to hand-pick the best of the year's entries from 32 categories in two days. Spanning from commercial, culture, arts, society and politics, the themes of the submissions were exhilarating as much as they were controversial and ambiguous. Despite the meticulous precautions taken on the entries collection, categorization, coding, judging, storing, winner notification and finally the exhibition, an error did occur.

At the HKDA, mistakes are treated with seriously. Through correcting, reflecting and improving, we grow bigger and stronger and gain the loyalty and support of our members. So what is the problem this year?

Preparation started last year as the new committee took their office and passed the amendments regarding the HKDA Awards. The event was postponed to 2005 as it was agreed there should be more time to study and reposition the project. Of course there was SARS in 2003 and the society was not ready for such a gala event. A permanent event emblem, chosen from members' submissions, was created to identify Hong Kong as a design centre-stage of Asia. The title of the award was re-named as HKDA Awards 05, reinforcing the significance of the Association and its instrumental role in the industry. From this year on, apart from the gold, silver and bronze awards, an endorsement mark will also be granted to the winners. They are authorized to use it in promoting their products and awards. Another new move is combining local entries with Asian counterparts in the competition, making it more challenging for Hong Kong designers.

On top of the strategic changes, the event organization is totally computerized for the first time. Participants submitted to the computer the amount, category and cost of their entries as well as related data for future publishing in the HKDA Awards 05 catalogue. Even the judges were impressed.

Just as overwhelming was the record-high amount of entries, the two days assigned for judging, as in the past, were not enough. To crack the dilemma, three panels of judges adjudicated separately for the graphics, products and interior categories simultaneously, only physically separated by windscreens.

Because of tight timing and some entries had to be re-assessed, two different sets of results came out. Without ratification, the winners were notified and the error was only discovered afterwards. Immediately the committee traced the root of the mistakes and found out fortunately only a few designers were affected. But then, for the HKDA, a small mistake is indeed a big one. Taking this opportunity, on behalf of the organizing committee, I would like to express our sincere regrets to those affected.

Another issue was controversy. The category that generated the most debates was graphic design. Below are some cases I'd like to share with the future committee.

Art or design?

Five judges of the graphics panel had fierce discussion on the determination of the artistic and graphic nature of some entries. They conceded that some entries were more a work of art than a functional design capable of being replicated. In the end, those entries were granted awards. On contemplating and distributing the award notifications, one question is raised among the committee: why do we regard posters as more artistic?

Poster is the favourite item for graphic designers, no dispute on that. In the past, because of the sheer number of entries, the committee would categorize them into commercial, cultural promotion and thematic sections in order to ease judging. Alas, that already was a tough job. Since the designers were not particularly clear about to which section their works belonged, it was up to the eyes of the committee members to decide based on the final ruling right of the Association. To avoid dispute, we see the need to clarify or get rid of the sub-categorizing in the future, especially among thematic and cultural posters where art vs design is a topic of constant brawl.

As design has entered a new age of cross-culture and multi-media, to draw a line between anything would be quite out of date. However, there are values, principles and visions that worth upholding behind a great competition. The above controversies will definitely contribute to the future of the HKDA Awards. Comments and suggestions from the international judges, local gurus and fellow members will be heeded. Together with the study of successful competition around the world and Asia, rules will also be improved.

Moral and social responsibilities.

The event confronted entries bearing moral controversy. For example, an exquisitely designed cigarette pack. Its parked off heated debates among the judges. Should design take up social responsibility? The unanimous answer, in the end, is yes. And out the cigarette pack exited. The incident served us a great lesson too. Following our tradition, every detail regarding the current situation, demand of the industry, experience from experts and international regulations were carefully considered while making macro and micro scale reforms for the event. The errors and achievements have both proven the HKDA Awards is indeed fair and open.

Let me thank again with all my heart to the participating Hong Kong and Asian designers and the esteemed international judges. We are grateful for the leadership of the Head of Organizing Committee of HKDA Awards 05, Kelly Sze, the coordination of our Vice-chairman Eddy Yu, and the comments from our committee members and judges Stanley Wong and Raymond Fung. Not to forget is the efforts of the numerous committee members, volunteers and students. Last but not least, the sponsors who support and recognize HKDA throughout the years are much appreciated. Without your engagement, how could we have discovered our virtues and sins.

主席致辭

吳秋全先生
香港設計師協會主席

創意向來是難以比併的一回事。

要從亞洲區所徵集到的2,700份作品中,精挑細選獲獎作品,繼而再評選金、銀、銅、優異、入選獎,以至「評審之選」,這是何等不易爲的事情。組成自不同國家、本身在其設計領域,包括平面、產品、室內設計、多媒體經已是卓越有成的十四位設計巨擘,連成一體,應邀請爲本會成立第三十三年、第二十屆舉行的『香港設計師協會獎』,擔任評審工作。要在兩天內,從三十二項組別中選出是年度傑出作品,其中涉及商業、文化、藝術、社會、政治題材,可想而知,當中不乏具爭議性、棘手和難以取捨的心頭好和毀譽參半的作品。比賽前林林總總的預測、提防和爭論,包括由徵稿、收件、分件、編碼、評審、入倉、發出獲獎通知,以至展覽,雖則已經過籌備委員會成員無數次的反覆推敲、危機預算、採排、預料的人爲失誤,始終還有百密一疏。

將發現的缺點、失誤,繼而作出糾正、反思和前瞻,是香港設計師協會長久獲會員信任和支持,並且賴以發展和壯大的不二法門。這一屆產生的問題又在哪裡?

應屆的大展籌備工作,因應去年初委員上任後的要求,一致作出新的修訂及通過,將原本在是年上任後,隨即馬上展開大展工作的急務,往後一年推遲。除了爲適應03年因非典型肺炎影響所及,市面一片蕭條的境況,更重要是爭取更多的時間,爲大展重新檢討和重新定位。我們向會員公開徵求大會永久標誌,給它建立新的形象,強化在亞洲區的認受性,以及考慮香港作爲亞洲區設計中心的位置,給它一個更鮮明的身份和恆久的地位。除此之外,有別於過往的『設計展05』等大獎稱號,重新正名爲『香港設計師協會獎05』,將主辦單位的權威性、認受性和影響力重新確立。從是屆開始,大會爲金、銀、銅獎爲主,另外頒發『獎項嘉許標徽』,並授權使用該標徽作推廣其所獲獎項之用。另一項重要變更,就是將香港區和亞洲區作品一併評選,從新發現香港的創意潛力和競爭力。

一連串新的策略性改革之外,是次大展亦率先引進全面化電腦運作程序,參賽者除可自行在電腦上輸入參賽作品量數、系列、總銀碼外,更須呈上參賽資料作日後獲獎年鑑排版之用。在評審過程中,全面電腦化計分方法無不給評審留下深刻印象。然而,事情發展總有例外一面。

應屆參賽作品爲歷屆之冠。過去經驗所及的兩日評審工作預計將應付不來,須三線評審同時進行,包括最嚴峻的時候,平面、產品和室內設計三大類必須以屏風分隔,同步三組評委分別評審。

因爲評審時間過於緊迫和部份入圍作品須放回重新審看,問題就出在來回間紀錄之誤差,因此導致入圍獲獎紀錄有兩個版本。最害的是,會內欠缺再三覆核。在發信通知獲獎後,才發現問題的嚴重性。籌委成員馬上開會追蹤錯失源頭,可幸的是,受影響的設計師只有三數位,作品誤報獲獎的僅廖廖數件而已。然而,小小錯失總是大錯,尤其發生在報稱爲亞洲認受性最強的『香港設計師協會獎』身上。在此,我謹代表本會籌委成員向受影響的設計師致最深的歉意。事情的另一個發展,再不是錯失,而是具爭論性的議題,此尤其出現在平面類別。本人在此簡錄當日的爭論觀點,好作爲下屆籌展者反思和參考。

是藝術或還是設計？

平面界別的五位評審，對參賽作品中某些設計和藝術成份的比重和本質，曾經作出過深入的爭議和討論。評審對一些藝術成份多於設計功能的作品應否入選有不同的見解，經再三反覆討論才確定它們入選或獲獎的資格。值得深思和反省的是，大會的平面大類中海報項目和上述所提的情況，出現兩個評審標準。爲甚麼海報項目就可以別具藝術性哩？ 這亦是籌委們於處理發放獲獎通知時，處於兩難的地方。

衆所周之，平面設計師都酷愛海報創作。在過去幾屆大展中，亦因爲海報項目參賽最多，爲評委易於分類及增加評審時效益起見，籌委將海報再細分爲商業、文化推廣和主題三大類。對於這種分法，評審們也不以爲甚，可是在分件過程中，籌委們已發現一般設計師對這種分法也不了了之，只好有勞我們十數雙眼一起鑑証每張海報的內容，將每一件重新分類。根據大會參與章程所述，本會「保留最終決議權去取消任何不符大會規格的作品」。籌委們也明白此種分法，建議有必要在下屆進一步釐清，或許也不設任何分法，以減少爭論。如是者，藝術與設計的問題在主題和文化海報產生衝突的情況尤其嚴重。

絕對同意二分法的觀念經已落伍，更何況現代設計已進入跨文化、跨媒體的領域。然而，每項大賽背後都有主辦機構的信念、宗旨、視野、遠景和提倡的功能，也不能因爲大勢所趨，而失卻各自的定位。值得肯定的是，上述爭議的出現，對來屆大展具有參考價值。見賢思齊，本會和籌委願意聆聽更多國際評審、本地設計權威和參考國際大賽的情況，按本會的宗旨、會員取向和香港，以至亞洲的情況，重新探討和修訂新的做法。

道德和社會責任

今屆作品亦出現設計應否助長遺害社會歪風、建立品牌責任和提倡設計道德的問題。部份煙包包裝設計非常出色，卻在評審團中出現分歧的意見，設計應否重視社會和道德責任？最後一致的決議認爲該予以出局。諸如上述的爭論，也讓我們上了寶貴的一課。本會和籌委依循過往傳統，按這年度的情況、設計界要求、專家的經驗和國際規範，經已重視每一細節，因此達成今屆大展的宏觀改革和微觀的修訂。見微知著，今屆的瑕疵和成就，再次肯定本會和『香港設計師協會獎』的公平、公正、公開的優良品格。

本人謹此再次感謝亞洲和香港設計師們的鼎力參與是次大賽，也感謝國際評審，遠道而來的評選工作；在籌委會主席施家禮帶領下，和副主席余志光的協助，加上本會委員及評審黃炳培、馮永基的寶貴意見，以及感謝幕後無數委員的心力；義務工作人員、學生和最重要的是，長期支持本會、肯定本會成就和貢獻的贊助商。沒有您們的參與，又怎能發現我們的完美和不完美。

About the HKDA Awards

Founded in 1972, the Hong Kong Designers Association is the first of its kind in Hong Kong, advocating increased visibility of public design and higher professional status for practising designers in government, cultural, entertainment, commercial and industrial sectors, as well as for full-time and part-time teachers and administrators in the academic field of design. HKDA now boasts three decades of history and growth since "The First Picture Show" was inaugurated in 1975. The Award ceremony was renamed to the HKDA Design Show in 1976 and held annually until 1980, when it became a biennial event. Since 1996, the call for entries has been extended to other Asia Pacific countries. This year, in celebration of the HKDA Design Show's 33rd anniversary, the ceremony is relaunched as HKDA Awards 05.

HKDA Awards 05 marks the first time that entries from all participating territories will be judged under a single banner, making this a truly regional event. This edition also introduces the Endorsement Mark scheme, offering winners the exclusive right to use the mark for promotional purposes.

HKDA Awards 05 called for entries in four main categories: Graphic, Product, New Media and Spatial, with a total of 32 sub-categories representing professional design specialisations, among which the latest addition is the "character" sub-category. This year welcomed over 2,700 entries from 36 cities, including Hong Kong, Macau, Beijing, Shanghai, Taipei, Bangkok, Tokyo, Osaka, Sydney, Singapore, Melbourne, Kuala Lumpur, Hanoi and many others — an increase of 21% over the last show, with local entries increasing by more than 35%.

About the Judges

Widely acknowledged by design peers as one of the most important multi-disciplinary design awards in the Asia-Pacific region, HKDA Awards 05 is the definitive benchmark for design professionals, as 2005 reflects the largest number of entries in its 33-year history. The judging panel features multidisciplinary design gurus from across the globe.

Graphic: Jonathan Barnbrook / Lu Jingren / Mervyn Kurlansky / Hideki Nakajima / Stanley Wong
New Media: Nick Law / Euna Seol / Jonathan Wong
Product: Gary Natsume / Chen Wen-Long / Lorraine Justice
Spatial: David Adjaye / Essy Baniassad / Raymond Fung

『香港設計師協會獎』簡介

香港設計師協會成立於1972年，是香港首個非牟利的設計專業組織。旨在推廣公眾對設計行業的興趣，並提高設計從業員的專業地位，包括從事政府、文化、娛樂、商業及工業界別的專業設計師，以及設計學術領域的全職、客席導師和行政人員。前身為1975年創辦的『圖畫展』年展；於76年易名為香港設計師協會『設計展』。80年改為每兩年舉辦一次。自96年起，接受其他亞洲地區參賽，包括中國內地、日本、馬來西亞、新加坡、泰國、南韓、台灣及印度。今年恰逢創立33周年，正名為『香港設計師協會獎05』。

今年的『香港設計師協會獎05』亦有多項突破。所有參賽地區的作品將會無分地域，一併評選，肯定其作為亞太區比賽的意義。這也將是『香港設計師協會獎』首次嘉許『認可標徽』，特別授權獲獎設計師使用該認可標徽推廣其獲獎作品。

『香港設計師協會獎05』共分平面、產品、新媒體、空間四大參賽作品類別，共設32個參賽項目，其中包括新增的『人物造型』項目，以表彰設計界別各項專業。今年的『香港設計師協會獎05』的參賽反應良好，共有2,700份來自香港及亞太地區的參賽作品，比02年舉行的『香港設計師協會設計展』增加了21%。本地作品的數目亦大大增加35%，亞太區的反應亦相當踴躍，有36個亞太區城市參賽，其中包括香港、澳門、北京、上海、台北、曼谷、東京、大阪、悉尼、星加坡、墨爾本、吉隆坡、河內等等。

評審團簡介

亞太區最重要的綜合性設計獎—『香港設計師協會獎』獲設計界同儕廣泛認同，並得到他們支持，組成了來自全球各個設計領域的大師比賽評審團，參賽地區的作品無分地域，一併評選，訂立了更專業權威基準。

平面： Jonathan Barnbrook / 呂敬人 / Mervyn Kurlansky / 中島英樹 / 黃炳培
新媒體： Nick Law / Euna Seol / Jonathan Wong
產品： Gary Natsume / 陳文龍 / Lorraine Justice
空間： David Adjaye / Essy Baniassad / 馮永基

Judges 評審團

Chen Wen-Long 陳文龍
Taiwan

President of Nova Design, with offices in Shanghai, Taiwan, the US, Italy and Malaysia, and more than 20 years of experience in design management and design leadership of over 100 transportation projects. He has served as Chairman of CIDA (China Industrial Designer Association) and Special Adviser for DesignToday of Japan. With a Master degree in Design from the Graduate School of Mechanical Engineering at Tatung University, he is an active lecturer in design and is currently the Visiting Professor of Shandong University in China.

Nova Design 的主席，於上海、台灣、美國、意大利和馬來西亞設有辦公室，並有 20 年的設計管理經驗和領導過超過 100 個運輸計劃。他曾任中華民國工業設計協會主席，和日本 DesignToday 特別顧問。他在大同大學機械工程研究院取得碩士學位，現在是一位活躍的設計講師，任中國山東大學客席教授。

David Adjaye
United Kingdom

Graduated from the Royal College of Art with a Master's degree in Architecture in 1993, he started a small practice in 1994. After building a solid and unique reputation in reconstructing cafes, bars and private homes, he reformed his studio as Adjaye Associates in 2000. The next year, Adjaye won the Idea Store Competition to design two new-build libraries in the London Borough of Tower Hamlets, later exhibited at the Venice Biennale in 2002 and 2004. Other recent projects include designing the Nobel Peace Center in Oslo, Norway, a prototype house in Nanjing, China and a new home for the Museum of Contemporary Art in Denver, USA.

1993 年於皇家藝術學院取得建築碩士學位，在 1994 年開始了小型業務。在重建咖啡店、酒吧和私人住宅方面建立了可靠和極好聲譽，他於 2000 年改組了他的工作室名為 Adjaye Associates。次年，Adjaye 贏得了 Idea Store 大賽，在 London Borough of Tower Hamlets 設計了兩家新建的圖書館，後來更在 2002 年及 2004 年的威尼斯雙年展中參展。他其他近期項目包括在挪威奧斯陸 Nobel Peace Center 的設計、一家在中國南京的模範屋，還有在美國丹佛的當代藝術館新館。

Euna Seol
South Korea

Co-founder and creative director of PostVisual.com, launched in Seoul in 2000 and specialised in digital campaigns for clients such as Nike, Samsung, Pantech & Curitel, Hyundai-card and Iriver. Her personal artsite "seoleuna.com", created in 1999, was exhibited in the 30th Rotterdam Film Festival and the 18th Sundance Film Festival in the Cine Online division. She has been awarded the Cannes Cyber Gold Lion, as well as at the London International Awards, Communication Arts Awards and the Flash Forward Film Festival in 2004.

在2000年在首爾成立的PostVisual.com始創人之一及創作總監，專門為Nike、Samsung、Pantech & Curitel、Hyundai-card和Iriver等客戶從事數碼計劃。她於1999年創製了個人藝術作品網頁seoleuna.com，並於第三十屆鹿特丹電影節和第十八屆Sundance電影節的網上電影組參展。於2004年，榮獲康城電腦金獅獎、倫敦國際獎、通訊藝術獎及Flash Forward電影節中的獎項。

Essy Baniassad
Hong Kong

Founder and general editor of Tuns Press, formerly Dean of the Faculty of Architecture at Dalhousie University, Canada. After practising and teaching architecture in North America and the UK, as well as conducting research in community architectural development in South America and Africa, he is currently Chair and Professor of the Department of Architecture at the Chinese University of Hong Kong.

Tuns Press 的始創人和總編輯，前加拿大 Dalhousie 大學建築學院院長。在北美和英國從事及教授建築，並於南美和非洲進行有關社區建築發展的研究，現任香港中文大學建築系系主任兼教授。

Gary Natsume
United States of America

Industrial Design Manager at ECCO Design, previously senior designer at frogdesign inc. Graduated from Aichi Prefecture University of Fine Arts (Japan), Parsons School of Design (New York) and received his Master of Fine Arts Degree from Cranbrook Academy of Art (Bloomfield Hills, Michigan). One of his award-winning designs was selected for the National Design Triennial, Design Culture Now exhibition at the Cooper-Hewitt National Design Museum and later acquired in the museum's permanent collection. His commercial work has also been shown at the San Jose Museum of Art.

ECCO Design 工業設計經理、前 frogdesign inc. 高級設計師，畢業於 Aichi Prefecture University of Fine Arts（日本愛知縣）和 Parsons School of Design（紐約），並在 Cranbrook Academy of Art（美國密西根州 Bloomfield Hills）取得美術碩士學位。他的其中一個得獎設計被 National Design Triennial 於 Cooper-Hewitt National Design Museum 的『當今設計文化展』（Design Culture Now）選中，後來更成為了該館的永久藏品。他的商業作品也曾在聖荷西美術館中展出。

Hideki Nakajima 中島英樹
Japan

Art director and graphic designer, established Nakajima Design in 1995. Since 1999 he participates in a unit called "code" with Ryuichi Sakamoto, Shigeo Goto and Norika Sora. Major awards include the Kodansha Prize for Book Design (2003), Chicago Athenaeum's Good Design Award (2001), Best Design in the Category of Books at the 19th International Biennale of Graphic Design Brno (2000), Tokyo ADC Award (1999), and five Golds and seven Silvers at the Art Directors Club Awards (1995-2000).

美術指導及平面設計師，於 1995 年成立了 Nakajima Design。自 1999 年起，他跟 Ryuichi Sakamoto、Shigeo Goto 和 Norika Sora 一起參與了一個名為「編碼」（code）的組織。主要獎項包括：the Kodansha Prize for Book Design（2003），芝加哥 Athenaeum 的 Good Design Award（2001）、第十九屆國際平面設計雙年獎（International Biennale of Graphic Design Brno）（2000）的書籍組最佳設計獎、東京的 ADC Award（1999），還有美術指導會大獎（Art Directors Club Awards）（1995-2000）中的五個金獎和七個銀獎。

Jonathan Barnbrook
United Kingdom

Famous in the world of font design, where he has extended his socio-political view by producing controversial typefaces based on historical forms with a contemporary subversive influence and titled in a confrontational manner (Manson, Exocet, Bastard). He founded the graphic design studio Virus in London in 1990, with four designers originating from England, Japan and Brazil. Non-commercial collaborations include art directing and producing work with the activist magazine Adbusters, as well as work which highlights political and social injustices, offered without copyright restrictions on www.barnbrook.net and www.virusfonts.com.

他的字體設計世界聞名，曾以歷史性的模式加上當代巔覆性的影響製作惹人爭議的鉛字字樣及以敢於正視的態度命名（Manson, Exocet, Bastard），擴闊他的社會及政治視野。他於 1990 年在倫敦聯同四位分別來自英格蘭、日本和巴西的設計師，創立了 Virus 平面設計工作室。非商業的項目合作包括藝術指導和替激進主義分子雜誌《Adbusters》創作，還有強調政治和社會中不平等的作品，以無版權的方式提供給 www.barnbrook.net 和 www.virusfonts.com。

Lu Jingren 呂敬人
China

Professor of Academy of Arts and Design at Tsinghua University, Deputy Director of National Book Graphic-design Art Committee, Director of the Book Graphic-designing Committee of all ministerial publishing houses, book designer, illustrator. Studied under the visual art designer Prof. Sugiurskohei of the College of Art Engineering in Kobe, Japan in 1989 and finally established Jingren Graphic Design House in China in 1998, as art-design inspector-general.

清華大學美術學院教授、全國書籍裝幀藝術委員會副主任、中央各部門出版社裝幀藝術委員會主任，中國美術家協會插圖裝幀藝術委員會委員。1989 年在日本神戶藝術工科大學院視覺藝術設計師杉浦康平教授門下學習，於 1998 年在中國成立了敬人平面設計公司並擔任藝術設計總監。

Jonathan Wong
Hong Kong

Graduated from San Jose State University in Calfornia, with a major in Mass Communications and Journalism and a minor in Arts. Worked as freelancer and art director in the advertising industry before joining Yahoo! at the US head office in 1999. As International Design Lead, he worked on globalizing and launching Yahoo! sites in Asia, Europe and South America, until he relocated to Hong Kong as Regional Lead of User Experience and Design for North Asia in late 2000.

畢業於美國加州聖荷西州立大學，主修大眾傳播和新聞，副修藝術。在 1999 年加入美國 Yahoo! 的總部前，曾在廣告業擔任自由職業者及藝術總監。作爲國際設計部主管，他致力於開發 Yahoo! 在亞洲、歐洲和南美洲的網站，並擴展至全球各地，直至 2000 年底來到香港擔任北亞洲地區使用者經驗及設計部的主管。

Lorraine Justice
Hong Kong

Currently Swire Chair Professor of Design and Head of the School of Design at Hong Kong Polytechnic University, while teaching higher education industrial design and human computer interface design for the past 17 years. She was previously Director of the Industrial Design Program in the College of Architecture at the Georgia Institute of Technology and Acting Chair and Associate Professor in the Department of Industrial, Interior and Visual Communication Design at Ohio State University. She was responsible for organizing the First Doctoral Education in Design Conference in Ohio, as well as the First China-USA Industrial Design Conference in Beijing.

現爲香港理工大學設計學院院長及 Swire Chair Professor of Design，而過去 17 年一直在高等院校教授工業設計和人類電腦界面設計。曾任喬治亞理工建築學院工業設計課程主任，及俄亥俄州立大學工業、室內及視覺通訊設計系署理系主任和副教授。她曾負責主辦俄亥俄州立大學設計博士教育首次會議，和北京中美工業設計首次會議。

Mervyn Kurlansky
Denmark

Born in Johannesburg, South Africa in 1936. He trained at the Central School of Art and Design in London, then freelanced before becoming graphics director of Planning Unit, the design consultancy service of Knoll International. In 1969 he joined Crosby/Fletcher/Forbes and in 1972 co-founded Pentagram, from which he resigned in 1993 to live and work in Denmark. Today he is active in design education, and his work is included in the permanent collection of the New York Museum of Modern Art. He conceived and designed the book "Watching My Name Go By", a celebration of New York's colourful graffiti.

1936年生於南非約翰尼斯堡，曾就讀於倫敦中央藝術及設計學院，在任職 Knoll International 設計顧問服務部策劃組平面總監之前，為自由職業者。於1969年加入 Crosby/Fletcher/Forbes；於1972年跟別人共同創立了 Pentagram 並於1993離職及遷居丹麥。今天，他在設計教育方面非常活躍。他的作品成為紐約現代博物館永久藏品系列之一，並構思和設計了頌揚紐約多姿多彩的塗鴉藝術的《Watching My Name Go By》一書。

Nick Law
Australia

After graduating from Randwick Technical College in Sydney, he began his career at Pentagram in London, working under the guidance of Alan Fletcher and John McConnell on a variety of international projects. He later founded the Australian-based creative firm Studio Dot, specializing in identity work and collateral. Since then he has worked as Senior Designer for the advertising agencies DMB&B (D'Arcy Masius Benton & Bowles) in London and Deifenbach Elkins (now FutureBrand) in New York, as Creative Director for FGI and finally as Multi-Channel Creative Director for R/GA.

從悉尼的 Randwick Technical College 畢業以後，他在倫敦的 Pentagram 開展事業，在 Alan Fletcher 和 John McConnell 的指導下從事各種國際性的項目。後來創辦了以澳洲為基地的創作公司 Studio Dot，專門從事主項目及其附屬活動。自此，他擔任倫敦 DMB&B (D'Arcy Masius Benton & Bowles) 廣告公司和紐約 Deifenbach Elkins 公司 (即現在的 FutureBrand) 高級設計師，FGI 創作總監及最後為 R/GA 擔任多頻道創作總監。

Raymond Fung 馮永基
Hong Kong

Architect, artist and promoter of visual environment, Senior Architect in the Hong Kong Architectural Services Department. Currently serving as Art Adviser of the Leisure & Cultural Services Department and Visiting Professor of the Central Academy of Fine Arts. In 1997, he was awarded an artist-in-residence scholarship at the Vermont Studio Center in the US. Since then, he has won over 30 awards, including 1990 Ten Outstanding Young Persons Award and Hong Kong Institute of Architects President's Prizes: Health Education & Exhibition Centre (1999), Hong Kong Wetland Park Phase 1 (2000) and Sai Kung Waterfront Park (2003).

作爲視覺環境建築師、藝術家及推廣者，馮先生已獲得超過30多個重要獎項：香港建築師學會會長獎狀，包括衛生教育及資源中心(1999)、香港濕地公園第一期(2000)及西貢海濱公園(2003)；他的作品多次入選全國美術作品展，香港藝術雙年展、香港設計雙年展及香港設計師協會獎。一九九七年獲獎學金赴美國維蒙爾藝術村深造。馮氏現職香港特區政府建築署。參與著作包括《建築師的見、觸、思》、《香港建築百年》及即將出版的《後九七之香港公共建築》。

Stanley Wong 黃炳培
Hong Kong

Stanley, Wong Ping-pui (alias anothermountainman), was born in Hong Kong in 1960. He graduated in 1980 from Hong Kong Technical Teachers' College (Design & Technology). Over the next 15 years he worked at Modern Advertising Ltd., Grey (HK) Advertising and J. Walter Thompson (HK) Advertising. In 1996, Stanley became the first Chinese to undertake an overseas position when he left Hong Kong to join Bartle Bogle Hegarty (Asia Pacific) in Singapore as regional creative director. Returned to Hong Kong in 1999 he take up the position of chief executive officer and executive creative director of TBWA (HK) Advertising. In 2000, Stanley joined Centro Digital as chief creative officer/film director. In July 2002, Stanley joint partner to set up Threetwoone Film Production Limited. In 2004, Stanley was invited to be member of AGI (Alliance Graphique Internationale). Throughout his career, Stanley has won more than 300 awards in graphic design, advertising & fine art both locally & internationally. In 2005, Stanley represented Hong Kong to exhibition in Venice Biennale.

黃炳培（又名又一山人）。1980年畢業於香港工商師範學院設計應用系，先後於現代（香港）廣告公司，精英（香港）廣告公司及智威湯遜（香港）廣告公司任職。1996年移居至新加坡並加入英國 **Bartle Bogle Hegarty**（亞洲）廣告公司爲亞洲創作總監，爲首位中國籍華人受聘此職位。1999年回港後出任 **TBWA**（香港）廣告公司之行政總裁及行政創作總監。至2000年，加入先濤數碼出任創作總裁及導演。2002年7月，以合夥形式成立三二一聲畫製作有限公司。2004年，被邀成爲 **AGI**（國際平面設計聯盟）會員。過去十多年間，黃氏之設計及廣告作品屢獲香港、亞洲及國際獎項三百多項。2005年，代表香港參加威尼斯藝術雙年展展出。

JUDGES' COMMENTARY & CHOICES
裁判論評と選択
판단자의 해석과 선택
评审委员会特选作品及评语

Essy Baniassad: Basheer Design Book Shop
David Adjaye: PMTD Headquarters
Hideki Nakajima: 妊紫嫣紅開遍 — 良辰美景仙鳳鳴
Gary Natsume: Decode Clock
Jonathan Barnbrook: Heromoism
Lu Jingren: 深圳 03 設計展作品集
Prof. Lorraine Justice: In-ear Gaming Headphone - SHG8010
Mervyn Kurlansky: Charlie Chan & The Secret Book Craft Print Yearbook 2002
Stanley Wong: Calendiary
Chen Wen-Long: Big Shot Professional Hairdryer with Ceramic Attachments HD552
Jonathan Wong: Little Prince is Depressed
Nick Law: Corroder
Euna Seol: Angelworld
Raymond Fung: Nil

Spatial_ Retail
t. Basheer Design Book Shop
e. d. Joey Ho

Essy Baniassad

The design submissions particularly in the spatial category displayed a generally good level of execution and signs of an active and highly skilled professional community of designers. However they left me with three impressions: richness of opportunities, limitation of originality, and limitations of scope in the choice and in the anner of submissions. Before going further I should mention that I write my thoughts directly because of my deep respect for the design community in Hong Kong. I don't think these comments are about the designers but they are about a combination of factors, which in Hong Kong seem to compromise the vast potential for design excellence.

Hong Kong clearly offers vast opportunities for design partly due to its pool of active and talented designers and partly due to the material wealth available to the clients. Match the investment in cars that the clients drive to what they can spend on their habitats. But the comparison ends there. In the case of cars the choice is clearly limited and pre-categorized. But in the case of places of habitation a similar condition to me suggests limitation of originality. I'll explain.

Hong Kong also contains great diversity of needs and client groups. One would expect to find that designers look for opportunities to address all sectors of this diverse group. No indication of any exceptional, exquisite and highly innovative designs, nor any examples of the most challenging area of design where measured improvements arising out of patient search and discovery in units of dense public housing would contribute greatly to raising the quality of daily life. I found the scope of submissions limited to a narrow middle band in terms of projects, design approach, client group, even the manner of submission. The submissions conveyed an evident sense of profusion be it at a reasonably high level, but not diversity. Which one is a better measure of quality?

Imagine how it would feel if someone tuned all the water you drink into fizzy soda water. Not for just an hour, not for just a day, not for just a holiday but for all your days- always. That's what I felt was happening as I looked at some 60 entries for the design award for residences. They were running into fizzy soda water residences (and losing much in the process). A house is about privacy. It is about the difference between you and others, not about public tags and trends. It's not a public bar. In a bar you can stay for an hour and leave with a memory but not leave it with a mark of your identity on it. A living room is not a furniture show room. A showroom is intended to show the furniture. A living room is intended to accommodate you supported by what becomes a part of you. It is not to put you on public display, not showy but comfy. It is a place to invite others into your private world, not one to confirm that you too have bought that designer brand chair! Am I right? What did I miss? I wonder.

Many of the design submitted seemed as empty as a showroom after closing hours. But they are homes! Who is living here? Where is the art? Where is the mess? Where is the relaxed person who has put the flowers on the windowsill in just a slightly not show-room photo-shot perfect position? For that matter where are the flowers? Art. Sign of life, your life, you? And where is the design with necessary originality to discover form in each case what is distinctly expressed and what can be in the background in the most artful and enriching way?

One project invited me to it. A bookshop, which I didn't know and visited after the jury. It had AN IDEA behind the FORM. Its submission was informative and lacked gloss. The idea behind it seemed to be promising in that it combined a number of pre-defined functions into a tight combination and therefore had a certain exploratory aspect. And the pictures and drawings in the submission were sufficiently informative to support the writing. I found that it was called, "Basheer" located at 1/F, Flat A, Island Bldg., 439-441 Hennessy Road, Causeway Bay. You could reach it through a pretty cluttered and tight staircase and lift. It turned out to be an engaging and rich collection of books tightly organized in an unobtrusive way that offered you a chance to be surrounded with what you came to see: books.

參賽的設計作品中，特別是空間組的作品，執行技術水平普遍很高，也反映出這裡有一群很活躍和專業的設計師。但他們也留給我三個印象：大量的機會、原創的局限和題材的局限。在說下去之前我要指出，我直接寫出我的感想，是因為我非常尊重香港的設計界。我不認為這些評語是指向設計師，而是指向多種看來使香港產生傑出設計的潛力有所減弱的成因。

香港明顯充滿很多設計的機會，一方面是因為它有很多活躍和有才華的設計師，客戶方面又有很充裕的資源提供。試比較客戶在他們駕駛的汽車和他們花在住宅的投資，但比較亦僅此而已。在汽車的例子上，選擇明顯是較為局限和預先已被分門別類；但在住宅方面，類似情況對我來說，是原創的貧乏，我會作解釋的。香港有大量各種不同的需求和客戶，很多時期望設計師會從中尋找機會發表他們對不同範疇的見解。在這項最富挑戰性的組別中，並沒有發現任何較優秀的、精美的和極富創意的設計，或者從研究稠密的公共房屋中提出適度的改善或發展出可以提升日常生活水平的設計。我發覺參賽作品的視野在計劃規模、設計手法、客戶類型、甚至態度均局限於狹窄的中間幅度。參賽作品傳遞了一個很明顯的奢侈意念，但卻欠缺多元化。哪一個才是較好質素的標準呢？

試想像，如果有人把你喝的水都變成有氣梳打水，你會怎樣？不是一小時、一天或者一個假期，而是天天如是。這就是我在看了60個住宅設計之後的感覺，它們都在變成有氣梳打水住宅（及在過程中喪失了很多）。房子是私隱的，它是展示你和別人的不同之處，而不是展示一個大眾標籤或潮流、它不是一間酒吧；在酒吧中，你可以流連一個小時及留下記憶，但不留半點你個人的特質。客廳不是個像俱陳列室，陳列室是要來展示傢俱的，而客廳是迎合你成為你的一部份，它不是要把你展示或炫耀於公眾眼前，而是要讓你感覺舒適。這地方是讓你邀請別人進入你的私人空間，沒有人要你證明你也買了某設計師牌子的椅子！我說得對嗎？我漏了甚麼嗎？我感到疑惑。

很多參賽作品都像關門後的陳列室一樣空洞。但它們是家呢！誰住在裡面？藝術在哪兒？那種紊亂呢？還有那個隨意地把花放在窗台，而不是放在一般陳列室照片所見的位置的人呢？如是者，那些花呢？藝術，是生活的象徵、你的生活還是你呢？以及那富創意，並每每以最豐富及藝術性的方法去探索「形式」所展現及藏於其背後的是甚麼的設計在那裏？

有一個作品吸引了我，它是一家書店，是我以前不認識的，在評審過後，我特地去了參觀。它的形式背後有一個意念，這參賽作品提交時很具資訊性又欠卻修飾。它背後的意念當中似乎大有可為，它把很多預設的功能緊密地結合，也因此頗堪探索。以及其照片和繪圖為說明文字提供了充足的資訊。它名字是『書得起』，座落於銅鑼灣軒尼斯道439-441號香島大廈一樓A座。走過一條又亂又窄的樓梯和電梯之後，便可以找到它。呈現於眼前的是一大堆有趣又豐富的藏書，緊密和平實的排放著，使你被包圍著，正是你到這裡來要看的東西 — 書本。

People + Book + Event

Spatial_ Office
t. PMTD headquarters
e. Design Systems Ltd.

David Adjaye

I was very impressed with the high standard of Asian design and thought it was comparable to anything happening in the rest of the world. The real challenge now for Asia is whether it can produce a distinct philosophy of design for the Asian world. I thought the judging was extremely well organized and efficient and a very enjoyable experience.

My favourite work was the "PMTD Headquarters" by Design Systems Ltd. because it was clear that they had to work with a very tight budget and had put a great deal of work into creating more with less and creating a very special environment. For the strengths of the HDKA, I think it is fantastic to have a representative body for Asian design while for the weakness, I think it would be good to include architecture as part of the whole and not have it seen as a separate thing.

In terms of improvement, I think it would be good to limit the number of boards per submission and also in the spatial category to request plans and sections are included to make the reading of the project simpler and easier to judge. I would urge Asian designers to search for a quality that is truly Asian, as the world becomes more merged and less individual, a unique quality will make you shine in the field.

亞洲設計水平之高，令我印象至深，足可與世界各地的同行媲美。亞洲現在面對的真正挑戰是她能否孕育出一套獨特的、屬於亞洲的設計哲學。我認為今次的評審策劃非常妥善且有效率，是一次愉快的經驗。我喜愛的作品是Design Systems Ltd.所設計的『PMTD總部』，很明顯他們要在緊拙的財政預算下，投入很多工作，去創造出以小為多，並營造出一個十分獨特的環境。

我認為香港設計師協會的長處，在於它讓亞洲擁有一個具代表性的設計組織；而弱點方面，我認為是對建築設計的處理，較佳方法是，把建築設計包括在作為整個設計體系的之中，而不是把它分開。至於改善方面，我認為最好能夠限制每份參賽作品的圖板數目，在空間設計類別要求提交平面圖和截面圖，讓評判能更簡單容易地審閱作品。我鼓勵亞洲的設計師探索真正的亞洲特質。因為整個世界已越趨融合，個體性越見減少，具備獨有的特質會令你鶴立雞群。

Graphic_ Book
t. The Blooming of Peony - the Memory
of Cantonese Opera Sin Fung Ming
奼紫嫣紅開遍 — 良辰美景仙鳳鳴
e. Les Suen

Hideki Nakajima 中島英樹

    I was glad that the Hong Kong Designers Association invited me to be their judge this year. Now the international world pays so much attention to Asia, and the Hong Kong Designers Association has a very international field of vision. All this is very important. At the same time, the judges were very serious and strict in the process of selecting works from designers around the Asian regions. It was really eye-opening and provided me with very valuable experience. Every work was an excellent piece of design and left me memorable impressions. I warmly congratulate all the participants, especially the awarded ones.

The winner of my Judges' Choice was Mr. Les Suen from Hong Kong and his work is "The Blooming of Peony - the Memory of Cantonese Opera Sin Fung Ming". I work on editorial design and I always have this question: Book medium already has a very long history. Is now the time for a new medium to appear?

I have always been thinking that way, so that when I saw this book during the judging, I was so shocked. I am afraid I do not have enough space to describe it here. I can only say that it "breaks the conventional mode." It has the feeling of harmony and I have not seen something like this before.

All in all, this book is so encouraging to me. It makes me believe that book medium still has a lot of potentialities. I firmly believe that this book will be passed through myriad ages.

今年,本人承蒙香港設計師協會邀請擔任評選工作,實在深感榮幸。時至今日,亞洲地區備受國際社會注視,而香港設計師協會對此亦顯示其國際視野。這些都是十分重要的。同時,各位評審員在評選來自亞洲各地的作品時,精挑細選,態度嚴謹,不但令人大開眼界,對我而言亦是非常寶貴的經驗。每件作品均設計出色,更令我留下深刻的印象。我謹向各位參賽者,特別是獲獎者,送上衷心的祝賀。

我的『評審之選』獲獎者是來自香港的孫浚良先生,他的作品是《妊紫嫣紅開遍 ─ 良辰美景仙鳳鳴》。本人也從事編輯設計,經常有這樣的疑問:書籍這種模式歷史已久,現在是否出現新模式的適當時候了?本人一直持有這種想法,故在評審期間看到這本書時,所受的衝擊尤為鉅大。篇幅所限,本人恐怕未能在此逐一具體描述,只能說這本書「打破了常規」,而它所具備的和諧感覺,更是我從未見過的。

總括而言,這本書令我大為鼓舞,讓我相信書籍這一模式仍然潛存著鉅大的發展空間。本人深信,這本書籍將會流傳後世。

Product_ Time Pieces
t. Decode clock
e. CHILLICHILLY

Gary Natsume

Design has become an international language, used by people from all over the world to connect with each other on an emotional level. At the same time, regional differences and originality in objects are becoming more and more important. Hong Kong is a unique place in the world. Because of its geographic location and history, it has the best from the East and the West in culture, food, architecture and fashion. It is also a place where the past and future coexist in beautiful harmony.

Much of the work I saw at this year's competition proved that Hong Kong designers can create contemporary objects with a deep appreciation of their own heritage while also maintaining sensitivity to new technologies. Instead of rejecting or over expressing the technology, many of the designs embraced it into a seamless solution. The most intriguing, underlying spirit I saw in all the work was "hospitality". Two chairs that interlock with each other, an ice stirrer that combines two functions in one, and a clock that tells time at one moment with unexpected surprise... They all make the visitor happy and comfortable. Probably the history of Hong Kong as a "Port City" nurtured this spirit over time by welcoming people from all over the world.

My Judges' Choice went to the clock with its mysterious symbols around the arm. The symbols looked like Braille or some other "digital signal". When the arm goes over the symbols, viewer will see the time. Clocks used to represent power, authority and technology. The one who knows time most accurately could rule the world. He or she would know when to harvest, how much to store and how to fight. Today, there is very little difference in the accuracy of clocks. Today, people don't need to wear a watch because their cellphone will tell the time, and even adjust automatically to new time zones. But I don't think clocks will disappear from our daily life, especially now when people spend most of their day inside without a sense of sunlight. Clocks should be here to show the transition from one mode of the day to another — from morning's preparation mode, to afternoon's communication and creation mode, to the evening's relaxing mode. There are many opportunities for designers to create clocks that will inform this transition in a more sensitive, poetic way to make people's life more joyful and fulfilling.

Technology is progressing rapidly every day, but the human nature of seeking comfort, joy and fulfilment will never change. I believe that is where the designer should contribute to keep objects closer to the human emotion. I would like Hong Kong to continue to be a place where designers from different regions can exchange ideas, knowledge and philosophy to make the best design for the rest of the world.

設計已成為一種國際語言，來自世界各地的人，以它在感性的層面上互相聯繫。與此同時，區域的差異及物件的原創性便越趨重要。香港是世界上一個很獨特的地方，由於它的地理位置和歷史，香港無論在文化、食物、建築及時尚潮流上，都能集東西方的優點於一身。這也是一處古舊與嶄新能美好和諧共處的地方。

我從很多的今年的參賽作品中可以証明，香港的設計師創作的當代作品，不單可以從一種對自身傳統具有很深入的瞭解，並對新科技保持很高的敏感度。在很多的作品中，既沒有抗拒或濫用科技，而是利用它與設計方案融為一體。在所有作品中，我看到一種最引人入勝的內在精神是「hospitality」。互相交錯的兩張椅子、一物二用的攪冰棒、以及在某時會以令人驚喜的方式顯示時間的時鐘。這些設計令人賞心悅目。香港，在歷史上作為一個「港口城市」，長久以來招待來自世界各地的人，這種精神可能便是由此孕育而成。

我的『評審之選』是一個有一些神祕的符號圍繞著時針的時鐘。這些符號看起來像盲人用的凸字或者一些「電子符號」。當時針疊在那些符號上，時間便會顯現出來。在過去，時鐘代表勢力 — 權力和科技。誰最準確地了解它，誰便能統治世界。他／她會明白該當何時收割，貯存多少，及如何作戰。今天，時鐘準確程度已大致相同。很多人甚至不再需要手錶，因為他們的流動電話也能顯示時間，更可以隨時區的轉變而自動調節。但是我不認為時鐘會在我們的生活中就此消失，尤其是人們現在大多數時間都生活在室內，對日光已欠缺敏感度。時鐘於此應提示一天中不同生活狀態的轉變 — 由早上的預備狀態，到下午的溝通及創作狀態，再到晚上的鬆弛狀態。實際上設計師還有很多空間去創作以更感性及更富詩意的形式去提示這些轉變的時鐘，使人們的生活更愉快和滿足。

科技正每天急速地發展，但是人類天性追尋舒適、喜悅和滿足感是不會改變的。我相信設計師應致力拉近物件和人類的感性。我希望香港能夠繼續成為一處可以讓來自不同地區的設計師交換意見、知識和人生觀的地方，為世界創造出最好的設計。

Poster_ Thematic Poster
t. Heromoism
e. Tommy Li Design Workshop Ltd.

Jonathan Barnbrook

It's some time since I have judged any design awards, what a shame because the HKDA reminded me of how much I can learn when I do so. Open debate about the nature of the work submitted can only help your own personal development. Also a forced medicine of looking at many pieces of work can revive eyes which normally look on the world of design in a very tired way.

I really did not know what to expect when looking the design from this area of the world, I have travelled widely in Asia but the design community, was almost unknown to me. What I found was not work that was looking to the Western design for inspiration but some examples which solidly reinterpreting many of the great Asian cultures in a contemporary way. Of particular interest was the work from China, a previously closed design community that was now opening up for us to see what they could do. One of my major hopes is that China does not make the same awful mistakes as the Western capitalist economies with the role of design, it is a force for positive social change and dialogue, and not just a service to manufacturers to increase profit.

Regarding my Judges' Choice, "Heromoism" by Tommy Li Design Workshop, I decided these two posters of artworks showed a playful spirit and a solid idea with a piece of text which simply talked about the legacy of Mao. A very strong piece which made me think about the complex issues facing society and design since the embracing of the market economy in China.

One very commendable decision by the invited judging panel was to throw out all of the work which was done for cigarette companies, A motion put forward originally by me, I felt that any design awards should provide a pointer to the design industry as to what designers should aspire to and value. Thankfully the other judges agreed, this contrasted to the many recent design awards recently particularly in Britain where awards were given to companies with very serious ethical practices simply because they had produced some 'nice' design. It made me feel that HKDA was seriously looking towards the future and that maybe my own country's design awards could look towards HKDA for some guidance about the effect they have on industry when they give an award.

我已經有一段時間沒有當設計比賽評審了,很慚愧,香港設計師協會提醒了我,當評審實在獲益良多。公開對作品性質進行討論只能幫助你個人的發展;再者,不得已的看很多不同的作品,可以重振看設計作品看得麻木的鑑賞力。

看著來自這地區的設計時,我真的不知能期望甚麼;我去過很多亞洲地方,但我對當中的設計社群卻一無所知。我在這些地方發現的並不是要從西方設計中找尋靈感的作品,而是一些實實在地以當代的方法重新詮釋偉大的亞洲文化的作品。特別有趣的是來自中國的作品,一個曾經對設計封閉的社群,現在正逐步開放給我們探視他們能做甚麼。其中一項我最希望看到的,就是他們不再重蹈設計的角色在西方資本主義經濟下的覆轍,設計應該是正面的社會改變和對話的力量,而不是只為生產商進一步謀利而提供的服務。

關於『評審之選』,我選擇李永銓設計廈的『毛英雄主義』海報的原因,是這兩張海報表達了一種嘲弄意味,和附有文字說明有關毛澤東遺留下來的精神的具體思想。這作品很有力,令我想到由市場經濟孕育的中國,對社會和設計所造成的複雜情況。

評審團其中一個值得讚揚的決定,就是拒絕所有為煙草公司而作的參賽作品。這原本是由我提出的,我認為任何設計獎項都應該作為設計專業的指標,為設計師提供方向和價值觀。很高興其他的評審也同意,這實在跟很多其他近期的設計大獎,特別是最近在英國的那些很不同。那些獎項頒給了一些有嚴重道德問題,而僅僅是由於它們是「很好」的設計。這令我覺得香港設計師協會對未來是認真的。我自己國家的設計獎項也應該向香港設計師協會借鏡它們所頒發的獎項對整個專業的影響。

Book
t. 深圳03設計展作品集
e. 韓家英

Lu Jingren 呂敬人

It is not easy to review a lot of works in just two days. After the other judges and I had finished our jobs, all of us "fell down" exhaustedly. It is my honour to be invited by Charles Ng, the chairman of HKDA, as one of the judges of this event. I also learnt a lot in the process of working with other judges from Hong Kong and around the world.

My first impression of this year's event was that there were a lot more entries from mainland China than before. Obviously, HKDA Awards is being more and more recognised in the mainland. It also means that Hong Kong plays a leading role in improving design in China and has inspired many young designers in China. Asian and Chinese design styles are very prominent in this year's HKDA Awards. They demonstrate a mixture of Eastern and Western cultures and mark a new visual language in contemporary China.

As I specialize in book design, I was particularly interested in Les Suen's "The Blooming of Peony - the Memory of Cantonese Opera Sin Fung Ming", Toshiyasu Nanbu's "Proto Type Font," Han Jiaying's "Shenzhen 03 Design Exhibition Catalogue", Equus Design Consultants Pte Ltd.'s "Charlie Chan & The Secret Book Craft Print Yearbook 2002." They manifested the paper medium's attractiveness and the beauty of reading. They made me feel that they were something alive, stimulating new possibilities in the atmosphere around them.

Digital technology has been changing people's lives nowadays. But we are not satisfied with the virtual world presented through a flat screen. We still want to get in touch with the traditional media. This time the competition showed numerous delightful creations of "spiritual materials." Behind a piece of materialized work, there are some deep-rooted traditions that cannot be seen. They bring happiness and beautiful things for us in this era.

Last but not least, what impressed me was that the involved people worked in such passionate, efficient, and orderly ways. It was really moving. They are very good models for our colleagues in mainland China. Thanks for their efforts.

Han Jiaying's "Shenzhen 03 Design Exhibition Catalogue" was really a "design feast" that I heartedly enjoyed very much. The book's very innovative design concept reveals that the author has a thorough consideration of elements in book design. From its formal structure to the expressed message, from the rhythm of colour and sign to the use of paper materials… from the whole of it to its details, from disorder to order, from space to time, from the book form to the contexts of expression, from logic to illusion… it made me feel that it is simultaneously poetic and philosophical. Hence "Collected Works of the Shenzhen 03 Design Exhibition" was my own Judges Choice.

在如此數量眾多、令人眼花繚亂的作品面前僅用兩天時間評出優秀作品，實在不易。我們五位評委評到最後一刻全部「躺倒了」。我十分榮幸受香港設師協會主席吳秋全先生之邀，擔任本次大賽的評委，並與各國及香港評委一起工作，受益匪淺。

本次大賽的第一印象是大陸作品比歷屆多了不少，顯見『香港設計師協會獎』大賽的知名度在大陸地區的影響逐年擴大。這也說明香港在引領中國設計進步所發揮的龍頭作用，從而激發許多大陸的年輕設計師們踴躍參與的熱情，也使得亞洲設計風、中國設計風的作品在本次融匯貫通東西文化的『香港設計師協會獎』大賽的舞台上突顯出順風上水的勢頭，展示了賦予時代印記的中國文化新視覺語言的一道風景。

也許是與本人的專業相關，本次大賽的書籍設計特別引我關注，孫浚良的《妊紫嫣紅開遍 — 良辰美景仙鳳鳴》（香港）、南部俊安的《PROTO TYPE FONT》（日本）、韓家英的《深圳03設計展作品集》（中國大陸）、Equus Design Consultants Pte Ltd.的《Charlie Chan & The Secret Book Craft Print Yearbook 2002》無不發揮紙品媒體的形態魅力與閱讀美感。更使我感受到這些作品不是停滯在某一凝固時間的靜止生命，而是在營造和指引周邊環境有生氣的元素。

當今流行的數碼技術確實改變了每一個人的生活，但人們已經不滿足於虛擬的視屏媒體的傳達，仍對傳統物化載體心存親近之感。本次大賽為我們呈現了無數令人欣喜的「物質之精神」的創造。在一件件物化作品的表面下，無形又不可見的恰恰是深藏其中的傳統，他們給人們帶來了快樂，也為這個時代留下了美好的東西。最後，令我感動的是，這次大賽的組織者和所有參與工作的人員，他們積極、熱情、高效、有序的工作給我留下美好的印象，也值得大陸的同行學習。謝謝他們所付出的辛勞。

韓家英設計的《深圳03設計展作品集》是我傾心享用的一道美味的書籍設計「佳餚」。這是一部有新的書籍設計概念的作品，從中可以看出作者悉心經營的書籍設計元素全方位的思考。從內容傳遞的形式結構到信息層次把握、從色彩符號的節奏處理到物化紙材語言的準確運用、從整體到細部、從無序到有序、從空間到時間、從書籍形態到傳達語境、從邏輯思考到幻覺遐想，令我感受有一種富有詩意，又具哲理的秩序控制的閱讀享受，為此選中《深圳03設計展作品集》作為我的『評委之選』。

Product_ Electrical Consumer Product
t. In-ear Gaming Headphone - SHG8010
e. Philips Electronics Hong Kong Ltd.

Lorraine Justice

The work exhibited this year was of great variety with strong products showing in the areas of electronics, gift items and furniture. Overall, these products from Hong Kong had an emphasis on materials, technology and functionality that are of international standard. An Asian design aesthetic is starting to emerge in the product areas of accessories and personal care items. This was a good group of products to judge. This particular piece of game equipment was well thought out and looks hand crafted because of the attention to detail. The choice of materials and shape make it a product that you want to pick up and use. The best part is it improves digital entertainment through an enhanced sensory experience, making "time out for games" more enjoyable. This is a great gift for anyone who plays games or for individual owners who love the latest in technology. In addition, the designers paid a lot of attention to ergonomic detail, handling and fit, no matter the size. It is an all around well-designed product worthy of the Philips Design.

今年，於電子/電器用品、禮品及傢俱等項目中均見不少出色之作。總體來看，香港的作品多強調物料、科技及實用性符合國際標準，而於飾物及個人用品項目中，則可見一股亞洲的設計風潮正乘時而起。對評審來說，這是一批好的作品。這件充滿玩味的作品，不單意念好，細緻的手工更使它看來像是手製品，而它的物料及外形，令人忍不住要拿上手看看，不過最精彩的，是它通過電子娛樂把感官體驗提升，令這「玩一玩」的玩意更好玩！不單愛玩的人，愛新科技的用家皆會對它愛不釋手。設計師在這件玩具作品上，對符合人體工學的細節、實際使用表現、外型以至體積等下了不少心思，令它各方面均表現突出，不愧為Philips Design的出品。

Graphic_ Annual Report
t. Charlie Chan & The Secret Book
Craft Print Yearbook 2002
e. Equus Design Consultants Pte Ltd.

Mervyn Kurlansky

During my long career in the field of graphic design, I have been privileged to participate in the judging of numerous design awards and have experienced a number of different methods of arriving at a fair selection. With regard to the HKDA Awards 05 the method devised by the executive members of the Hong Kong Designers Association was in my opinion the most efficient and democratic I have yet witnessed. The members of the jury and their hosts conducted their task with due diligence and it was a pleasure and an honour to serve with them.

The international spread of the jury also ensured that sound consideration was given to the cultural differences amongst the entries. It has also been my experience that one can usually expect to find that on average only approximately 15% of the work entered in awards of this kind are of a good standard. Occasionally this can be as high as 25% and this was the case in several categories on this occasion. I was least impressed by the visual identity system category and most impressed by the book design section but my favourite piece was to be found amongst the annual reports. Every now and then I come across a piece of visual communication that warms my heart and lifts my spirit, and reminds me why I became a graphic designer.

The "Craft Print Yearbook 2002" is one of the most innovative and surprising annual reports I have seen in a long time. The approach is intelligent, inventive and witty. ("The Concise Oxford English Dictionary" defines wit as sudden, unexpected, intellectual pleasure.) The concept is entirely appropriate to the subject matter and the work is beautifully crafted with great attention having been paid to every detail throughout the entire publication.

在我從事平面設計的漫長歲月中，曾經在無數設計大獎中擔任評審，也有嘗試以不同方法達至公平結果的經驗。『香港設計師協會獎05』的評選方式是由該會的執行委員訂定的。我認爲它是我所見過最有效率和最民主的評審方式。評審團的成員和其他參與者都非常認眞及投入。能和他們一起工作實在是一種榮譽。國際化的評審團也確保能顧及到不同參選作品之間的文化差異。按我的經驗，在這類比賽中，大概可以預期平均約有15%的參賽作品入選，這已是不錯的水準了。這次，部份組別的入選率竟高達25%。視覺形象系統組別的作品對我比較欠缺吸引力，書籍設計卻給我最深印象。不過我最喜歡的作品是在年報組別中發現的。

偶爾我會看見一些作品讓我心頭一暖、心情興奮和提醒我爲何要成爲平面設計師。《Craft Print 2002年年報》是我多年來見過其中一份最具創意和最令人驚喜的年報設計。它的表現手法是明智、創新和巧妙的。(《牛津簡明英語辭典》把巧妙解釋爲突然、意想不到和聰穎的樂事)作品的概念跟題材非常配合，而作品的工藝出色，在每個細節上都下了不少工夫。

Graphic_ Assorted Promotional Item
t. Calendiary
e. CoDesign Ltd.

Stanley Wong 黃炳培

1. After I had agreed to be one of the judges, I began to regret. It was of course honourable to be the representative of Hong Kong. But not being able to compete with other great Asian designers is indeed a pity.

2. Asia has a lot of excellent designers. There were so many great works in the last three years. When I look back, I am glad that I did not participate and bump into disappointment.

3. I have been the judge of different international and local competitions. I do not know why, only approximately 0.5 to 1 % of the entries are really excellent. Apart from congratulating and admiring their designers, I cared so much about the proportion between good and excellent works. This reflected the quality of design works of that year. In a sense, it is also the reason why design awards are so appealing. If you ask me about the quality of this year's entries, I would say: they still need to improve a lot.

4. To me, design, culture, and art are not separate. Creation is a process of communication. For many years, there were a lot of cultural features in Asian and global poster competitions. So many good works there were of course their designers' meticulous creations. And because of market demand, the poster categories of a lot of design awards initiate cultural features in order to create spaces between graphic design and cultural/artistic works. Some overseas judges felt uncomfortable with this group of works in the review process this time. They did not know what the criteria were. This year, there were several excellent entries (they were not posters). To be fair, whether you

have commercial clients or not, you still need to take care of the audience/market size while you create your works. It was really hard to compare them, and sometimes people did doubt whether the comparison was fair. What was more unfortunate was that the rules of the awards did not spell out (or define) the criteria. The judges found it really hard to make decision. I cannot deny that there might be some unfair and improper situations for the participated designers. I apologize for that. It is time for us to discuss how we should define and manage design awards in the future.

5. I reviewed the works all night long until morning. I chose a book titled "Amount" (多少). You have to read it from cover to cover and experience the idea that the more you put down the more you earn in your heart. It is really good… I read it several times and found the coils in it very fussy, pretentious, and unnecessary. They are exactly the opposite of what the book is about…

6. My two other cups of tea are a calendar "Calendiary" and a poster about the year Hung Lam was born. They are very solid, not fussy at all. And more importantly, they give their audience some inspiration. At last I chose the calendar "Calendiary" because it gave me positive inspirations. A commercial project for a paper company can provide not only designs but also a lesson on the philosophy of life for people to appreciate. This is utterly the utmost of the power of design!

1. 答允大會邀請出席評審後，一度十分後悔。身為香港代表當然光榮，不能參賽與亞洲各出色設計師觀摩切磋，心總是癢癢的。

2. 亞洲高手林立，過去三年佳作不少。回心一想，也幸好沒有投稿「送死」，換來失意。

3. 當過很多國際/本地不同的比賽評審；不知為何，出色叫絕的作品往往都是大概佔0.5-1個百分點。恭賀羨慕他們之餘，其實我每次都關心展中介乎一般好及絕頂好之作品的比率高否，這正是反映年度地域的設計成績水準的最好讀數。又或者是個比賽吸引號召力另一解讀方法。若果問我今屆這黃金指數，我會答：離高還有一大距離。

4. 對我來說，從來不刻意將設計、文化和藝術劃分清楚，創作就是溝通。多年來亞洲以至全球的文化專題海報觀摩比賽的眾多項目，產生了無數的非商業甚至近乎沒面世和大眾溝通的海報作品。裡面佳作當然是眾設計師個人匠心獨運，所以不久以前因市場的需要，很多設計展海報項目已特別開一個文化/專題的類別，以方便這批乎乎平面設計和文化藝術間作品作龍虎榜。今次評審過程中，一些海外評判一直對這一環節抱著很不習慣，並不知怎落墨評分的表現和意見。今屆參展作品中，有數件（非海報）極之出色的作品又來到這個空間。憑心而論，有商業客戶與否，要照顧觀眾/市場的大小，在一個比賽中同一比拼是十分困難，有時甚至引來不公平之說。更不幸的是與會的比賽章程未有詳細列明（或很難定界線），所以令眾評審很難決定。無可厚非，對這些參展設計師有不公平及沒有最安善之安排，也要多說一句抱歉。日後設計比賽的定義及界限怎樣處理，是時候讓我們來一個討論。

5. 評審至第二天早上，滿以為挑定一本名為《多少》的書作為我評審心頭選。一本要你由首頁翻看到尾，就親身經歷放下和人生佔有更少；心裡就擁有更多的道理，真的很好。細看多遍發覺它中間結紮的線圈真的花巧、造作及多餘。與書要介紹的態度完全違背。

6. 另外兩件心頭好是《Calendiary》日曆及林偉雄出生年海報。兩作品都給我不花巧，言之有物的感覺，更重要是，它倆都給觀眾得到一點啟示。最後我選了《Calendiary》日曆，因它給我的啟示是正面積極和明天的。一個紙行的商業項目能給人欣賞設計之餘，亦上了一課人生哲理，這可就是設計至大的力量吧。

Product_ Electronic & Electrical Appliance
t. Big Shot Professional Hairdryer with Ceramic Attachments HD552
e. Kenford Industrial Co., Ltd.

Wen-long Chen 陳文龍

Recently, I have been invited to review designs in different places, including mainland China, Taiwan, as well as certain international competitions. From its planning, poster, website, to arrangement of activities, this event was very professional and international. In Greater China district, Hong Kong is the most international city in terms of both time and depth. Thus Hong Kong's path to internationalization is extremely advantageous. This time, I could feel that both the Hong Kong government and the people of Hong Kong zealously intend to develop strategies of design, articulate the core of Asian design, and improve the status of Hong Kong design. It is not difficult to design a sophisticated commodity like hair dryer. But excellent and refreshing designs are still very recommendable! The product's shape is very simple. The collocation of its materials and the texture of its colours show its functions. The delicacies (like the connection of different parts and materials) and accessories demonstrate the quality of the product's making and the value of such an innovation!

最近我應邀到不同地方作設計評審，包括中國大陸、台灣與及一些國際性的比賽。從整體規劃、海報、網頁設計到活動的安排，這次活動都是很專業和國際化的。香港是大中華區無論在歷史、深度也是最國際化的城市。因此，香港在國際化的路上擁有絕對的優勢。這次，我感受到香港政府與香港市民都熱衷發展設計策略、清晰展現亞洲設計核心及提升香港的設計地位。要設計像風筒這種發展成熟的商品並不困難，但出類拔萃的設計，仍是很值得推崇的！這產品的簡潔造型，物料的應用搭配與顏色的質感充分表現其功能。細節部份（如不同零部件與物料之間的連繫）及配件展現產品的生產質素與這新穎設計的價值！

New Media_ Educational Website
t. Website Development
e. Westcomzivo Ltd

Jonathan Wong

The website of "Little Prince is Depressed" (www.depression.edu.hk) is my Judges' Choice. It's a very informative and interactive educational site for people learning and understanding more what depression is. It's also in bilingual with both traditional and simplified Chinese. The site is nicely designed with illustration, animation and music background. A character "little prince" is created and used to represent someone who has depression symptom. It's a hearty idea because it gives a human touch to the users and hence draws more of their attention to the contents. Also, the website is well structured. It's user-friendly with self-explanatory menu, good user flows and navigation. The design drives users to go through the rich contents inside with comfortable music background. Also it's very important that the developer would have put a user survey at the bottom of the pages that makes users feel that their comments and suggestions are welcomed. It's very important to impress users with good user experience. I think it is the best among other finalists in terms of its creativity, contents, execution, usability and great presentation. It proves a very positive user experience.

網站『憂鬱小王子之路』（www.depression.edu.hk）是我的『評審之選』。它是個很富資訊性和互動性的教育網站，讓人認識並了解抑鬱症。它提供雙語並備有繁體和簡體字版本。這是個設計精緻的網站，並配有插圖、動畫和背景音樂。網站塑造了「小王子」這個角色代表那些患有抑鬱症病徵的人。這是個很用心的意念，使用者能感到一點人性，因此更引起了用者對內容的注意。另外，網站的結構完善、目錄一目了然、導覽流暢，容易使用。這些設計帶領用者在令人舒暢的背景音樂下，瀏覽網站中豐富的內容。此外，在網頁底部還有一項使用者調查，讓用者感到自己的意見和提議是受重視的。以愉快的經驗令用者留下深刻印象，是非常重要的。在所有入選作品中，我認為它在創意、內容、執行、易用性和外觀設計等各方面都最好的。它帶出了一種很正面的瀏覽經驗。

New Media_ Other New Media Graphic
t. Corroder 饕餮
e. Rice 5

Nick Law

What I found most interesting about the work was it's cultural distinctiveness. At this time of creeping global culture, in this most universal of mediums, an authentic regional aesthetic was apparent. There was a tendency towards an energetic visual density. I found this layering particularly compelling when applied to installations. The "WKCD Exhibition", the "Style HK 2004" and the "Toa Heung Museum" work were all beautiful, lush examples of this approach. Because they didn't demand precise interaction they were able to surround the viewer with a breathtaking symphony of immersive stimuli. For the websites this chaos was at times obscuring function. When it did work, it was because the complexity was ordered and given a clear hierarchy. One of my favourite pieces was not a website or an installation, it was the simple animated short "Corroder". It demonstrates what powerful work can emerge as a result of digital technology democratizing the tools of filmmaking. It is a haunting, beautifully crafted story fusing lurid live action environments with starkly primitive black and white characters. It felt grounded in a region, in this instance not because of its density, but because of it's off kilter simplicity.

於今次比賽中，令我最感到有興趣的是作品的文化特徵。在這個文化逐漸變得全球化的年代，媒體亦變得一體化，真實又地道的文化美便變得十分突出。我也發覺越來越多作品使用強烈的視覺表達手法。當運用到大型裝置時，效果更是強烈。而『WKCD Exhibition』、『Style HK 2004』和『Toa Heung Museum』，正是漂亮的好例子，因為它們無須互動的關係，更可令觀眾全心全意地享受眼前的視覺刺激。這個表達手法運用到網頁設計時，可能會遮蓋了網頁的功能，但若能把複雜變得井井有條、層次分明，則是可行的。於今次比賽中，最得我心的不是網頁設計或裝置作品，而是一條短短的動畫片『饕餮』，它充分表現了電子科技把影像製作自主化的威力。一個儕人的故事，配合真實的環境及粗糙、黑白的角色，迫力十足，但反而是它的平實，令人感到沉重不已。

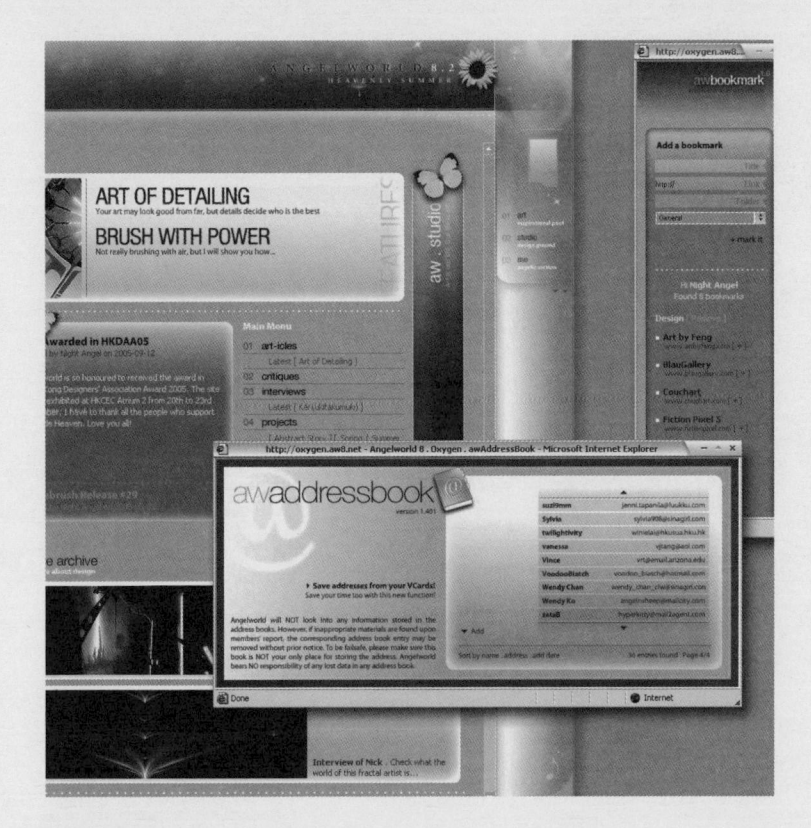

*New Media_*
Business & Consumer Website
t. Angelworld
e. Vincent Lai Wing Him

Seol Euna

I consider that it was a great chance for me to have a wider vision to the works of Asian circle to participate in the HKDA Awards 05 as a judge. One thing I feel lack of it is that most submitted works were below standard except for the prize-winning works. I hope this can be served as a momentum for the improvement in quality of the works of Asian circle in the future. It is very hard to maintain certain works consistently from the beginning to the end. Especially, it is very unusual that the site with the level as "AngelWorld" has the unity in both design and navigation on the whole. "AngelWorld" shows a superior level in technique as well. With all of these factors, I choose "AngelWorld" as my Judges' Choice with no hesitation.

我認為當『香港設計師協會獎05』的當評審,是對亞洲設計有更多認識的機會。唯一不足的是除了得獎的作品外,參賽的作品都在水平以下。我希望這次比賽會是將來提升亞洲設計水平的動力。要從頭到尾保持一些作品的連貫性是很困難的。尤其是要在像『AngelWorld』這樣水平的網站中把設計和瀏覽結合為一個整體。此外,『AngelWorld』在技術上也是超高水準的。基於這些因素,我毫不猶豫地選了『AngelWorld』作為我的『評審之選』。

Raymond Fung 馮永基

In this year's submissions in the category of Spatial Design, there was a record high in numbers, which implying that the HKDA Awards, as often perceived as a predominantly graphic competition, has already gained recognition by interior designers, from both local and abroad, as one of the most remarkable professional events in the field. Apart from local big firms which submitted the largest share of high quality works, I am delighted to have seen many more individual new comers, whose works had demonstrated its attempts to depart from a stereotyped approach. These were presumably designers' own premises which would allow oneself to have total freedom to manifest space, light, composition and more importantly building materials that are tasteful, and yet being excluded in a commercial world as such. Regrettably, I had decided to giving up my own Judges' Choice, because I was not convinced of such an important prize is to be totally judged upon one's own subjectivity. It is therefore worth reviewing if such category of award is still in-line with prevailing adjudication system, especially when this HKDA Awards has progressively established to become an international competition, catering for the whole of Asia Pacific Region.

On the overall, the submissions maintained to be of very high professional standard, nevertheless the three judges were eager to see signature works that could be much more inspiring. It is evident that the submissions were so much restrained by market-driven clients, whom would not be interested to expose to new ideas and challenges.

今屆參加空間設計組別的作品空前踴躍，反映出這個向來被視為由平面設計主導的『香港設計師協會獎』，已深受海內外室內專業設計師認同，且被高度評價為業內最受歡迎的盛事。除了本地的主要公司提交最大部份的高質作品外，更高興的，是看見個別新人輩出。誠然，他們能夠擺脫傳統，主要是反映於自資的項目中，才得以自由地發揮空間、光源和構圖之間的變奏；而更重要是，當事人可以唾棄俗套，洒脫地運用有品味的建築材料。我放棄挑選『評審之選』的決定，是不苟同其過份依重個人主觀判斷。尤其這項比賽已提升至亞太地區的層次，我們更值得檢討這個特別獎項是否還配合現行的審評制度。

整體來說，參賽的作品都保持極高的專業水平。惟三位評判都期待能有強調個人風格而具啓發性的作品參賽。事實所見，它們還未能逃離市場主導的枷鎖。

Index 索引

Award*

Gold 金獎
Silver 銀獎
Bronze 銅獎
Excellent 優異獎
Merit 入選獎

*All works included in this book are award winning designs.
Credits without award label refer to Merit Award winning works.
本書收錄本屆比賽之各項獲獎作品。沒有獎項標籤的乃獲入選獎的作品。

Credit

a. = Animation 動畫師
ad. = Art Director 美術總監
ap. = Application Programmer 應用程式編寫員
at. = Artist 藝術家
c. = Construction 建製
cd. = Creative Director 創作總監
ce. = Computer Effect 電腦效果
cl. = Client 客戶
cp. = Color Separation 分色
cs. = Customer Service 客戶服務
cw. = Copywriter 撰稿員
d. = Designer 設計師
da. = Design Assistance 設計助理
dd. = Design Director 設計總監
e. = Entrant 參賽者
ed. = Editor 編輯
et. = English Translator 英語翻譯員
gd. = Graphic Design 平面設計
i. = Illustrator 插畫師
ia. = Information Architect 訊息規劃
m. = Manufacturer 製造商/製作公司
mo. = Model 模特兒
mp. = Multimedia Programmer 多媒體程式編寫員
o. = Others 其他
p. = Photographer 攝影師
pb. = Publisher 出版商
pc. = Printing Consultants 印刷顧問
pd. = Producer 監製
pj. = Project Director 項目總監
pm. = Project Manager 項目主任
pp. = Print Production 印刷製作
pr. = Photo Retouch
pt. = Printing 印刷
re. = Remarks 注意事項
s. = Sound 音效設計
sd. = System Design 系統設計
t. = Title 主題
w. = Website 網站

Full set of works may not be exhibited as a series; we reserve the right to edit all materials included in this book.
大會保有全書之編輯權利，系列作品未必全數編列於本作品集中。

GOLD AWARDS 金賞
금상수상 金奖作品

The Gold Awards recognise the highest quality of design and most outstanding innovations of the year.

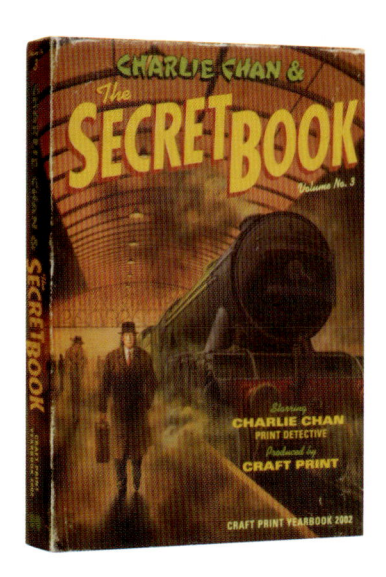

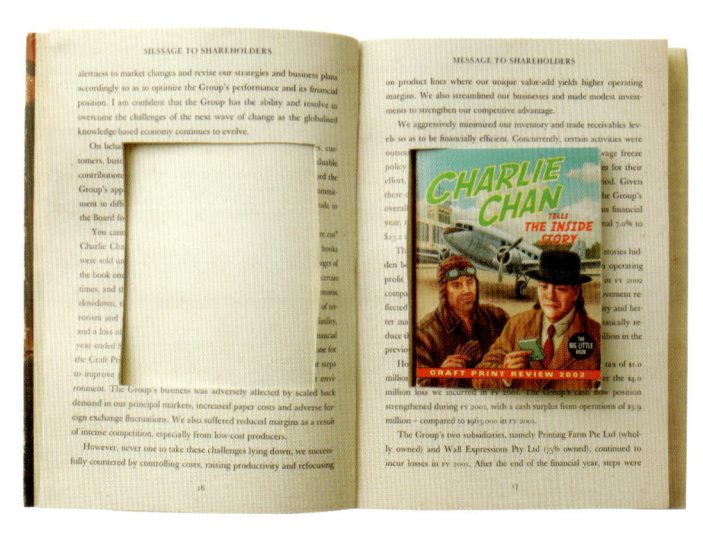

Gold
1_ Annual Report

t. Charlie Chan & The Secret Book
Craft Print Yearbook 2002
e. Equus Design Consultants Pte Ltd.
cd. Andrew Thomas
d. Chung Chi Ying, Gan Mong Teng
i. Michael Lui
cw. Andrew Thomas
sp. pt. cl. Craft Print International Ltd.

46

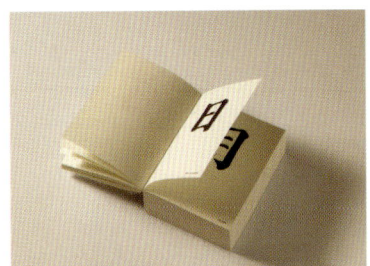

Antalis Gold Award
2_ Assorted Promotion item
t. Calendiary
e. CoDesign Ltd.
dd. Eddy Yu, Hung Lam
d. Ken Lo, Teresa Hui
cw. Foronica Lam, Ken Lo
pt. Wai Man Book Binding (China) Ltd.
cl. Heiwa Paper Co., (H.K.) Ltd.
ca. Ou Da Wei

Antalis Gold Award
3_ Assosrted Promotional item
t. Proto Type Font
e. ad. d. Toshiyasu Nanbu
cl. Taste Inc.

48

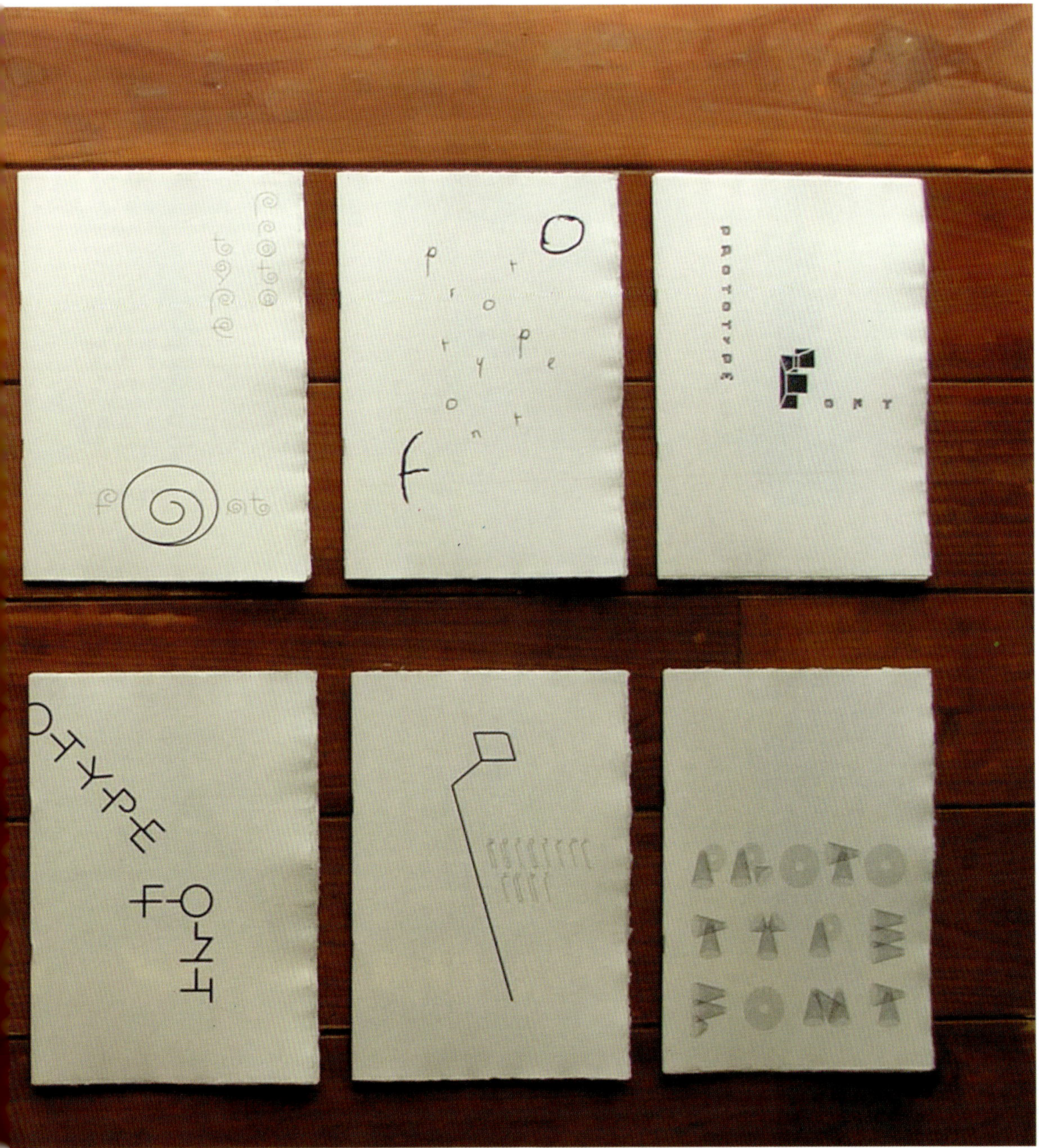

3

OZONE

May the ozone hole expanded now after it is pointed out that the ozone hole has expanded because of the environmental destruction?It is correct that the influence increases to men by the thing that a large amount of ultraviolet rays pours down.

the whirl is existence from the outside to the inside that looks like the circuit that connects the outside from the inside.

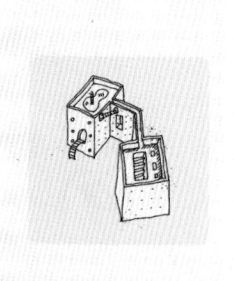

minimal house where office was made to be mated to house of resort type.

STRUCTURE

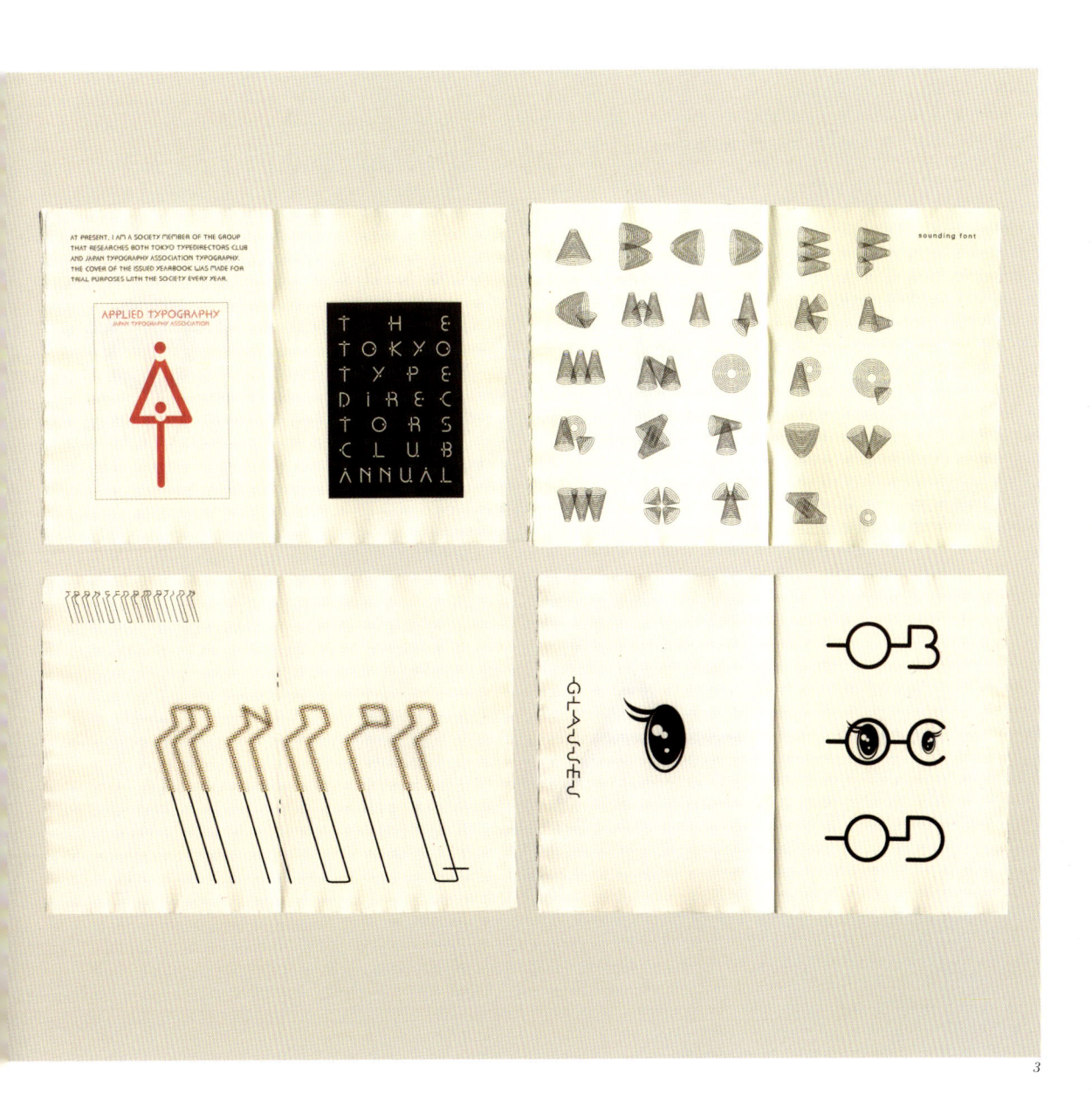

AT PRESENT, I AM A SOCIETY MEMBER OF THE GROUP
THAT RESEARCHES BOTH TOKYO TYPEDIRECTORS CLUB
AND JAPAN TYPOGRAPHY ASSOCIATION TYPOGRAPHY.
THE COVER OF THE ISSUED YEARBOOK WAS MADE FOR
TRIAL PURPOSES WITH THE SOCIETY EVERY YEAR.

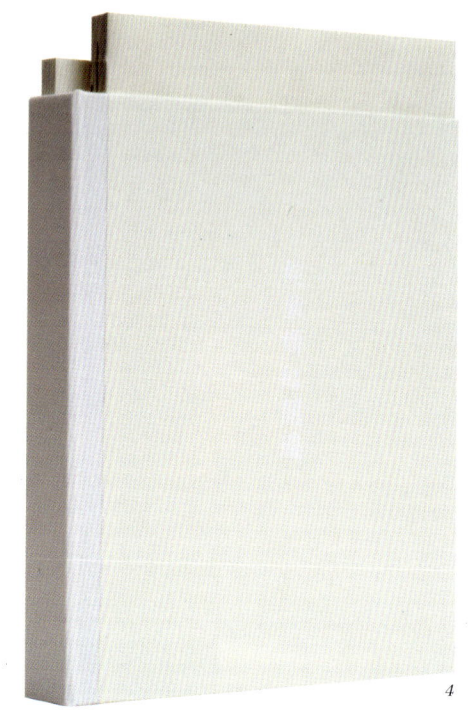

Gold
4_ Book

t. The Blooming of Peony - the Memory of
 Cantonese Opera Sin Fung Ming
 姹紫嫣紅開遍—良辰美景仙鳳鳴
e. cd. ad. d. Les Suen
pt. Kee Mei Printing Co., Ltd.
cl. Joint Publishing (HK) Co., Ltd.

白蛇新傳

再世紅梅記
仙鳳鳴劇團第九屆演出特刊

任劍輝

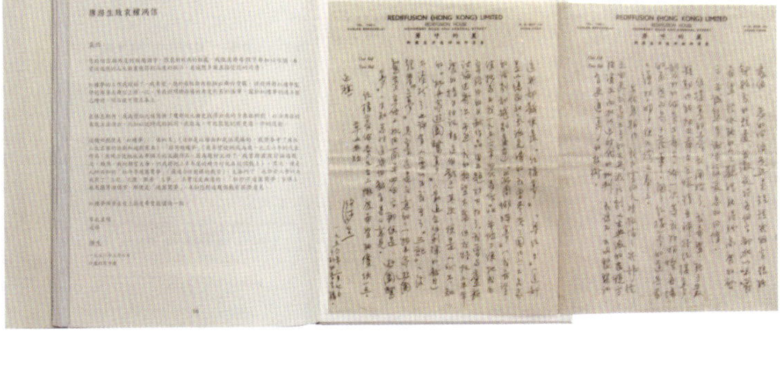
REDIFFUSION (HONG KONG) LIMITED
REDIFFUSION (HONG KONG) LIMITED

P.S. ALL OF THESE ARTICLES ARE TRUE, EXCEPT FOR ONE LITTLE LIE. P.S. TUTTI QUESTI ARTICOLI SONO VERI, A PARTE UNA PICCOLA BUGIA.

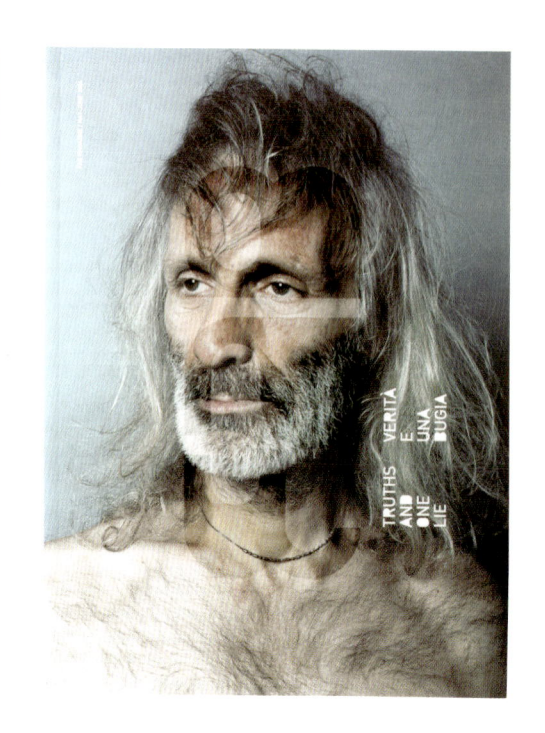

AND THEN, AFTER ALL, THERE WAS STILL SOMETHING ELSE WE WANTED TO SAY. / E POI, DOPO TUTTO, C'ERA QUALCOS'ALTRO CHE VOLEVAMO DIRE.

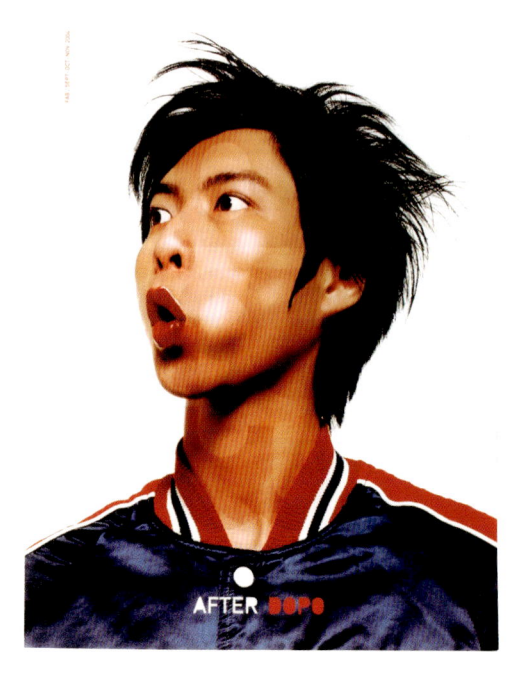

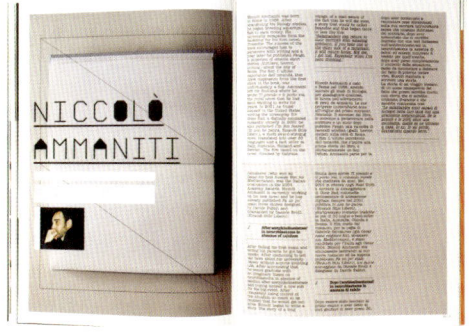

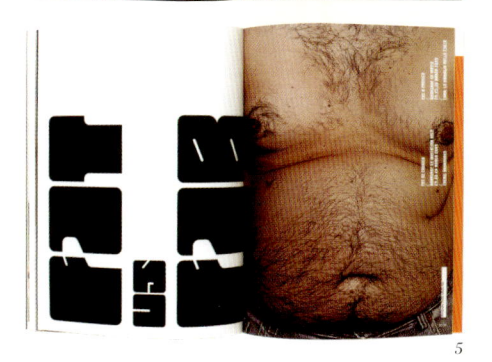

BEWARE OF IDEALS.
THE BEST THEY CAN DO
IS TO BE JUST THE SAME
AS YOUR EXPECTATIONS./
DIFFIDATE DEGLI IDEALI.
IL MASSIMO CHE POSSONO
FARE È QUELLO DI
CORRISPONDERE ALLE
VOSTRE ASPETTATIVE.

TRUTHS AND ONE LIE
VERITÀ E UNA BUGIA

NICCOLÒ AMMANITI

Gold
5_ *Editoral*
t. "FAB" Issue 1 - 3
e. MILKXHAKE
ad. MILKXHAKE, Fab Creative Team
cw. Creative Writing Department, Fabrica
cl. Fabrica, Italy

心靈環保禪淨中心（非牟利）有限公司
PEACE OF MIND ZENTER (NON PROFIT MAKING) LTD
灣仔天樂里2至4號金豐商業大廈6字樓
6/F, KAM FUNG COM'L BLDG, 2-4 TIN LOK LANE, WANCHAI, HK

T 2572 7892　F 2572 7717

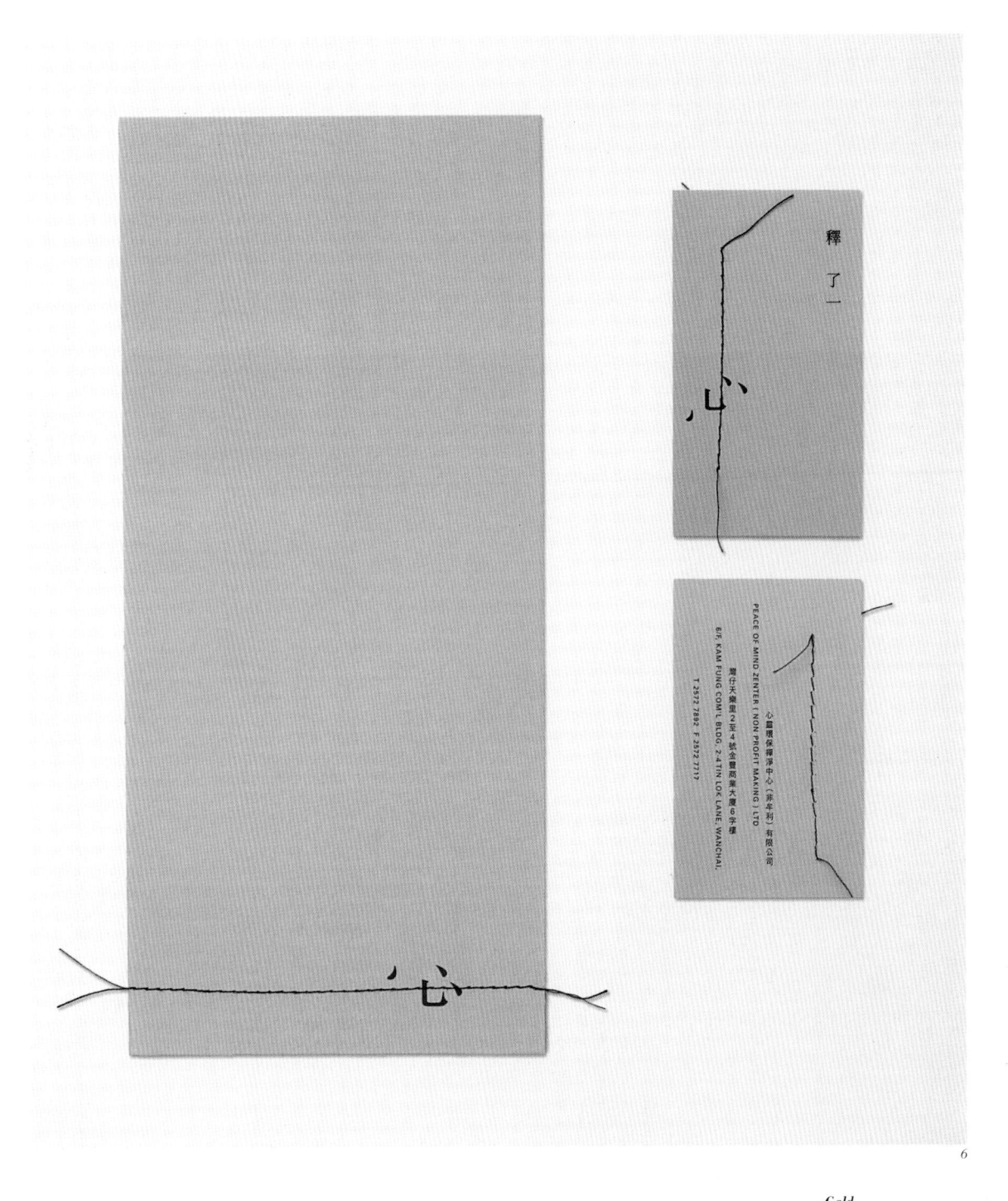

Gold

6_ *Stationery*

t. Peace of Mind Zenter
e. CoDesign Ltd.
dd. *d*. Hung Lam
pt. L.Force Printing Co., Ltd.
cl. Peace of Mind Zenter

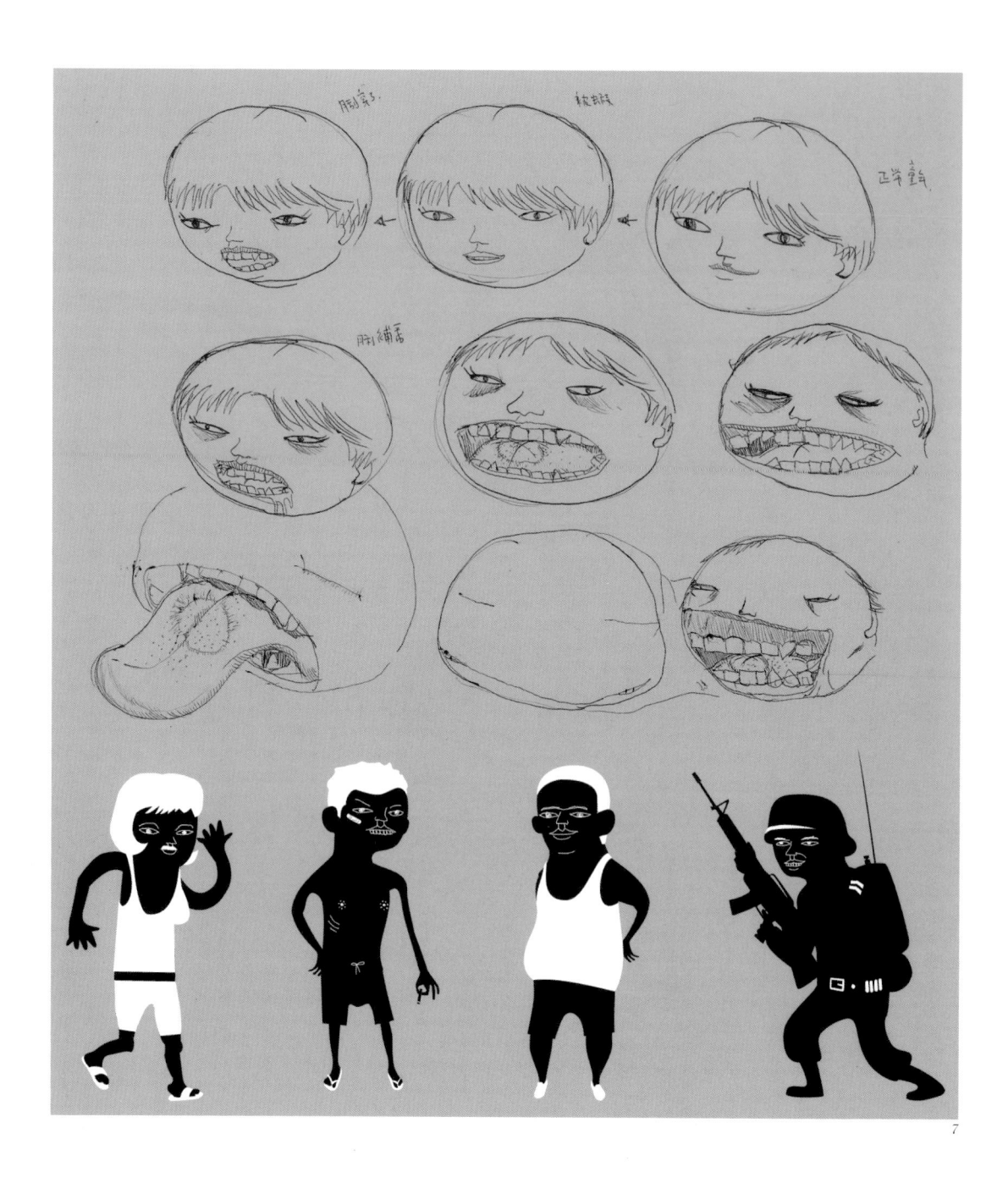

Gold
7_ Other New Media Graphic
t. Corroder 饕餮
e. Rice 5
cd. Kevin Tsang, Tom Shum
ad. d. i. a. Kevin Tsang, Tom Shum, Andrew Lee
p. Tom Shum, Andrew Lee
cw. Andrew Lee
s. Alok
cl. Hong Kong Arts Centre

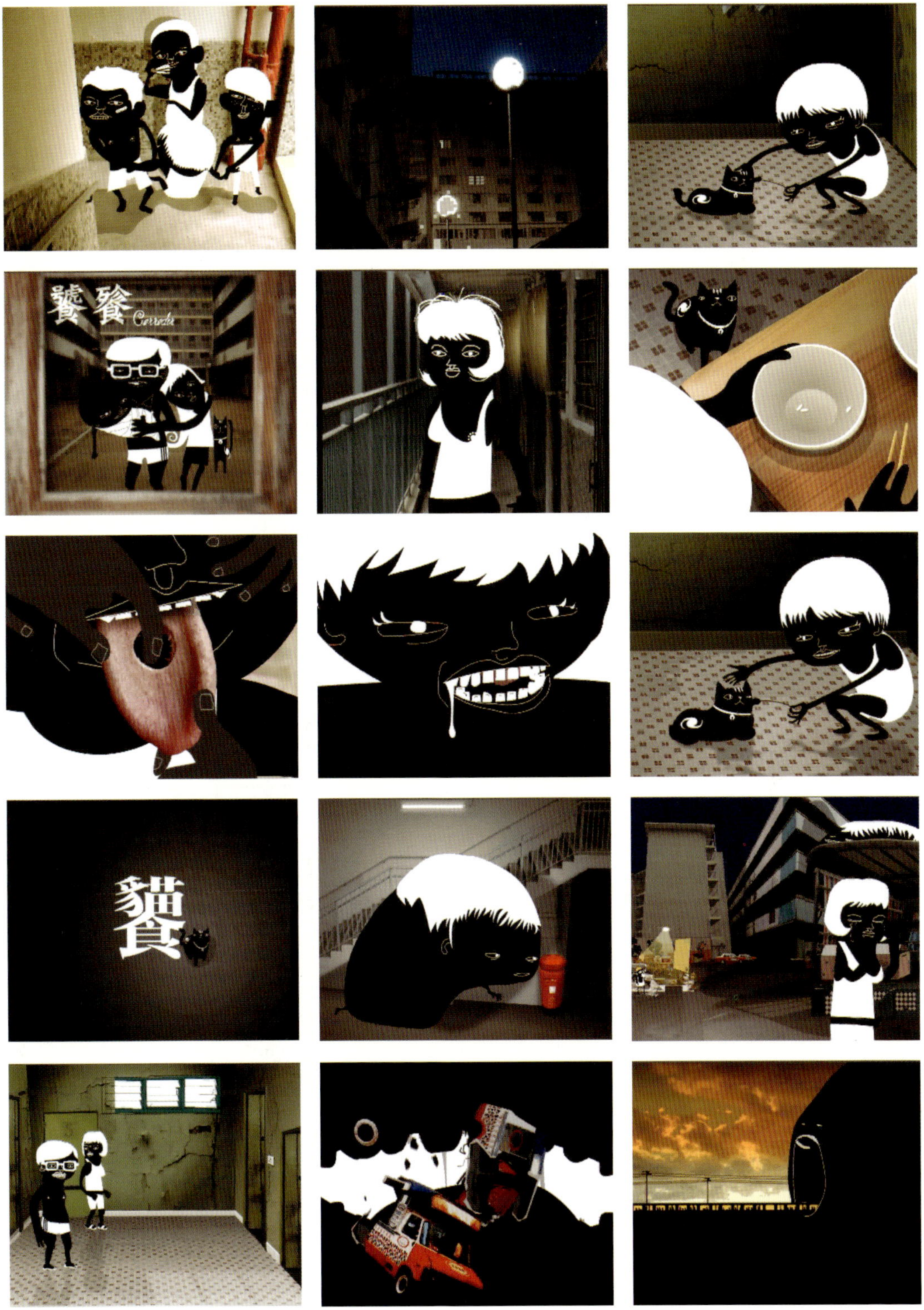

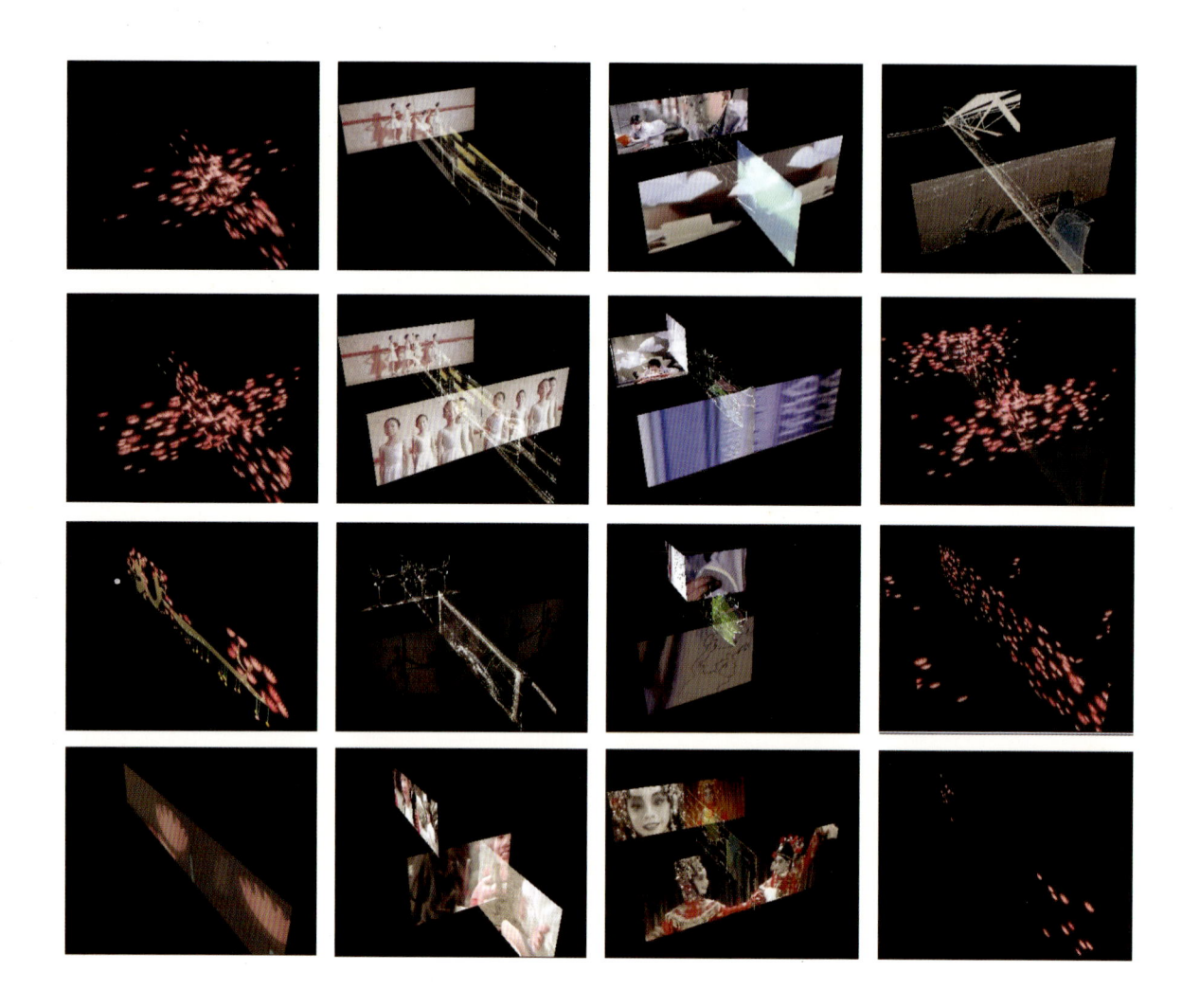

Gold
8_ *Other New Media Graphics*
t. WKCD Exhibition
e. Draughtzman
cd. dd. Ziggy Koo
ad. Alliot Cheng
d. Godwin Ko, Josephine Ching
p. cw. QiQihar
s. Wilson Tsang, Poon Tak Shu
a. Dino Technology
ap. i. NTlab
cl. Henderson Land Development Co., Ltd.

8

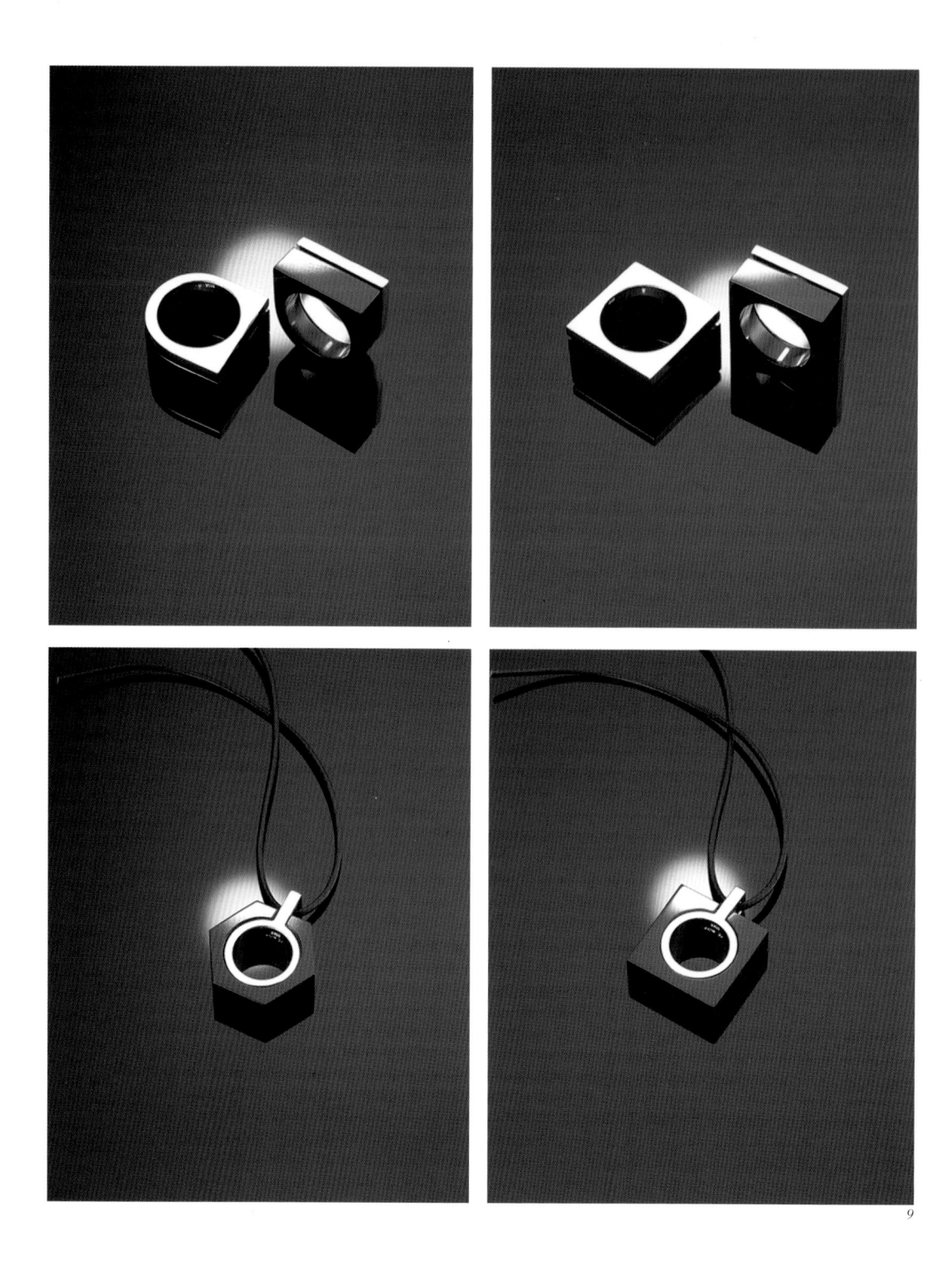

Gold
9_ Fashion Accessories
t. Jade Collection
e. Barrie Ho Architecture Interiors Ltd.

Gold
10_ *Electronic & Electrical Appliance*
t. 5.8 GHz Premium Telephone
e. VTech

Gold
11_ *Electronic & Electrical Appliance*
t. Big Shot Professional Hairdryer with Ceramic Attachments HD552
e. m. Kenford Industrial Company Ltd.
d. Michael Keong Wai Ho
cl. Remington

12

Gold
*12_* Furniture
t. Dik & Dak
e. Kan & Lau Design Consultants
dd. ad. d. cl. Freeman Lau Siu Hong

Gold

13_ Time Pieces

t. Decode Clock
e. CHILLICHILLY
d. Arthur Yung, Clement Cheung
dd. Arthur Yung
ad. cs. Clement Cheung
m. Seedz Ltd.
cl. CHILLICHILLY by Seedz Ltd.

66

14

Gold
14_ Charactger Design
t. Gardener 6"
e. cd. dd. ad. d. Michael Lau
cl. Crazysmiles Co., Ltd.

PUBLICATION 出版
출판 出版物及刊物

As the printed page competes more and more with the scrolling screen, these editorial publications - books, magazines, even annual reports - are specimens of good design for both literature and leisure reading.

Annual Report
Book
Editorial

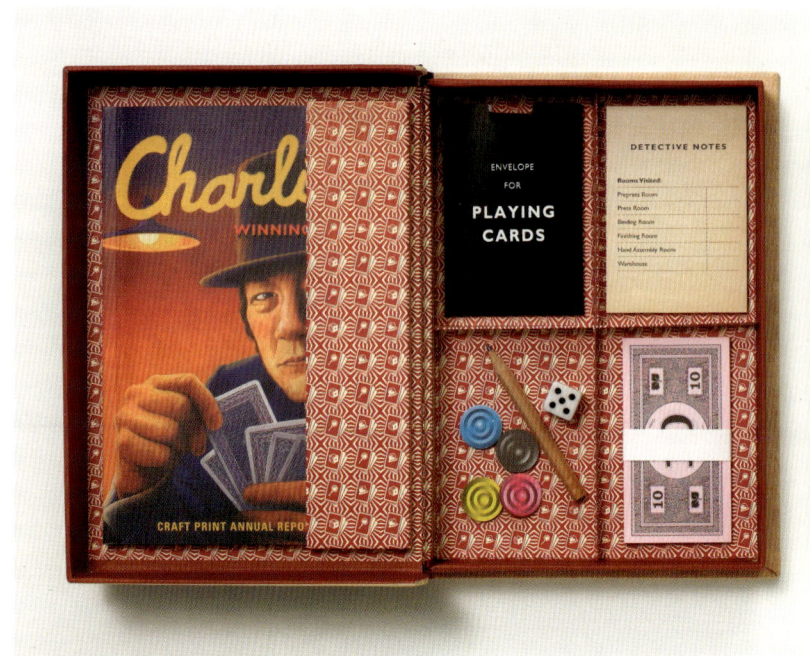

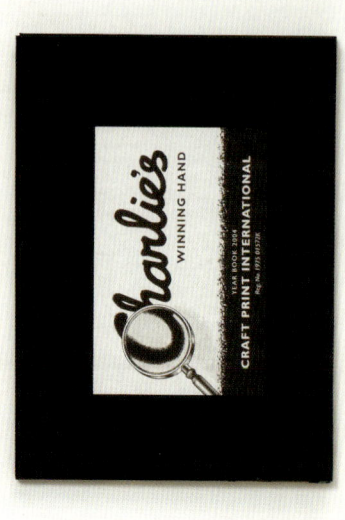

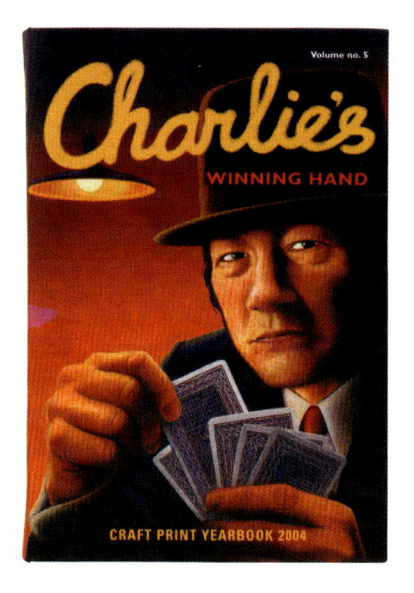

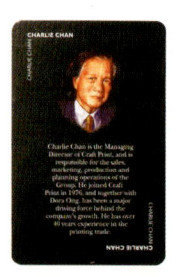

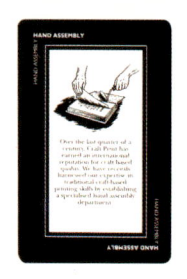

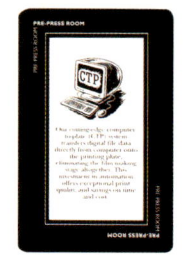

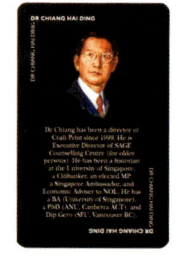

Silver

15_ Annual Report

t. Charlie's Winning Hand Craft Print Yearbook 2004
e. Equus Design Consultants Pte Ltd.
cd. Andrew Thomas
d. Chung Chi Ying, Tay Chin Thiam
i. Michael Lui
cw. Andrew Thomas
cl. pt. cp. Craft Print International Ltd.

71

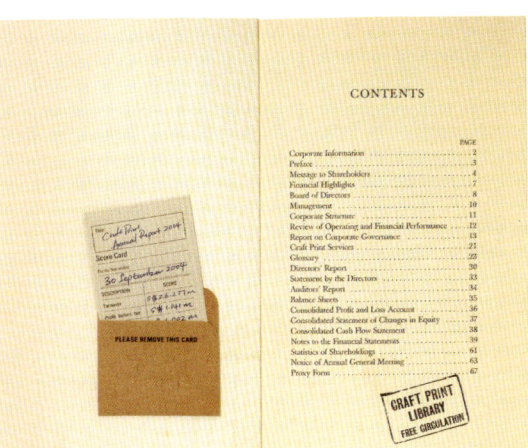

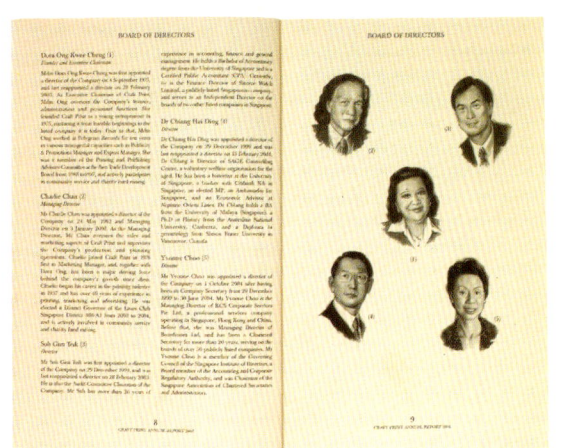

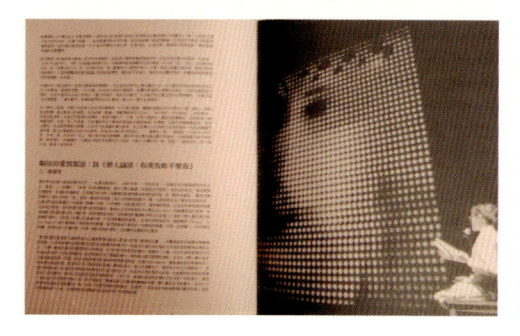

Bronze
16_ Annual Report
t. Zuni Icosahedron Annual Report 02 - 03
e. Les Suen
ad. Les Suen
d. Geoff & Les Suen
cl. Zuni Icosahedron
pt. Kee Mei Printing Co., Ltd.

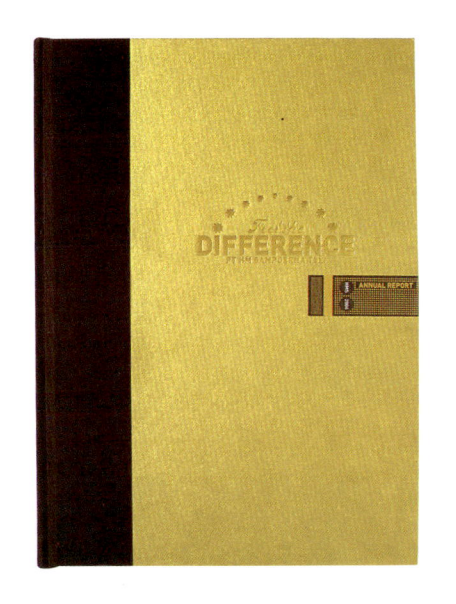

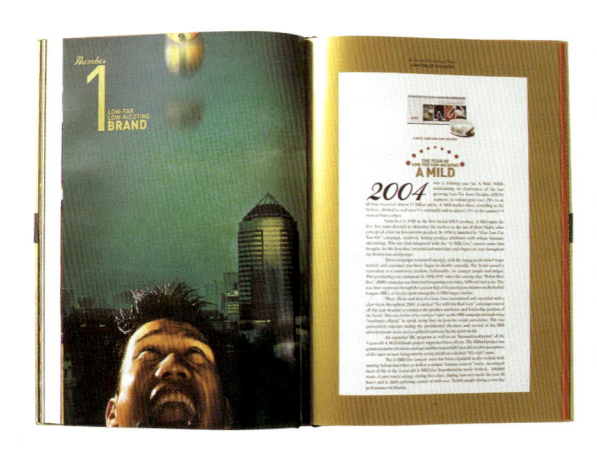

17_ Annual Report
t. Feel the Difference
e. Epigram
cd. Edmund Wee
d. Zann Wan
p. Tigor
cs. Cynthia Tay
cl. PT HM Sampoerna Tbk.

73

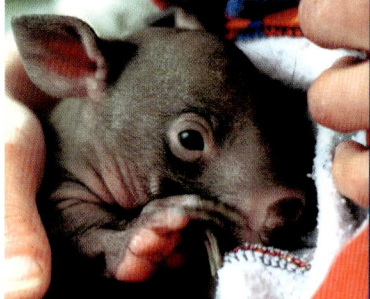

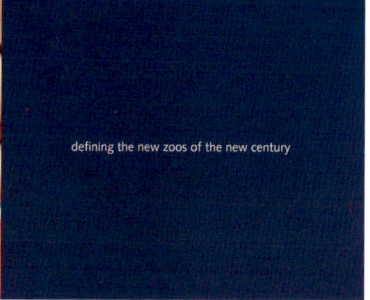

18_ Annual Report
  t. Shangri-La Asia Ltd 2004
     Annual Report
  e. Step Design Consultants Ltd
  cd. Stephen Barry
  ad. d. Michelle Miralles
  i. Jimmy Cheung
  cs. Sarina Ramjahn
  cl. Shangri-La Asia Ltd
  pp. pt. cp. SNP Vite

19_ Annual Report
  t. Zoos Victoria Annual Report
  e. Eade + Evans
  cd. Iain Evans
  ad. dd. d. Tony Alessi
  cl. Zoological Parks and Gardens
     Board of Victoria

20_ Annual Report
  t. Zoos Victoria Annual Report
  e. Eade + Evans
  cd. Iain Evans
  ad. dd. d. Tony Alessi
  cl. Building Commission of Victoria

21

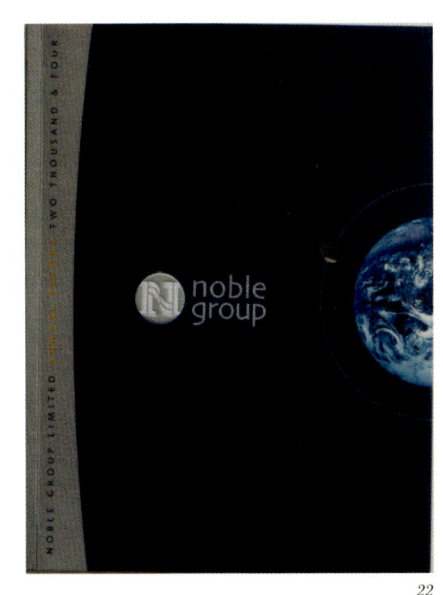

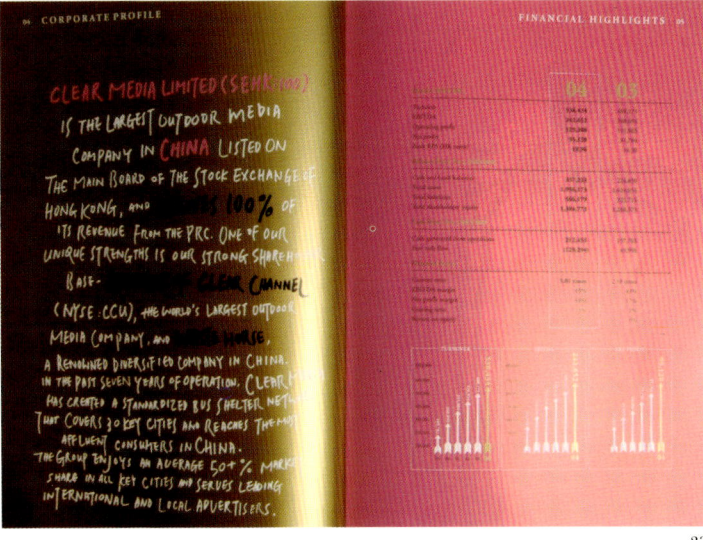

22

23

21_ *Annual Report*
t. Next Media Ltd. Annual Report 2001/02
e. Yellow Creative (HK) Ltd.
cd. Wong Chun Hong
d. Amy Woo
cw. iPR Asia Ltd.
cl. Next Media Ltd.

22_ *Annual Report*
t. Noble Group Ltd. Annual Report 2004
e. Graphicat Ltd.
cd. dd. Colin Tillyer

23_ *Annual Report*
t. Clear Media Ltd. Annual Report 2004
e. Yellow Creative (HK) Ltd.
cd. Wong Chun Hong
d. Amy Woo
cw. iPR Asia Ltd.
cl. Clear Media Ltd.

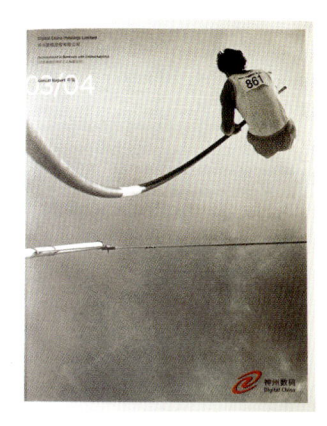

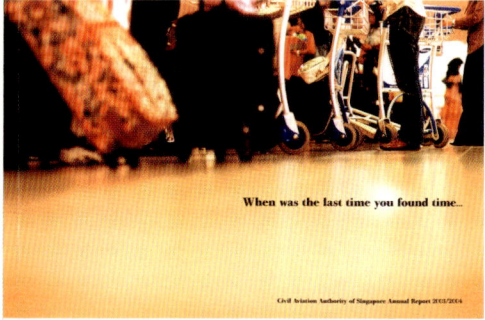

24_ Annual Report
- *t.* Digital China Annual Report 2003/04
- *e.* Monopoly Design Ltd.
- *dd. d.* Kevin Yuen
- *cl.* Digital China Holdings Ltd.

25_ Annual Report
- *t.* When was the last time you found time...
- *e.* Epigram
- *cd.* Edmund Wee
- *d.* Zann Wan
- *p.* Nicholas Leong
- *cs.* Cynthia Tay
- *cl.* Civil Aviation Authority of Singapore

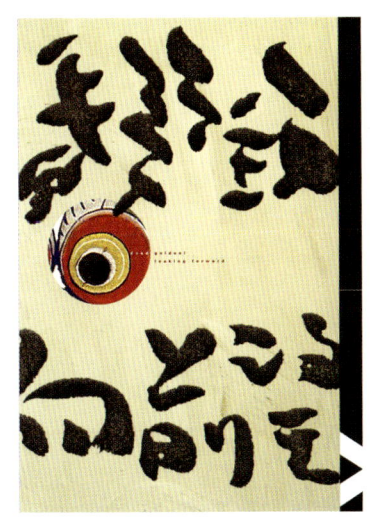

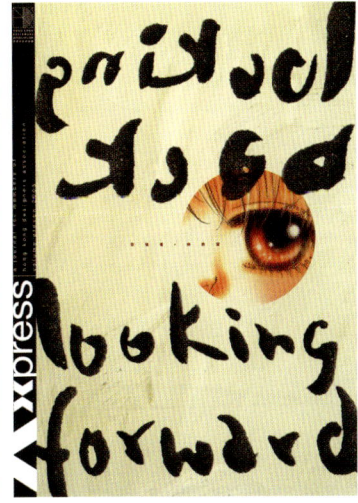

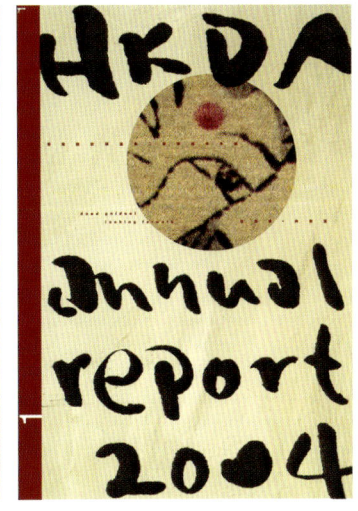

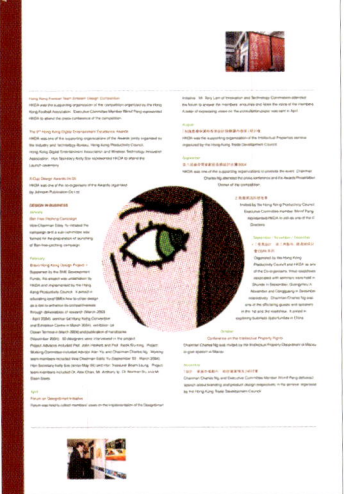

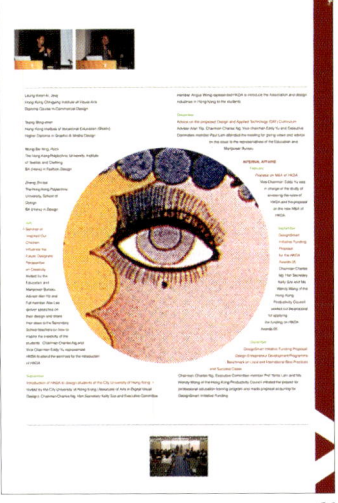

26_ Annual Report
t. HKDA Annual Report 2004
e. Circle Design Ltd
cd. Clement Yick
d. Cheung Man Kit
cl. Hong Kong Designers Association

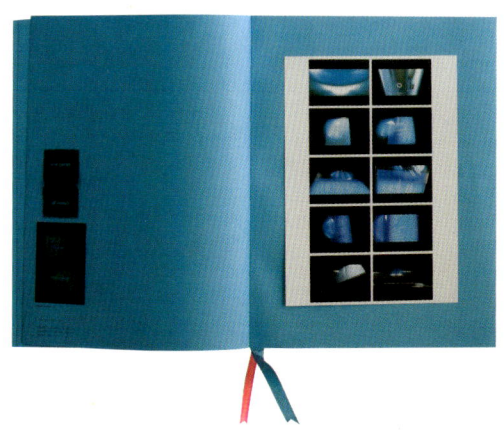

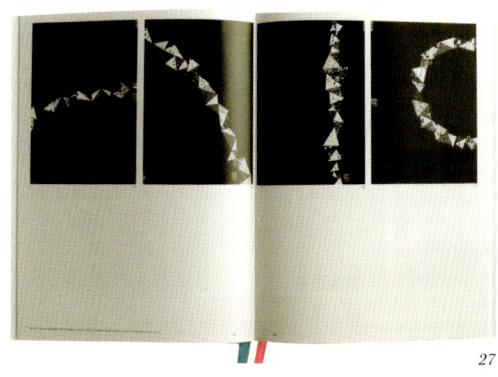

Silver
27_ Book
t. 深圳03設計展作品集
e. cd. dd. ad. 韓家英
cl. 深圳03設計展

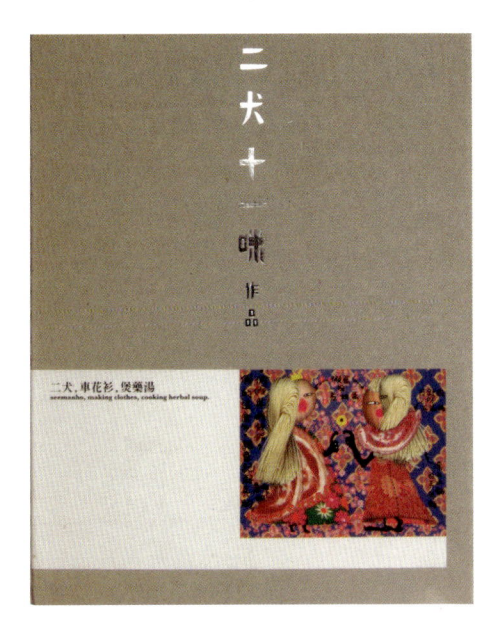

Bronze
28_ Book
t. Seemanho, Making Clothes, Cooking Herbal Soup.
e. Shellmoonsite
cd. ad. d. Lee Man Chung
pt. Elegance Printing & Bookbinding Co., Ltd.
cl. Artopia Publishing Ltd.

Bronze
29_ Book
t. Bauhaus Dessau / Mikiya Takimoto
e. ad. d. Masayoshi Kodaira
p. Mikiya Takimoto
sp. pt. Toppan Printing Co.,Ltd.
cl. PIE Co., Ltd.

29

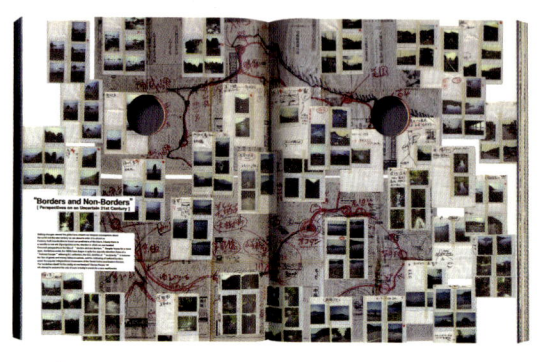

Bronze
30_ Book
t. Visualization
e. Keiko Yoshida
cd. dd. Katsumi Yutani
ad. Shotaro Sakaguchi, Keizo Tada, Kenichi Hatano, Emi
p. Masamitsu Morisawa, Isao Kimura
cw. Katsumi Yutani
cl. Dentsu Inc., Dentsu Communication Institute
pd. Chinami Aoki

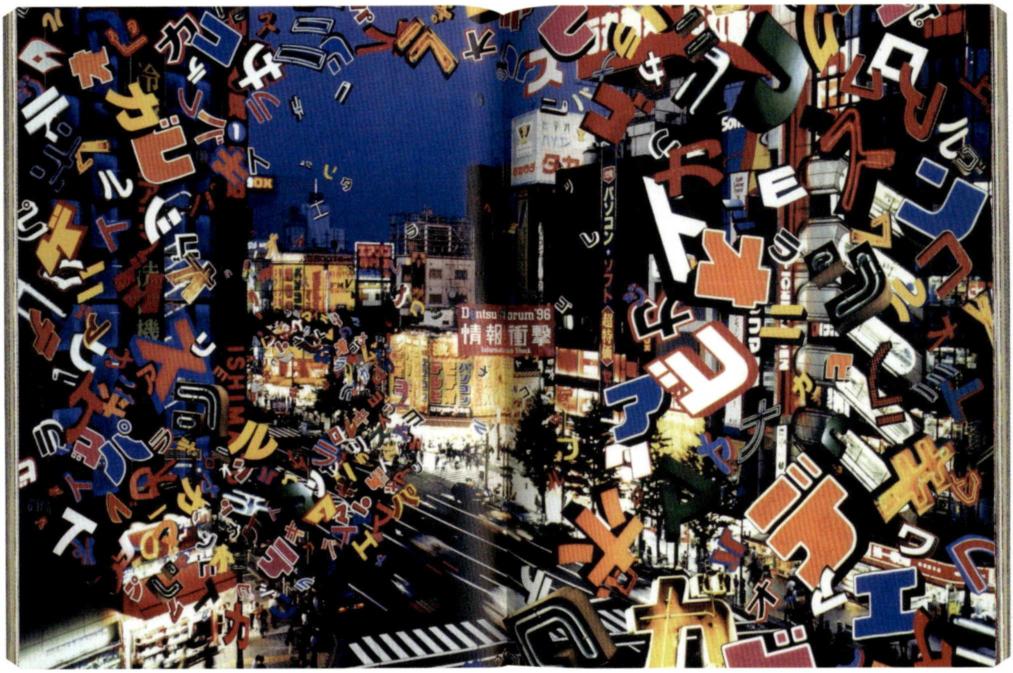

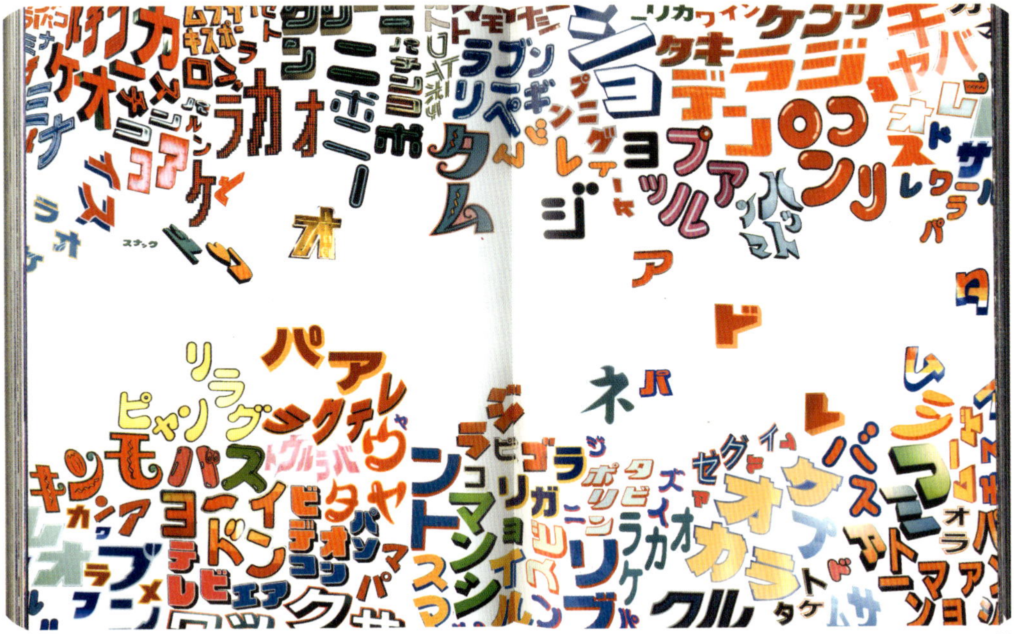

30

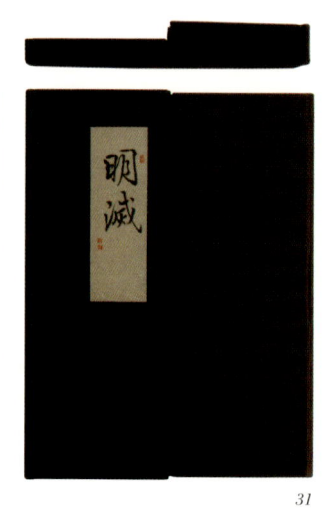

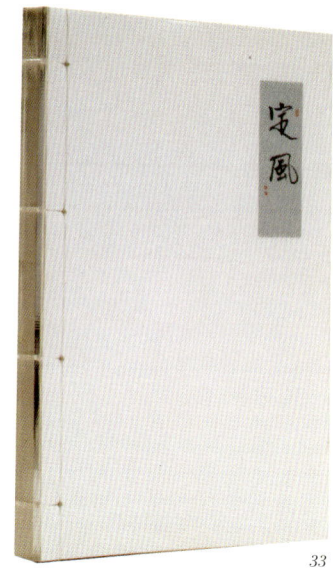

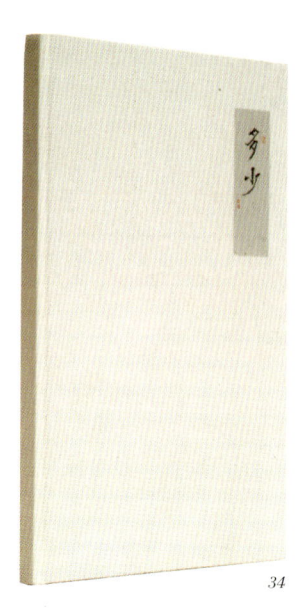

Excellent
31_ Book
t. 明滅
e. cd.dd. ad. cl. 陳俊良
d. Chang Hui-Wen

32_ Book
t. 放下
e. cd.dd. ad. cl. 陳俊良
d. Chang Hui-Wen

Bronze
33_ Book
t. 定風
e. cd.dd. ad. cl. 陳俊良
d. Chang Hui-Wen

Excellent
34_ Book
t. 多少
e. cd.dd. ad. cl. 陳俊良
d. Chang Hui-Wen

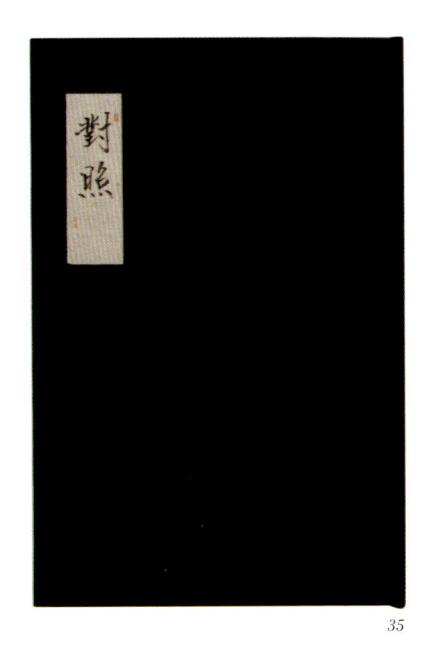

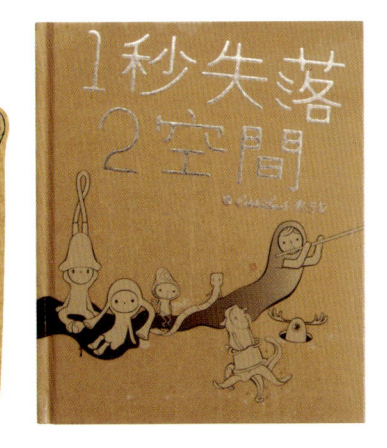

35_ Book
t. 對照
e. cd.dd. ad. cl. 陳俊良
d. Chang Hui-Wen

Bronze
36_ Book
t. Photographs Billy Cheung + Benny Au
e. ad. d. Benny Au Tak-shing
p. Billy Cheung, Benny Au
pt. Suncolor Printing Co., Ltd.
cl. miniminigallery

Bronze
37_ Book
t. Chaos No.1（1秒失落2空間）
e. cd. ad. Les Suen
d. Eddie Lau & Les Suen
i. Eddie Lau
pt. Kee Mei Printing Co., Ltd.
cl. Enrich Publishing Ltd

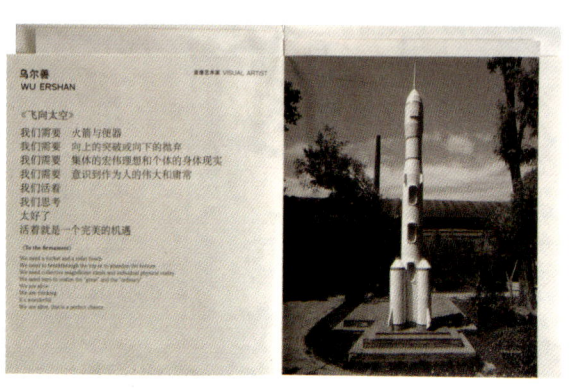

Bronze
38_ Book
t. Modern Style In East Asia 2004
e. cd. ad. d. Les Suen
p. Teruaki Nagamine
pt. Kee Mei Printing Co., Ltd.

長坂 輝明
TERUAKI NAGASAKINE

テレデザイン
tele-design

福津 宣人
NOBUTO FUKUTSU

みかんぐみ
MIKAN

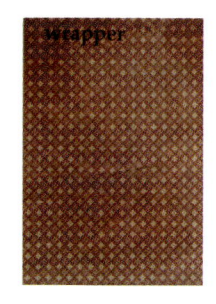

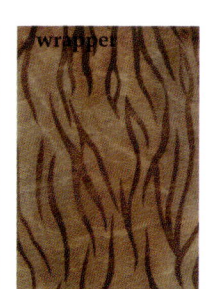

Excellent
39_ Book
t. Wrapper
e. cd. dd. cd. ad. d. He Jun
p. An Li, Duan Meng
cl. Ganggu Paper Trading Co., Ltd.

40_ Book
t. 韓家英設計有限公司
e. cd. d. p. cw. i. 韓家英

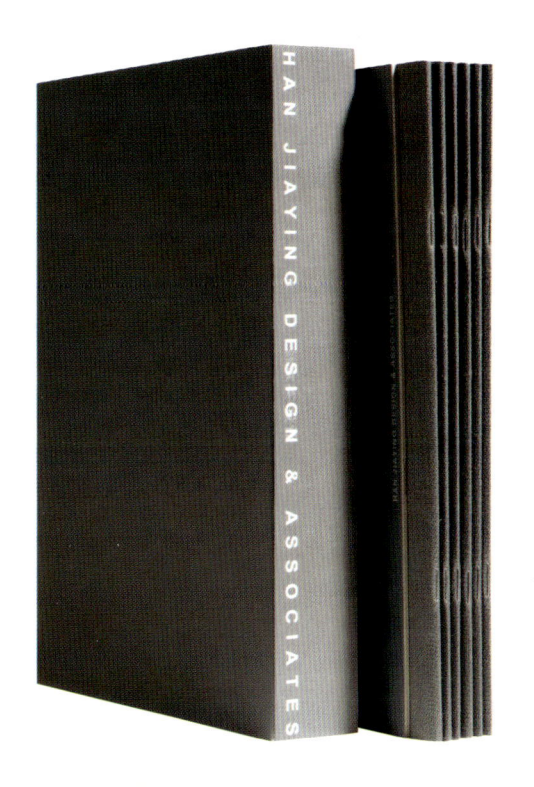

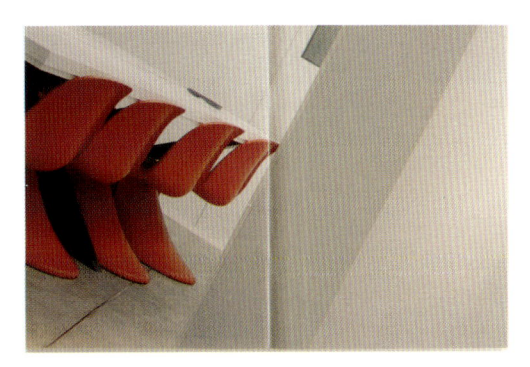

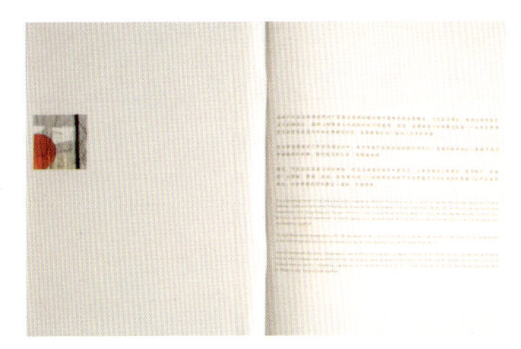

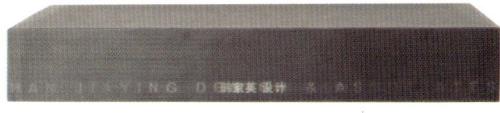

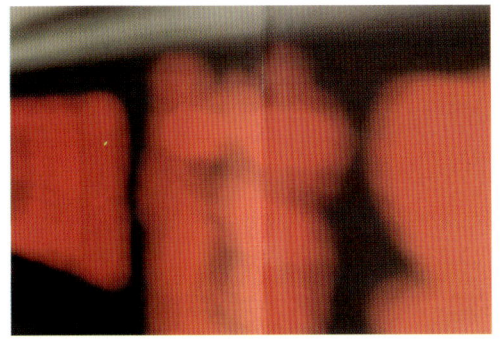

t. Nara Yoshitomo / Hirosaki
e. cd. ad. d. Masayoshi Kodaira
p. Mikiya Takimoto
sp. pt. Toppan Printing Co.,Ltd.
cl. NPO harappa

4 1

*42_* Book
t. ARCHIGRAM : Experimental Architecture 1961 - 1974
e. ad. Masayoshi Kodaira
cd. Comtemporary Art Center, Art Tower Mito
d. Masayoshi Kodaira, Namiko Otsuka
p. Kozo Takayama, Hiroki Nakashima
at. Archigram
sp. pt. Toppan Printing Co., Ltd.
cl. PIE Co., Ltd.

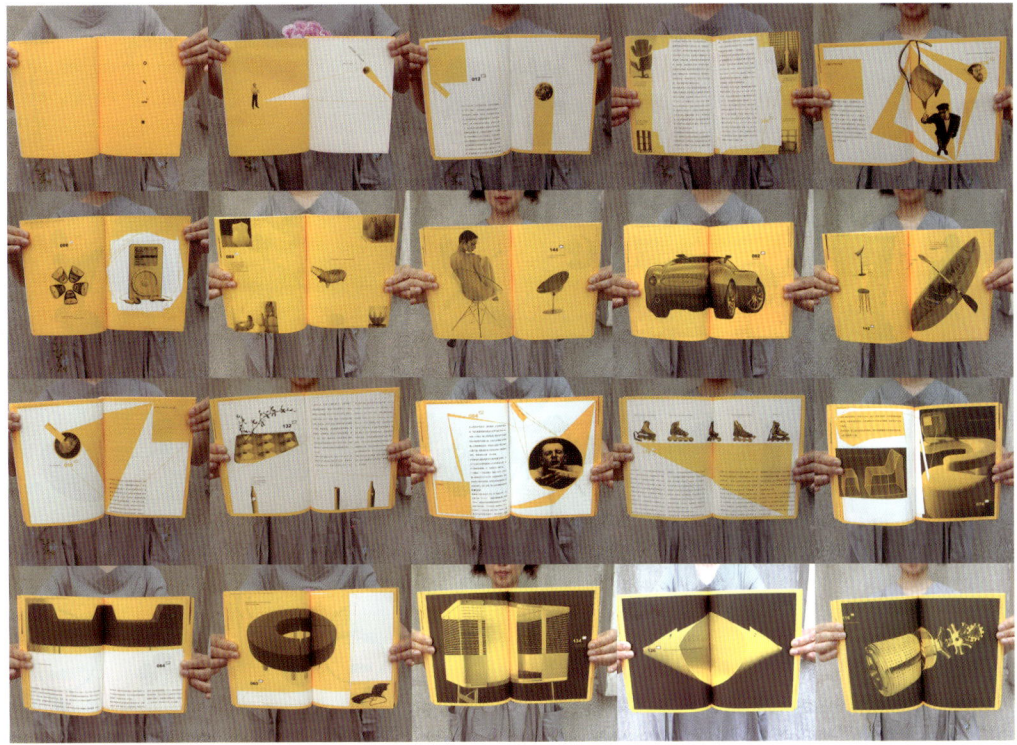

43_ Book
t.《王受之講述—建築的故事》
　　《王受之講述—產品的故事》
e. cd. dd. ad. d. 小馬哥 橙子
cs. 中國青年出版社
sp. 北京圖文天地
p. 北京中科印刷廠
cl. 中國青年出版社

44_ Book
t. Herman Miller
e. ad. d. Osamu Misawa
p.p. Dai Nippon Printing Co., Ltd.
cl. X-knowledge Co., Ltd.

*45_* Book
t. n_ ext: New Generation of Media Artists
e. ad. d. Kazuya Kondo
cl. NTT InterCommunication Center

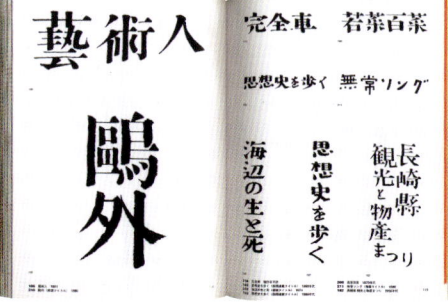

Excellent
46_ Book
t. Yoshio Hayakawa His Design, Times and Osaka
e. dd. ad. Shinnoske Sugisaki
cd. Tomio Sugaya
d. Shinnoske Sugisaki, Chiaki Okuno
pt. Nissha Printing Co., Ltd.
cl. Osaka City Museum of Modern Art (Planning Office)

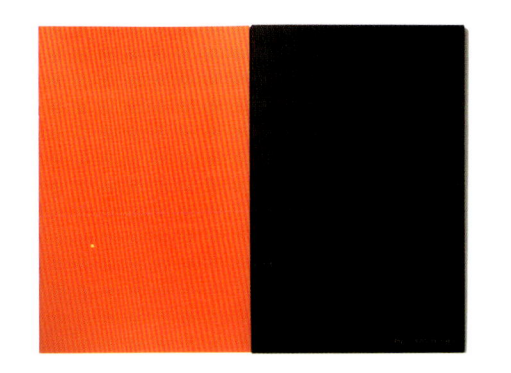

Excellent
47_ Book
t. Amazing Magazine #1
e. ad. d. p. i. cw. Benny Au Tak-shing
e.*t.* Teresa Chan, Betty Chan
pt. Suncolor Printing Co., Ltd.
cl. Amazing Angle Design Consultants Ltd.

48_ Book
t. Chaneration
e. dd. Alan Chan
d. Peter Lo
cw. anothermountainman
et. Wong Kee Chee
p. Stanley Wong, Sam Wong, Sandy Lee, Almond Chu, Alvin Chan
pt. Suncolor Printing Co., Ltd.
cl. Hong Kong Heritage Museum

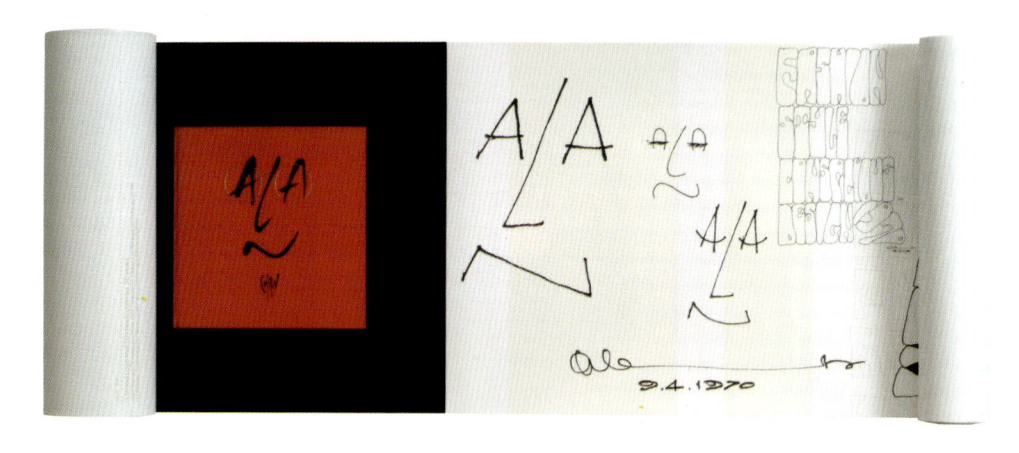

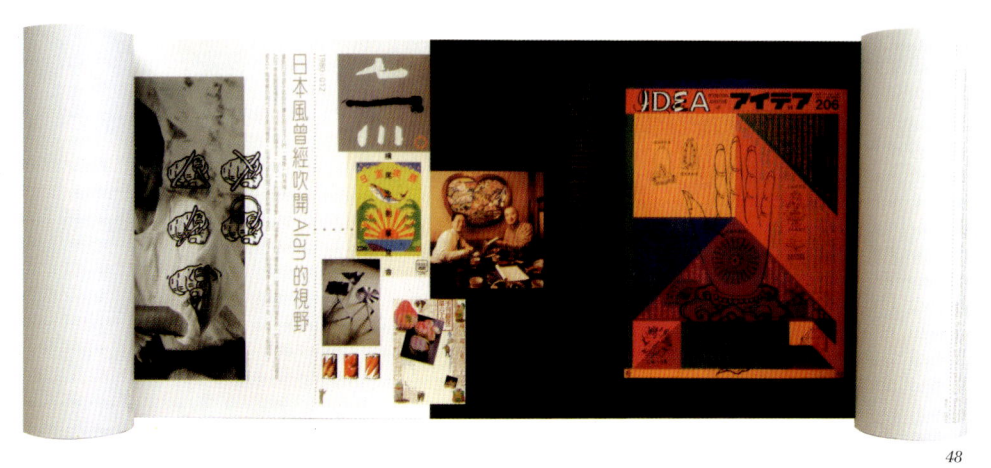

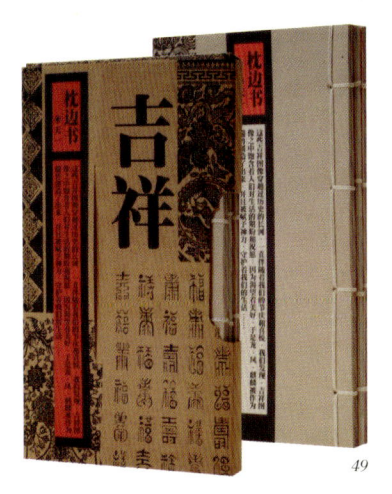

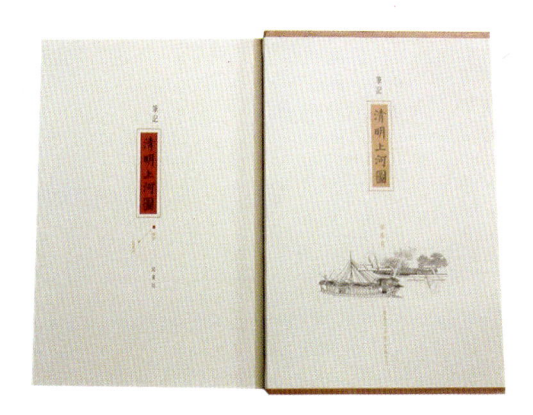

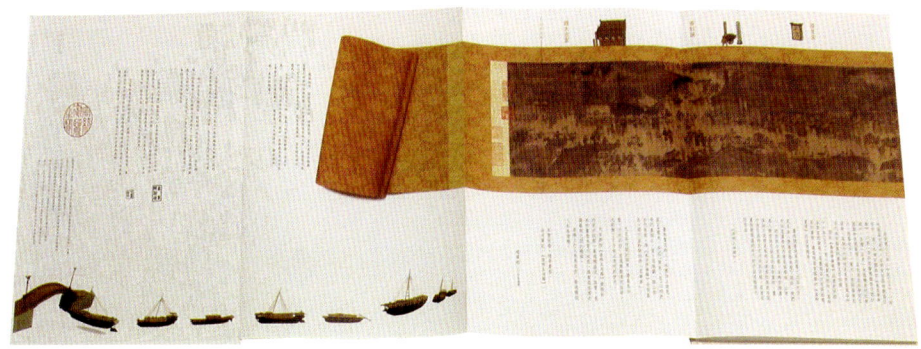

49_ Book
t. 齊魯風雅頌
e. 廣東天一文化有限公司
cd. dd. ad. 天一
d. p. i. cw. 天一創作群
cl. 山東省集郵公司

50_ Book
t. Strolling Along the Ching Ming River :
　Notes on a Famous Painting of Sung Dynasdy
　(筆記清明上河圖)
e. 三聯書店(香港)有限公司
d. Chiu Kwong Chiu, Lilly Lam, Kwok Chiu Wai
pt. C&C Offset Printing Co., Ltd.

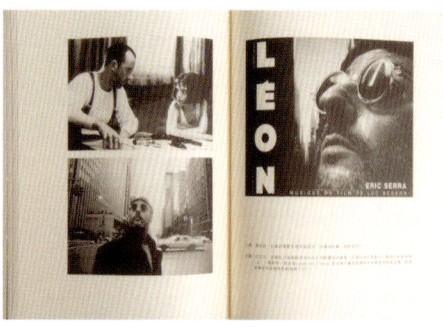

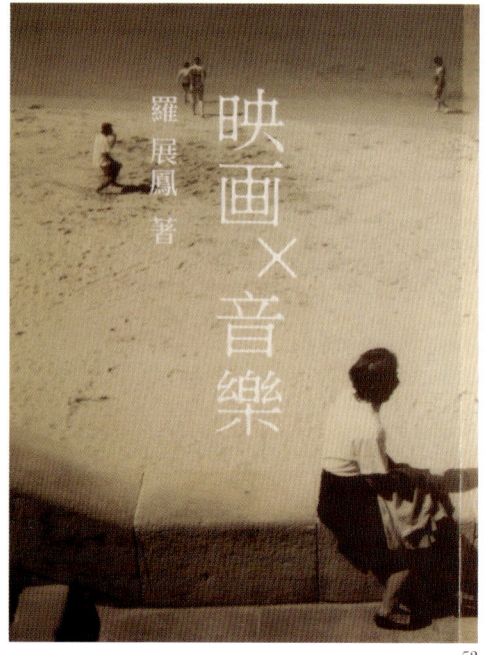

51_ Book
t. SEVEN
e. ad. d. Benny Au Tak-shing
pm. Teresa Chan
pt. Suncolor Printing Co., Ltd.
pc. Little Wai Wai
cl. Amazing Angle Design
  Consultants Ltd.

52_ Book
t. Film × Music（映畫×音樂）
e. 三聯書店(香港)有限公司
d. Les Suen
pt. Kee Mei Printing Co., Ltd.

53

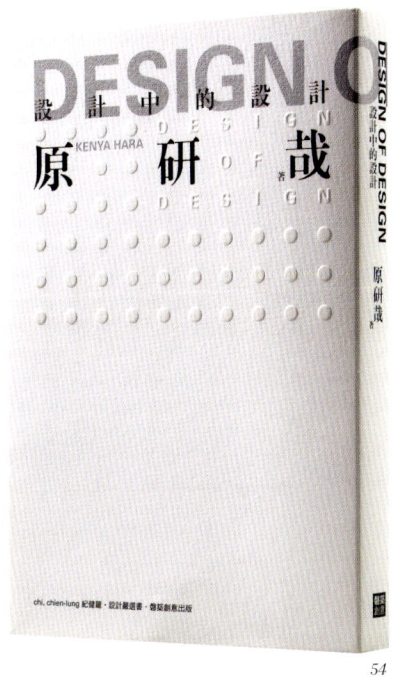

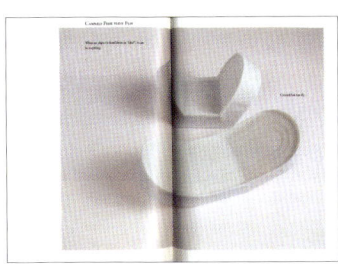

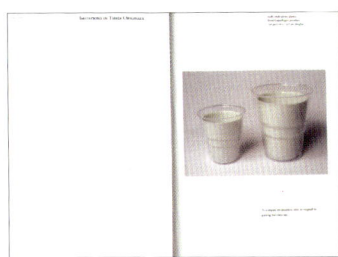

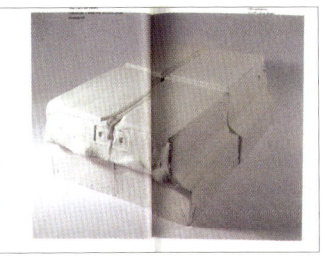

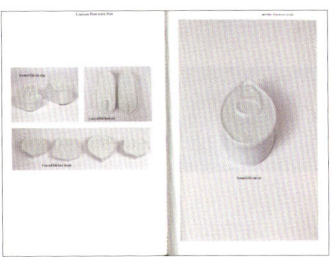

54

55

53_ Book
t. Lam Tsuk Tsui . Destiny
e. cd. ad. Eric Chan
d. i. Ryan Yeung, Niro Chan
cl. China Translation & Printing Services Ltd.

54_ Book
t. design of design 中文版
e. cd. dd. ad. d. Chi Chien-Lung
cl. Pan Zhu Creative Co., Ltd.

55_ Book
t. Moulding World - A Summer in Denmark
e. CoDesign Ltd.
dd. Hung Lam
d. Teresa Hui
p. cw. Annie Wan
pt. Willey Printing & Production Ltd.

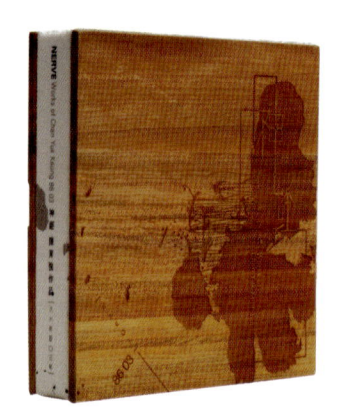

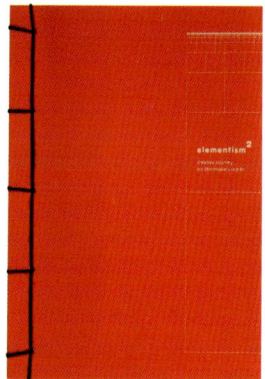

Excellent
*56_* Book
- *t.* Superwoman Exhibition Catalogue
- *e.* Sandy Choi Associates Ltd.
- *dd.* Sandy Choi
- *d.* Becky Yeung
- *ed.* Margaret Leung
- *cs.* Angela Lee
- *cp.* Colorlink & Associates Ltd.
- *pt.* Colorprint HK Co., Ltd.
- *cl.* Hong Kong Poster League
  Hong Kong Heritage Museum

Excellent
*57_* Book
- *t.* NERVE Works of Chan Yuk Keung 86 03 - Wooden Cover
- *e.* Kan & Lau Design Consultants
- *cd. dd.* Freeman Lau Siu Hong
- *d.* Freeman Lau, Justin Yu, Luk Chi Cheong, Chan Yuk Keung
- *p.* Gary Leung, Chan Kwok Fu, Bert Li, Chan Yuk Keung
- *i. cl.* Chan Yuk Keung
- *sp. pp.* Luk Chi Cheong of ISreading Culture Co., Ltd.

Bronze
*58_* Book
- *t.* Elementism 2
- *e.* CoDesign Ltd.
- *cd.* Shinnoske Sugisaki
- *dd. d. p. cw.* Hung Lam
- *pt.* Sun Color Printing Co., Ltd.
- *pb.* MCCM Creations

Excellent
59_ Book
t. Man & God
e. cd. Joseph Foo
dd. Joseph Foo, Tan Wei Ming
d. Tan Wei Ming, Joseph Foo
p. David & Allen of Studio DL
cw. Iching Chan, Tan Soo Inn, Rev Thomas Low
sp. Prestige Colour Scan Sdn Bhd
pt. Percetakan Osacar Sdn Bhd
cl. Art4soul

60_ Book
t. Reflection
e. Bliss Partners Int'l Ltd.
cd. Ivan Leung

*61_* Book
t. Shaw Films Series 邵氏光影系列
e. 三聯書店(香港)有限公司
d. Les Suen
pt. Kee Mei Printing Co., Ltd., C & C Offset Printing Co., Ltd.

邵氏
光影系列
SHAW
FILMS
百美千嬌
Shaw Beauties
天映娛樂 策劃
武俠
功夫片
天映娛樂 策劃
Musical &
Melodrama
《南國電影》
《香港影畫》總目錄

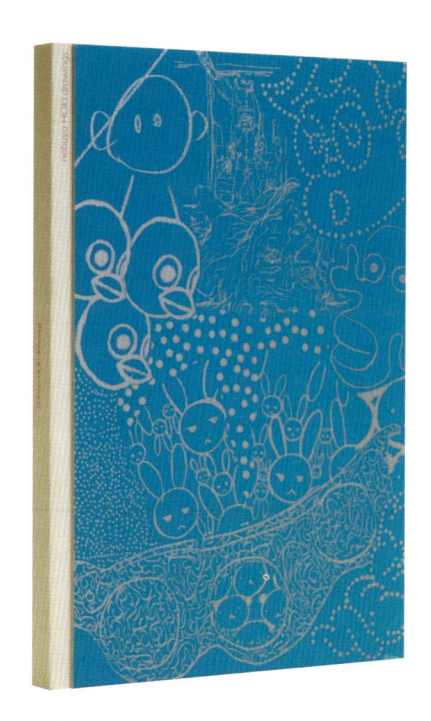

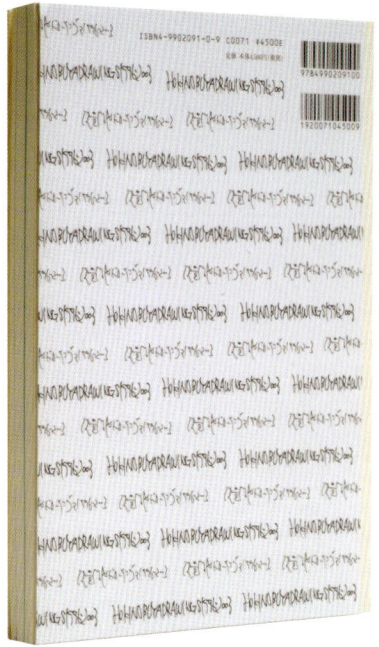

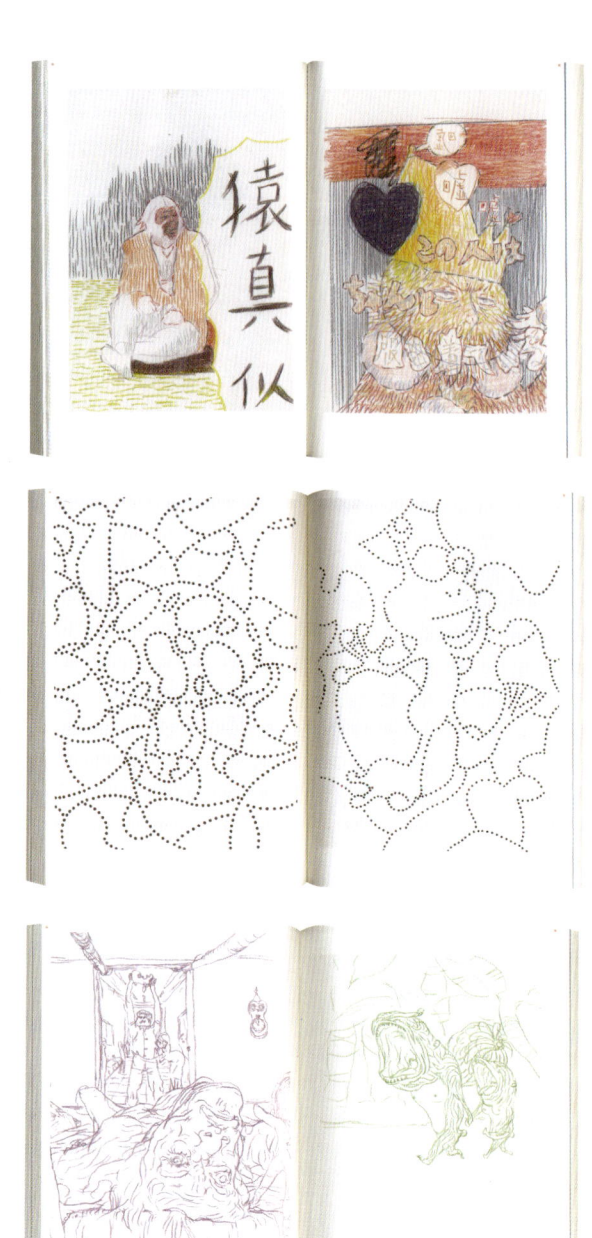

Bronze
62_ Book
t. Nobuya HOKI Drawings
e. ad. d. Akihiko Tsukamoto
at. Nobuya Hoki
pt. Kashimura Co., Ltd.
cl. Daiwa Radiator Co., Ltd., Taro Nasu Gallery

63

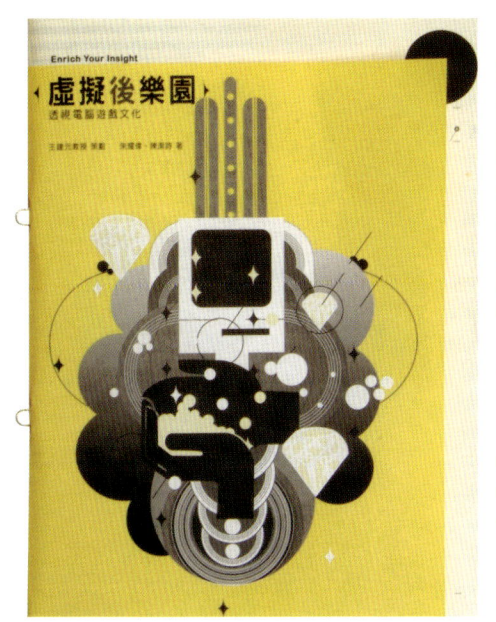

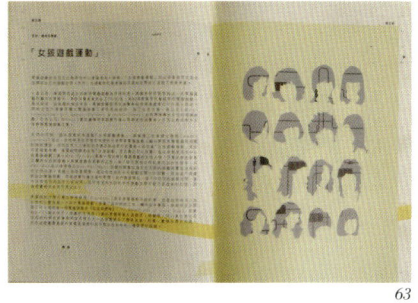

64

Excellent
63_ Book
t. Enrich Your Insight 01 虛擬後樂園
e. cd. ad. Les Suen
d.i. Ng Chi Wai
pt. Kee Mei Printing Co. Ltd.
cl. Enrich Publishing Ltd.

64_ Book
t. Navigating Design
e. RC Communications Ltd.
cd. Alice Lo, Ronald Yeung
d. Leo Lei Lap-ian, Winifred Leung
cp. Silver System Ltd.
pt. Sunshine Press Ltd., Hong Kong
cl. School of Design,
   Hong Kong Polytechnic University

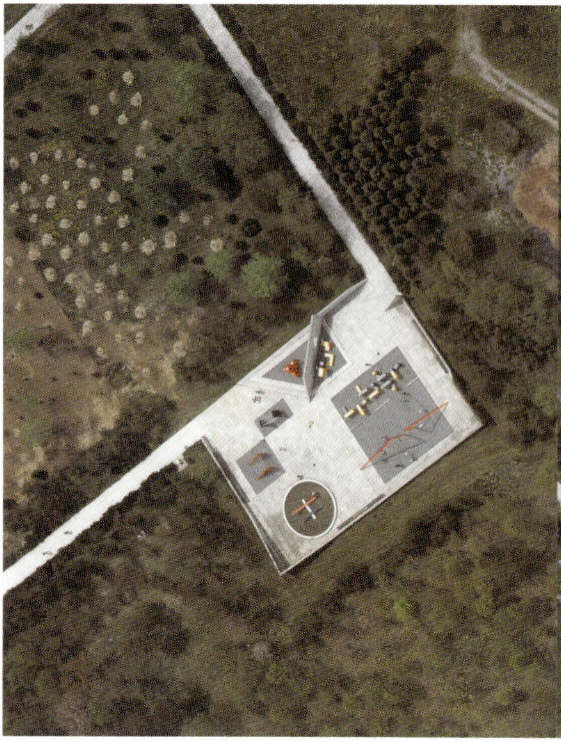
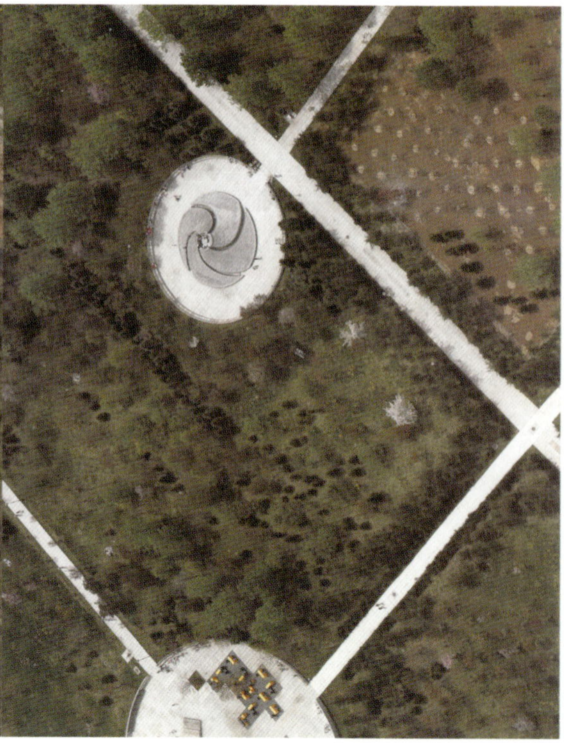
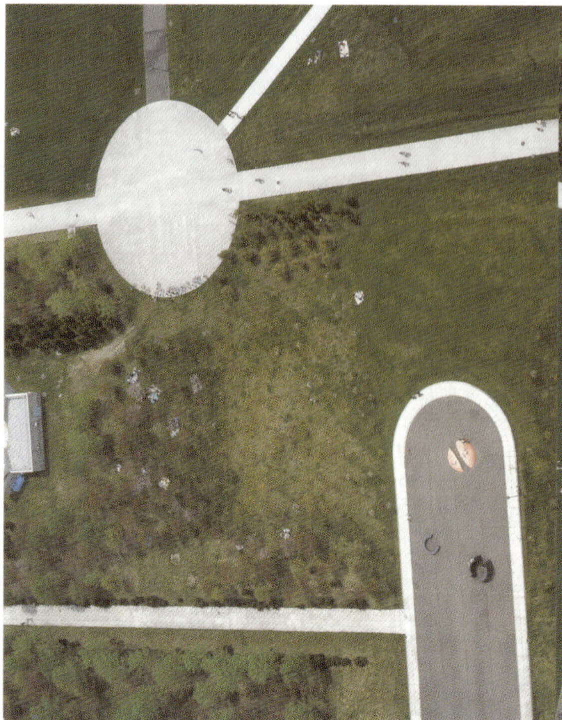
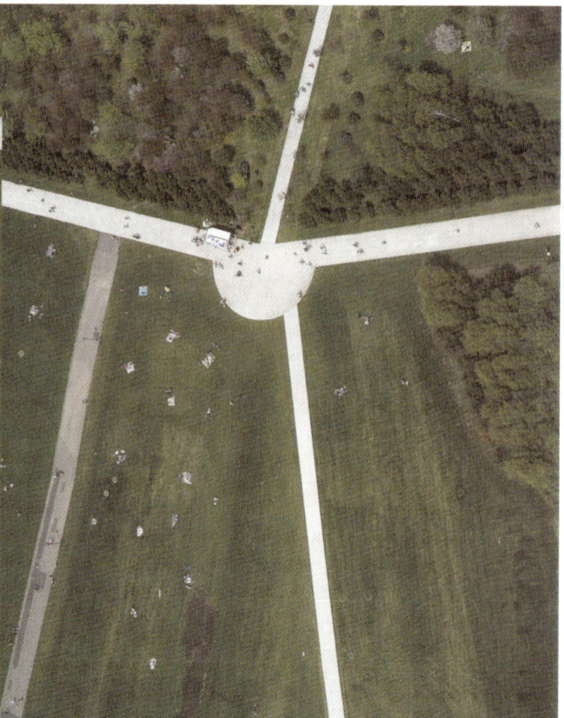

65

Bronze
65_ Editorial
t. X - Knowledge HOME
e. ad. d. Masayoshi Kodaira
p. Taiji Matsue
cp. pt. Dai Nippon Printing Co.,Ltd.
cl. X-knowledge Co., Ltd.

Excellent
66_ Editorial
t. "Travelling, Travelling Oh, Travelling for Good"
e. cl. Kan & Lau Design Consultants
cd. ad. Kan Tai-keung
d. Kan Tai-keung, Justin Yu

Excellent
67_ Editorial
t. West Kowloon - No Fighting
e. CoDesign Ltd
dd. d. Eddy Yu
p. Ducky Tse
cw. Raymond Fung
pt. Green Production
cl. Hong Kong Designers Association

68_ Editorial
t. Good Design 2002 2003
e. ad. d. Masayoshi Kodaira
p. Kozo Takayama
cp. pt. Kowa Printing Co., Ltd.
cl. Japan Industrial Design Promotion Organization

GOODDESIGN20022003
JAPAN INDUSTRIAL DESIGN PROMOTION ORGANIZATION

First Published in Japan on January 21, 2003
by copyright JIDPO
(Japan Industrial Design Promotion Organization)
4th Floor Annex, World Trade Center Bldg.
2-4-1, Hamamatsu-cho, Minato-ku, Tokyo 105-6190, Japan
Tel. +81-3-3435-5633 Fax. +81-3-3432-7346
URL: http://www.jidpo.or.jp/ http://www.g-mark.org/
Distributed by Maruzen Co., Ltd
2-3-10, Nihonbashi, Chuo-ku, Tokyo 103-8245, Japan

Publisher: Hikoharu Kure
Editors: Yuichi Yamada, Sae Suzuki, Naomi Yui,
Tatsuro Urata, Jun Akimoto, Noriko Kurahashi
Associate Editors: Eizo Okada,
Keiichiro Fujisaki, Erimi Fujihara
Art Director: Masayoshi Kodaira, FLAME, inc.
Photographer: Kozo Takayama, Taro Mizutani
Printing: Kowa Printing Co., Ltd
Printed in Japan
All rights resereved.
No part of the contents of this book may be reproduced
without the permission of the publisher.

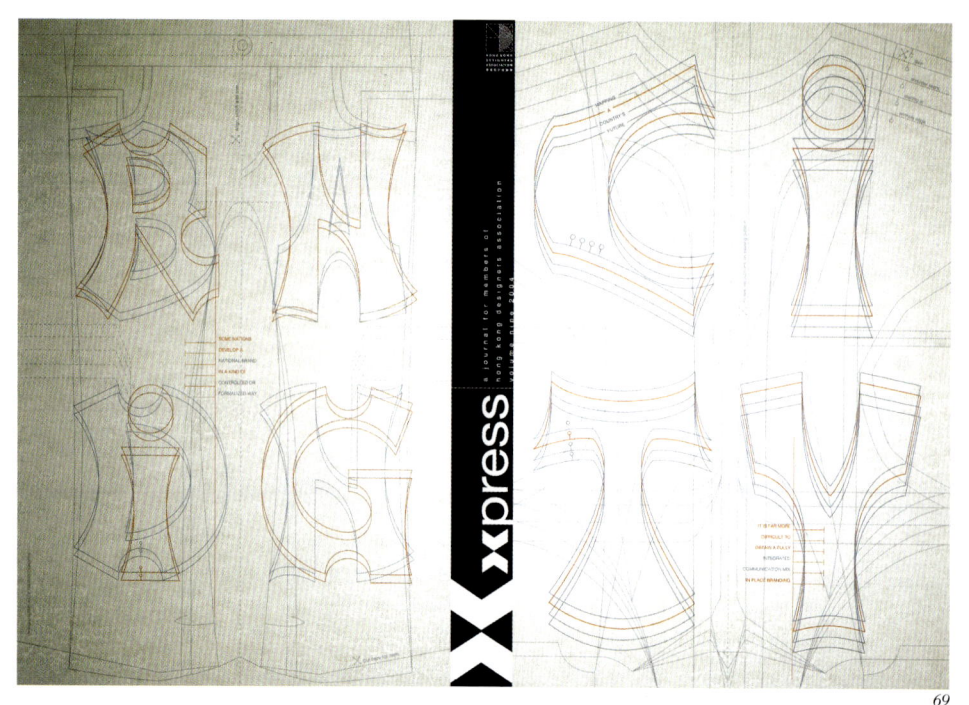

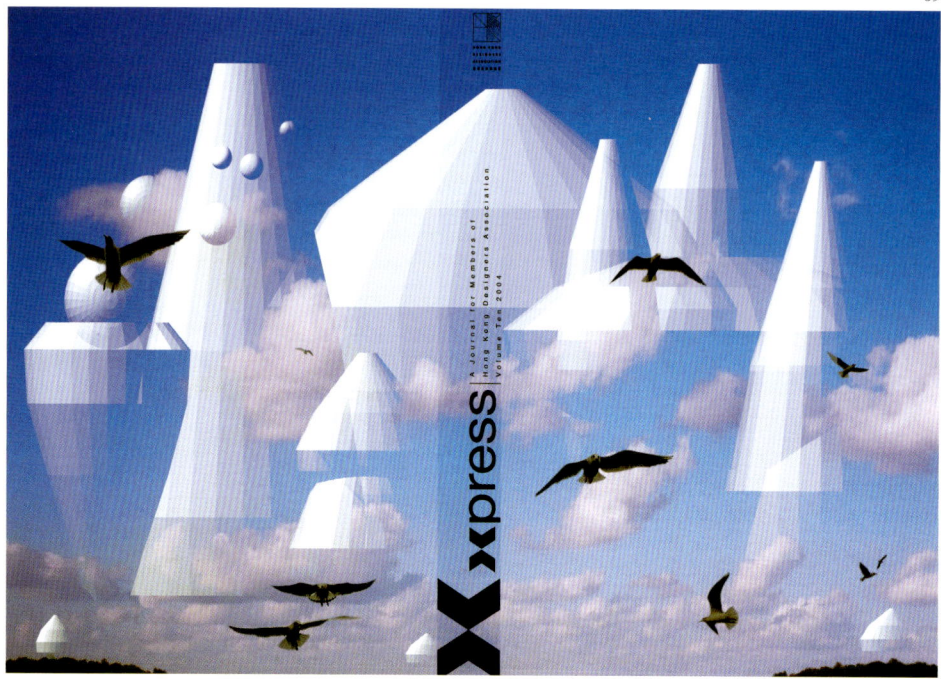

69_ Editorial
t. Xpress Vol 9 2004 Issue Cover
e. cd. Eric Chan
d. Eric Chan, Iris Yu, Ryan Yeung
p. Lau Kwok Tim of Tim Photography
i. Iris Yu, Ryan Yeung
cw. Cat Tyrell
cl. Hong Kong Designers Association

70_ Editorial
t. Mapping Design Collectives in Hong Kong
e. ad. d. i. Benny Au Tak-Shing
cl. Hong Kong Designers Association

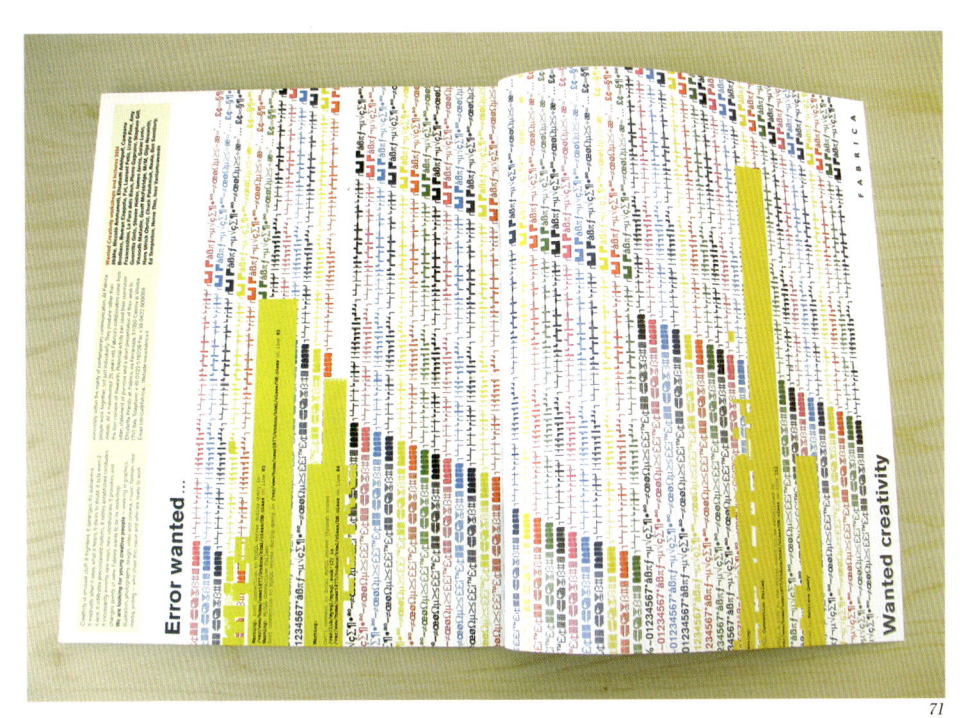

71_ *Editorial*
t. Wanted Creativity - "error Wanted ..."
e. ad. Milkxhake
cl. Fabrica, Italy

72_ *Editorial*
t. 茜利性經 Hyrer - Sutra
e. dd. ad. d. Lawrence Choy
cl. Characters Publications Ltd.

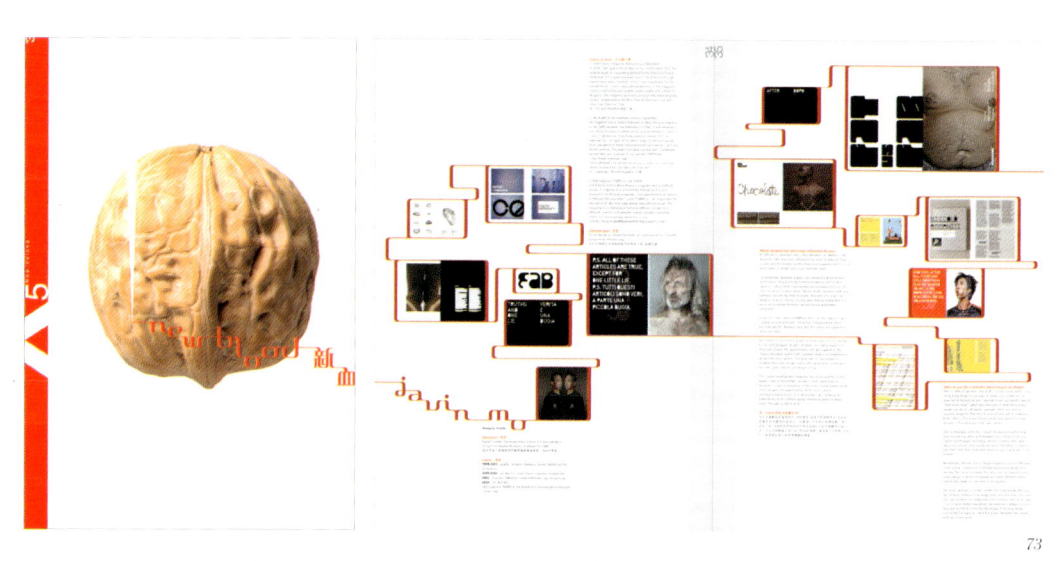

73

74

75

73_ Editorial
t. New Blood
e. Token Workshop
cd. dd. Kenneth To Po Keung
d. Danes Chong
p. Danny Chiu
cl. Hong Kong Designers Association

74_Editorial
t. CO1 Design 04 Show
e. Paul Lam Design Associates
cd. Paul Lam
d. Paul Lam, Cheng Kar Wai, Tequila Chan, Anissa Cheng, Patrick Chan, Queenie Shek
i. Patrick Chan
cp. Art Point Production
pt. Hoi Kwong Printing Co., Ltd.
cl. CO1 School of Visual Arts

75_ Editorial
t. di Magazine
e. dd. Alan Chan
d. Peter Lo
cp. Jessica Choi
cl. Design and Architecture & TIANHUA Advertisement

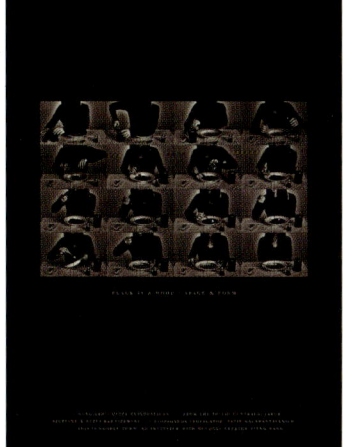

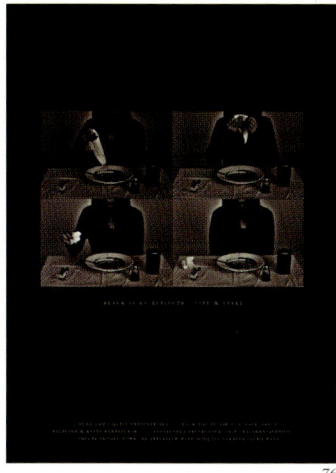

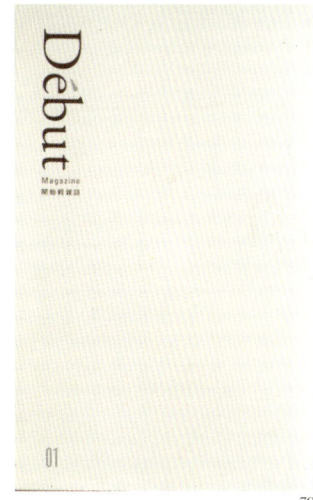

76_ Editorial
t. Black is
e. CoDesign Ltd.
dd. d. p. Hung Lam
cl. ish Magazine

77_ Editorial
t. "FAB" - Issue 1-3 Cover Design
e. Milkxhake
ad. Milkxhake, Fab Creative Team
p. Namiko Kitaura, Japan
   Rebekka Ehler, Denmark
cw. Creative Writing Department, Fabrica
cl. Fabrica, Italy

78_ Editorial
t. Xpress Vol. 11 (Hot Gossip)
e. Genemix
cd. dd. ad. d. James Leung Wai-Mo
p. Andy Wong Studio Point
   (Concept Photos Only)
cw. Hong Kong Designers Association
cl. Hong Kong Designers Association

Excellent
79_ Editorial
t. 開始輕雜誌
e. cd. dd. ad. Chen Jun-Liang
d. Chang Hui-Wen
p. Cheng Chih-Jen
cl. Ching Shang Phoenix Co., Ltd.

Market Research for Designers

Angelica Leung

Market research is much more than just conducting focus groups. When used properly, it is a time and cost effective way to find out insights on the behaviour and attitudes of your customers, and to track the performance of your designs. Angelica Leung talks to Eva Leung, Associate Director at ACNielsen to find out more about what market research tools are available.

Service industries and fast-moving consumer goods manufacturers have used various forms of market research for many years to monitor the sales performance of their products, consumers purchase behaviour and the attitudes that users and non-users have towards their brands. The information is a valuable guide to brand development, sales strategies and initiate repackaging. Designers tasked with developing a new corporate identity, packaging or shop layout, benefit from having the same level of understanding and access to information as their clients possess. And this information provides a clear understanding of the basis of their decisions.

Here are some common market research tools that some of your clients may already be using. Possible implications for designers are provided.

Retail Measurement

On a monthly basis, point of sale bar code scanning data from supermarket and drug store chains, such as Jusco, Watsons and Wellcome is merged with data from a sample of independent retailers are analysed to monitor key measurements such as availability of the product in each sales channel, sales volume and value. This data can be as detailed to each SKU (Stock Keeping Unit. For example, a packaged drink in 350ml and 500ml sizes are two different units). Data from chain stores can be even analysed on a weekly level.

Brand Equity Monitoring

Banking, transport and service industries continually track people's attitudes and preferences towards their brands. Key references include brand awareness, knowledge, usage and preference, even at a premium cost and positioning in the marketplace. Several research tools can be employed, such as focus groups and telephone/street interviews.

During a focus group, a pre-screened group of respondents are asked a series of questions by a trained facilitator. The responses and comments were noted by observers hidden behind one-way mirrors. Eva Leung explains that the two key areas of quality control for market research – randomness and representation of the respondents – are mainly regulated during the screening process of qualified candidates. According to the information requirements of the client, a series of check questions are posed to candidates, such as whether they have used or bought a particular product in the last few weeks and to show proof of purchase. Demographic information (age, gender, income) is also matched to target groups.

Implications to designers

Eva Leung mentions that increasingly, corporations are inviting designers to sit in and observe focus groups to get first hand information, especially when testing various design prototypes for advertisement, corporate identity and packaging. Designers now have end user information to complement their intuition and professional training. Use of focus groups also means that new ideas can be tested and modified before full-scale production, avoiding potentially costly failures.

New Packaging Testing and Shop Design

3-D images of products are put in a virtual shelf and respondents select which design they like most through an internet interface. New products and their displays can be tested in small numbers of trial stores and simulated shopping experiences. The sales results are then compared with a set of control stores to forecast the performance at a official launch.

It is even possible to conduct shadow-shopping, when a researcher accompanies a shopper to monitor decision-making behaviour and their movement through different parts of the shop.

Implication for designer

After the first aspects of a new product design, the increase of sales value/volume can be monitored immediately. This proof of increase in current share is a useful addition to the company portfolio and can be used in future project bidding.

The market research agency often has many years of data that can be analysed for trend identification. For example, a category full of brands of a similar product, such as packaged drinks, batteries and shampoos can be analysed for packaging trend information such as the popularity of cartons versus bags, large versus small pump versus pour. Without needed information, designers often resort to a 'snap-shot' visual survey of existing products in the market. This increases the risk of unknowingly proposing a design that is losing popularity with consumers.

Ad hoc Studies

Market research companies often publicly announce top-line findings of ad hoc surveys through newspapers, journals or their own websites. For example, here are two samples of research that was published by ACNielsen:

a) Hong Kong people are the highest impulse shoppers in Asia
b) 61% frequent a fast food restaurant at least once a week.

Could this information be proactively used by designers to propose brand strategies, packaging or interiors to suit the changing needs of your client's clients?

China/Global Research Network

The benefits of working with an international market research company, says Eva, is the access of world wide information through a local contact point. Clients are able to make meaningful worldwide comparisons as the data is collected and analysed in a similar methodology in all markets.

Implication for designers

Your company is bidding for a job to design product packaging for a beverage for a remote region of China. The initial designs need to be ready in only three weeks and you have no prior experience of the beverage market in that area. Using this global service, you could buy market research of this region and commission the agency to run various analyses on the category, such as top 10 brands, best-selling SKUs (size and packaging monitoring) and distribution analyses. These sales are split between different sales channels? In this way your proposal is more likely to impress the client by your understanding of the local market.

The next time you have an information need, consider employing professional market researchers. When used properly, they can provide invaluable insights in a time and cost-effective way. Meanwhile, keep an eye out for regular findings shared by various research companies.

Benefits of Hiring an Agency

Market research is a highly specialised profession. There are many cost benefits such as the structure of the processes of how to design the culture, not your information and experience and training. The culture – not your information is:
• Access to specialised client sources of data are not available to outsiders, such as scan of chain stores
• Save time and cost – design do not have the manpower to conduct large scale interviews of...

Cost of market research

As a guideline, the price of the information is dependent on how much manpower is required to collect and analyse the information and whether it is expensive to buy or collect the raw data. For example, buying a percentage increase or decrease in market share of " brand (such as growth by 8% over 3 months) will be cheaper than the market size in sales value of an entire category (such as 1 million dollars in sales per month), as the latter requires the aggregate analysis of many brands. Similarly, an exclusively commissioned study will be more expensive than adding 1,2 questions in list of questions in regularly conducted face-to-person or face-to-face survey, where the cost is shared by many clients, each sharing the responses to their commissioned questions only.

118

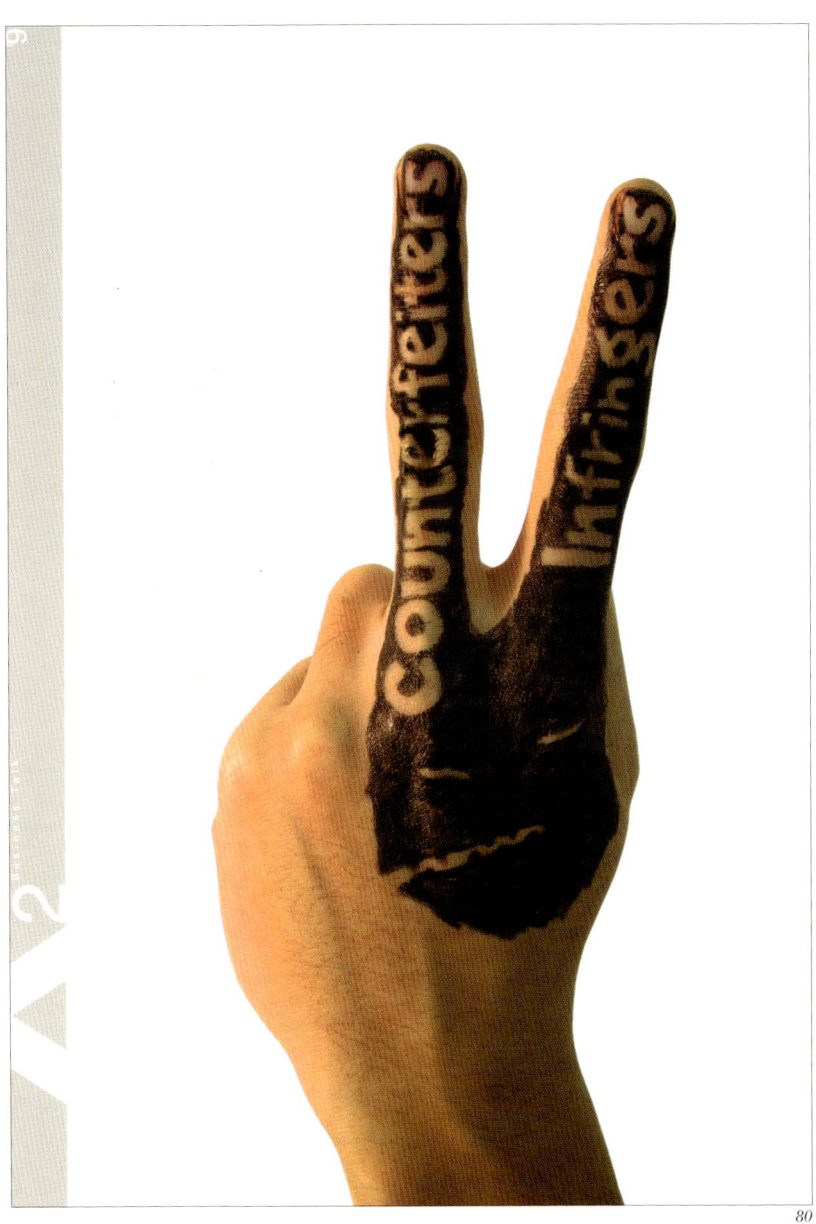

80_ Editorial
t. DA Xpress - Business Talk
e. cd. ad. d. p. Hong Ko
cl. Hong Kong Designers Association

PROMOTION プロモーション
판촉 宣传品

Advertising is all about catching the eye, and these promotional items - ranging from institutional brochures to cutting-edge packaging - are all eye-candy in the marketplace.

Assorted Promotional Item
Institutional & Marketing Literature
Packaging

Silver
81_ Institutional
t. 之間
e. cd. dd. d. 畢學鋒
cl. 廣東美術館

Bronze
82_ Institutional
t. 深圳六人展
e. cd. dd. d. 畢學鋒

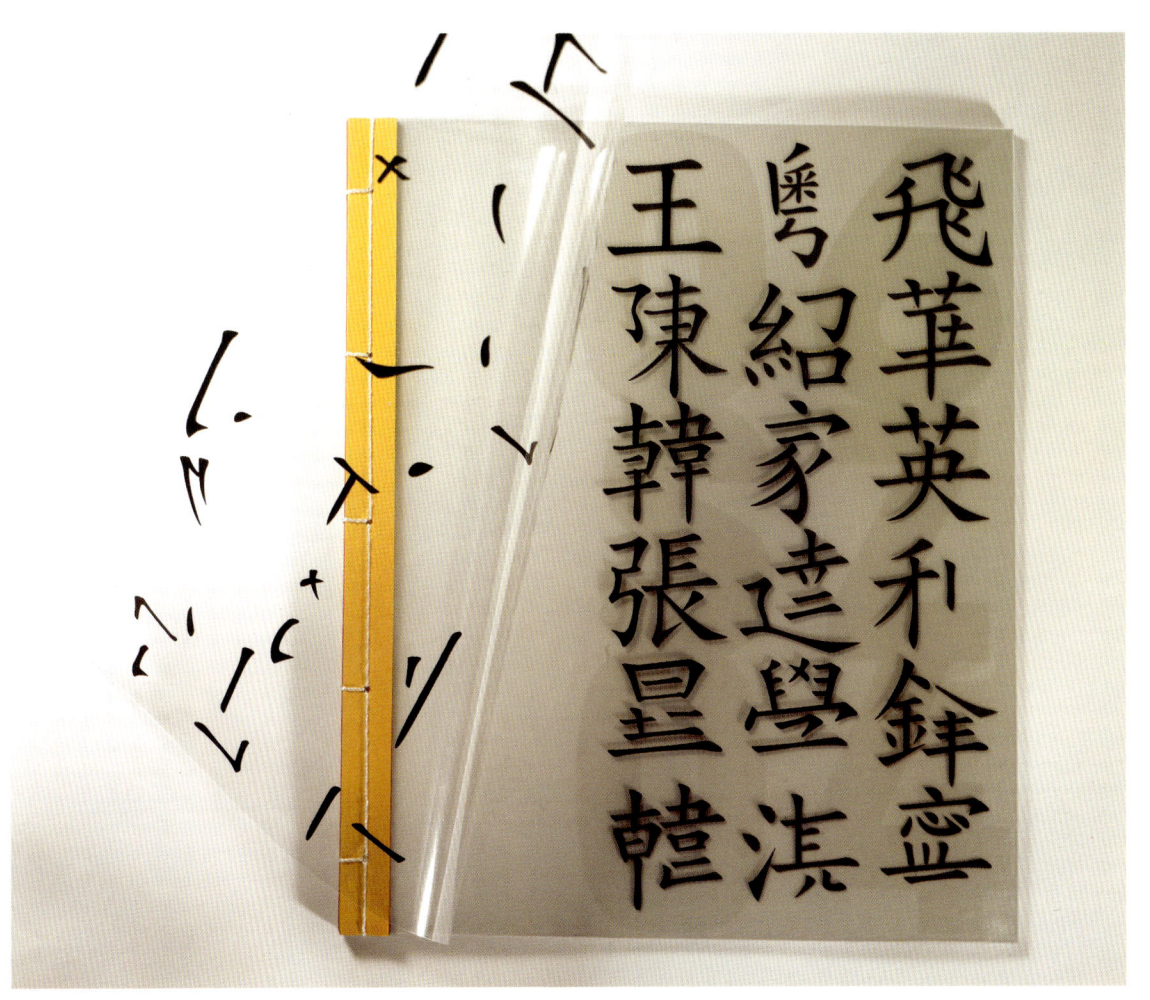

HAR MON Y HO USE

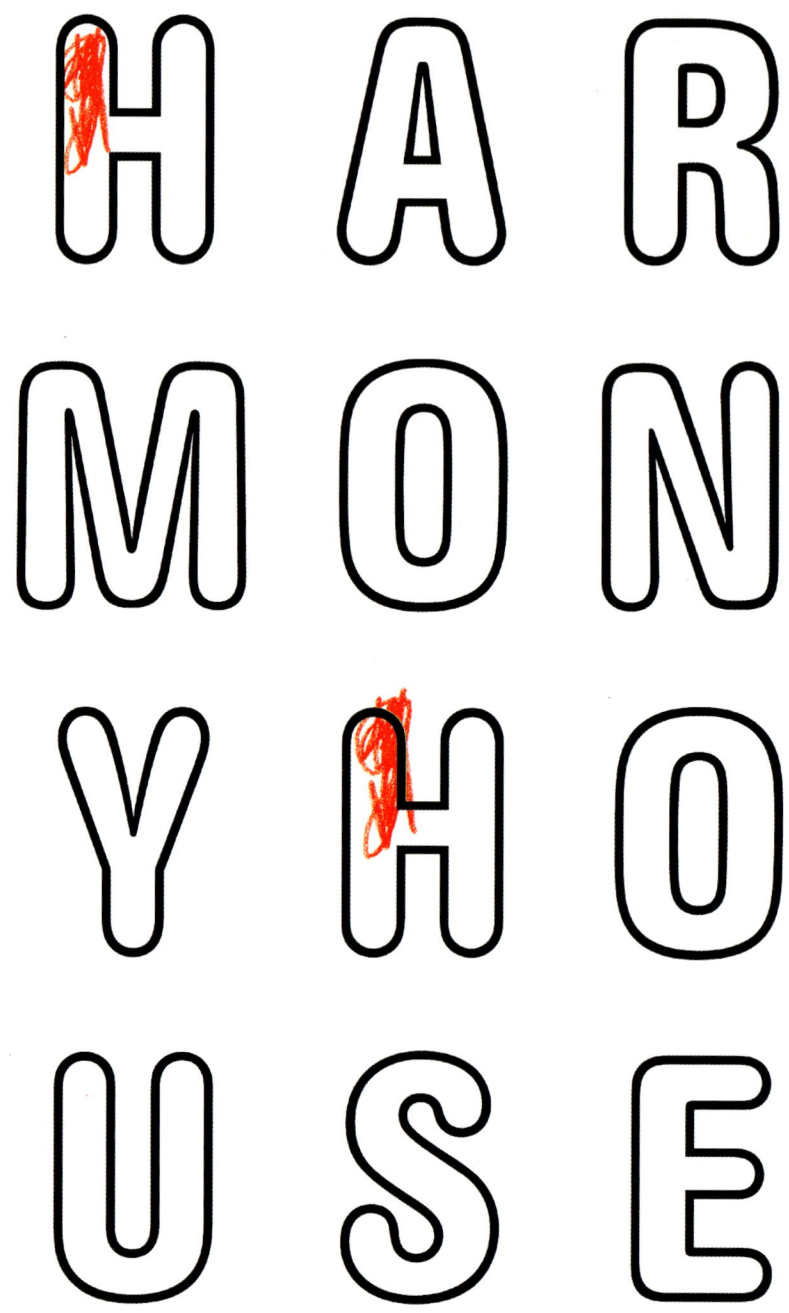

Bronze
83_ Marketing Literature
t. Harmony House
e. Sandy Choi Associates Ltd.
dd. Sandy Choi
d. Thor Lee
i. Maxine Choi, Thor Lee, Goldie Wong
cs. Angela Lee
pp. Art Factory
p. Print-Point Co., Ltd.
cl. Harmony House

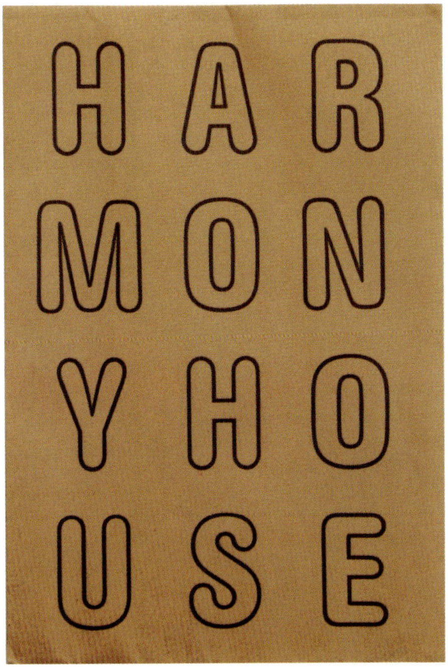

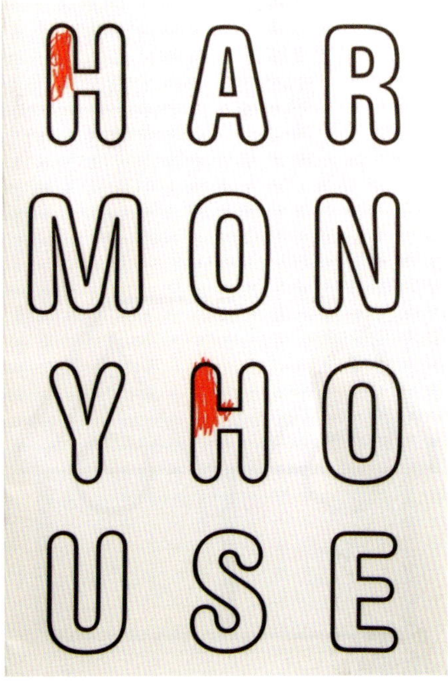

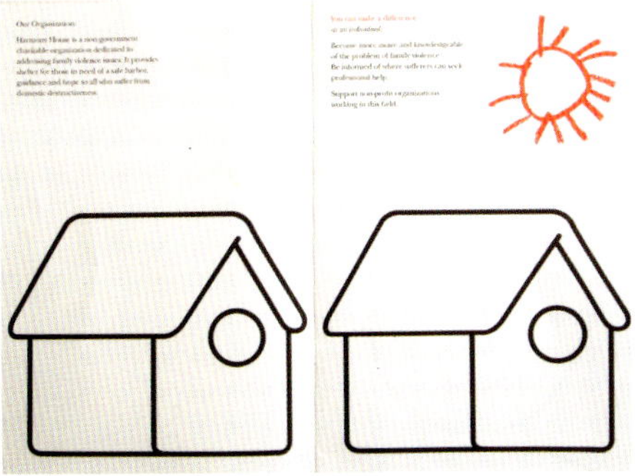

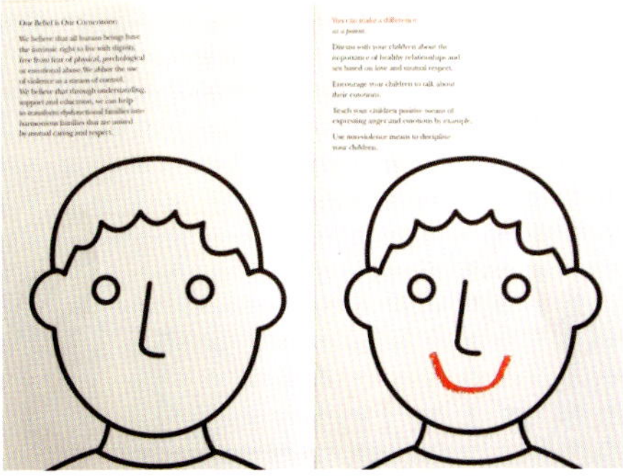

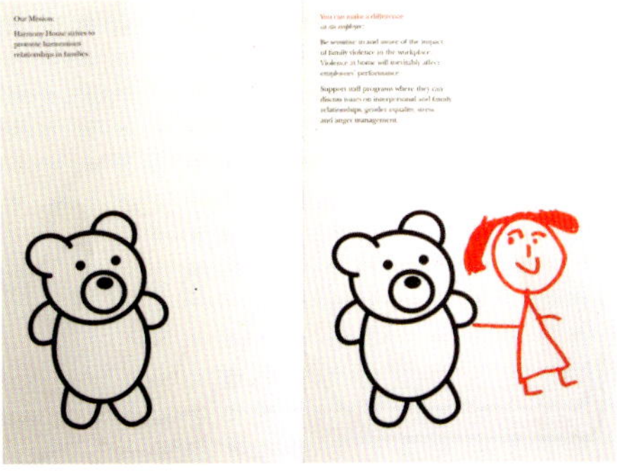

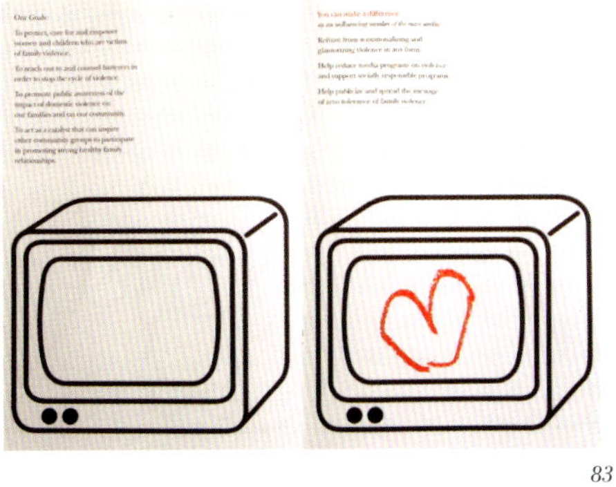

83

84

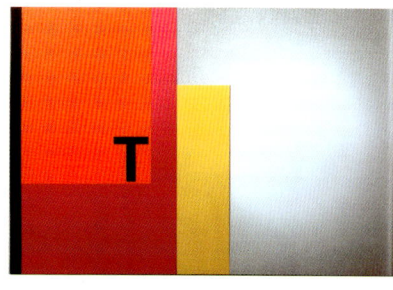

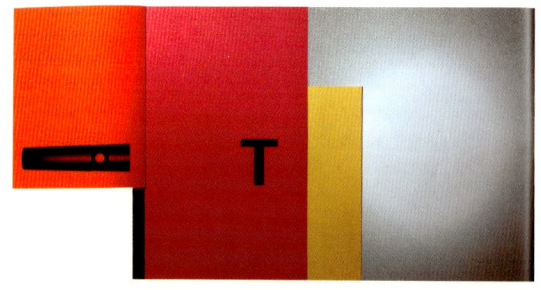

85

Bronze
84_ Marketing Literature
t. Fame
e. dd. ad. d. cw. cl. Ken-Tsai Lee

Bronze
85_ Marketing Literature
t. Shine On You
e. ad. d. i. Benny Au Tak-Shing
p. Dick Chan, Billy Cheung, Benny Au
pt. Suncolor Printing Co., Ltd.
cl. Tai Tak Takeo Fine Paper Co., Ltd.

Bronze
86_ Institutional
t. 元記 — 長江藝術与設計學院簡介
e. 長江藝術与設計學院
cd. d. 吳勇
cw. cl. 汕頭大學長江藝術与設計學院
cp. pt. 深圳寶峰印刷有限公司

87

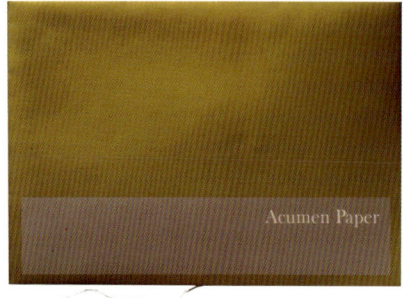

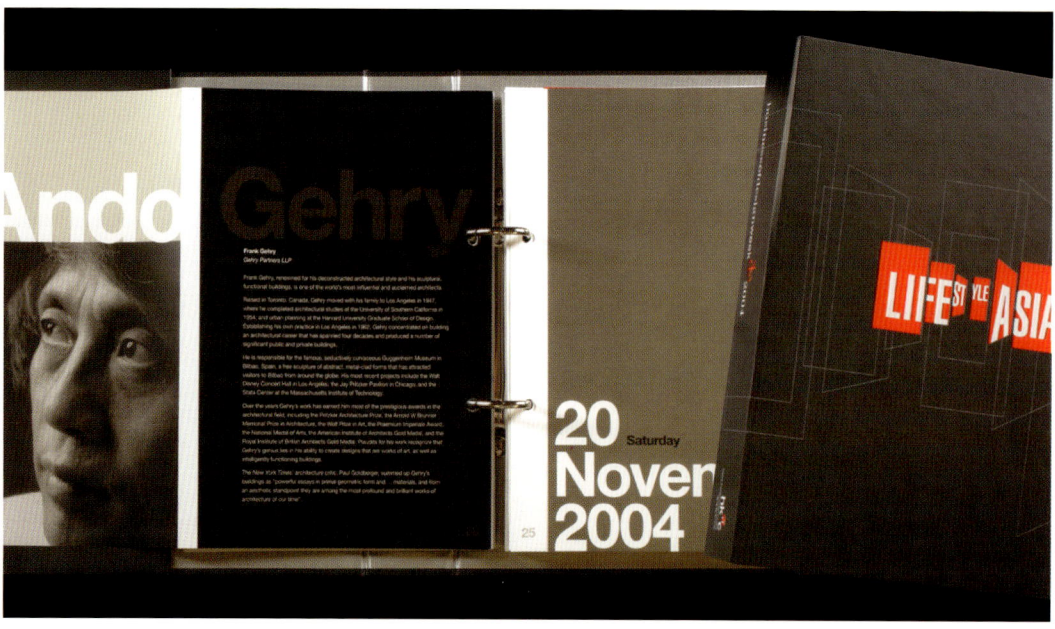

88

87_ Marketing Literature
t. Acumen Paper- Promotion Items
e. Acumen Paper
cd. dd. ad. d. Benny Tak-shing Au
cl. Acumen Paper

88_ Marketing Literature
t. Lifestyle Asia Programme Guide 2004
e. Sandy Choi Associates Ltd.
dd. Sandy Choi
d. Goldie Wong, Lau Sui Wah
cs. Emma Chan
cl. Hong Kong Design Centre

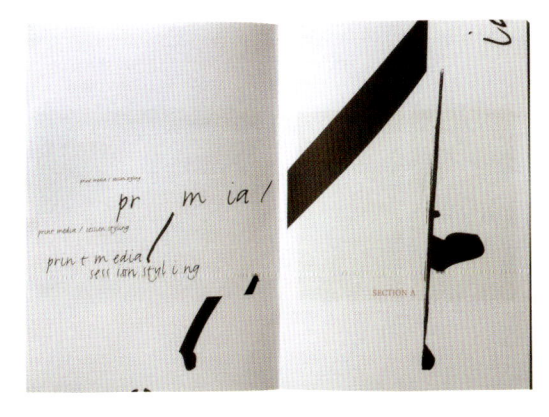

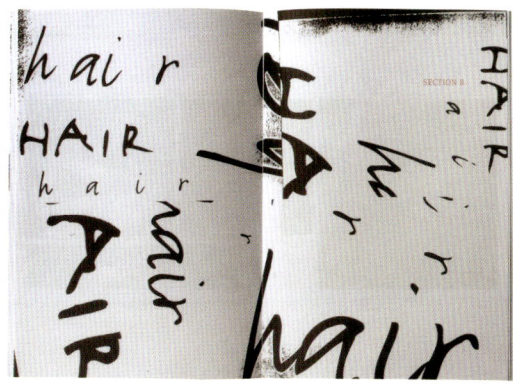

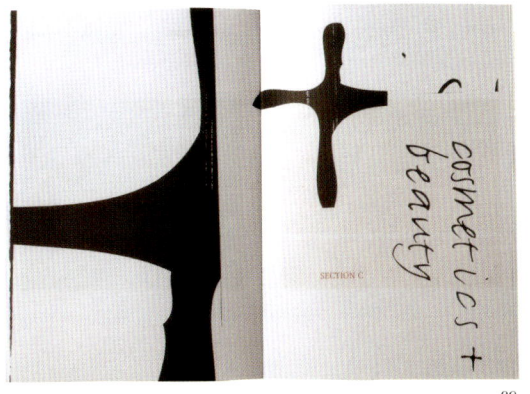

Excellent
89_ *Marketing Literature*
t. Colour Cosmetica Education
e. Voice
cd. d. Anthony Deleo
dd. Anthony Deleo, Scott Carslake
ad. Anthony Deleo, Angela Pastore
p. David Solm
cw. Angela Pastore, Gavin Oliver
cp. pp. pt. Finsbury Print
cl. Colour Cosmetica

90_ Marketing Literature
t. 2046 - Movie Booklet
e. Acorn Design Ltd.
ad. d. Frank Chan Wah Hung
cp. Simple Art Ltd.
pt. General Printers
pr. Chan Hon Lai
cl. Fortissimo Films, Block 2 Pictures Inc.

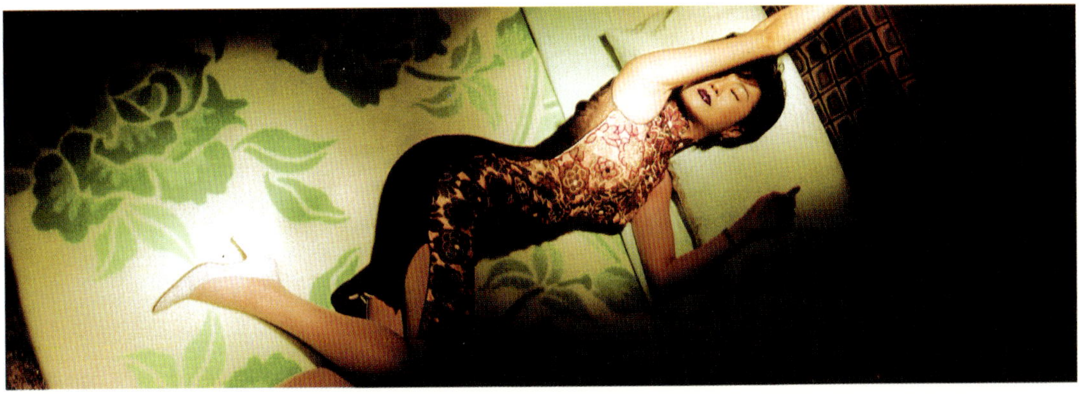

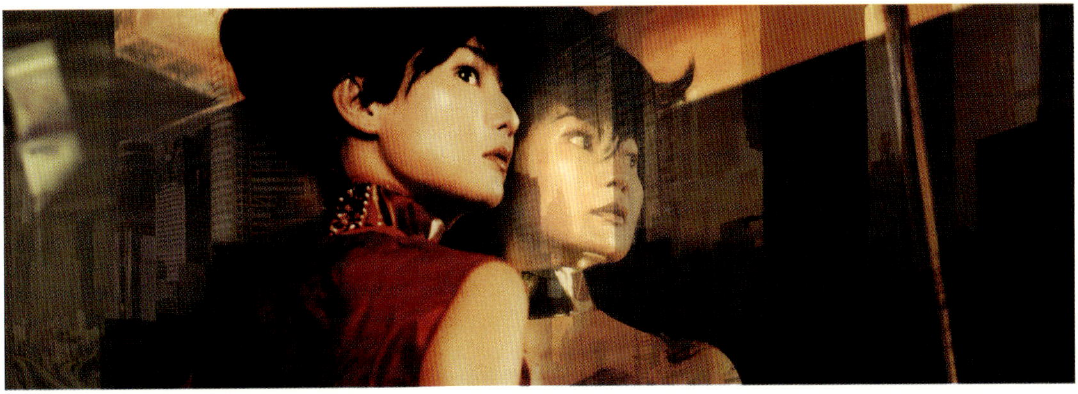

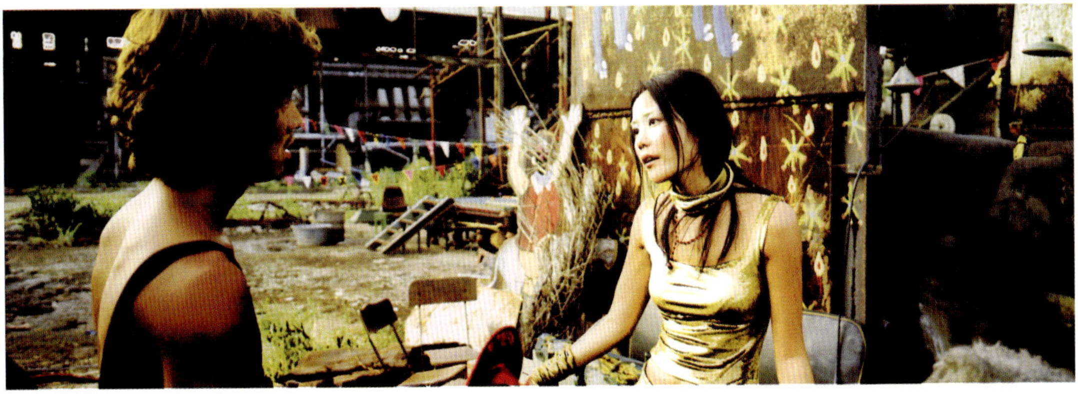

90

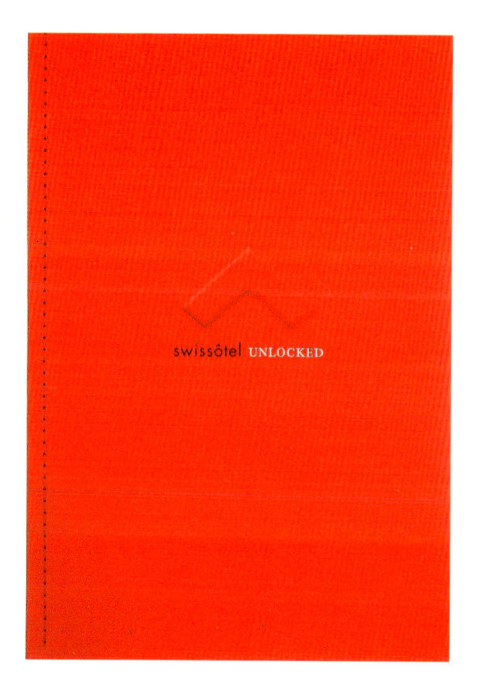

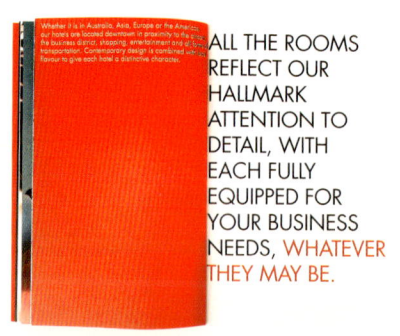

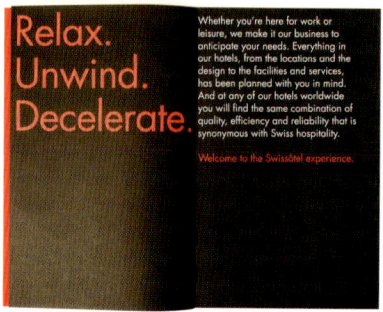

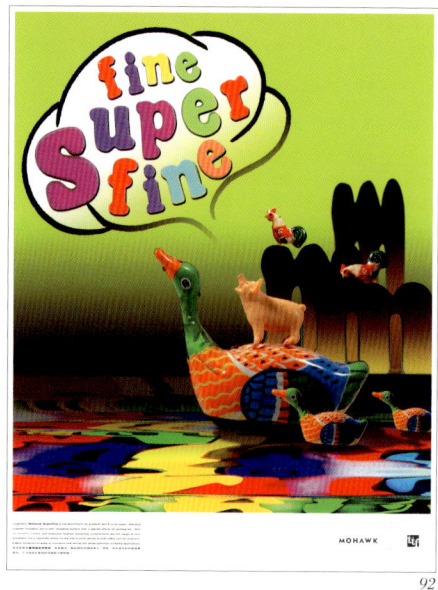

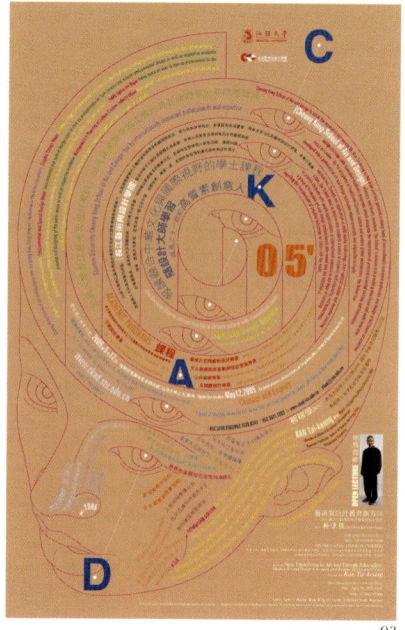

91_ *Marketing Literature*
t. Swissotel Unlocked
e. Equus Design Consultants Pte Ltd.
cd. Andrew Thomas
d. Tay Chin Thiam
p. Ken Seet
cw. Andrew Thomas, Cheah Su Fei
cp. pt. Colourscan Co., Pte. Ltd.
cl. Swissotel Hotels & Resorts
   (Managed by Raffles International
   Hotels & Resorts)

92_ *Marketing Literature*
t. Fine! I'm Superfine
e. ad. d. i. Benny Au Tak-Shing
p. Dick Chan
pt. Suncolor Printing Co., Ltd.
cl. Tai Tak Takeo Fine Paper Co., Ltd.

93_ *Institutional*
t. 長江藝術与設計學院05—香港招生
e. 長江藝術与設計學院
cd. d. 吳勇
cw. cl. 汕頭大學長江藝術与設計學院
cp. pt. 深圳佳信達印刷有限公司

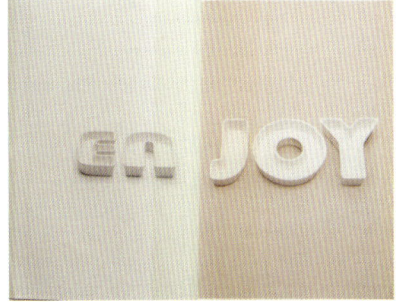

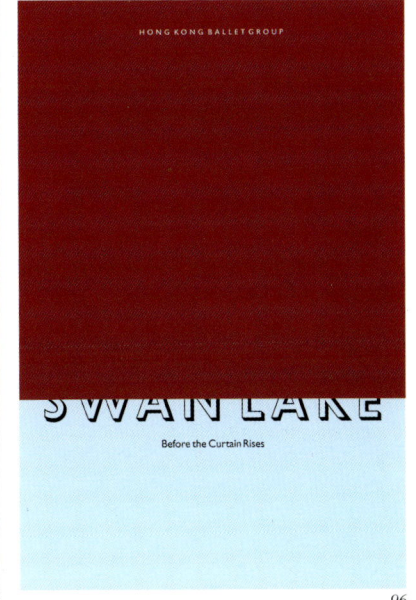

94_ *Marketing Literature*
t. Corporate Brochure for "da dolce"
e. Tommy Li Design Workshop Ltd.
cd. Tommy Li
dd. Choi Kim Hung
d. Wong Siu Kwan
p. Danny Chiu
cw. Yao Shun Language Services Ltd.
cs. Lancy Chiu
pt. T. A. Production & Printing Co. Ltd.
cl. Fu Gar International Ltd.

95_ *Marketing Literature*
t. Proad Design Corp.
e. 知本設計廣告有限公司
cd. Proad Design CORP.
dd. ad. d. p. Jennifer Tsai
cl. Proad Design CORP.

96_ *Marketing Literature*
t. Swan Lake : Before the Curtain Rises
e. Sandy Choi Associates Ltd.
dd. Sandy Choi
d. Goldie Wong, Mo Won Kit
p. Cheung Chi Wai
cs. Angela Lee
pt. Corporate Press (HK) Ltd.
cl. Ricoh Hong Kong Ltd.,
   Hong Kong Ballet Group

97_ *Marketing Literature*
t. Sinowood Folder and Brochures
e. Monopoly Design Ltd.
cd. Andy Blank
ad. d. Vivian Law
p. James Fung
cl. Sino-Forest Corporation Ltd.

98_ *Marketing Literature*
t. AXA HK8 Newsletter & Notebook
e. Monopoly Design Ltd
dd. Kevin Yuen
d. Kevin Yuen, Kin Wong, Brit Nehmeyer, Neville Lam
cl. AXA China Region Insurance Co., Ltd.

99_ *Marketing Literature*
t. Stretching The Boundaries
e. Equus Design Consultants Pte Ltd.
cd. cw. Andrew Thomas
d. Gan Mong Teng, Nicholas Paul
p. Roy Zhang
cp. pt.. cl. Colourscan Co Pte Ltd.

100

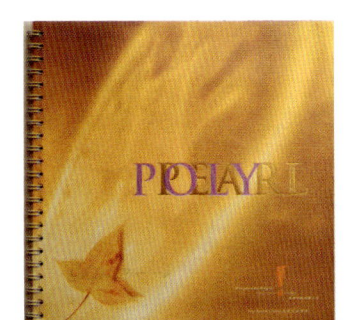

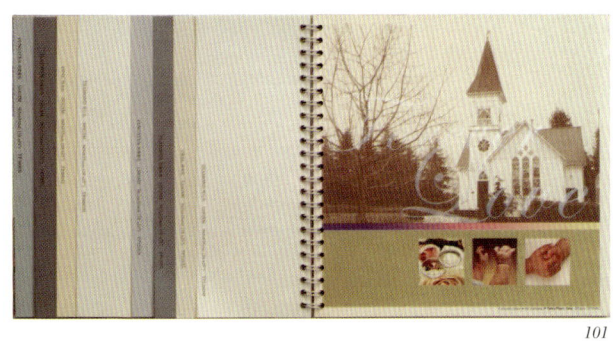

101

102

Excellent
100_ Marketing Literature
t. HKDA 02 Show Programme
e. Sandy Choi Associates Ltd.
dd. Sandy Choi
d. Becky Yeung
cl. Hong Kong Designers Association

101_ Marketing Literature
t. Polytrade Twins Pearl Booklet
e. Ameba Design Ltd.
cd. dd. ad. d. Gideon Lai
cl. Polytrade Paper Corp. Ltd.

102_ Marketing Literature
t. Heiwa Neenah Paper
   Hang-tag Booklet
e. Ameba Design Ltd.
cd. dd. ad. d. Gideon Lai
cl. Heiwa Paper (HK) Ltd.

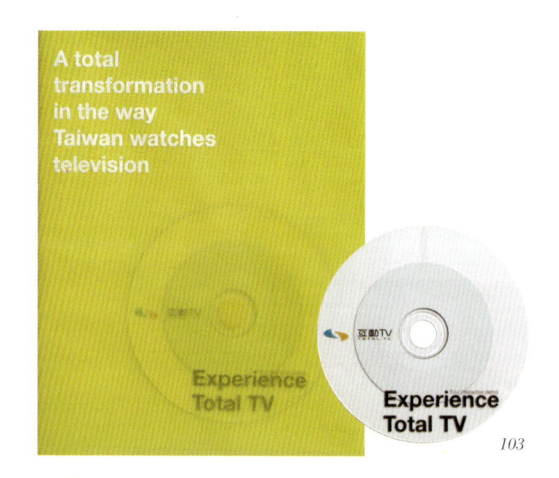

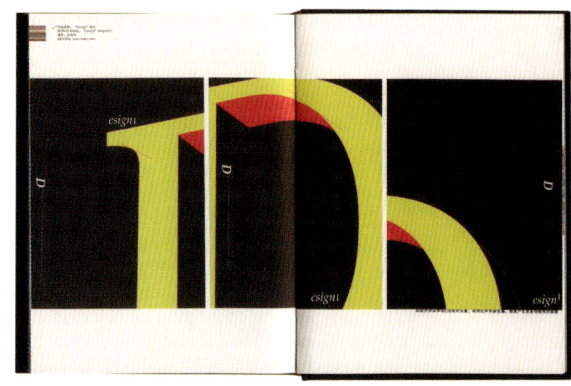

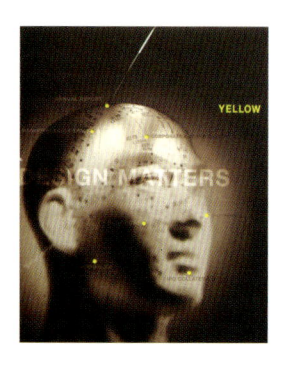

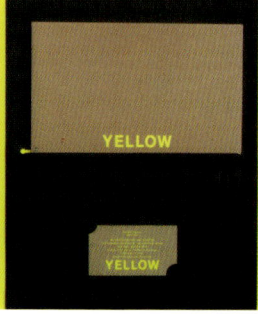

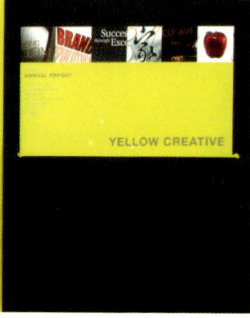

103_ Marketing Literature
 t. Total TV Brochure (Int'l Version)
 e. STAR Group Ltd.
 cd. d. Cat Lam Siu Hung
 p. Woody Wu
 pp. Winsome Ho
 cl. Total TV

104_ Marketing Literature
 t. Double Yearbook Of JHT Design
 e. cd. dd. d. Peng Ke
 p. Wang Ha
 i. Zhou Xiu-Zhen
 cw. Tao De-Hui
 cl. Shanghai JHT
    Packaging Corporation

105_ Marketing Literature
 t. Yellow Creative (HK) Ltd. - Brochure
 e. Yellow Creative (HK) Ltd.
 cd. Wong Chun Hong
 cl. Yellow Creative (HK) Ltd.

136

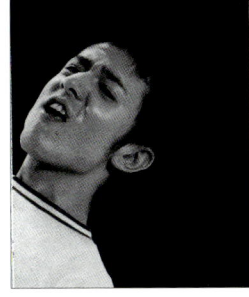

106_ *Marketing Literature*
t. Levis Wild Wide Wash Catalogue
e. Acorn Design Ltd.
ad. d. Frank Chan Wah Hung
p. Lester Lee
pt. Chan Hon Lai, Shum Cho Yu
cl. Levi Strauss, USA., LLC- Taiwan Branch

107_ *Marketing Literature*
t. Tangents & Dispersions Booklet
e. Genemix
cd. dd. ad. d. James Leung Wai Mo
p. Bertha Ma, Eva Chan, James Leung
cl. Tangents & Dispersions

108_ *Marketing Literature*
t. Lane Crawford Book
e. Monopoly Design Ltd.
cd. Andy Blank
ad. d. Vivian Law
cl. Lane Crawford (Hong Kong) Ltd.

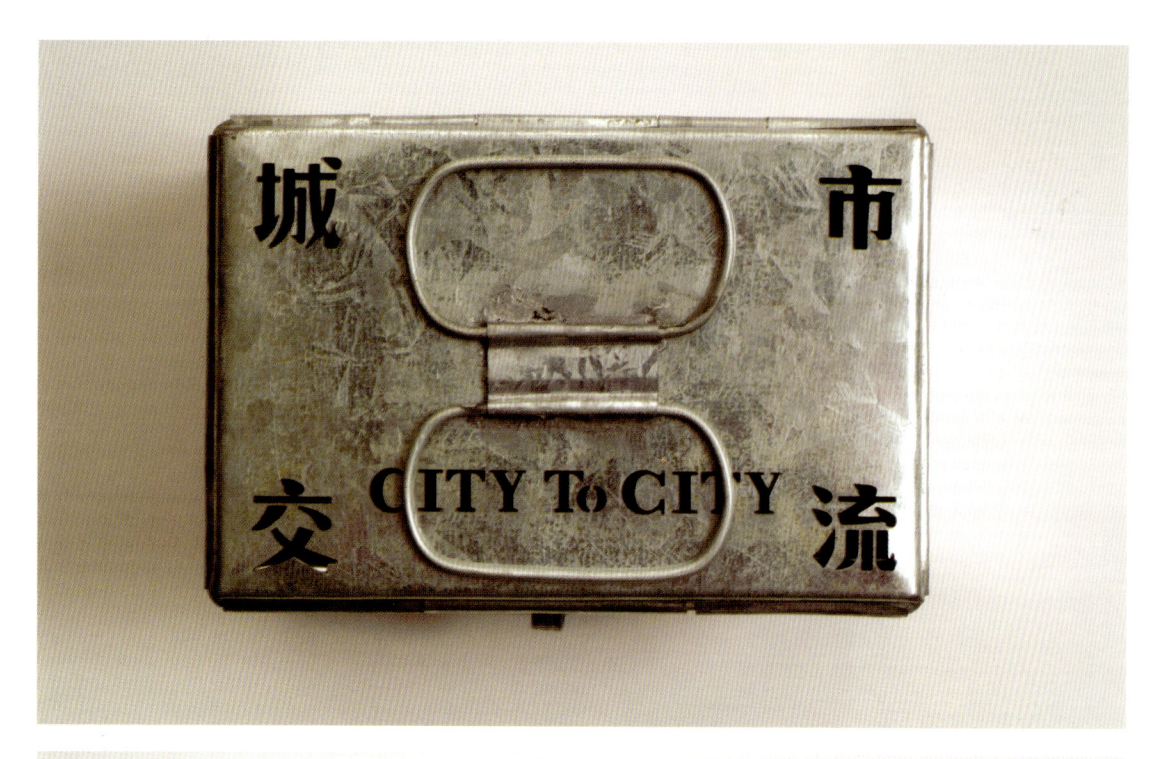

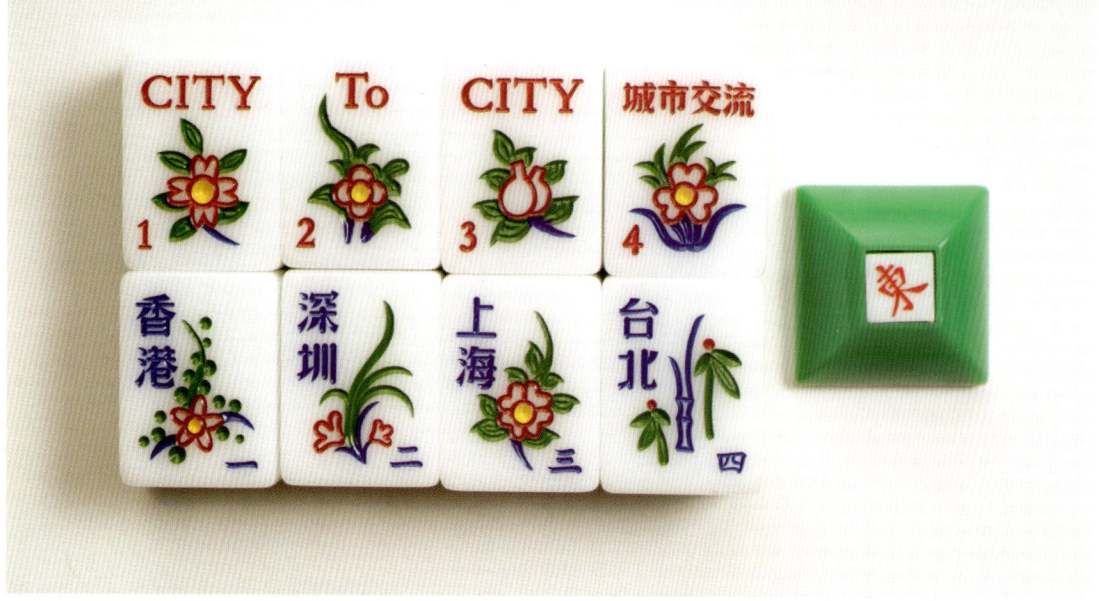

Bronze
109_ Assorted Promotional Item
t. City to City - Promotion Materials
e. Kan & Lau Design Consultants
cd. Freeman Lau Siu Hong
ad. Freeman Lau Siu Hong,
  Veronica Cheung
d. Freeman Lau Siu Hong, Serrine Lau,
  Margaret Chui
cl. Hong Kong Institute of
  Contemporary Culture

110

Bronze
110_ Assorted Promotional Item
t. Traditional Trades & Handicrafts Stamps
e. adjective
cd. d. i. Michael Fung
cl. Hongkong Post

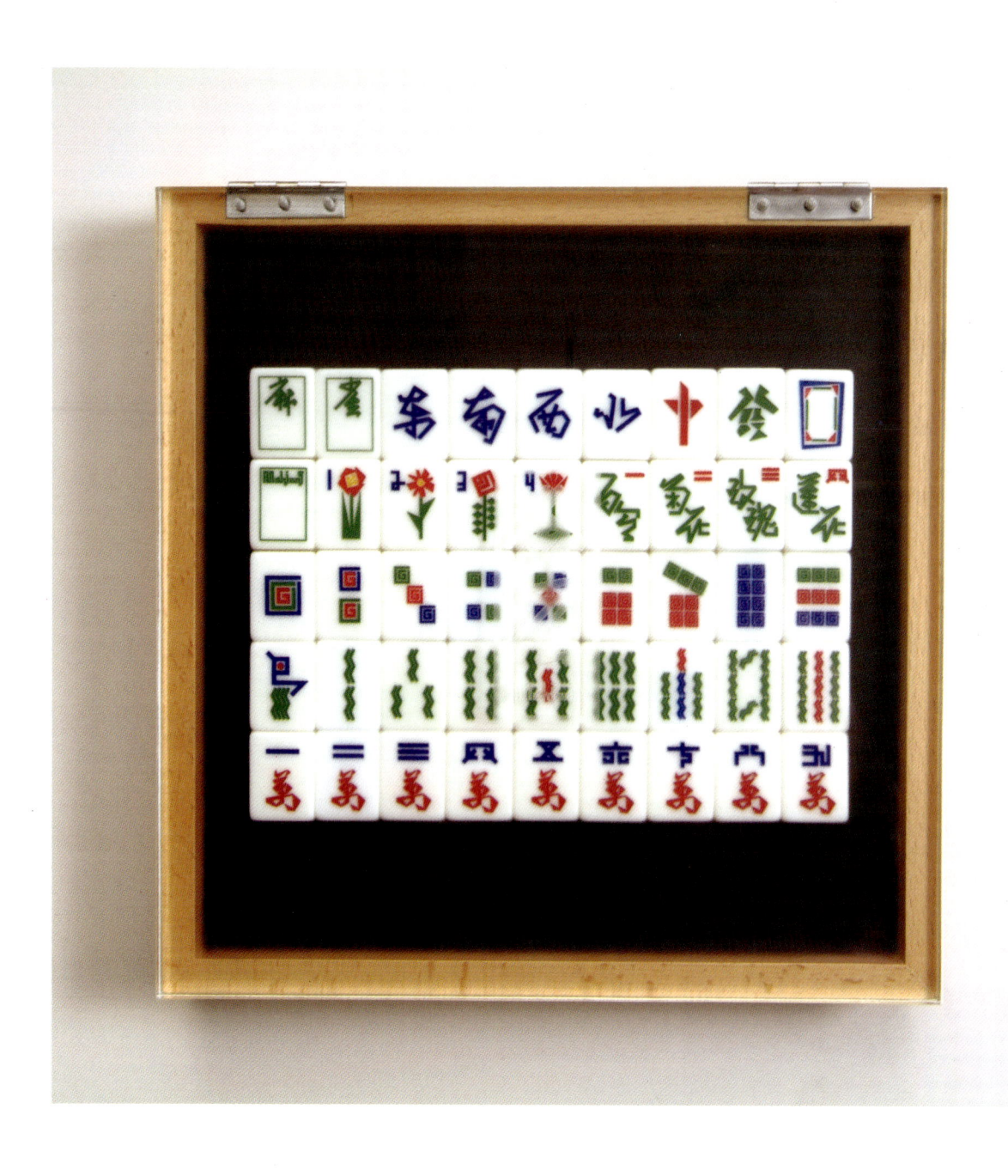

111_ Assorted Promotional Item
t. 麻雀 Mahjong
e. dd. ad. d Lawrence Choy

112

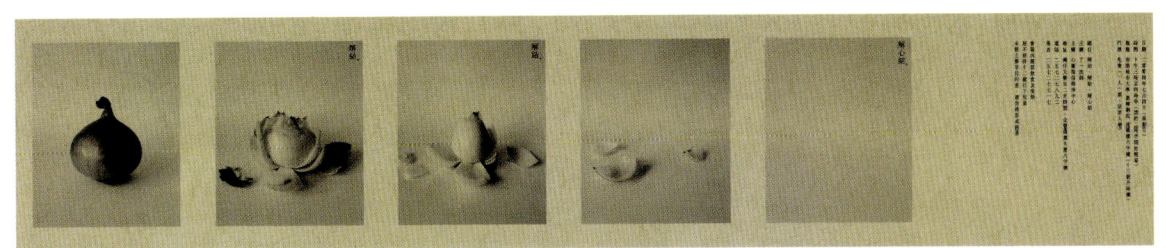

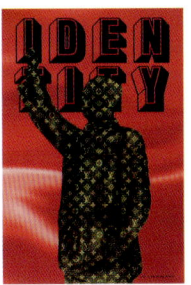

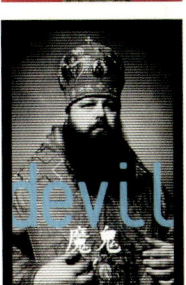

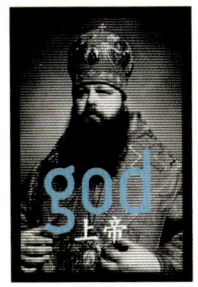

113

Excellent
112_ Assorted Promotional Item
t. 解結、解結、解心結
e. CoDesign Ltd.
dd. d. p. Hung Lam
cw. Liao Yi
pt. Printact Production Co.
cl. Peace of Mind Zenter

Excellent
113_ Assorted Promotional Item
t. 宣傳品
e. 深圳朗圖公司

Excellent
114_ Assorted Promotional Item
t. Boom 06
e. Unioncult
cd. p. Michael Cheung
d. Kim Wong, Ben Yeung
cw. John So
cs. Owen Ngau, Nakanishi Taka
pt. Suncolor Printing
cl. Speak For

142

114

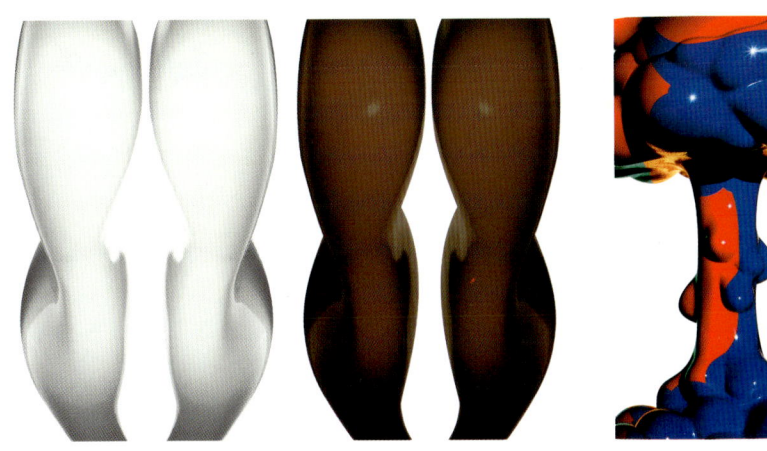

115_ Assorted Promotional Item
t. Supreme Cover Promotion Booklet
e. CoDesign Ltd.
dd. Eddy Yu, Hung Lam
d. GiGi Cheng
p. Bobby Lee
i. Ngie Lo Lo
cw. Eddy Yu, GiGi Cheng
cl. Tai Tak Takeo Fine Paper Co., Ltd.

116_ Assorted Promotional Item
t. dshot
e. ad. d. Benny Au Tak-shing
pt. Suncolor Printing Co., Ltd.
cl. Dick Chan, dshot

117_ Assorted Promotional Item
t. IGOO Shanghai Opening Invitation Card
e. IGOO
cd. ad. Ben Lui
cl. IGOO Communications Ltd.

Excellent
118_ Assorted Promotional Item
t. Motclub903 Remade Project
e. ad. p. Milkxhake
cl. Hong Kong Commercial Radio

119_ Assorted Promotional Item
t. Yoho Town - Promotion Package Design
e. Kan & Lau Design Consultants
cd. Freeman Lau Siu Hong
ad. Freeman Lau Siu Hong, Ko Siu Hong
d. Freeman Lau Siu Hong, Ko Siu Hong, Karen Li
cl. Sun Hung Kai Properties Ltd.

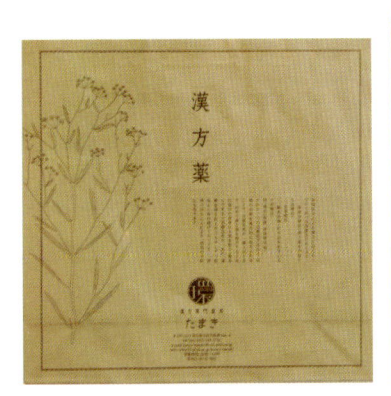

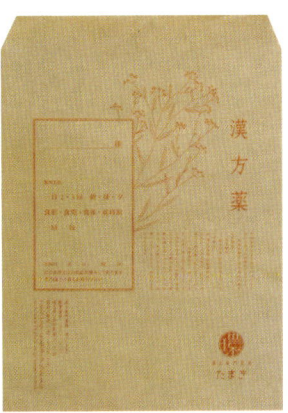

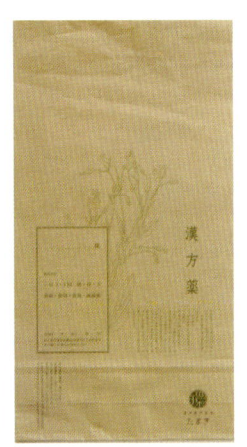

120_ Assorted Promotional Item
t. Package of TAMAKI
e. ad. Osamu Misawa
d. i. Satomi Kajitani
pp. Dai Nippon Printing Co., Ltd.
cl. TAMAKI

121_ Assorted Promotional Item
t. Karling & Lawrence Wedding Card
e. dd. ad. d. Lawrence Choy

122_ Assorted Promotional Item
t. Thank You Card
e. Creation Design
cd. i. Lok Tsun Man
pt. Chi Tak Printing
cl. Creation Design

Silver
123_ Assorted Promotional Item
t. E & E Paper calendar
e. cd. dd. ad. i. Ken-tsai Lee
d. Ken-tsai Lee, Yao-feng Chou
cl. Fonso Interprise Co., Ltd.

*124_* Assorted Promotional Item
t. Alphabet Stamps
e. cd. d. p. Benny Lau Siu-tsang
cl. Hongkong Post

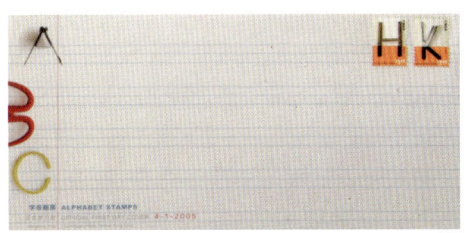

*125_* Assorted Promotional Item
t. Rich Your File
e. 陳俊良
cd. dd. ad. Chen Jun-Liang
d. Chang Hui-Wen
p. Luke Studio
cl. Freeimage Design

149

開演時間

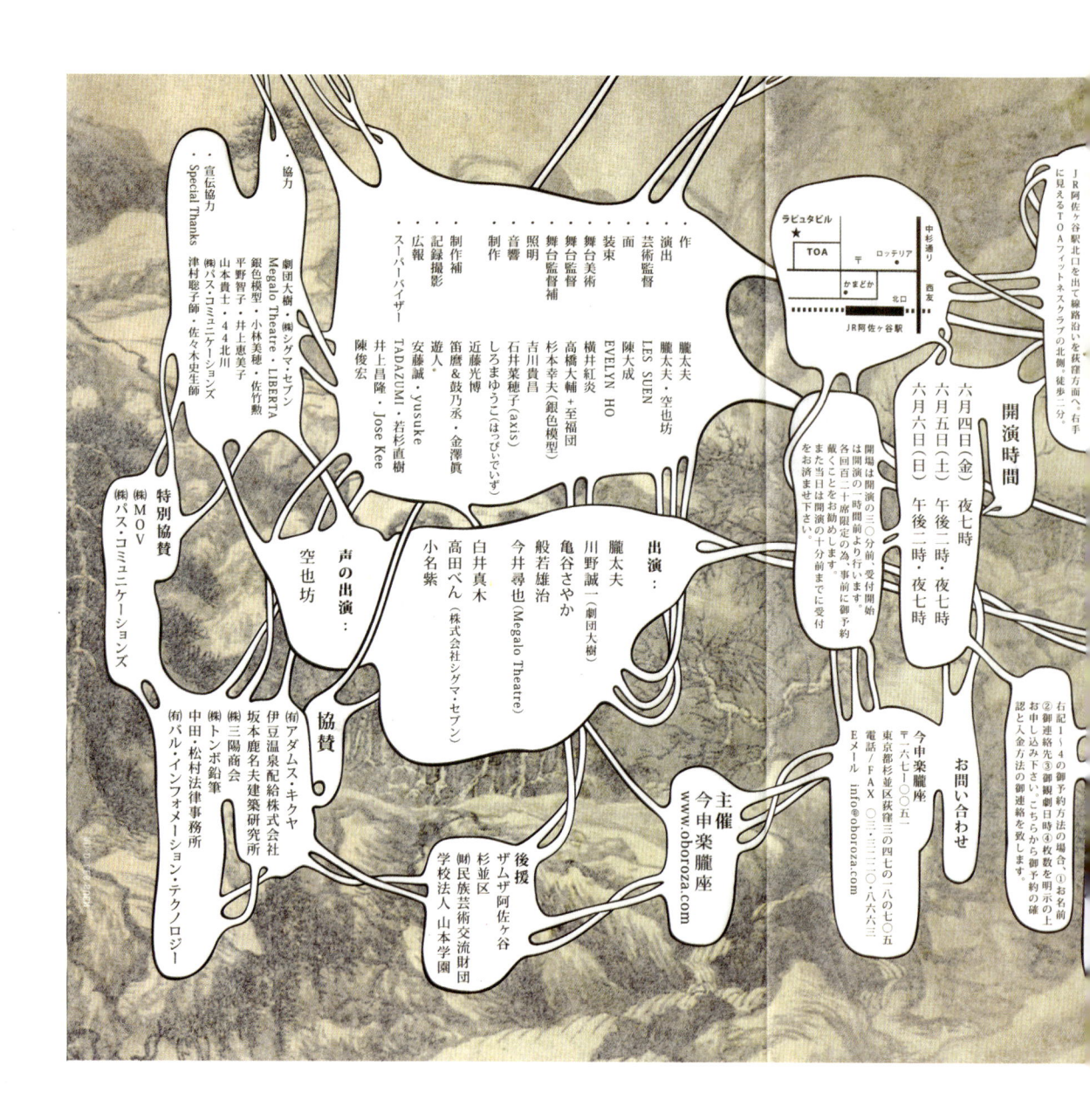

六月四日（金）夜七時
六月五日（土）午後二時・夜七時
六月六日（日）午後二時・夜七時

開場は開演の三〇分前より受付開始、開演の一時間前より行います。各回百二十席限定の為事前に御予約頂くことをお勧めします。また当日は開演の十分前までに受付をお済ませ下さい。

お問い合わせ

今申楽朧座
www.oboroza.com

〒167-0051
東京都杉並区荻窪三の四七の二八の七〇五
電話／FAX 03-3220-8663
Eメール info@oboroza.com

右記1〜4の御予約方法の場合①お名前②御連絡先③御観劇日時④枚数を明示の上お申し込み下さい。こちらから御予約の確認と入金方法の御連絡を致します。

作
朧太夫

演出
朧太夫・空也坊

芸術監督
LES SUEN

面
陳大成

装束
EVELYN HO

舞台美術
横井紅炎

舞台監督
高橋大輔＋至福団

舞台監督補
杉本幸夫（銀色模型）

照明
吉川貴昌

音響
石井菜穂子（axis）

制作
しろまゆう」（はっぴぃでいず）

制作補
近藤光博

記録撮影
笛鷹＆鼓乃承・金澤眞

広報
安藤誠・yusuke

スーパーバイザー
井上昌隆・Jose Kee
陳俊宏

出演：
朧太夫
川野誠一（劇団大樹）
亀谷さやか
般若雄治
今井尋也（Megalo Theatre）
白井真木
高田べん（株式会社シグマ・セブン）
小名紫

声の出演：
空也坊

協賛
（有）アダムス・キクヤ
伊豆温泉配給株式会社
坂本鹿名夫建築研究所
（株）三陽商会
（株）トンボ鉛筆
中田・松村法律事務所
（有）バル・インフォメーション・テクノロジー

後援
ザムザ阿佐ヶ谷
杉並区
（財）民族芸術交流財団
学校法人 山本学園

主催
今申楽朧座
www.oboroza.com

特別協賛
（株）MOV
（株）パス・コミュニケーションズ

協力
劇団大樹
（株）シグマ・セブン
Megalo Theatre・LIBERTA
銀色模型・小林美穂・佐竹勲
平野智子・井上恵美子
山本貴士・44北川

宣伝協力
パス・コミュニケーションズ

Special Thanks
津村聡子師・佐々木史生師

今中樂朧庵

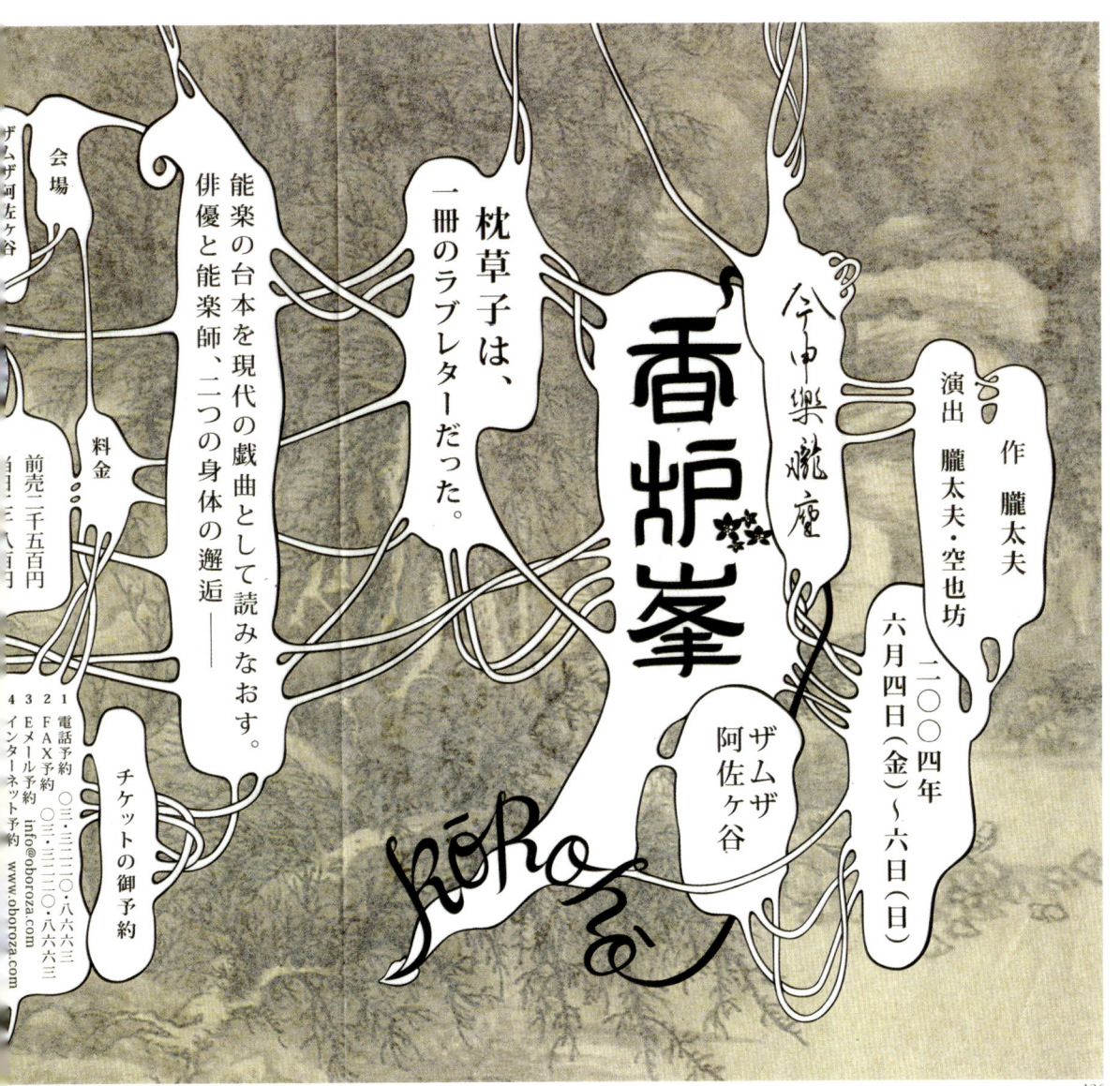

香炉峯

枕草子は、一冊のラブレターだった。

能楽の台本を現代の戯曲として読みなおす。
俳優と能楽師、二つの身体の邂逅──

作　朧太夫
演出　朧太夫・空也坊

二〇〇四年 六月四日（金）〜六日（日）

会場　ザムザ阿佐ヶ谷

料金　前売二千五百円

チケットの御予約
1 電話予約　〇三-三三三〇-八六六三
2 FAX予約　〇三-三三三〇-八六六三
3 Eメール予約　info@oborozza.com
4 インターネット予約　www.oborozza.com

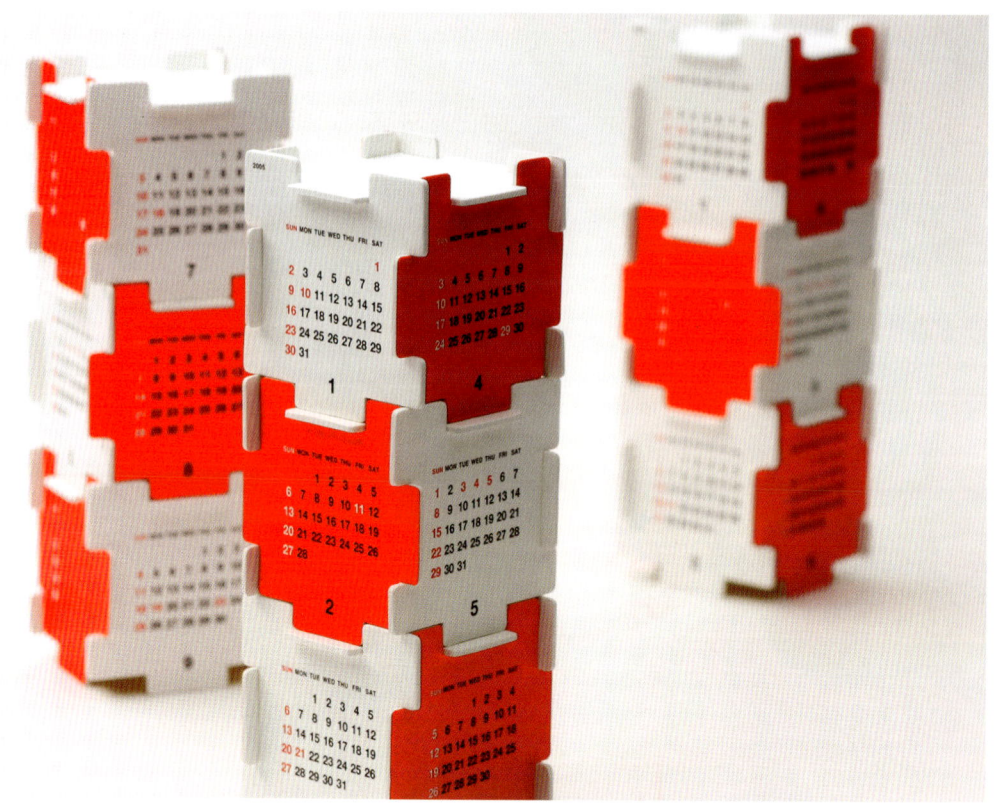

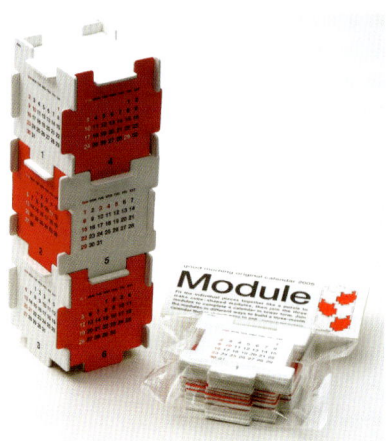

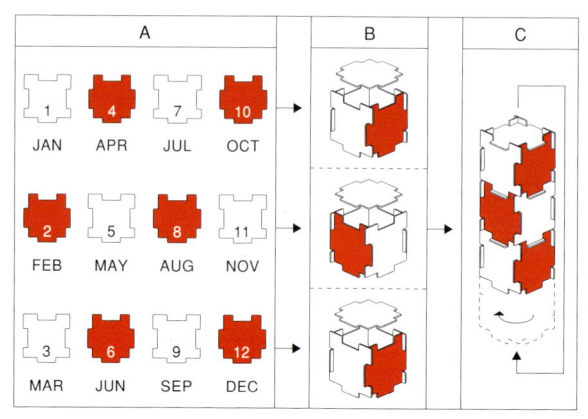

127_ Assorted Promotional Item
t. Module
e. Good Morning Inc.
cd. ad. Katsumi Tamura
d. Kohei Miyasaka
pp. Sonobe Co., Ltd.
cl. Good Morning Inc.

128_ Assorted Promotional Item
t. Color Cartridge
e. Good Morning Inc.
cd. ad. Katsumi Tamura
d. Kohei Miyasaka
pp. Sonobe Co., Ltd.
cl. Good Morning Inc.

129_ Assorted Promotional Item
t. JCD Design Award 2004
e. ad. d. Masayoshi Kodaira
pt. Mochizuki Printing Co.,Ltd.
cl. Japanese Society of Commercial
   Space Designers

130_ Assorted Promotional Item
t. New and the Very Best of TTF
e. ad. d. i. Benny Au Tak-shing
pt. Suncolor Printing Co., Ltd.
cl. Tai Tak Takeo Fine Paper Co., Ltd.

131_ Assorted Promotional Item
t. Curious Collection '05
e. ad. d. Akihiko Tsukamoto
i. Harumi Kimura, Kumiko Yamaguchi, Tetsuro Minorikawa
cw. Masayuki Minoda
cl. ArjoWiggins Fine Papers

132_ Assorted Promotional Item
t. Twist
e. Good Morning Inc.
cd. ad. Katsumi Tamura
d. Akira Katagiri, Hiroyuki Fukazu
pp. Sonobe Co., Ltd.
cl. Good Morning Inc.

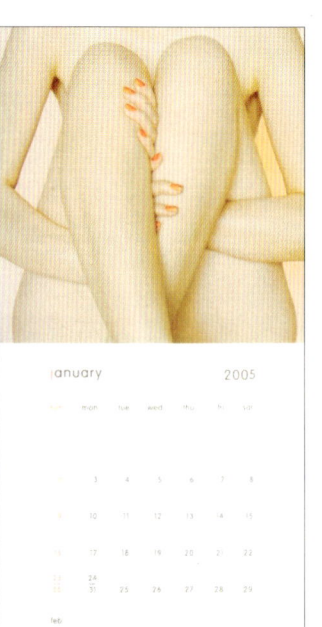

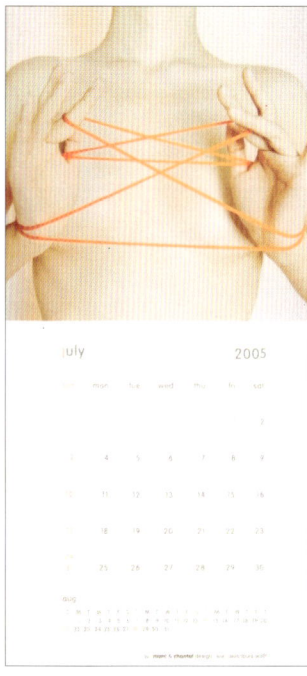

133_ Assorted Promotional Item
t. Marc & Chantal Design - New Year Gift 2003
e. Marc & Chantal Design
cd. Chantal Rechaussat, Marc Cansier, Marc Brulhart
d. Ivan Chiu

156

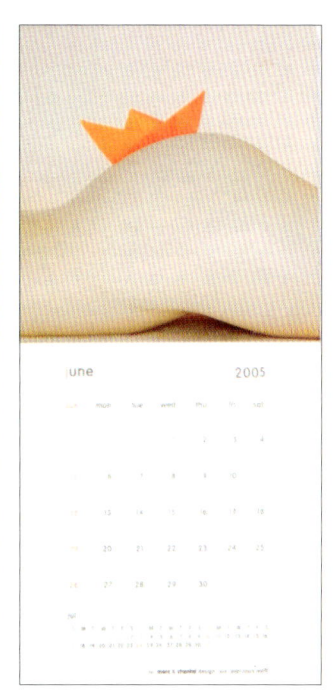

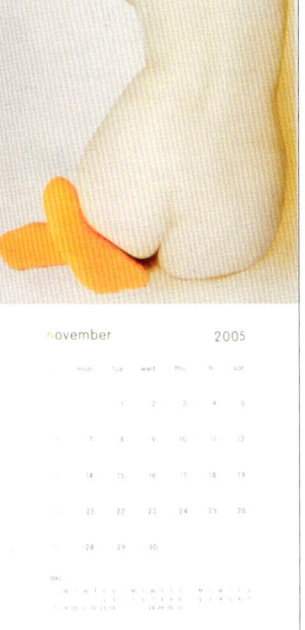

157

134

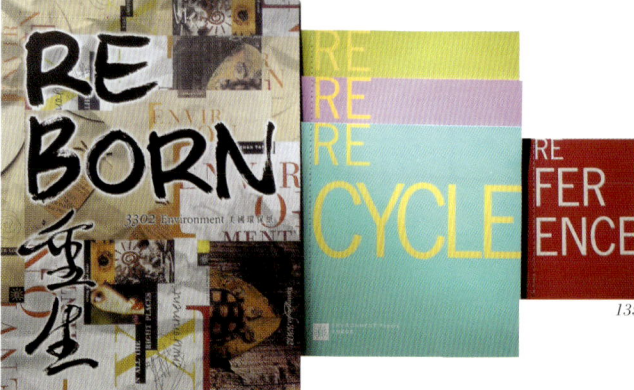

135

136

137

134_ Assorted Promotional Item
t. World Heritage - China
e. The Graphis Company Ltd.
cd. d Bon Kwan
cl. Hongkong Post

135_ Assorted Promotional Item
t. REBORN 3302 Environment
e. BrandsNation Limted
cd. dd. cw. Eric Cheung
d. Eric Cheung, Isabella Chan
p. Danny Chiu
cp. FingerPrint Ltd.
pt. Colham Printing Co., Ltd.
cl. Heiwa Paper Co., Hong Kong Ltd.

136_ Assorted Promotional Item
t. GPC Shanghai 04
e. Leo Burnett Shanghai
cd. Ruth Lee, Dennis Ou
ad. Lemon Dao
d. i. Patrick Wang
pp. Jason Kong

137_ Assorted Promotional Item
t. SVF
e. Circle Design Ltd
cd. d. p. Clement Yick
cl. Tai Tak Takeo Fine Paper Co., Ltd.

158

138_ *Assorted Promotional Item*
t. Curious Collection
e. ad. d. Akihiko Tsukamoto
i. Frank Viva
cw. Masayuki Minoda
cl. ArjoWiggins Fine Papers

139_ *Assorted Promotional Item*
t. TTF Calendar 2003
e. ad. d. i. Au Tak-shing, Benny
d. Dick Chan
p. Suncolor Printing Co., Ltd.
cl. Tai Tak Takeo Fine Paper Co., Ltd.

140_ *Assorted Promotional Item*
t. 一鳴驚人
e. Stony
cd. dd. 程湘如

141_ *Assorted Promotional Item*
t. Game
e. Circle Design Ltd
cd. Clement Yick
ad. Leung Wai Yin
d. i. Phyllis Koo
cl. Polytrade Paper Corporation Ltd.

142

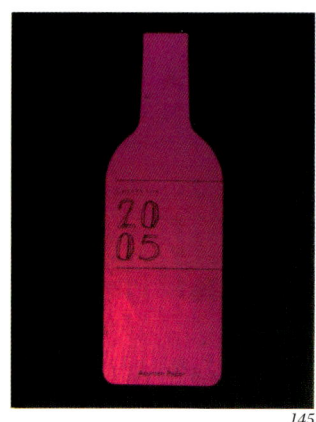

143

144

145

142_ Assorted Promotional Item
t. Hong Kong Sports
e. The Graphis Company Ltd.
cd. d. Bon Kwan
i. Patrick Wong
cl. Hongkong Post

143_ Assorted Promotional Item
t. 香港 FUN 秘物（賀卡）
e. Master Character Profile Company
cd. dd. Max Mak
d. Clarence Chiu

144_ Assorted Promotional Item
t. Nicole Chu & Jo Lo Wedding Day
e. Jo Lo
cd. cw. Nicole Chu, Jo Lo
dd. i. Jo Lo
ad. d. Nicole Chu
cp. Avantgarde Adertising Studio
pt. Regal Printing Ltd, Chung Mei Printing Ltd.

145_ Assorted Promotional Item
t. Acumen Paper-Diary 2005
e. Acumen Paper
ad. d. i. Benny Au Tak-shing
p. Can Wong
pt. Suncolor Printing Co., Ltd.

160

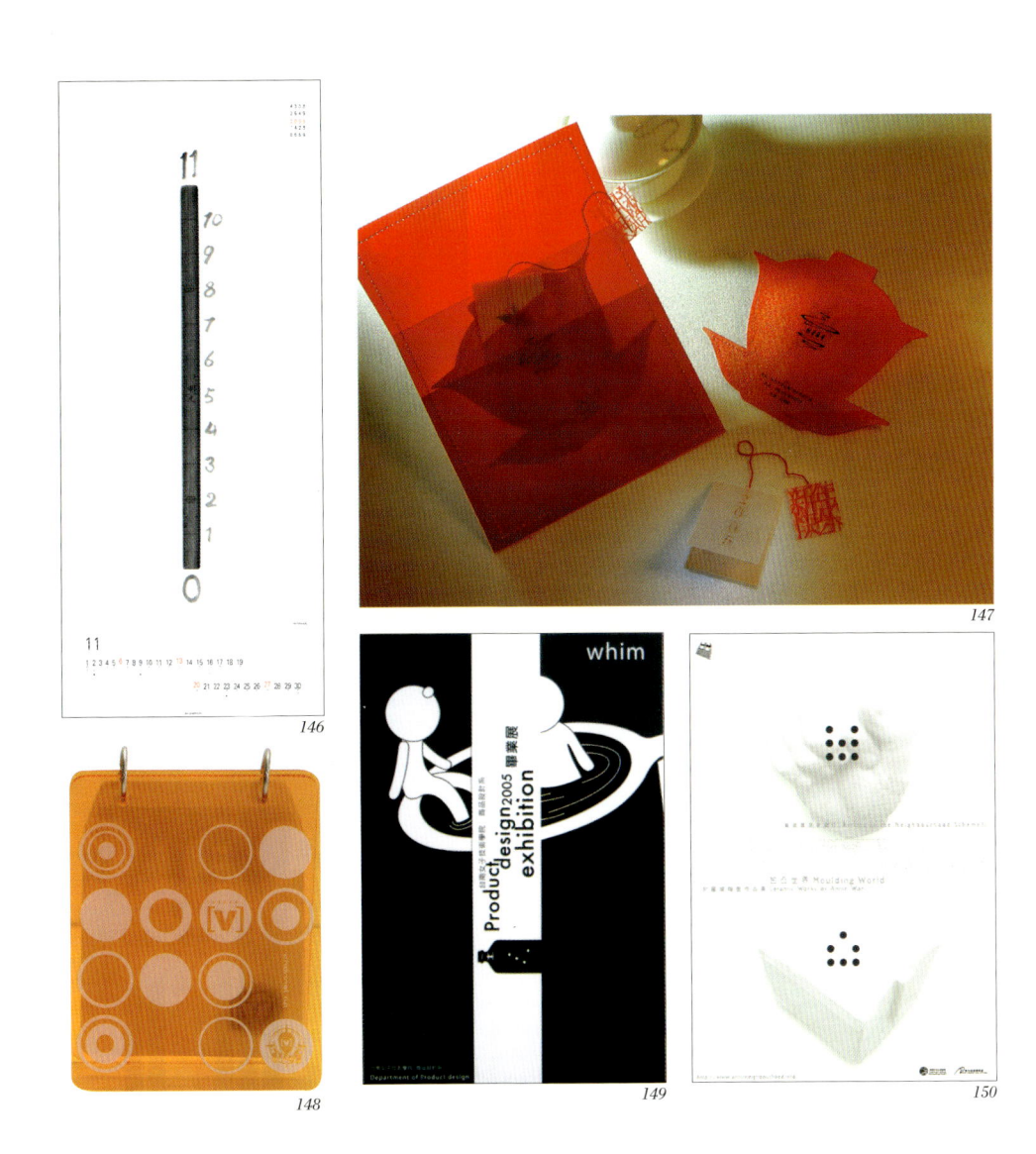

146_ *Assorted Promotional Item*
t. Kan Tai-Keung - 11月安尚秀月曆
e. Kan & Lau Design Consultants
cd. ad. d. Kan Tai-Keung
cp. G.L. Graphic Co., Ltd.
cl. Kan & Lau Design Consultants

147_ *Assorted Promotional Item*
t. 青藤茶館賀卡
e. cd. dd. ad. d. p. i. cw. Wuyuanmin
cl. 青藤茶館

148_ *Assorted Promotional Item*
t. V Photo Frame
e. STAR Group Ltd.
cd. Cat Lam Siu Hung
d. Cat Lam, Angel Tsang
pp. Winsome Ho
cl. Channel V

149_ *Assorted Promotional Item*
t. Product Design 2005 Exhibition
e. I-Hsuan, Cindy Wang
d. Cindy Wang

150_ *Assorted Promotional Item*
t. Leaflet & Postcard for "Moulding World Ceramic Works by Annie Wan"
e. Tommy Li Design Workshop Ltd.
cd. Tommy Li
d. Choi Kim Hung
p. Larry Hou
cs. Lancy Chiu
cl. Art Promotion Office

161

Bronze
151_ Packaging
t. Landscape of Architectures
e. ad. Masayoshi Kodaira
d. Masayoshi Kodaira, Namiko Otsuka
pt. KCOM
cl. UPLINK Co.

152

Bronze
152_ Packaging
t. 鏗鏘集得獎作品集1982-2004
e. cd. Les Suen
d. Les Suen, RTHK Design Team
cl. RTHK 香港電台

153

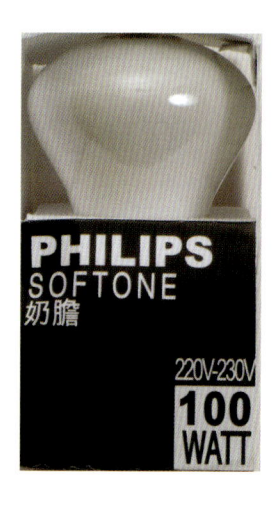

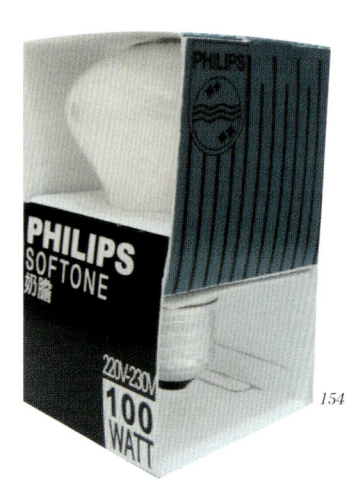

153_ Packaging
t. Mr Chan Fine Tea
e. Alan Chan Design Company
dd. Alan Chan
d. Peter Lo
cl. Alan Chan Creations

Bronze
154_ Packaging
t. Simple Design
e. Woo Ka Yee

154

155

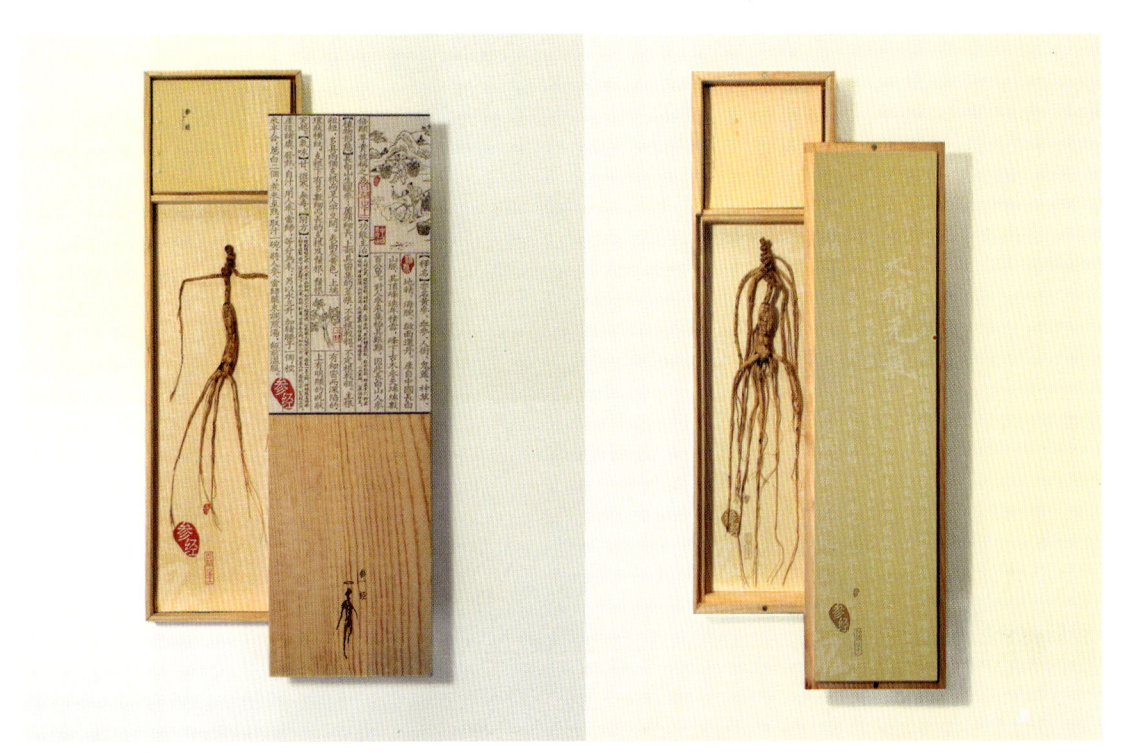

Excellent
155_ Packaging
t. Saint Ginseng
e. Tommy Li Design Workshop Ltd.
cd. Tommy Li
d. Choi Kim Hung
cl. Saint Ginseng, Shanghai

156

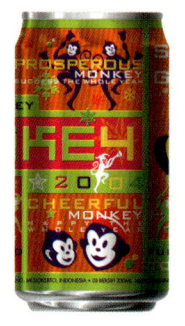

157

156_ Packaging
t. Galaxy Bunch Tee Box
e. cd. d. Michael Kwong
cl. Locomotive Productions Limited

Excellent
157_ Packaging
t. United Can
e. Alan Chan Design Company
dd. Alan Chan
d. Peter Lo
cs. Candas Yeung
cl. PT Multi Bintang Indonesia Tangerang, Mojokerto, Indonesia

166

158

159

160

161

158_ Packaging
t. Packaging - ISIMARU Udon
e. d. Tam Yu Hin, Demo

159_ Packaging
t. Amoy - Premium Soy Sauce
e. Grey Wba HK Ltd.
cd. ad. David Lo
d. Liver Ng
cs. Kathy Wong
cp. Best Pack Enterprises Company
pt. Mayor Packaging Enterprises (1968) Ltd.
cl. Amoy Food Limited

Excellent
160_ Packaging
t. 懷慶府酒包裝設計
e. cd. dd. ad. d. p. i. cw. 劉文
d. 深圳市柏星龍包裝設計有限公司

161_ Packaging
t. 百年老店
e. 共同品牌策略顧問 共同包裝設計
cd. d. 張曉明
dd. ad. 馬深廣
i. 馬深廣, 張曉明
cl. 宜賓五糧液股份有限公司

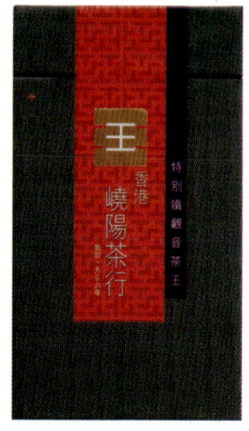

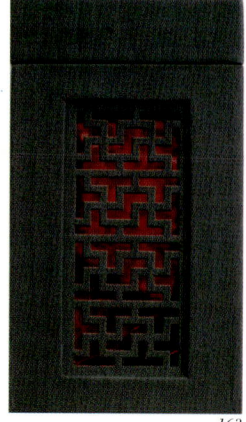

162_ Packaging
t. MAESTROWU Gift Box
e. cd. d. Chiu, Hsien-nen
pt. Chart Design Ltd.
cl. Chin Ho Li Steel Knife Factory

163_ Packaging
t. Geow Yong Tea Hong (Hong Kong) Ltd.
 - Gift Tea Pack
e. Kan & Lau Design Consultants
cd. ad. Freeman Lau Siu Hong
d. Freeman Lau Siu Hong, Ko Siu Hong
cl. Geow Yong Tea Hong (Hong Kong) Ltd.

164_ Packaging,
  Assorted Promotional Item
t. Phoenix Wooden Stamp
e. STAR Group Limited
cd. Cat Lam Siu Hung
d. Cat Lam, Stephen So
pp. Winsome Ho
cl. Phoenix

Excellent
164_ Gift & Premium
t. Phoenix Wooden Stamp
e. STAR Group Limited
cd. Cat Lam Siu Hung
d. Cat Lam, Stephen So
pp. Winsome Ho
cl. Phoenix

165

166

167

*165_* Packaging
t. Oolong Oolong Tea
e. Alan Chan Design Company
cd. dd. Alan Chan
d. Peter Lo
cs. Candas Yeung, Jessica Choi
cl. JT Tabacco Inc, Japan

*166_* Packaging
t. Watsons' Water - General & Hotel Bottle Pack Design
e. Kan & Lau Design Consultants
cd. ad. Freeman Lau Siu Hong
d. Freeman Lau Siu Hong, Karen Li
cl. Watsons' Water

Bronze
*167_* Packaging
t. Watsons' Water - Centennial Bottle
e. Kan & Lau Design Consultants
cd. ad. Freeman Lau Siu Hong
d. Freeman Lau Siu Hong, Karen Li
cl. Watsons' Water

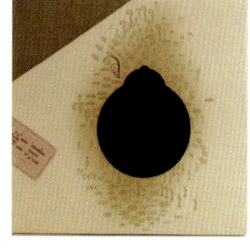

168_ Packaging
t. 蒙頂甘露茶
e. 共同品牌策略顧問共同包裝設計
cd. dd. d. 馬深廣
ad. 張曉明
i. 馬深廣, 胡子
cl. 四川蒙頂皇茶茶業有限公司

169_ Packaging
t. 祺禎名茶
e. 共同品牌策略顧問共同包裝設計
cd. dd. d. 馬深廣
ad. 張曉明
i. 馬深廣, 胡子
cl. 祺禎茶業有限公司

170_ *Packaging*
t. Eason 4 a chance
e. Token Workshop
cd. ad. d. Kenneth To Po Keung
p. Lewis Ho
cl. Emperor Entertainment Group

171_ *Packaging*
t. Lhasa Ice Beer
e. Kan & Lau Design Consultants
cd. ad. Kan Tai-keung
d. Kan Tai-keung, Serrine Lau, Vinci Fung
cl. Carlsberg Brewery Hong Kong Ltd.

172_ *Packaging*
t. 陽光地帶乾紅葡萄酒
e. 共同品牌策略顧問共同包裝設計
cd. dd. ad. d. i. 馬深廣
cl. 煙台陽光地帶葡萄釀酒有限公司

173_ Packaging
t. if
e. Tommy Li Design Workshop Ltd.
cd. Tommy Li
dd. Tami Leung
d. Douglas Mak
p. Danny Chiu
cs. Lancy Chiu
cl. Inspiring Fascination Co., Ltd., Macau

174_ Packaging
t. Basheer Design Books Shop Bag
e. dd. Eric Chan
d. Eric Chan, Iris Yu
cl. Basheer Design Books Shop

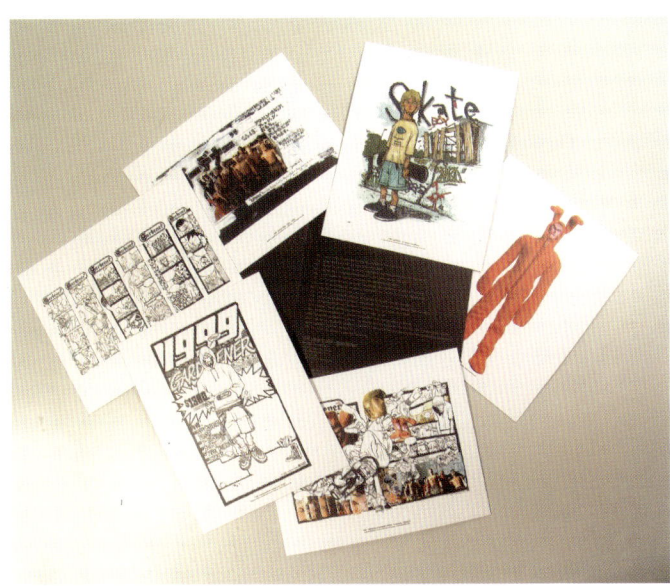

175_ Packaging
t. Sixs Year Old - Gardener
e. cd. dd. ad. d. Michael Lau
pp. pt. Miracle Printing Co., Ltd.
cl. Crazysmiles Co., Ltd.

176_ Packaging
t. 科技系列
e. 袁世文

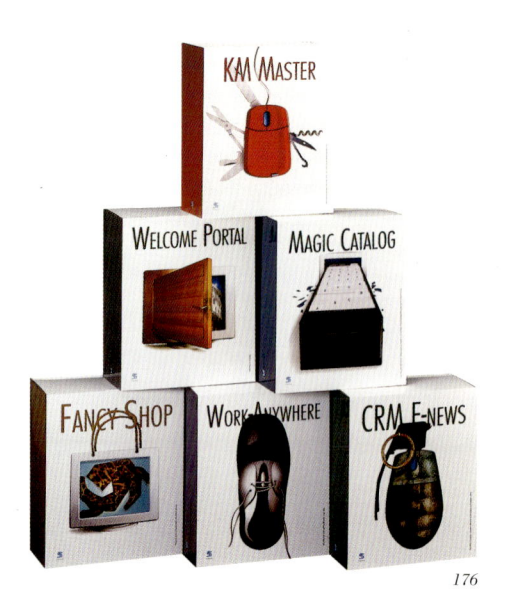

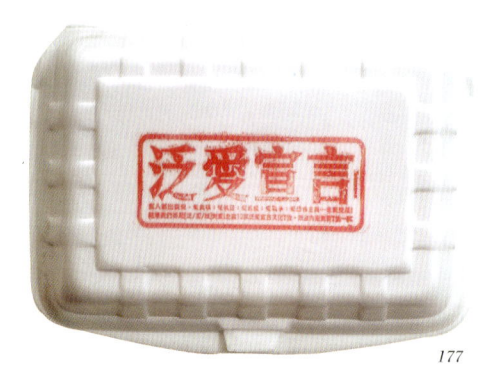

177_ Packaging
t. Lovism T-shirt by Ta-Ma-DeSign
e. Charles Ng & Maxi Communications Ltd.
cd. dd. ad. cw. Charles Ng
d. i. Young Hoi Chun
cl. Ta-Ma-DeSign

178_ Packaging
t. Saint Honore Moon Cake
e. Alan Chan Design Company
cd. dd. Alan Chan
d. Tina Ng
cs. Jessica Choi
cl. Saint Honore Cake Shop Ltd.

174

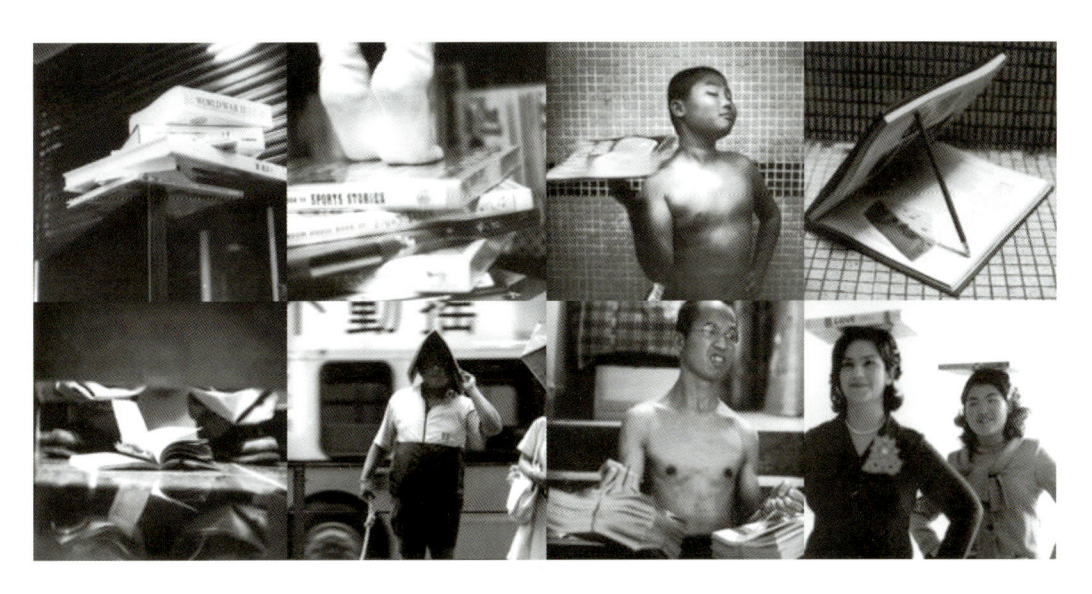

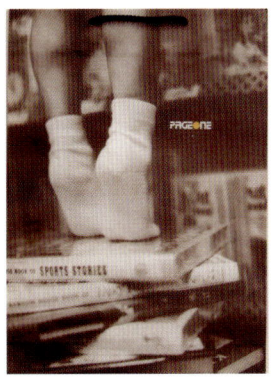

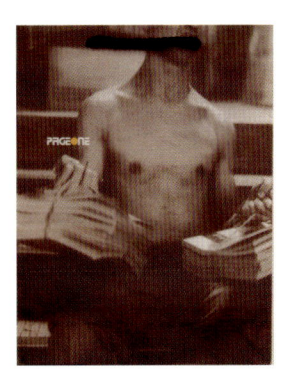

Excellent
179_ Packaging

t. Living with books
e. 28aDesign
cd. dd. ad. Leo Kwok
d. Kit Yeung
p. Lewis Ho @ Studio Incline
cp. Smartmax Int'l Ltd.
pt. Fortunate Printers Ltd.
cl. Pageone Bookshop

POSTER ポスター
포스터 海报

Posters plaster the public space with everything the consumer needs to know - these cover commercial and cultural promotion in a variety of thematic campaigns.

Commercial Poster
Cultural Promotion Poster
Thematic Poster

Adobe Silver Award
180_ Commercial Poster
t. Paper Living Show
e. ad. d. p. i. Au Tak-shing, Benny
pt. Suncolor Printing Co., Ltd.
cl. Tai Tak Takeo Fine Paper Co., Ltd.

181

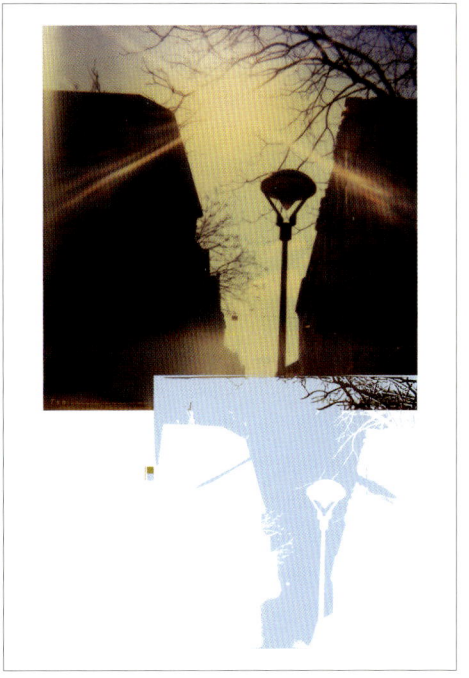

Bronze
181_ Commercial Poster
t. Tiantu Sunny Advertising VI
e. cd. dd. ad. d. He Jun
p. Peng Yangjun
cl. Tiantu Sunny Advertising

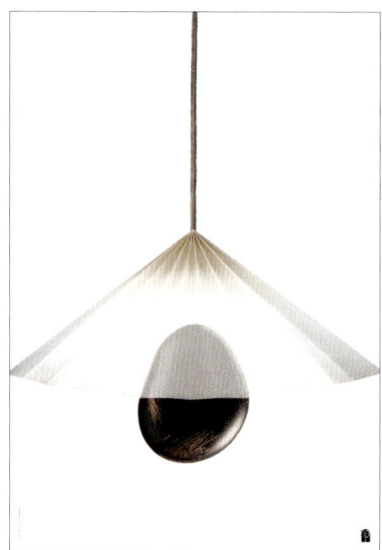

Bronze
182_ Commercial Poster
- *t.* Panta Rei Ltd. - Poster Series
- *e.* Kan & Lau Design Consultants
- *cd. ad.* Kan Tai-keung
- *d.* Kan Tai-keung, Wilson Heng
- *p.* C K Wong
- *cl.* BG Lighting Co., Ltd.

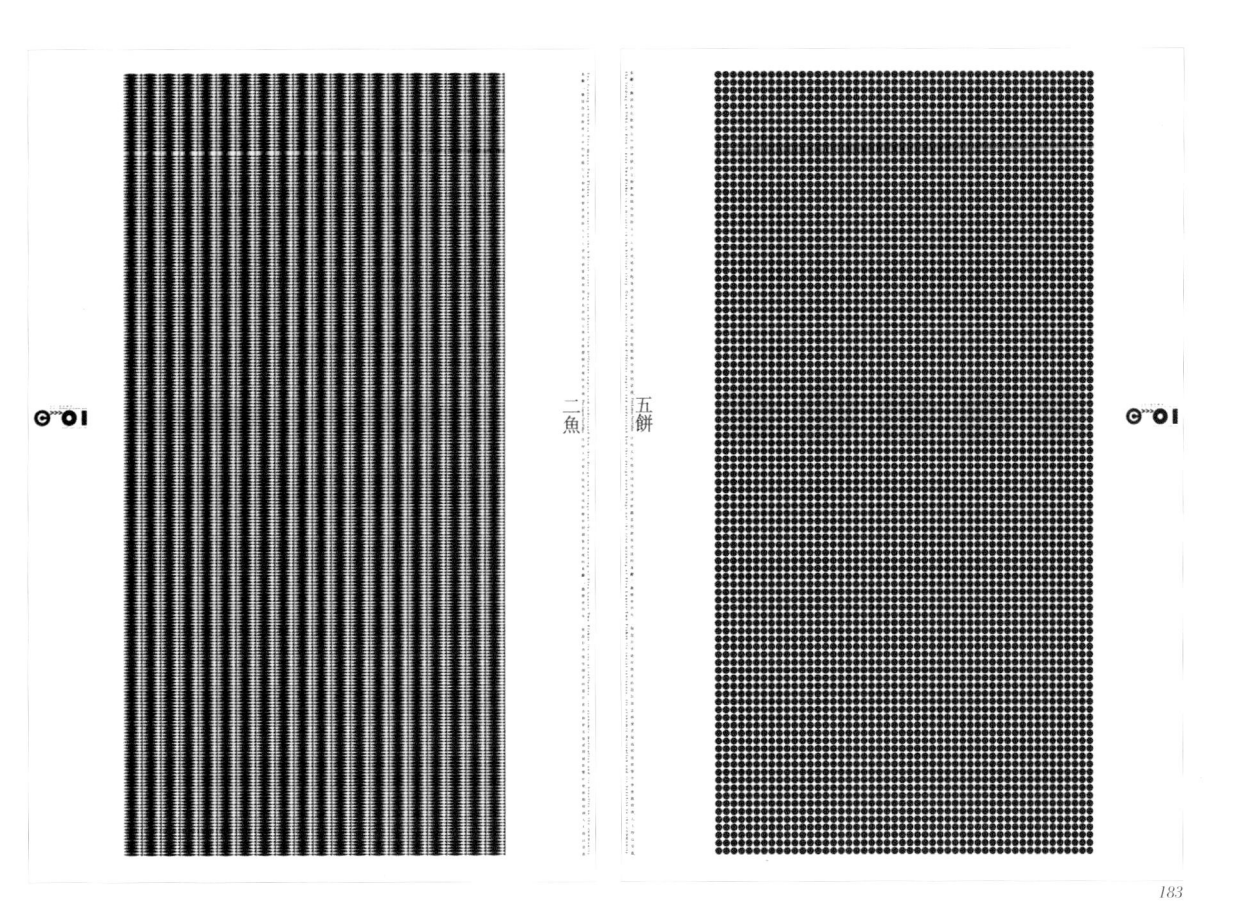

Bronze

183_ Commercial Poster

t. Five Loaves, Two Fishes
e. Paul Lam Design Associates
cd. Paul Lam
ad. Anissa Cheng
d. Queenie Shek, Patrick Chan
cw. Maria Angela Lee, Phoebe Wong
pt. Hoi Kwong Printing Co., Ltd.
cl. CO1 School of Visual Arts

MIKIYA TAKIMOTO EXHIBITION
APRIL 7 - 11, 2005
SPIRAL GARDEN
5-6-23, Minami-Aoyama, Minato-ku, Tokyo 107-0062 Japan Tel: 03-3498-1171 http://www.spiral.co.jp Presented by: Organizing Committee for the Exhibition
Sponsored by: Onion inc. / SUNTORY LIMITED / Shingata Inc. / TOHOKUSHINSHA FILM CORPORATION / ROBOT COMMUNICATIONS INC. Provided by: ARC-SYSTEM
CHROMART LABORATORY INC. / 10BAN STUDIO / TRY-TRY LTD. / PIE BOOKS / FLAME, inc. Space Cooperation Provided by: Wacoal Art Center Space Coordination

Bronze
184_ *Cultural Promotion Poster*
t. BAUHAUS DESSAU / MIKIYA TAKIMOTO
e. ad. d. Masayoshi Kodaira
p. Mikiya Takimoto
cp. pt. Toppan Printing Co., Ltd.
cl. Organizing Committee for the Exhibition
  "BAUHAUS DESSAU, MIKIYA TAKIMOTO"

Bronze

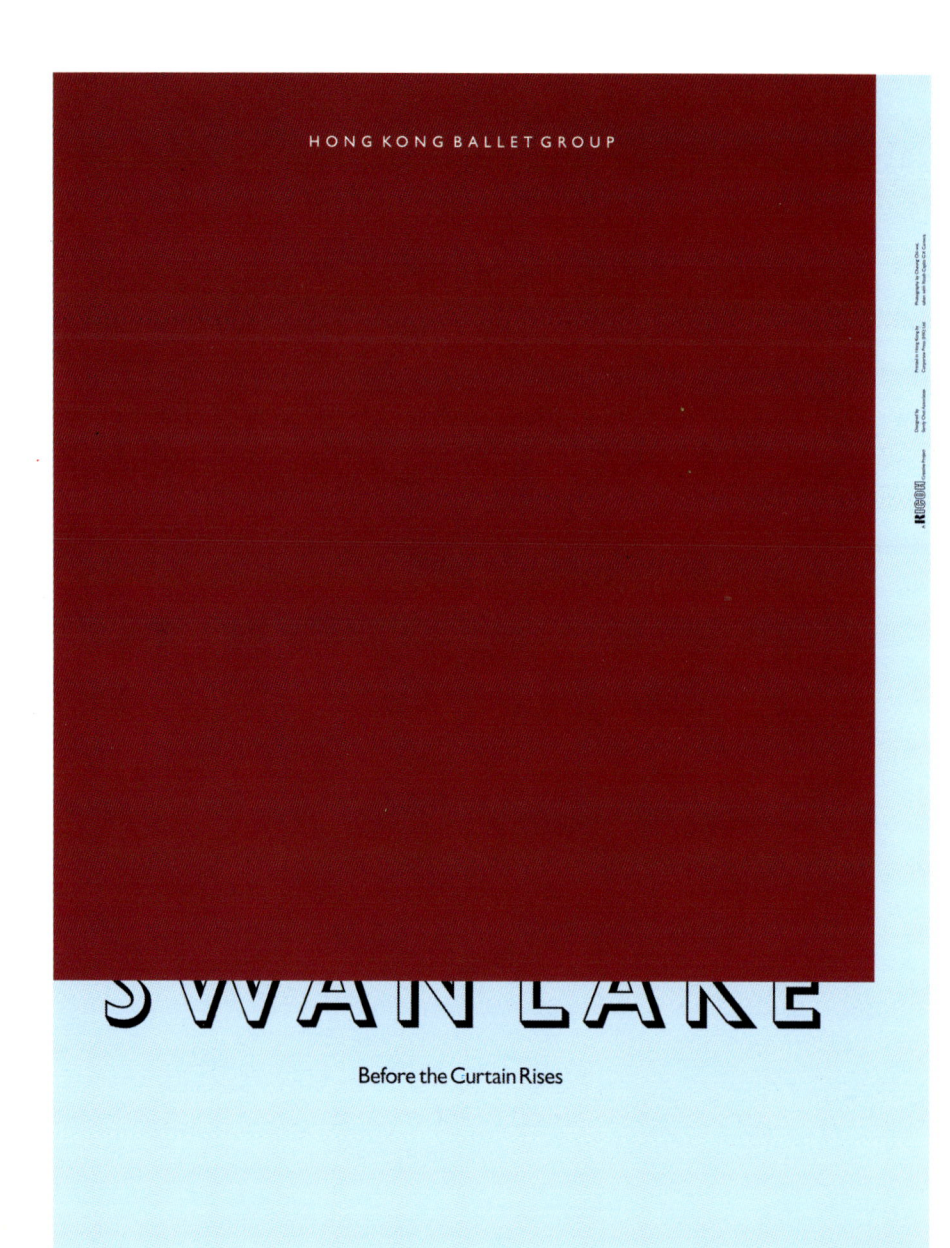

185_ Commercial Poster
t. Swan Lake : Before the Curtain Rises
e. Sandy Choi Associates Ltd.
dd. Sandy Choi
d. Lau Sui Wah
cs. Angela Lee
pp. Art Factory
cl. Ricoh Hong Kong Ltd., Hong Kong Ballet Group

Bronze
186_ Cultural Promotion Poster
t. ARCHIGRAM : Experimental Architecture 1961-1974
e. ad. Masayoshi Kodaira
d. Masayoshi Kodaira, Namiko Otsuka
cp. pt. Toppan Printing Co., Ltd.
o. Images, Archigram Archives

zettai H na syousetsu

Hanamura mangetsu / Fukumori Nanmei
Amakasu Ririko / Hinata Tomogi

kongetsuno Gokujou Tenohira no monogatari kurumatani cyokitsu

okuda Hideo
「Tokyo hatsu NewYork keiyu」

suzuki koji
Hachinenburi no Horror cyohen
「edge・city」

Yamada Tosuke / Yamamoto Fumio / Kakuda Michiyo
Eiga「chakusin ari」

絶対Hな小説/花村萬月/芙蓉南溟/甘糟りり子/日向蓬
今月の極上てのひらの物語車谷長吉
特集・奥田英朗8年ぶりのホラー長編「エッジ・シティ」
鈴木光司が8年ぶりのホラー長編
一白百恵原デビュー二十周年特別
山本文緒の書下ろし日記
大好評!作家の読み物時代
映画『着信アリ』特集

角川書店

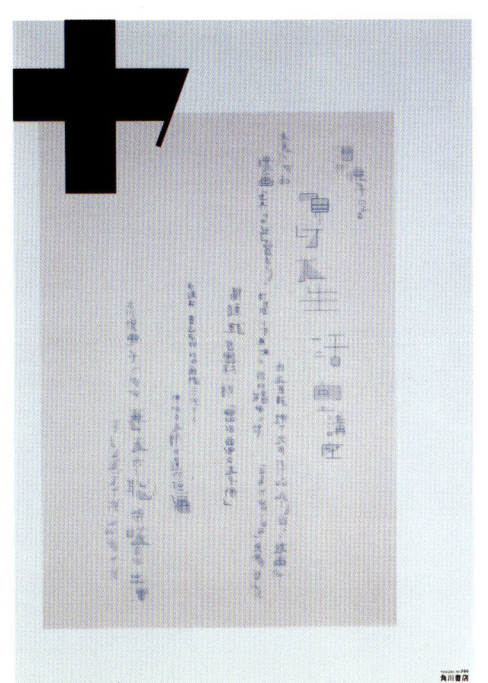

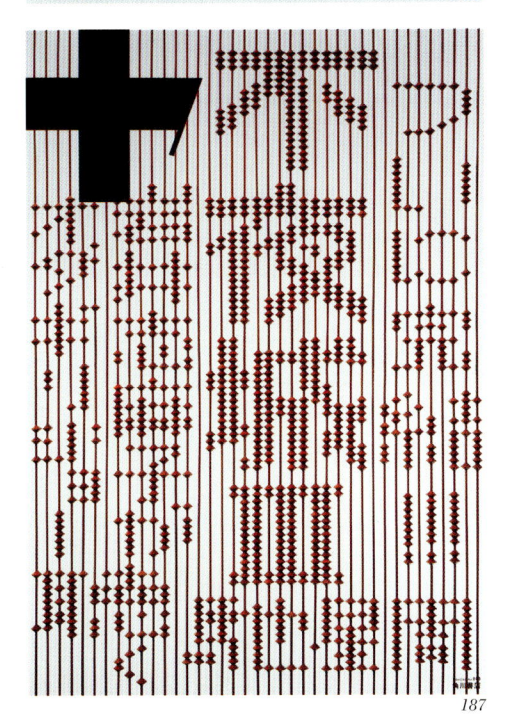

Bronze
187_ Commercial Poster
t. YASEI JIDAI
e. ad. Norito Shinmura
d. Yuka Watanabe
p. Kiyofusa Nozu
cl. Kadokawa Shoten Co., Ltd.

Bronze
188_ Cultural Promotion Poster
t. HONG KONG : HUG & KISS
e. ad. milkxhake
cl. Hong Kong

Bronze
189_ Cultural Promotion Poster
t. BADE *CO1*
e. ad. d. i. Au Tak-shing, Benny
pt. Suncolor Printing Co., Ltd.
cl. CO1 School of Visual Arts

Bronze
190_ Cultural Promotion Poster
t. Life line for visually impaird person
e. Daiko Advertising Inc.
cd. Susumu Fujii, Masahiro Ogawa
ad. Toshiomi Takahashi
d. Kouichi Oda
p. Yuji Sawa
cw. Hiroe Harada, Takeo Takahashi
cl. Japan Ad Council

Silver

191_ Thematic Poster

t. Heromoism
e. Tommy Li Design Workshop Ltd.
cd. cw. Tommy Li
d. Joshua Lau, Choi Kim Hung
p. Larry Hou
pt. Hin Lee Plastic & Screen Printing Ltd.
cl. Tommy Li Solo Exhibition @ MTR ARTtube

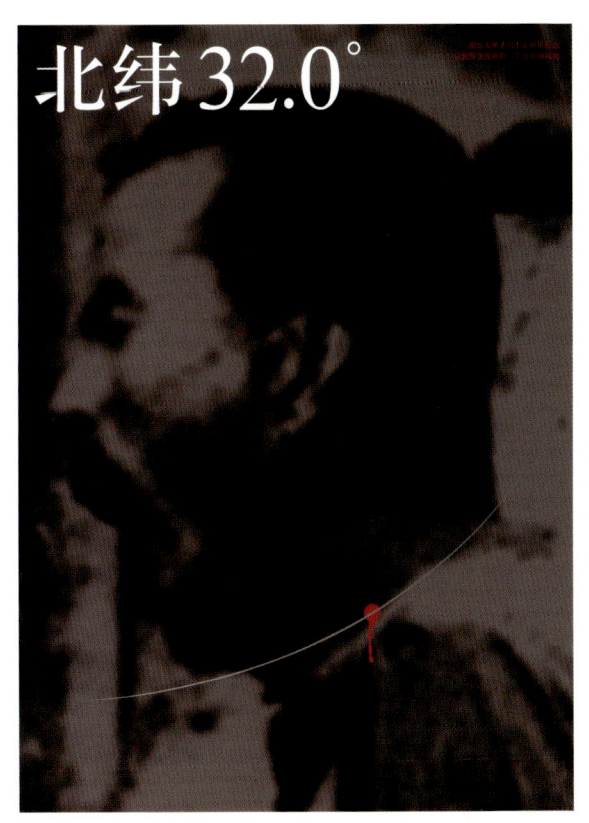

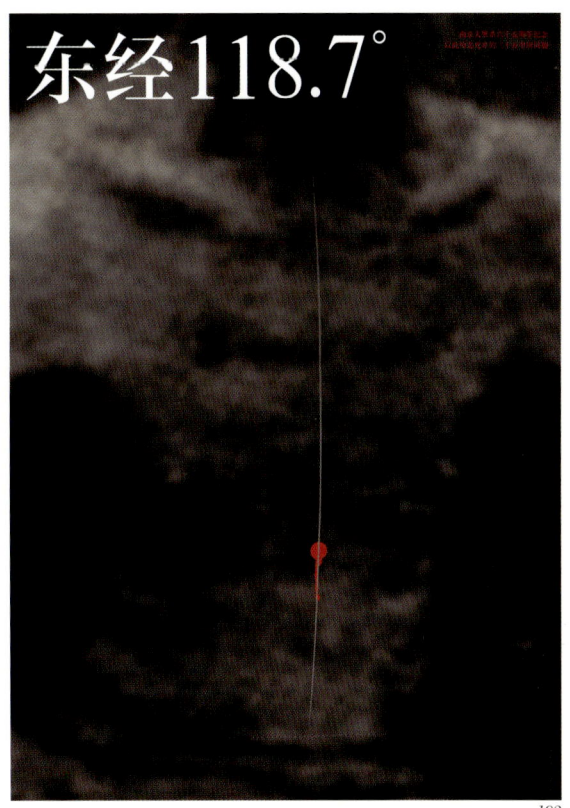

Bronze
192_ Thematic Poster
t. North Latitude 32.0 Degrees / East Longtitude 118.7
e. Eric Cai Design Co.
cd. ad. d. Cai Shi Wei, Eric
cw. Cai Shi Wei, Eric, Xu Zhi Hong
cl. Nanjing Massacre Memorial

Bronze
193_ Commercial Poster
t. AADS Opening
e. ad. d. Benny Au Tak-shing
pt. Suncolor Printing Co., Ltd.
cl. Amazing Angle Design Consultants Ltd.

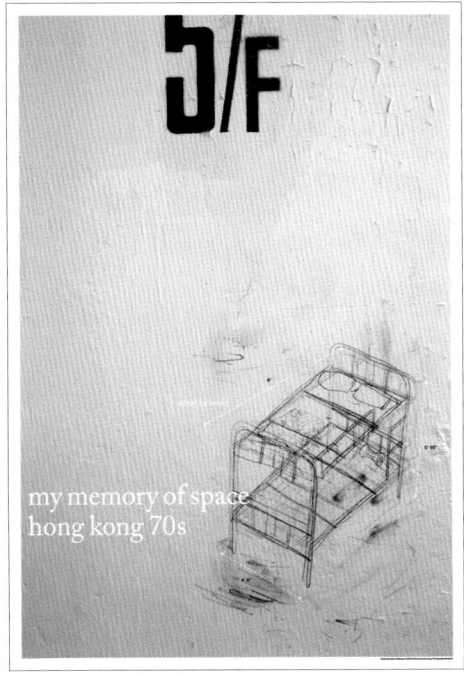

Bronze

194_ Thematic Poster

t. My Memory of Space, Hong Kong 70s
e. CoDesign Ltd.
dd. d. Hung Lam
p. Ducky Tse
i. Tak Yeung
cw. Eddy Yu, Hung Lam
cl. The 3rd International Poster Triennial, Heritage Museum, Hong Kong, 2004

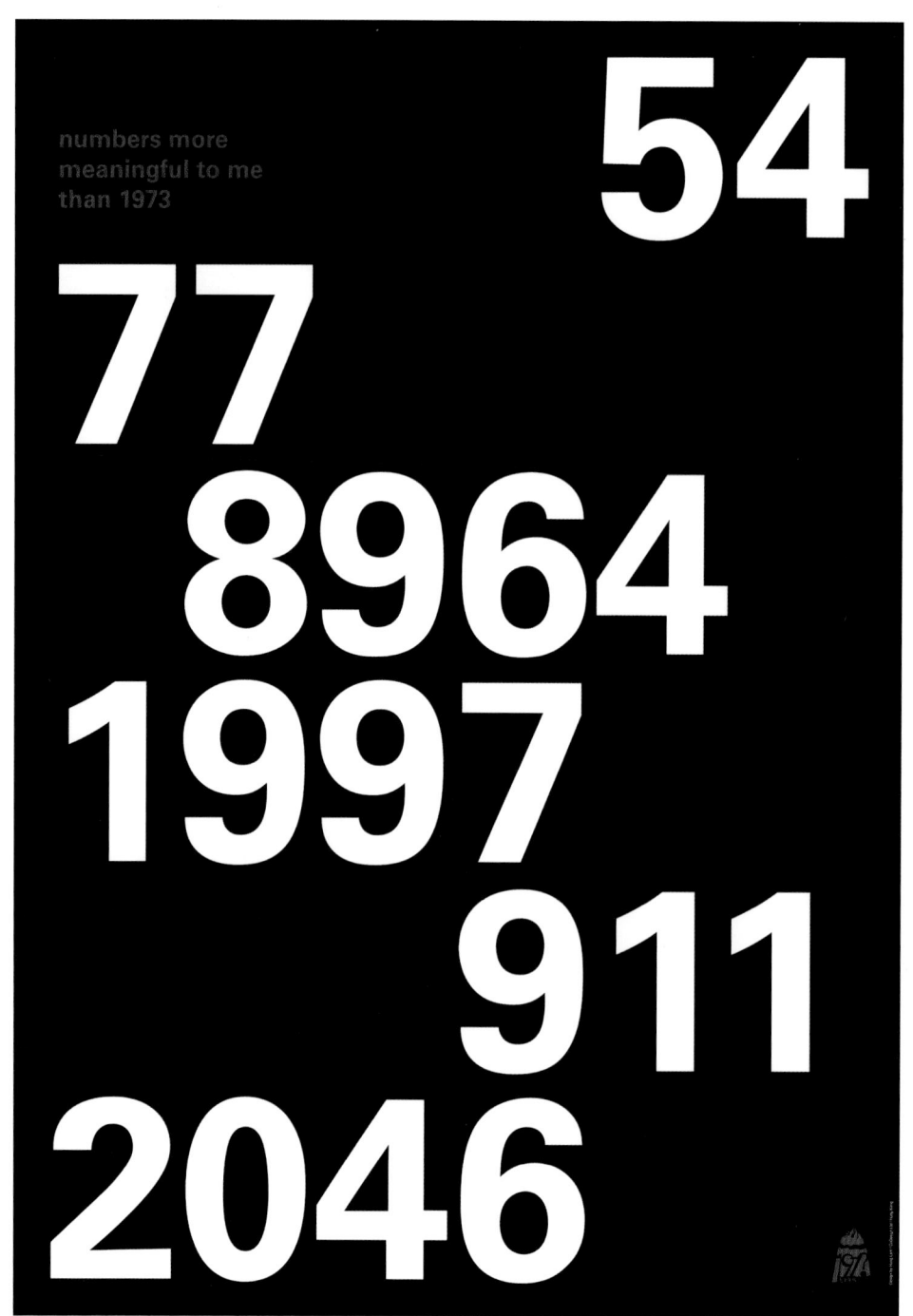

Bronze
195_ Thematic Poster
t. Meaningful Numbers
e. CoDesign Ltd.
dd. d. Hung Lam
cl. Born in 70's Poster Exhibition

Bronze
196_ Thematic Poster
t. 巴黎國際藝術城
e. cd. dd. d. 畢學鋒
cl. 法國巴黎國際藝術城

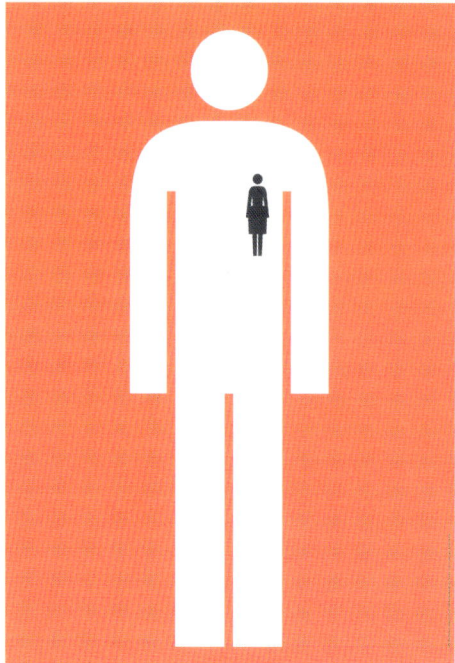

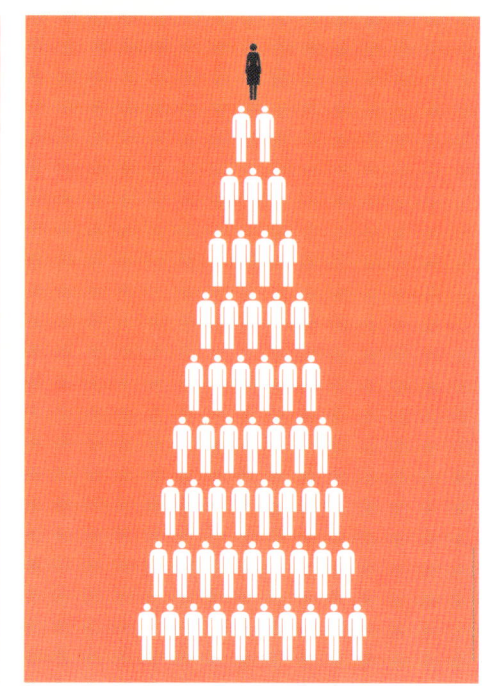

Bronze

197_ Thematic Poster

t. Superwoman 5, 6, 7, 8
e. Sandy Choi Associates Ltd.
dd. Sandy Choi
d. Becky Yeung
cs. Angela Lee
pp. Art Factory
cl. Hong Kong Poster League, Hong Kong Heritage Museum

Lucky Tea Co.,Ltd.

Bronze
198_ Commercial Poster
t. 棋禎茶業
e. 共同品牌策略顧問共同包裝設計

cd. dd. d. 張曉明
ad. 馬深廣
i. 張曉明, 胡子
cl. 棋禎茶業有限公司

Bronze
199_ *Thematic Poster*
t. 漢字
e. cd. dd. 陳永基
ad. 陳永基, 葛湘瑛
d. 葛湘瑛
cl. 台灣海報設計協會

200

201

Bronze
200_ *Commercial Poster*
t. 0 + C Furniture "Music Note Chair"
e. Bliss Partners Int'l Ltd.
cd. Ivan Leung

Bronze
201_ *Commercial Poster*
t. "Wood You Care"
e. Bliss Partners Int'l Ltd.
cd. Ivan Leung

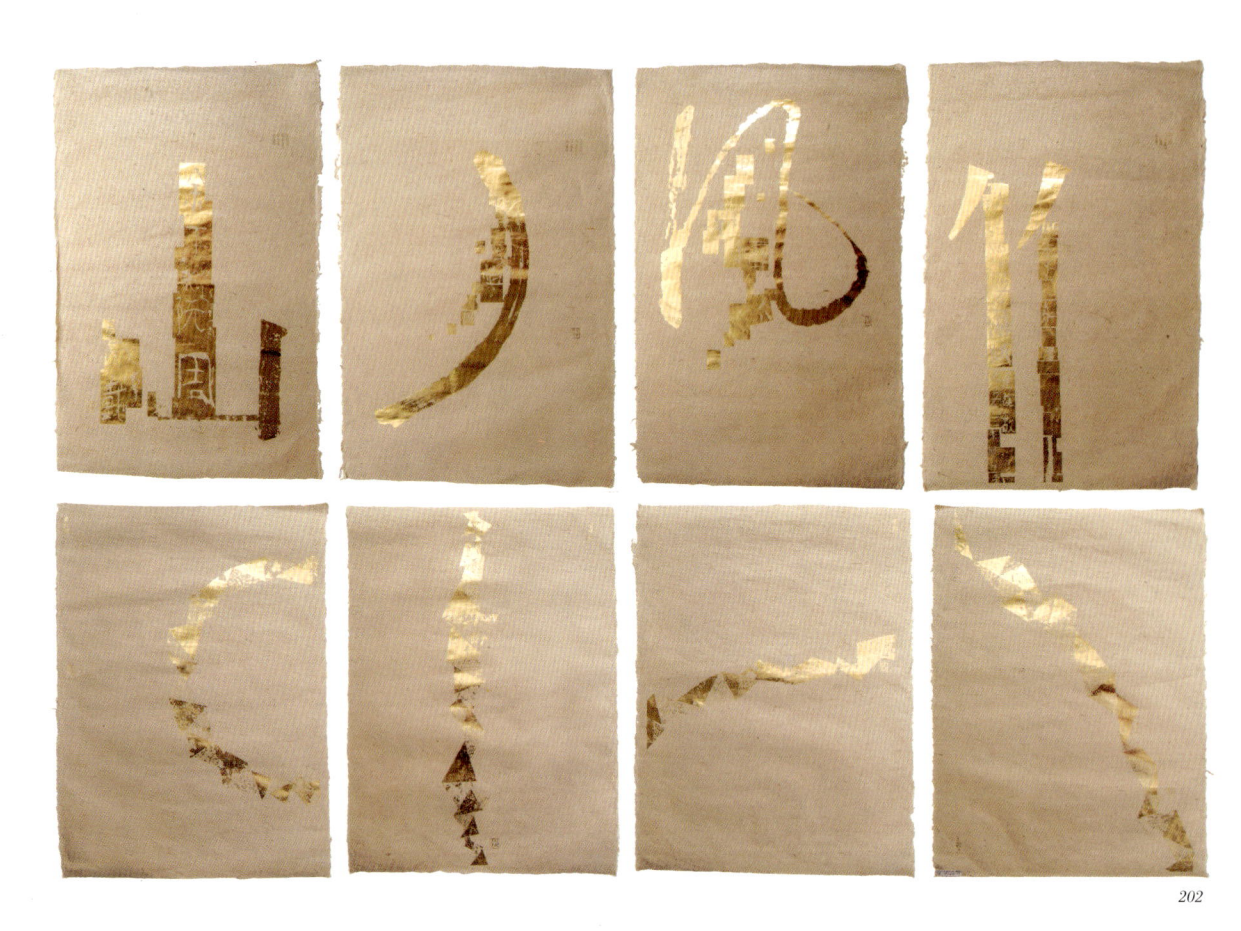

Bronze
202_ Thematic Poster
t. 2003-2004 天涯海報系列
e. cd. dd. ad. d. 韓家英
cl. 《天涯》雜誌社

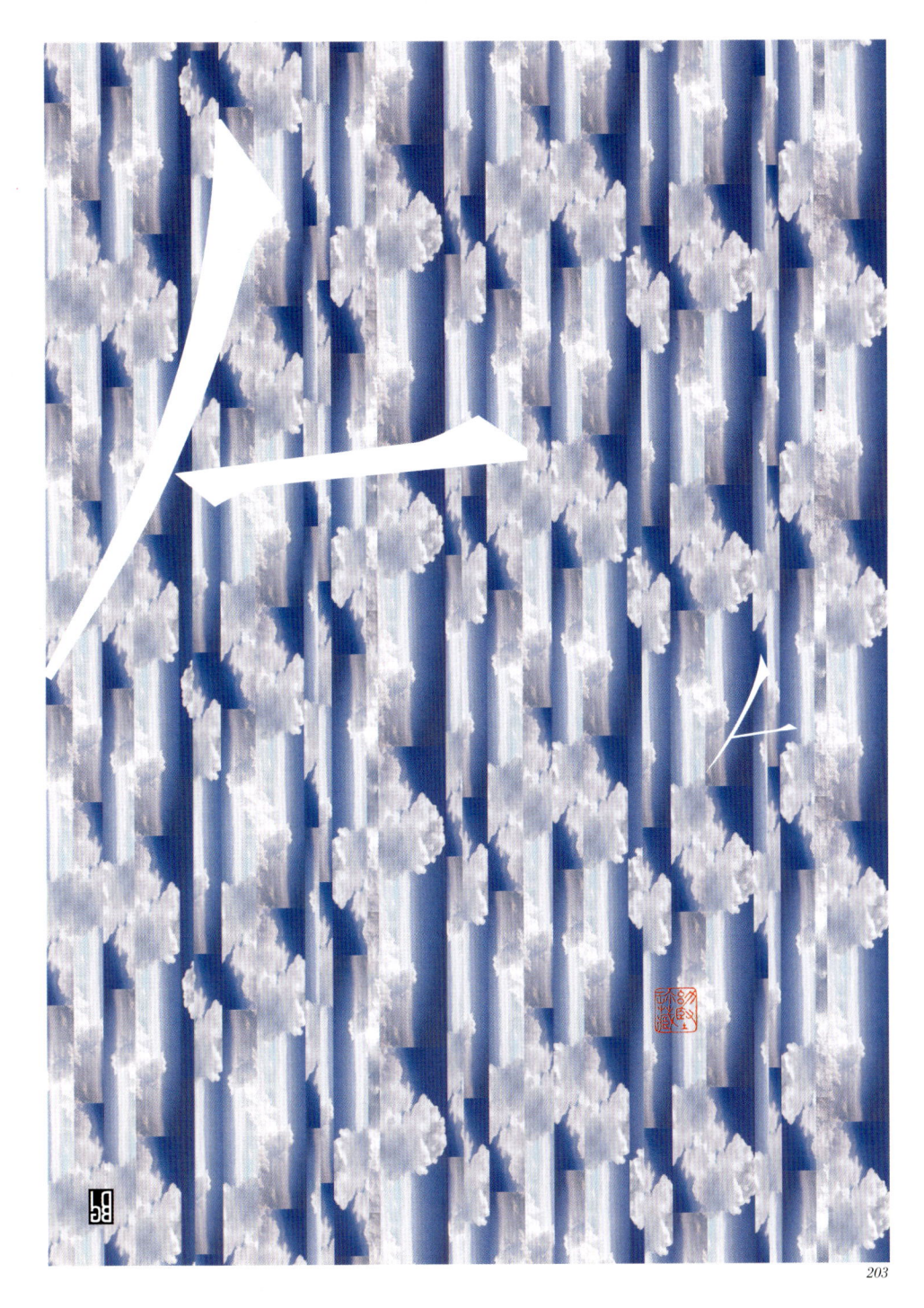

203_ *Thematic Poster*
t. In Love with Bamboo
e. cd. dd. d. Alan Chan
pt. Artron (HK) Ltd.
cl. The 3rd International Poster Biennial, Ningbo, 2004

204_ *Cultural Promotion Poster*
t. 中國傳統圖形與現代視覺設計
e. cd. dd. 陳永基
ad. 陳永基, 翁岱鍵
d. 翁岱鍵
cl. 清華大學美術學院, 汕頭大學長江藝術與設計學院

205_ *Cultural Promotion Poster*
t. 向達利致敬設計與藝術
e. cd. dd. ad. 陳永基
d. 鄭竹涵
cl. 台灣海報協會, 誠品書局

August 6 - 8, 2005　Tokyo International Forum, Exhibition Hall

Open Hour: 10:00 - 20:00 (until 17:00 Last Day)　Initiated by: ART FAIR TOKYO Committee　Sponsored by: ITOCHU Corporation / Veolia Water Japan K.K. / M Factory Corporation GIORGIO ARMANI JAPAN CO., LTD. / SECOM CO., Ltd. / Pictet Financial Management Consultants Co., Ltd. / MY INVESTMENTS LTD. / MONTBLANC
Supported by: The Ministry of Foreign Affairs of Japan / Ministry of Economy, Trade and Industry / The Commercial Service of the U.S. Embassy, Tokyo / Embassy of Israel / Embassy of Italy Austrian Embassy / Royal Netherlands Embassy / Korean Cultural Service, Embassy of Korea / Embassy of the Federal Republic of Germany
Admission: 1Day Free Pass　Adult ¥1,000 / Students ¥800　Free for children who are grade school age and younger.
Advance Ticket: 1Day Free Pass　¥800 (Adult Only)　e-plus [www.eplus.co.jp/artfair-tokyo] / Ticket Pia [P-code: 686-072　Tel: 0570-02-9999] / LAWSON TICKET [L-code: 33502　Tel: 0570-063-003]

「日本はもっとアートが好きな国になりませんか。」
「このアート、やばいよ。」「技術もすごいけれど、考え方がすごいなあ。」「このアートを買った、というより、やっと手に入れた。」「ココロがシーンとするアートもあるし、ココロがザワザワするアートもある。」「いいものを観ると、自分もがんばろうと思える。」「ほう、あなたは、そういうアートを気に入る人でしたか。」「どこ観てるんですか？そのアートの。」「お目が高い、というか、お目が厳しい。」「好きなアートや好きな人に会うと、欲しくてたまらなくなる。」「金銭感覚がなくなる。」「この人の家には、金はないけど、アートならある。」「映画デートもいいけど、アートデートもいいな、と思った。」「こういうアートフェアが日本の文化になれるといいのだけれど。」

ART FAIR TOKYO

アートフェア東京　2005年 8月6日［土］・7日［日］・8日［月］　東京国際フォーラム・展示ホール

www.artfairtokyo.com

206_ Cultural Promotion Poster
t. ART FAIR TOKYO
e. cd. ad. d. Masayoshi Kodaira
cw. Hideki Azuma
pt. GRAPH Co., Ltd.
cl. ART FAIR TOKYO Committee

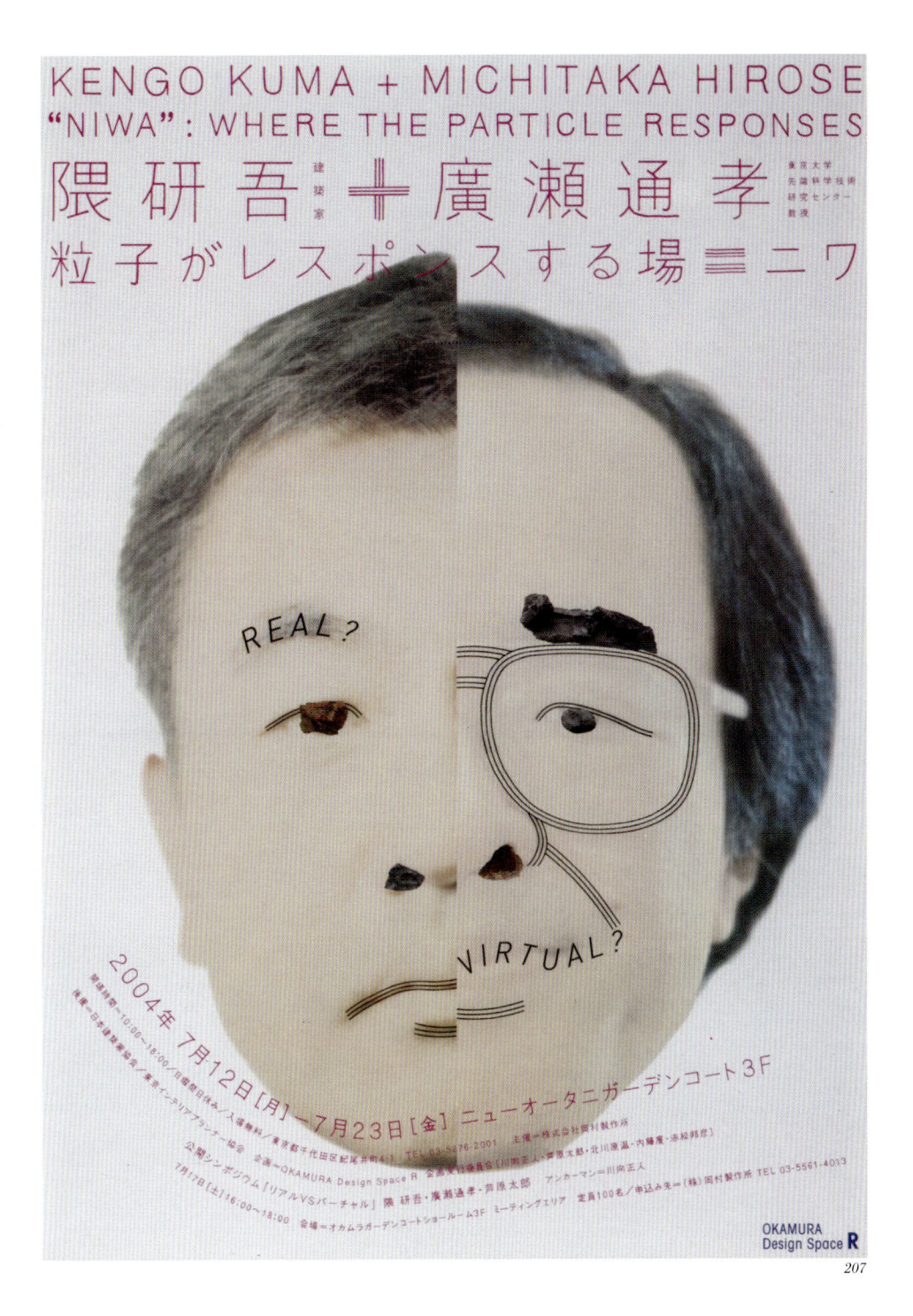

207_ Cultural Promotion Poster
t. KENGO KUMA + MICHITAKA HIROSE
e. ad. d. Masayoshi Kodaira
cp. pt. Toppan printing Co., Ltd.
cl. Okamura Corporation

208_ Cultural Promotion Poster
t. Homage to IKKO TANAKA :
　with and without IKKO TANAKA
e. ad. d. cw. Katsuhiro Kinoshita
pp. W - cLock
pt. Digital Print
cl. Tokusyu Paper Mfg. Co., Ltd.

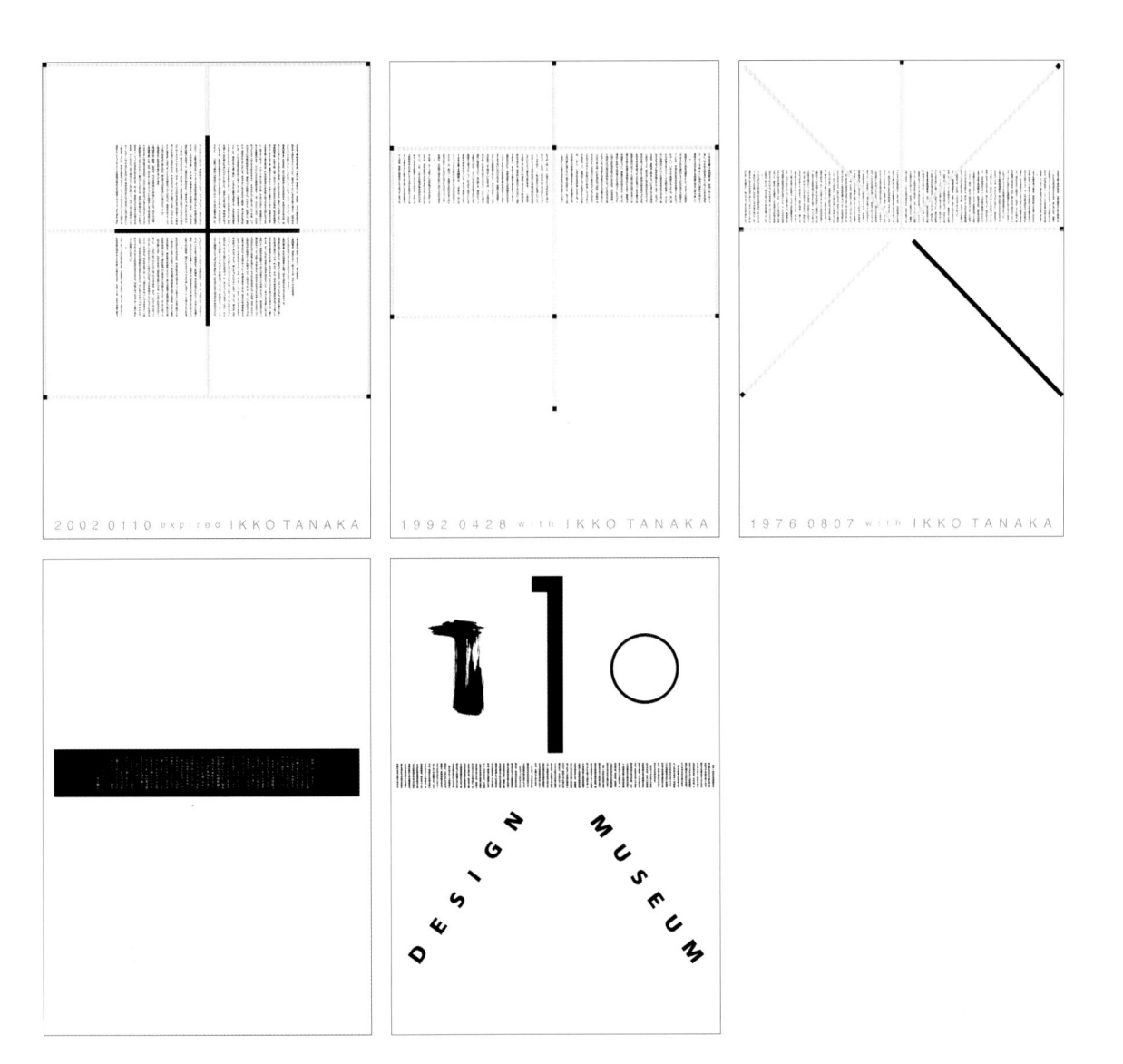

2002 0110 expired IKKO TANAKA   1992 0428 with IKKO TANAKA   1976 0807 with IKKO TANAKA

DESIGN MUSEUM

Excellent

209_ *Thematic Poster*
t. Hong Kong Good Dong Xi
e. Tommy Li Design Workshop Ltd.
cd. Tommy Li
d. Tami Leung
p. Danny Chiu
cw. Tommy Li, Tami Leung
cl. "Hong Kong Good Dong Xi" Poster Exhibition

今ほどの豊かさが本当に必要なのでしょうか？地球温暖化がこのまま進むと、海水の膨張や氷河の融解により、21世紀末には海面が15〜95cm上昇します。日本では、海面以下の地域が2.7倍にひろがり、人口410万人が危険にさらされ

Excellent
210_ Thematic Poster
t. Global Warming
e. ad. d. Norito Shinmura
p. Ko Hosokawa
cw. Hiroyuki Koyama
cl. TRACK 16 GALLERY

211_ *Thematic Poster*
t. Turn "WAR" into "WARM"
e. ad. d. Au Tak-shing, Benny
pt. Suncolor Printing Co., Ltd.
cl. Tai Tak Takeo Fine Paper Co., Ltd.

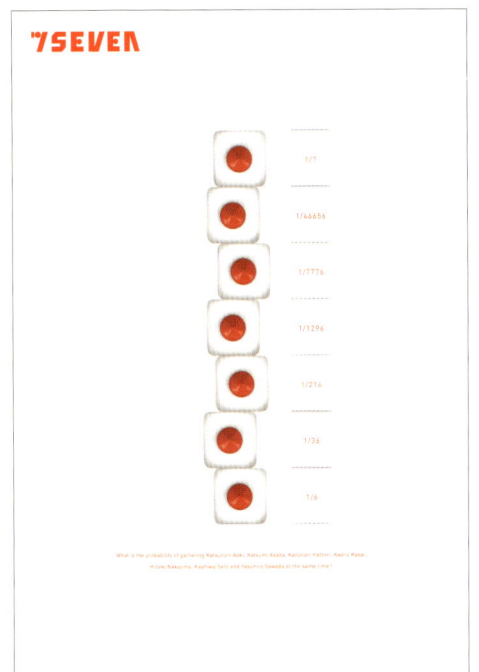

212_ Thematic Poster
t. SevenInOne
e. d. Ken Lo
cl. Amazing Angle
   Design Consultants Ltd.

213_ Thematic Poster
t. SEVEN
e. cd. d. Yuen Chun Kit
cl. Amazing Angle
   Design Consultants Ltd.

214_ Thematic Poster
t. $9 + 4 - 10 \times 3 \div 5 = 7$
e. cd. d. Lam Hon Hing
cl. Amazing Angle
   Design Consultants Ltd.

215_ Thematic Poster
t. Sed Unuz
e. ad. d. i. Au Tak-shing, Benny
pt. Suncolor Printing Co., Ltd.
cl. Amazing Angle
   Design Consultants Ltd.

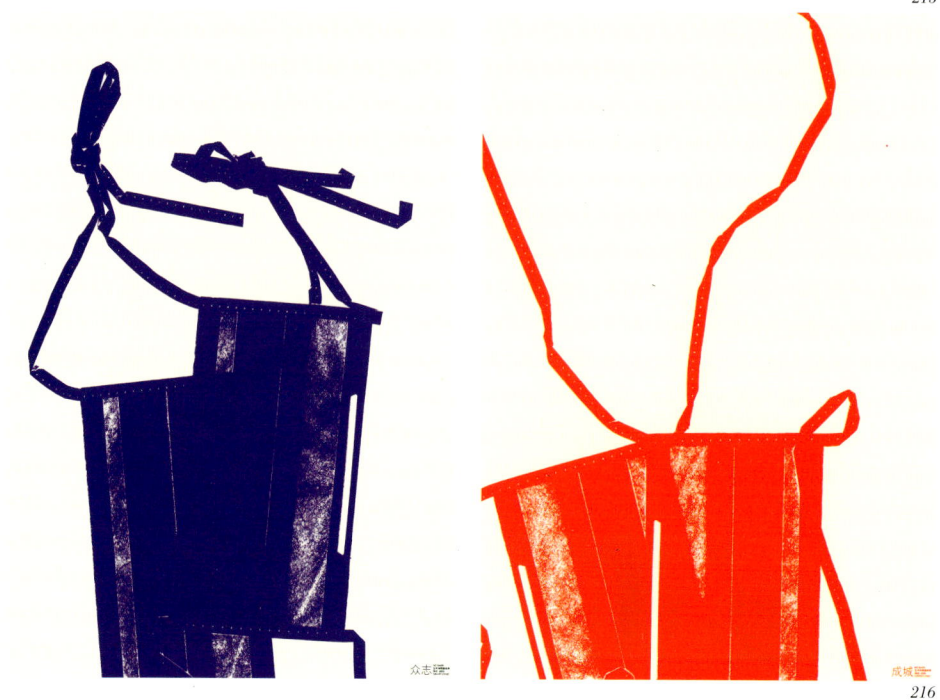

216_ Thematic Poster
t. Anti SARS
e. ad. d. Au Tak-shing, Benny
cl. Poster Art Exhibition, Shenzhen

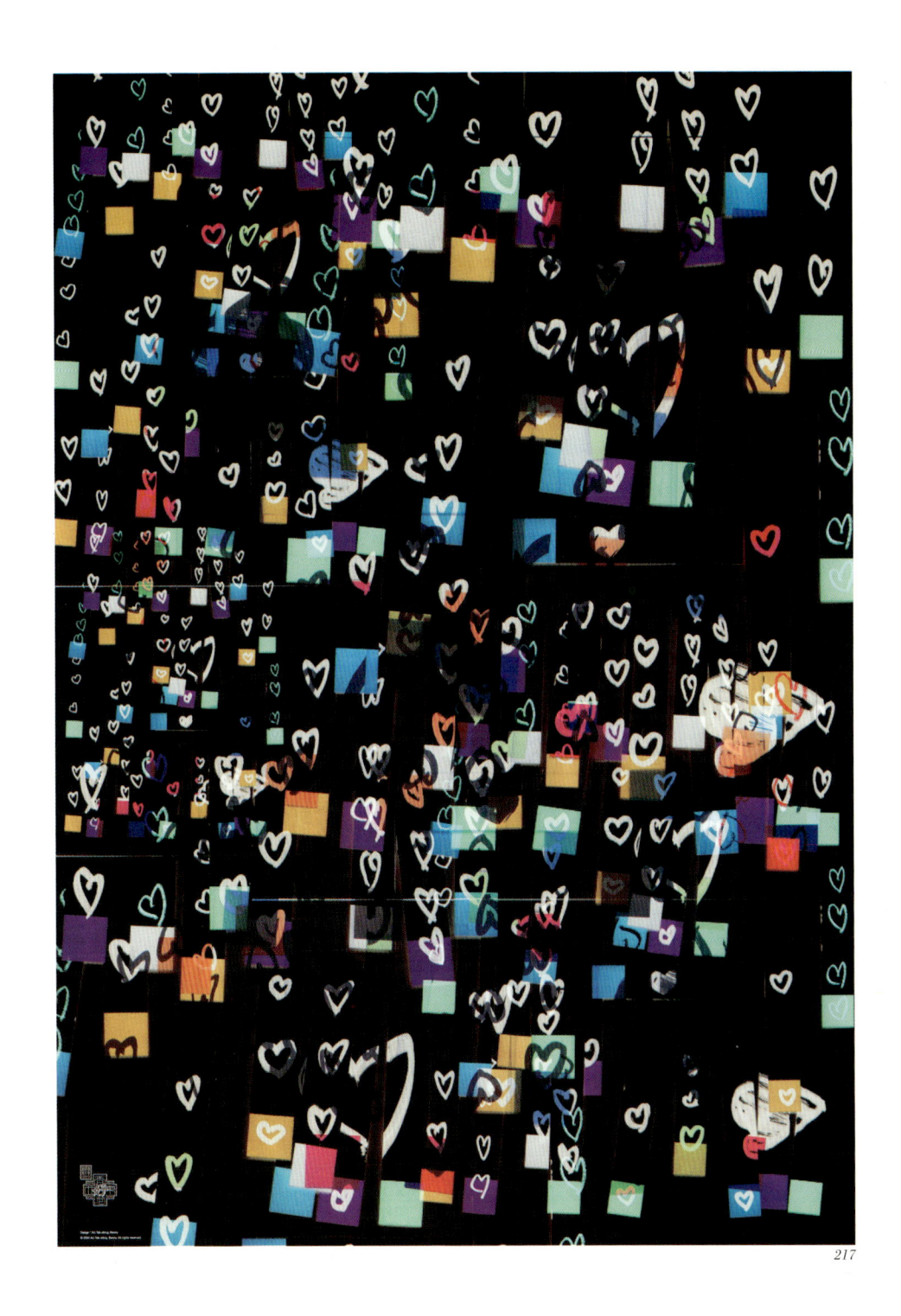

217_ Thematic Poster
t. Hong Kong Good Dong Xi
e. ad. d. i. Au Tak-shing, Benny
pt. Suncolor Printing Co., Ltd.
cl. Hysan Development Co., Ltd.

Excellent
218_ Commercial Poster
t. Be a Happy Camper
e. ad. d. Norito Shinmura
cl. Ryohin Keikaku Co., Ltd.

219_ Thematic Poster
t. Karling & Lawrence's Wedding
e. dd. ad. d. Lawrence Choy

Harmony House

You can make a difference
as an individual:

Our Organization:

Harmony House is a non-government charitable organization dedicated to addressing family violence issues. It provides shelter for those in need of a safe harbor, guidance and hope to all who suffer from domestic destructiveness.

Become more aware and knowledgeable of the problem of family violence.

Be informed of where sufferers can seek professional help.

Support non-profit organizations working in this field.

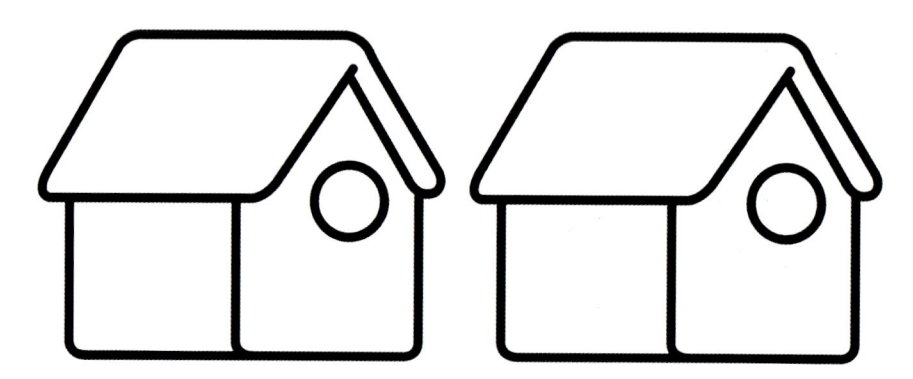

Harmony House
P.O. Box 99068, Tsim Sha Tsui Post Office
Kowloon, Hong Kong

Phone 2794 9300
Email hhl@harmonyhousehk.org
www.harmonyhousehk.org

Commercial Poster

t. Harmony House
e. Sandy Choi Associates Ltd.
dd. Sandy Choi
d. Goldie Wong
i. Maxine Choi, Thor Lee, Goldie Wong
cs. Angela Lee
pp. Art Factory
cl. Harmony House

Harmony House

You can make a difference *as a parent*:

Our Mission:

Harmony House strives to promote harmonious relationships in families.

Discuss with your children about the importance of healthy relationships and sex based on love and mutual respect.

Encourage your children to talk about their emotions.

Teach your children positive means of expressing anger and emotions by example.

Use non-violence means to discipline your children.

Harmony House
P.O.Box. 99068, Tsim Sha Tsui Post Office
Kowloon, Hong Kong

Phone 2794 9300
Email hhl@harmonyhousehk.org
www.harmonyhousehk.org

楽しい考え。

221_ Commercial Poster
t. HONDA CLIO KYORITSU POSTER
e. dd. ad. Setsue Shimizu
cd. cw. Kozo Koshimizu
d. Souzu Etsue
p. Shigeru Tanaka
i. Sino
cl. HONDA CLIO KYORITSU

明るい考え。

222_ *Thematic Poster*
t. No Peace No Boom
e. Unioncult
cd. Michael Cheung
d. Henry Kwok
cs. Nakanishi Taka
cl. Livi Co., Ltd.

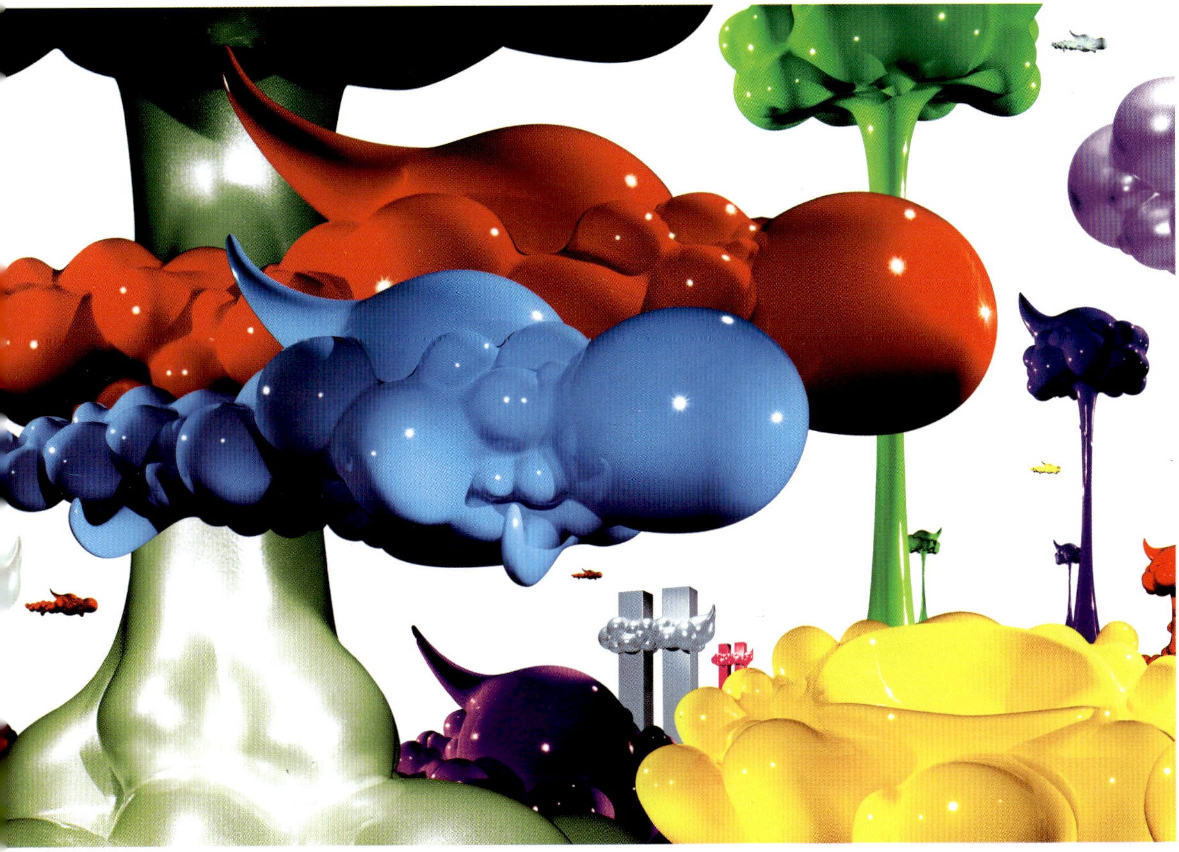

Make Home. Make Future.

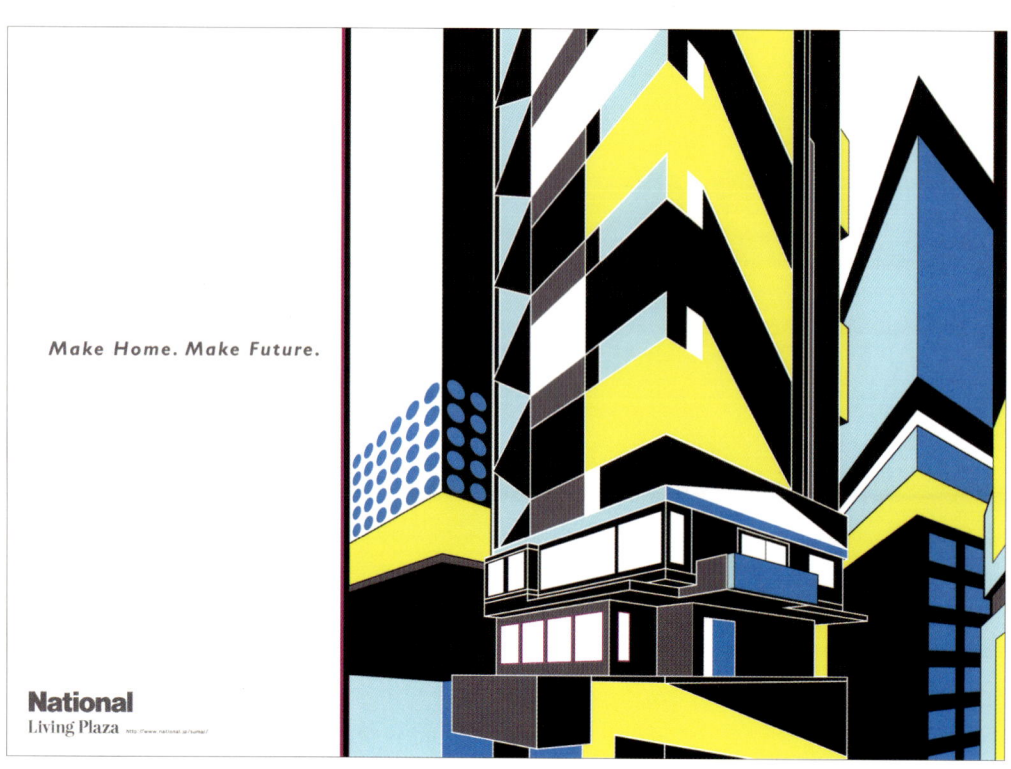

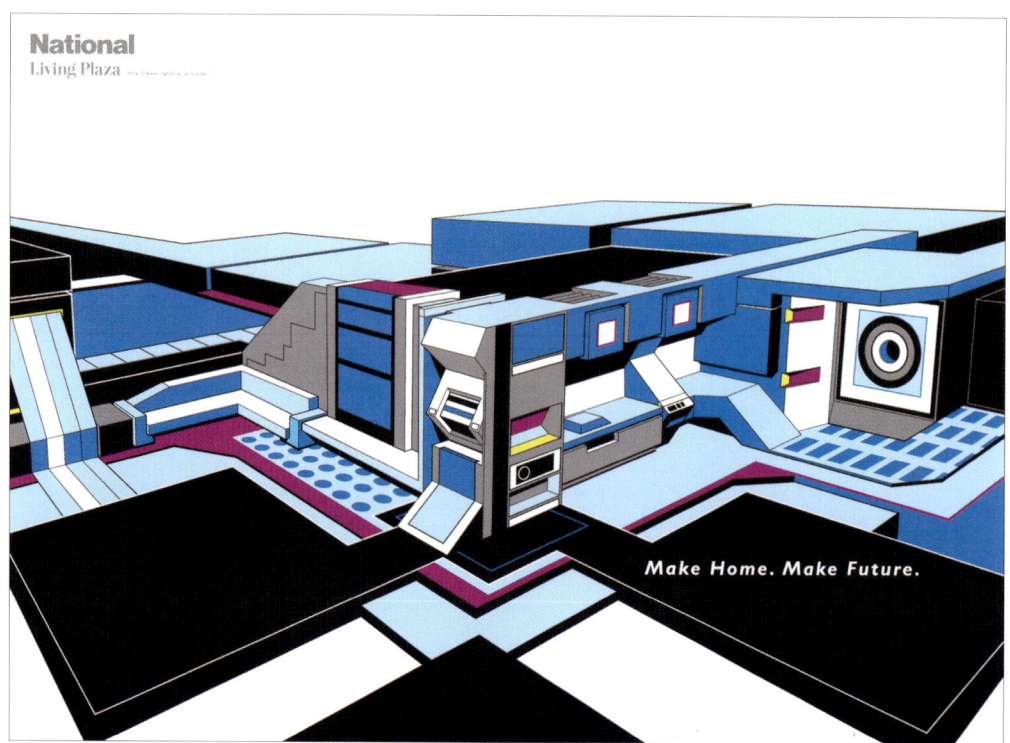

National
Living Plaza

National
Living Plaza

Make Home. Make Future.

223_ Commercial Poster
t. National Living Plaza 03
e. Daiko Advertising Inc.
cd. Noboru Yamawaki
ad. Takuya Suzuki, Toshiomi Takahashi
i. DELTA
cw. Kumiko Aso
pt. Style Printing
cl. Matsushita Electric Industrial Co., Ltd.

National/Panasonic
Make Home. Make Future.
National Living Plaza

National/Panasonic
Make Home. Make Future.
National Living Plaza

224_ Commercial Poster
t. National Living Plaza 02
e. Daiko Advertising Inc.
cd. Noboru Yamawaki
ad. Takuya Suzuki, Toshiomi Takahashi
i. Miwako Akatsu
cw. Kumiko Aso
pt. Style Printing
cl. Matsushita Electric Industrial Co., Ltd.

225_ *Thematic Poster*
t. Destruction & Construction
e. ad. d. i. Au Tak-shing, Benny
pt. Suncolor Printing Co., Ltd.
cl. Amazing Angle Design Consultants Ltd.

Building Hong Kong **Destruction**
Construction redwhiteblue exhibition

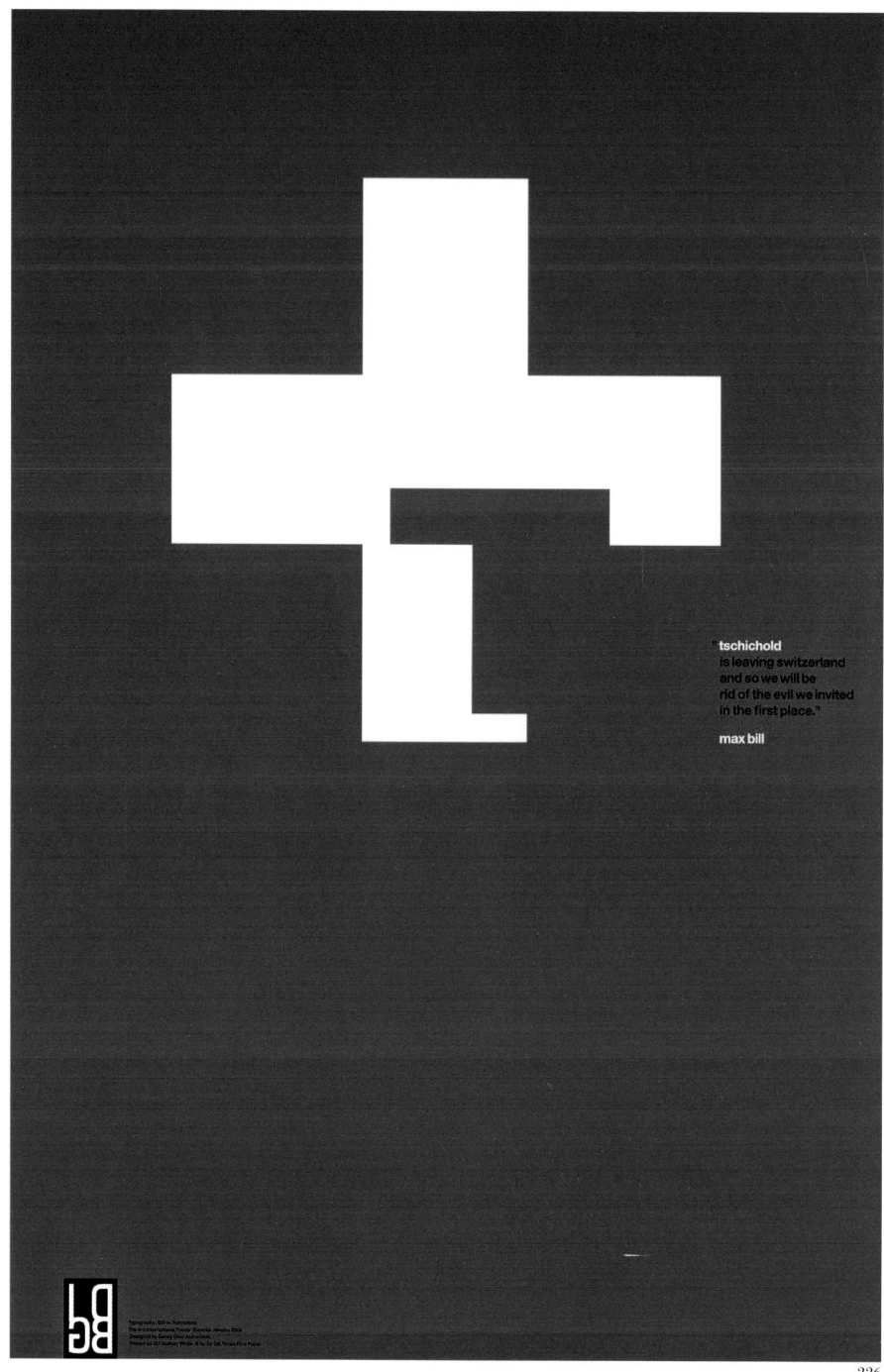

Excellent
226_ Thematic Poster
t. Typography : Bill vs Tschichold
e. Sandy Choi Associates Ltd.
dd. Sandy Choi
d. Goldie Wong
pp. Art Factory
cl. Sandy Choi Associates Ltd.

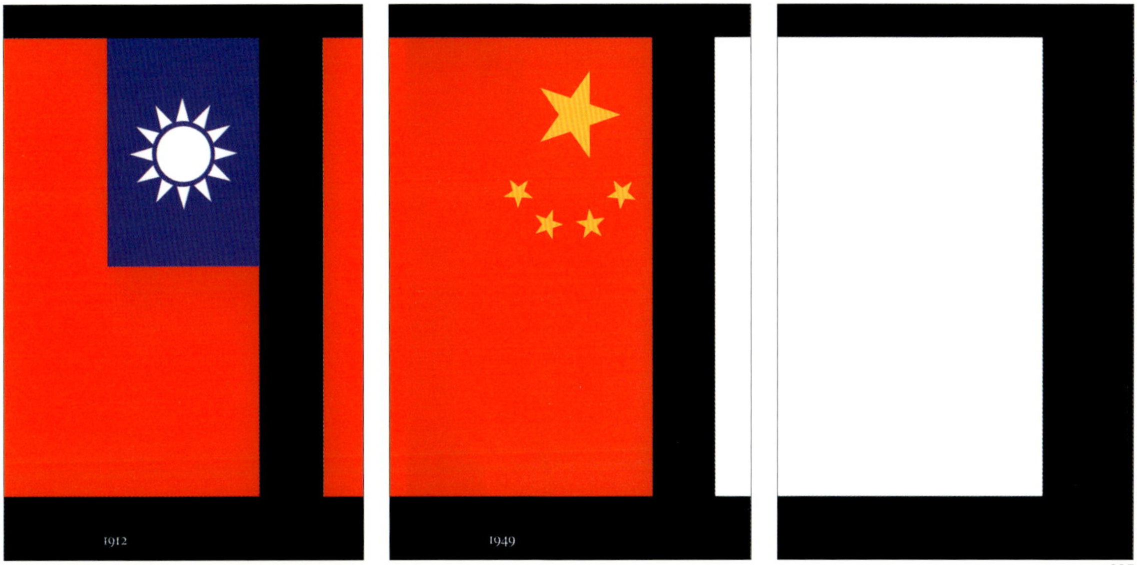

Excellent
227_ Thematic Poster
t. Space
e. Sandy Choi Associates Ltd.
dd. Sandy Choi
d. Thor Lee
pp. Art Factory
cl. Hong Kong Heritage Museum

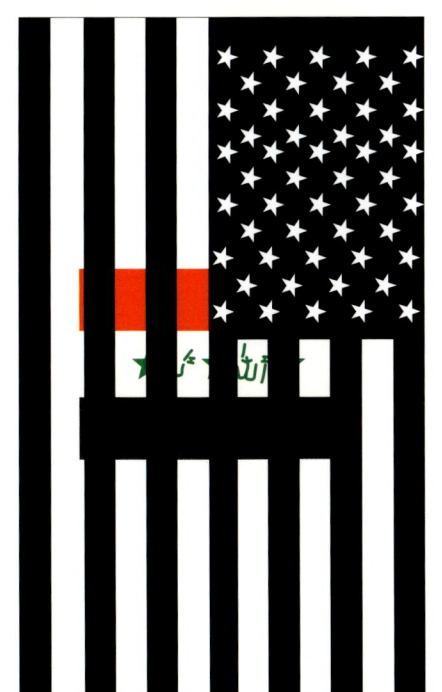

Excellent
228_ Thematic Poster
t. Prison and Protection
e. cd. dd. ad. d. cw. cl.
Ken-tsai Lee

Excellent
229_ Thematic Poster
t. Japan, 2005?
e. cd. dd. ad. d. cw. cl.
Ken-tsai Lee

三昧美術館

230_ *Commercial Poster*
t. 27 Art Museums Selected by Terunobu Fujimori
e. ad. d. Katsuhiro Kinoshita
cw. Terunobu Fujimori
pp. Tosho Printing Co., Ltd.
pt. Digital Print
cl. TOTO Ltd.

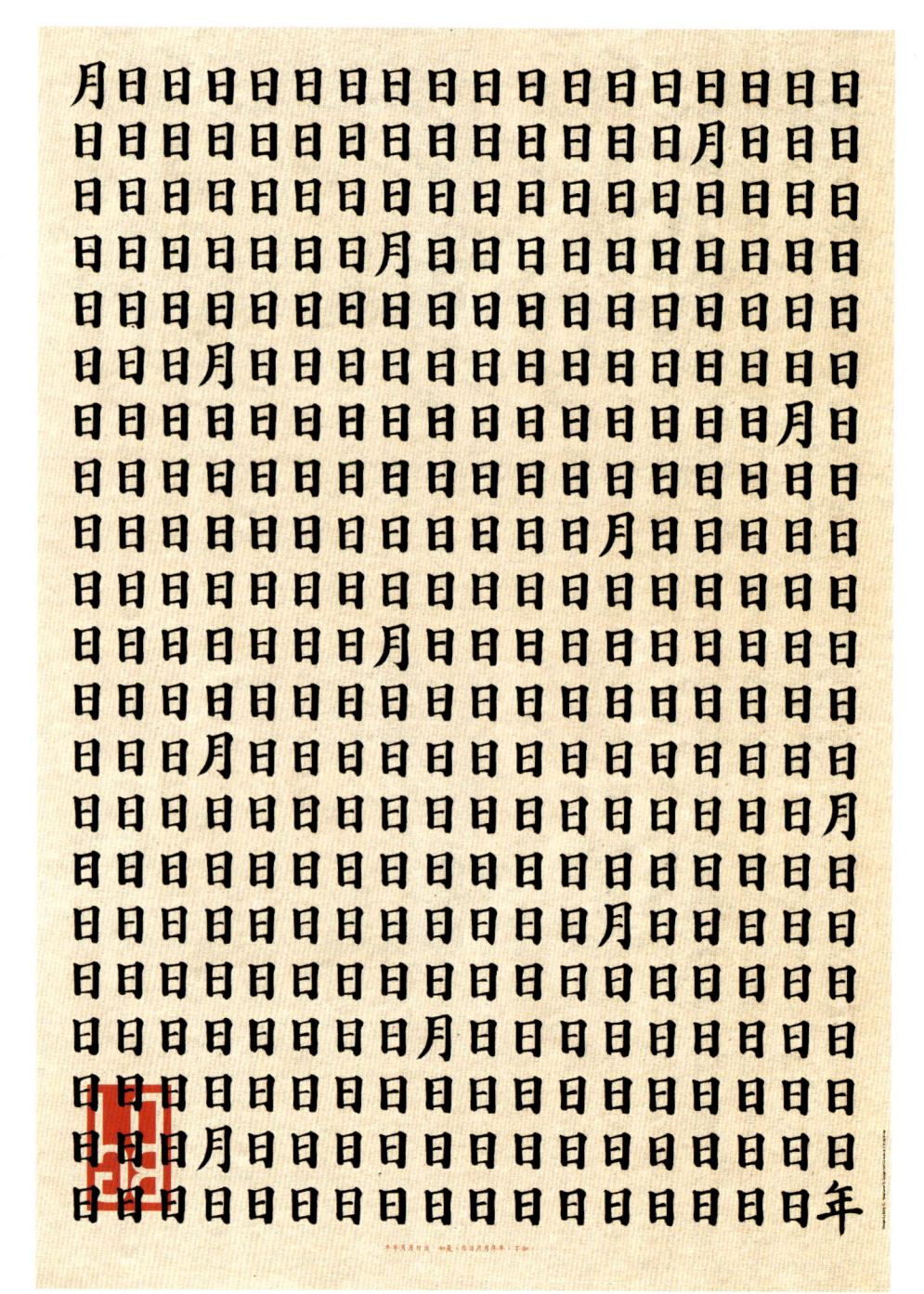

231_ *Thematic Poster*
t. DayMonthYear
e. CoDesign Ltd.
dd. Eddy Yu, Hung Lam
d. Ken Lo
cw. Foronica Lam, Ken Lo
cl. 3rd International Poster Competition, Ningbo, China, 2004

*232_* Commercial Poster
t. Gardener
e. cd. Michael Lau
dd. ad. shya-la-la workshop
cl. Michael Lau

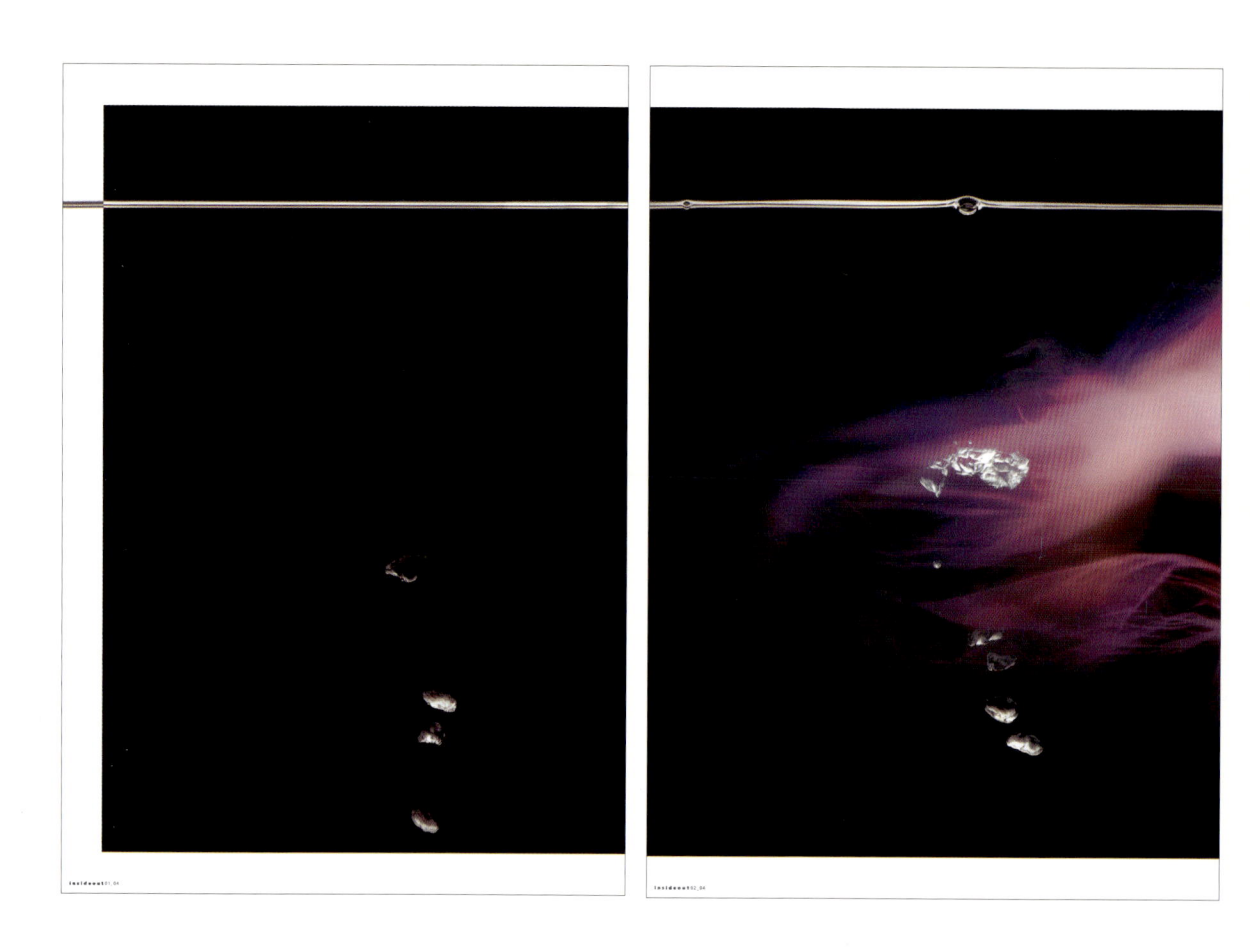

233_ *Thematic Poster*
t. InsideOut - I
e. ingDesign
dd. ad. d. Chau So-hing
p. C.K. Wong
ce. Matthew Ku

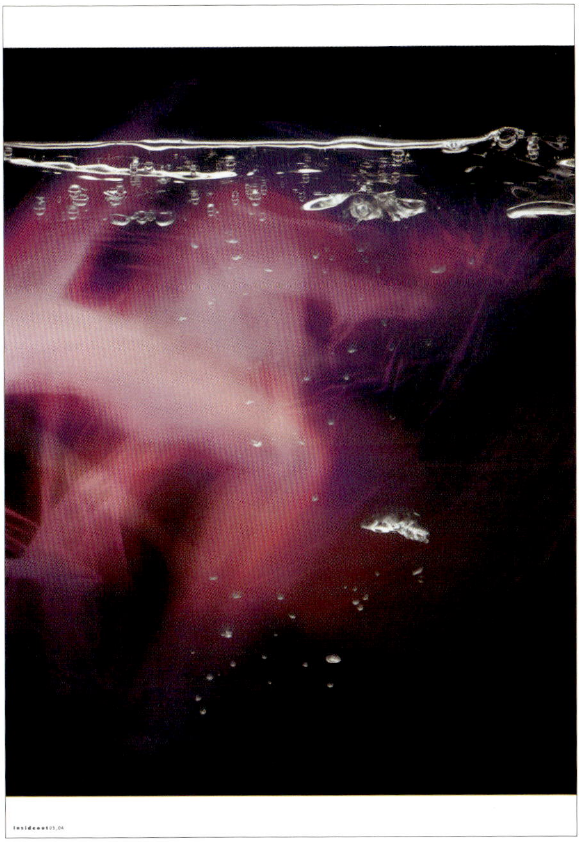
insideout03_04

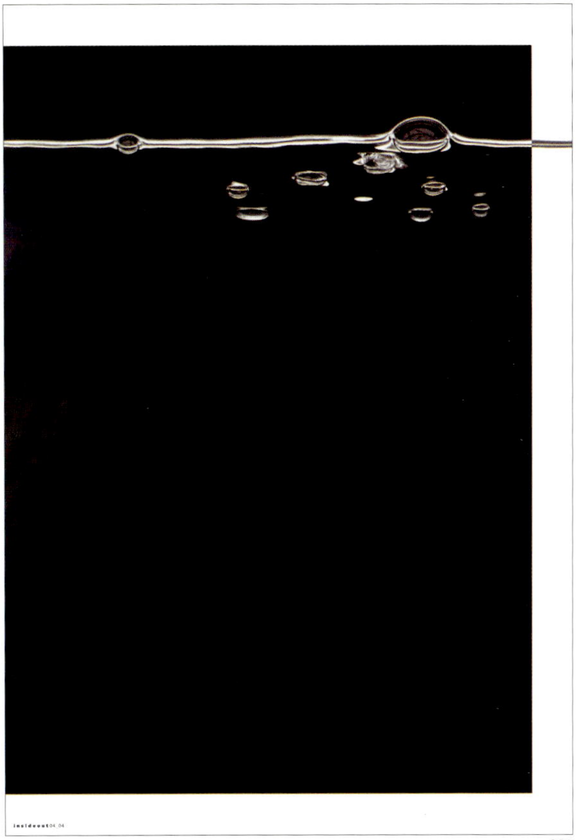
insideout04_04

整合·
UNITE中国精神
Chinese spirit

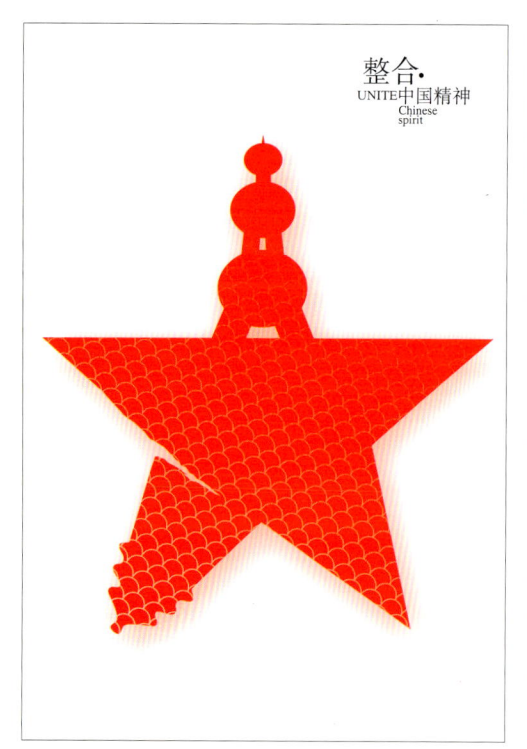

烙印·
BRAND中国符号
Chinese symbol

合壁·
COMBINE中西血脉
Eastern&western culture

234_ Thematic Poster
t. Unite Chinese Spirit
e. cd. dd. Wu Yibo

Excellent
235_ Commercial Poster
t. Koubo Guide poster
e. Setsue Shimizu
cd. Kozo Koshimizu
dd. ad. Iku Sato
d. Raita Kimura
cw. Hiroshi Sasaki
pp. C'co., Ltd.
cl. Koubo Guide Co.

236_ Commercial Poster
t. eeny meeny miny mo
e. ad. Masayoshi Kodaira
cd. Masayoshi Kodaira, Hideki Azuma
d. Masayoshi Kodaira, Namiko Otsuka
p. Mikiya Takimoto
cw. Hideki Azuma, Natsumi Morita
pt. Toppan Printing Co., Ltd.
cl. Mitsubishi Corp. - UBS Realty Inc.

RESTAURANT HIRAMATSU

eeny meeny miny mo
8953 HAKATA RIVERAIN

KITCHO

LA MANINA

eeny meeny miny mo
8953 HAKATA RIVERAIN

KUROBUTA

237_ Thematic Poster
t. In hopes of preserving this beauty
   eternally SERIS B
e. cd. dd. ad. d. p. cw. Yoshiteru Asai
cl. Peaceful Uses Atomic Energy Association

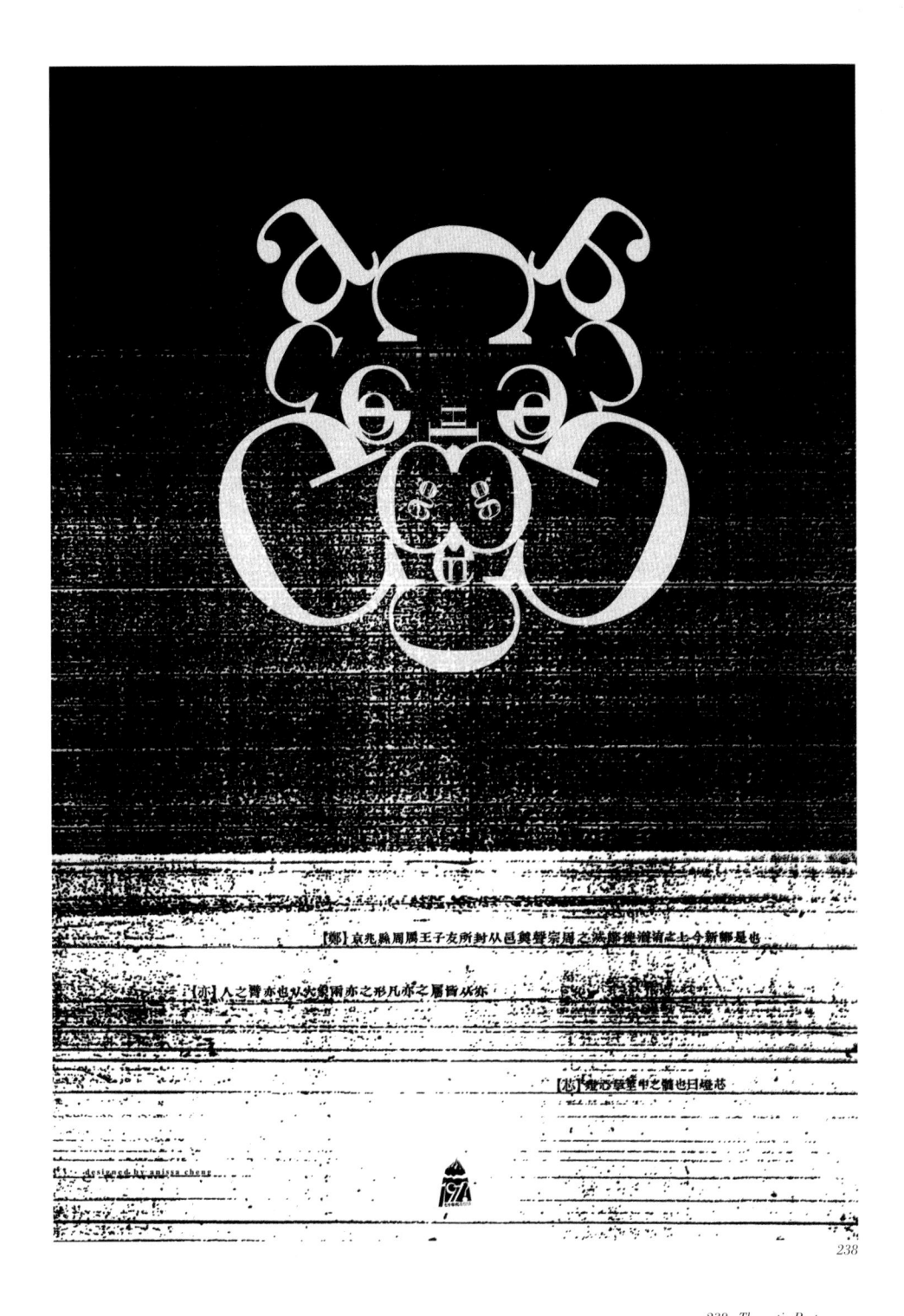

238_ Thematic Poster
t. 1971
e. cd. d. Anissa Cheng
pt. Wide Ocean Printing Co., Ltd.
cl. Suzhou Art & Design Technology Institute

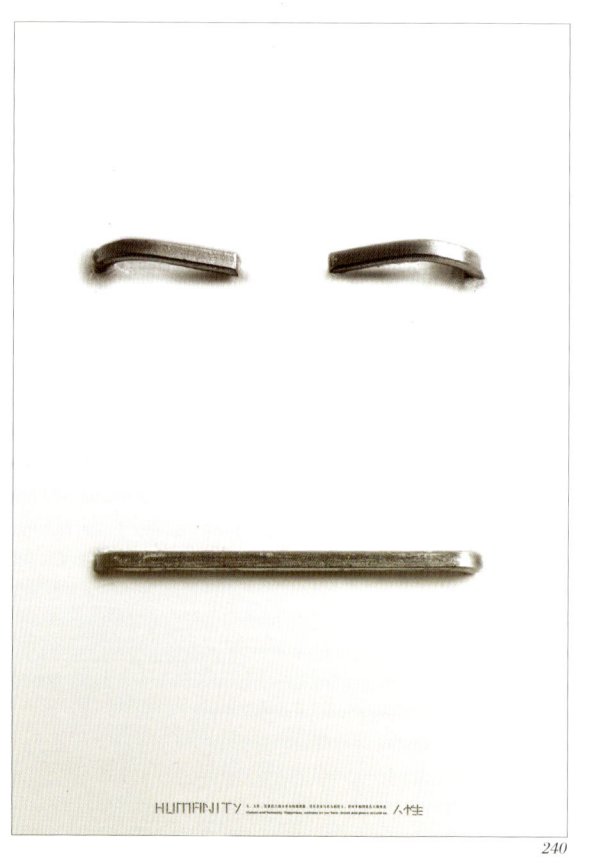

239_ *Thematic Poster*
t. Hong Kong Good Things
   - Mr.Kan Tai Keung
e. d. Eric Chan
p. Lau Kwok Tim of TIM Photography
i. Iris Yu
cl. Hysan Development Co., Ltd.

240_ *Thematic Poster*
t. Humanity
e. cd. dd. ad. p. cw. Chen Hong
cl. 《人性》極限設計 - 04/05 國際連線全球競賽

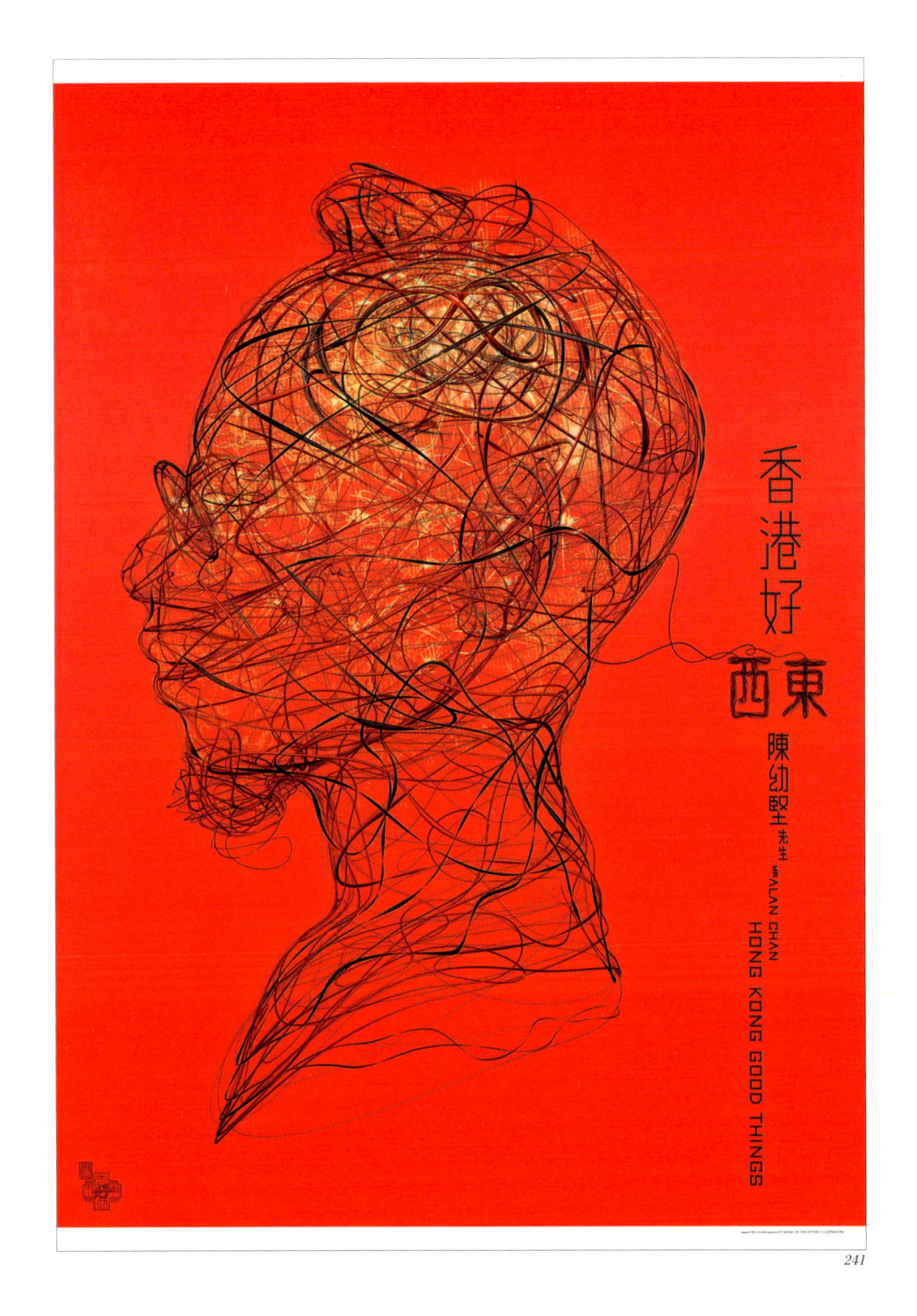

241_ Thematic Poster
t. Hong Kong Good Things - Mr. Alan Chan
e. d. Eric Chan
i. Fei Wong of Fine Effort Illustration
cl. Hysan Development Co., Ltd.

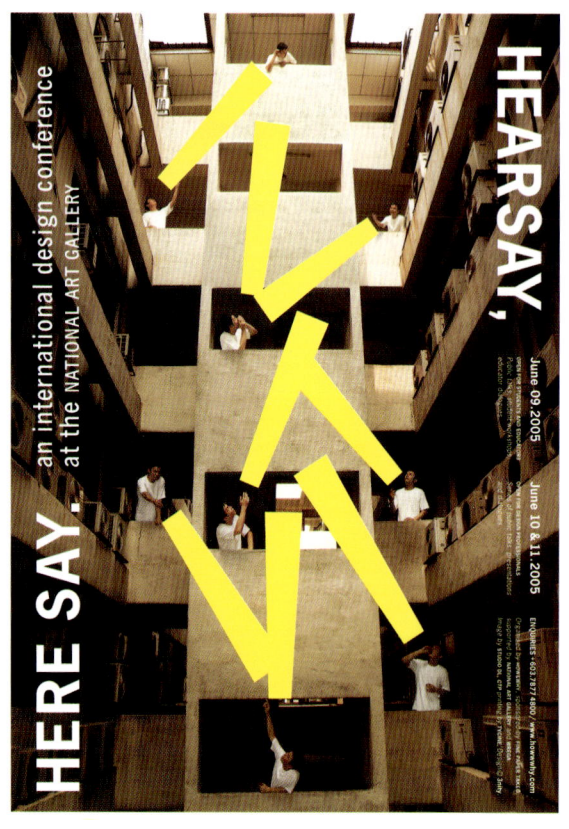

242_ *Cultural Promotion Poster*
t. Hearsay, Here say
e. cd. dd. Joseph Foo
d. Raymond Lai, Ling Hooi Wan
p. Studio DL
cw. Kay Khoo, Jesmin Chua
cp. pt. Tye Cine Colour Separations Sdn Bhd
cl. How&Why

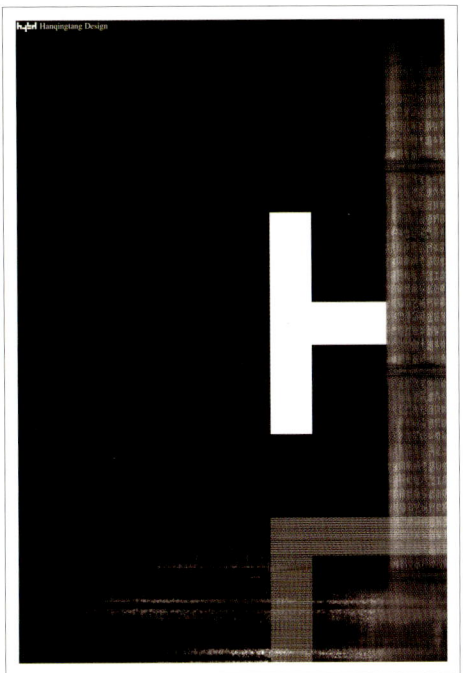

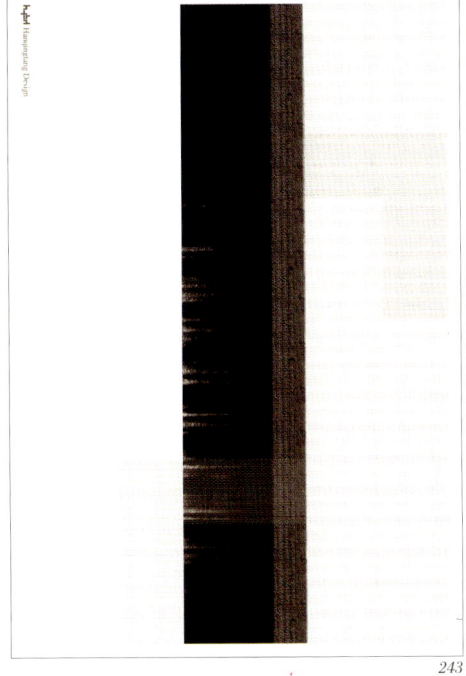

Excellent
243_ Thematic Poster
t. Han Qing Tang
e. cd. dd. ad. d. Zhao Qing
i. Jiang Chang Hong

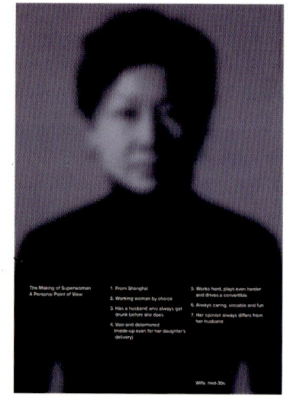

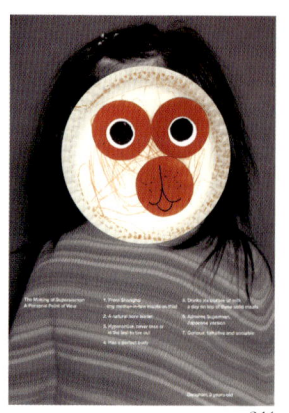

244_ *Thematic Poster*
t. Superwoman 1, 2, 3, 4
e. Sandy Choi Associates Ltd.
dd. Sandy Choi
d. Becky Yeung
p. Ringo Tang
cw. Sandy Choi, Margaret Wong
cs. Angela Lee
pp. Art Factory
cl. Hong Kong Poster League,
　　Hong Kong Heritage Museum

245_ *Thematic Poster*
t. Love & Peace = Joy
e. Ameba Design Ltd.
cd. dd. ad. d. Gideon Lai
cl. New Idea Magazine

246_ *Thematic Poster*
t. NO SARS
e. cd. dd. ad. d. 石小帆
p. 林烏農
cl. 關山月美術館

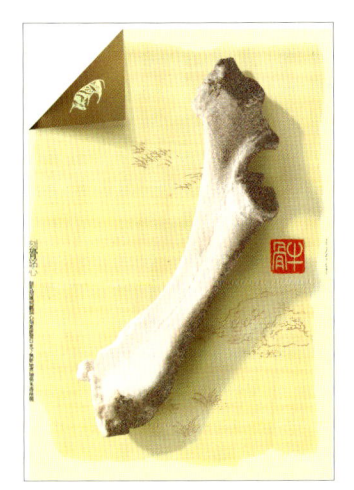

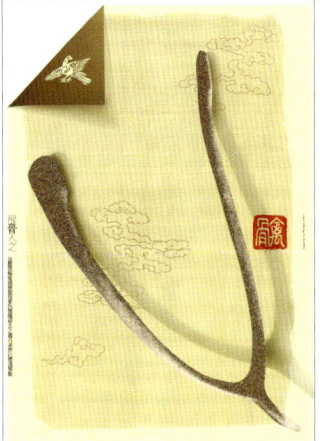

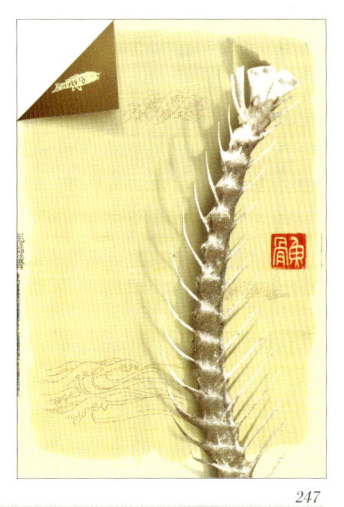

247_ Thematic Poster
t. InsideOut (A)
e. Ameba Design Ltd.
cd. dd. ad. d. Gideon Lai
cl. 8 Designers Show

248_ Thematic Poster
t. Consume Less
e. CoDesign Ltd.
dd. Eddy Yu, Hung Lam
d. cw. Eddy Yu
cl. The Chubu Creators Club, Asian Environmental Poster Exhibition, 2005

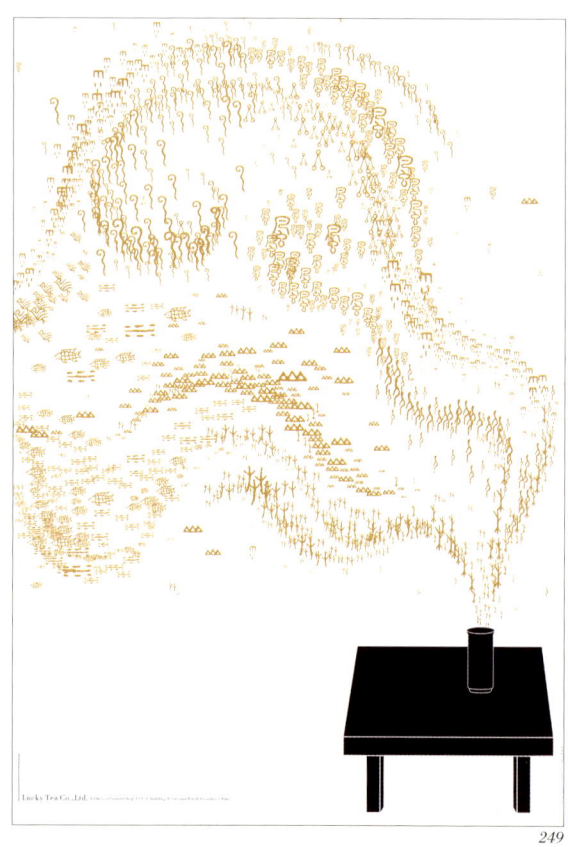

249_ Commercial Poster
t. 祺楨茶業推廣海報
e. 共同品牌策略顧問共同包裝設計
cd. dd. ad. d. 馬深廣
i. 胡子
cl. 祺楨茶業有限公司

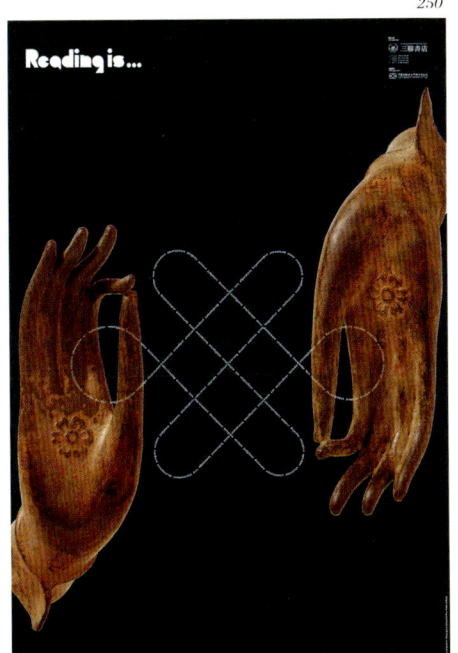

250_ *Thematic Poster*
 t. Homage to Ikko Tanaka
   by Kan Tai-keung
 e. Kan & Lau Design Consultants
 cd. ad. d. Kan Tai-keung
 i. Benson Kwun
 cp. G.L. Graphic Co., Ltd.
 cl. Kan & Lau Design Consultants

251_ *Cultural Promotion Poster*
 t. Regeneration
 e. cd. d. Yip Yee Ki
 p. Kwong Kwok Wing
 cl. CO1 School of Visual Arts

252_ *Thematic Poster*
 t. Reading Is ...
 e. Token Workshop
 cd. ad. d. p. Kenneth To Po Keung
 cp. pt Output Plus Workshop Ltd.
 cl. Joint Publishing

253_ *Thematic Poster*
 t. Super Women
 e. Alan Chan Design Company
 cd. Alan Chan

254_ Cultural Promotion Poster
t. Kan Tai-keung Culture, Kan & Lau Design
  Shenzhen Zhongshan Exhibition
e. Kan & Lau Design Consultants
cd. ad. d. Kan Tai-keung
p. Bong Ng
cp. G.L. Graphic Co., Ltd.
cl. Kan & Lau Design Consultants

[GLOBALITY]

[GLOBALITY]

255

255_ *Thematic Poster*
t. Globality
e. 共同品牌策略顧問共同包裝設計
cd. dd. ad. d. i. 馬深廣
p. 文建軍
cl. 廣州平面社會

256_ *Thematic Poster*
t. Condomania Tokyo "The Goddess of Rubbers"
e. ad. d. Akihiko Tsukamoto
i. Radical Suzuki
cw. Masami Ouchi, Masayuki Minoda
cl. Sea Road International Corporation

257_ *Thematic Poster*
t. Love Earth Love Children
e. ad. d. Akihiko Tsukamoto
cd. Hiromi Inayoshi
i. Radical Suzuki
pt. Twin-Eight Co., Ltd.
cl. NGO Kirara No Kai

258_ *Thematic Poster*
t. Wannabee Chinese!
e. milkxhake
ad. milkxhake, Ben Tseng
p. Shane Nash, USA,
   Sebastiano Scattolin, Italy
cl. Fabrica, Italy

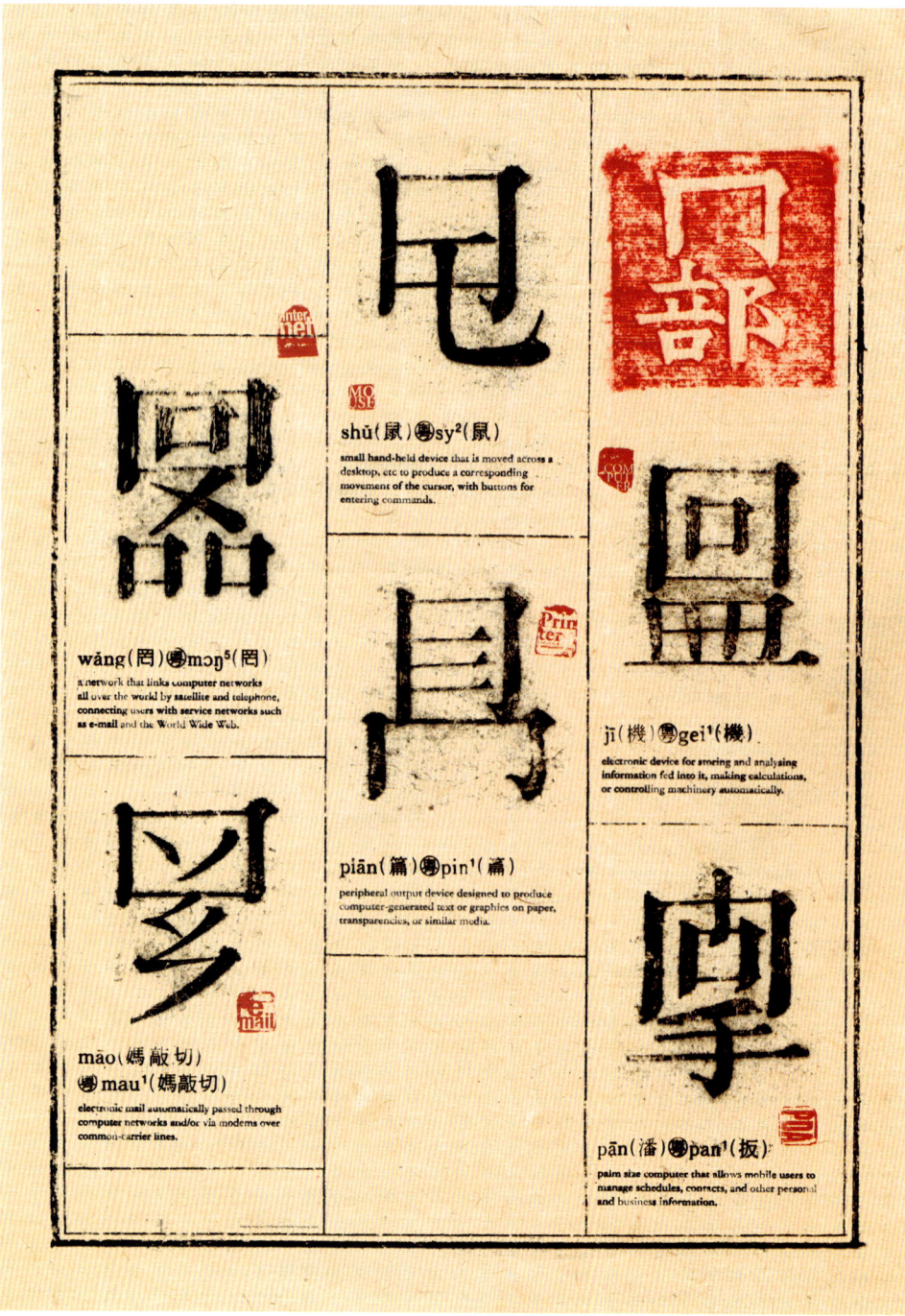

Excellent
259_ Thematic Poster
t. Chinese Character
e. CoDesign Ltd.
dd. d. cw. Hung Lam
cl. "Chinese Character"
International Poster Exhibition, Taipei, 2003

Excellent
260_ *Thematic Poster*
 t. Orange PrayStation
 e. CoDesign Ltd.
 dd. d. cw. Hung Lam
 p. Ducky Tse
 cl. Man & God Showcase in Stuttgart Design Centre, Germany International Poster Exhibition, 2005

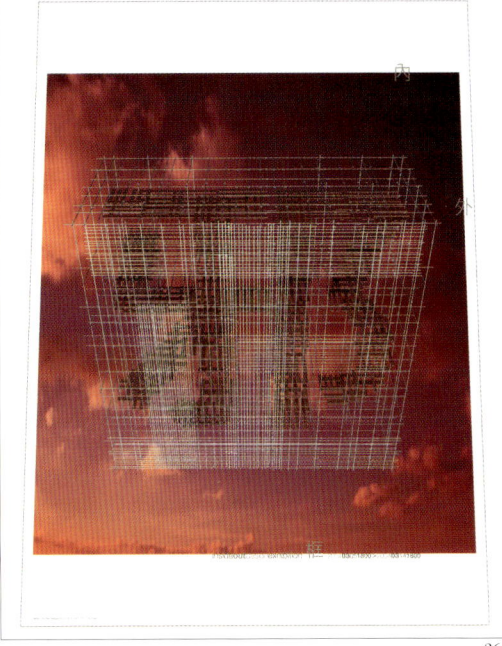

Excellent
261_ *Thematic Poster*
 t. 2 Faces of Humanity Series
 e. cd. d. Eric Chan
 i. Fei Wong of Fine Effort Illustration
 cl. Insideout 8 Designers Show

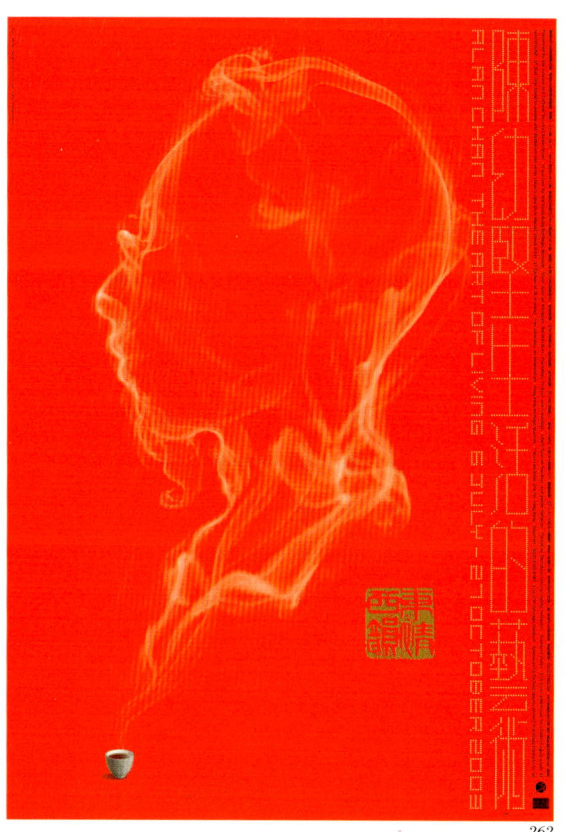

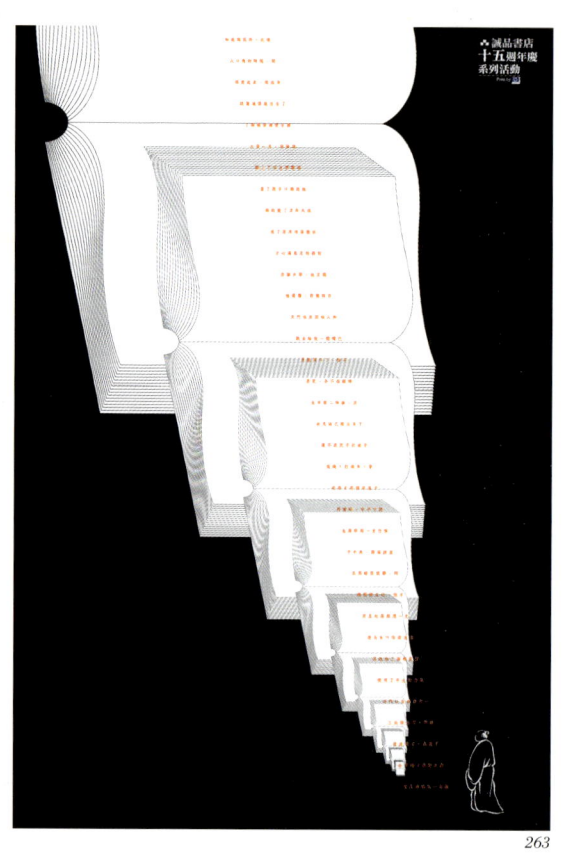

262_ Cultural Promotion Poster
t. Chaneration
e. Alan Chan Design Company
dd. Alan Chan
d. Alan Chan, Peter Lo
i. Fei Wong
cl. Hong Kong Heritage Museum

263_ Cultural Promotion Poster
t. ESLITE Bookstore
e. Kan & Lau Design Consultants
cd. ad. d. Freeman Lau Siu Hong
cp. G.L. Graphic Co., Ltd.
cl. Kan & Lau Design Consultants

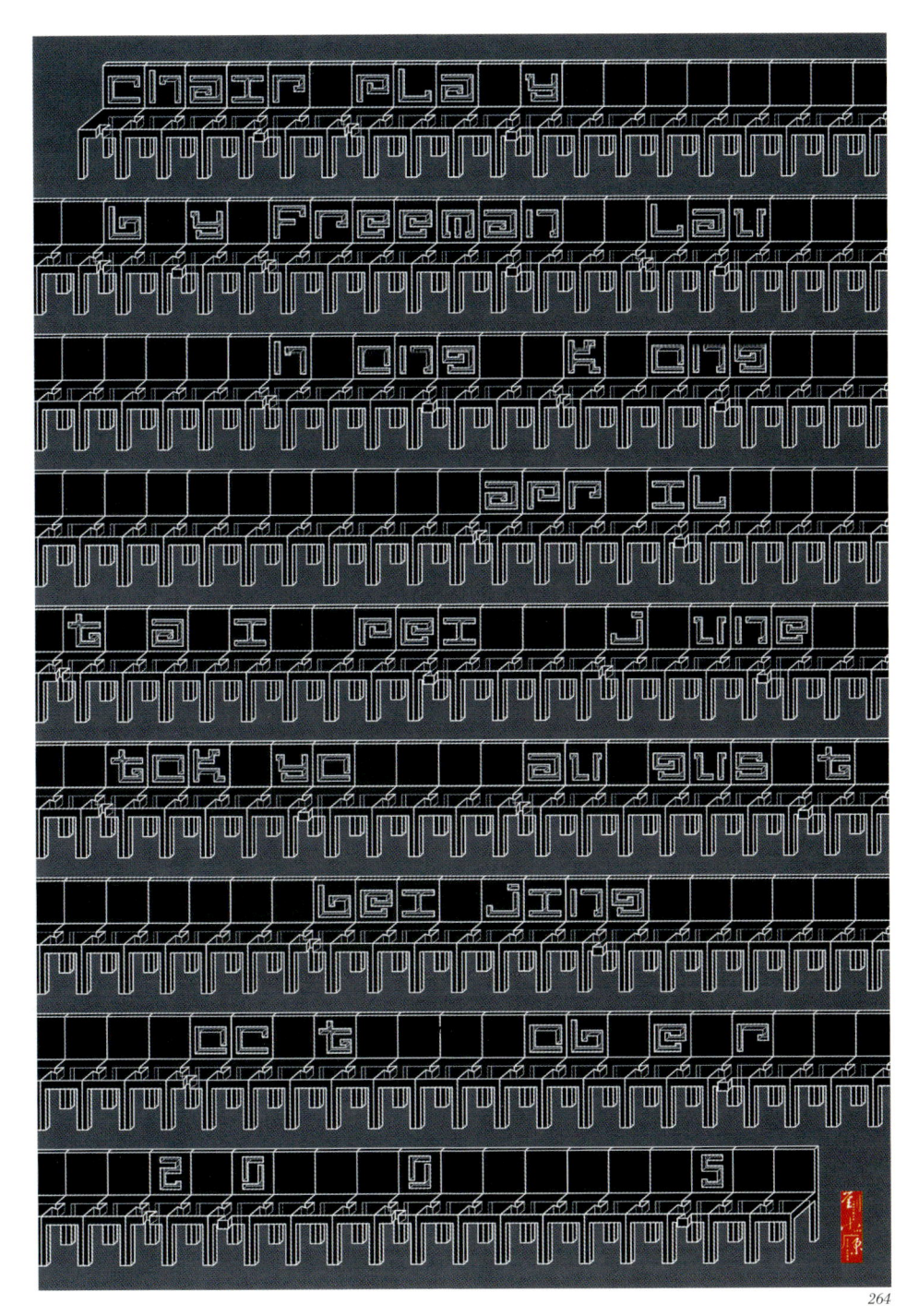

264_ Cultural Promotion Poster
t. Chair Play by Freeman Lau
e. Kan & Lau Design Consultants
cd. ad. Freeman Lau Siu Hong
d. Freeman Lau Siu Hong, Vinci Fung
cp. pt. G.L. Graphic Co., Ltd.
cl. Kan & Lau Design Consultants

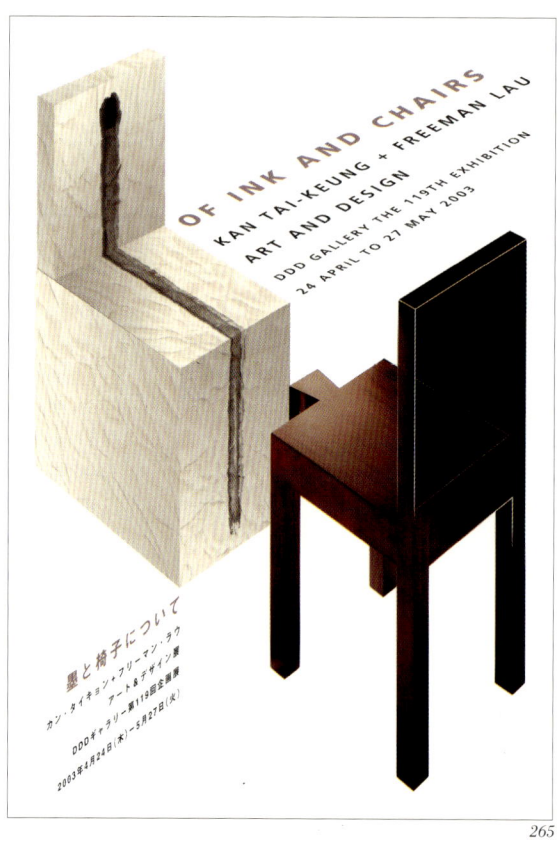

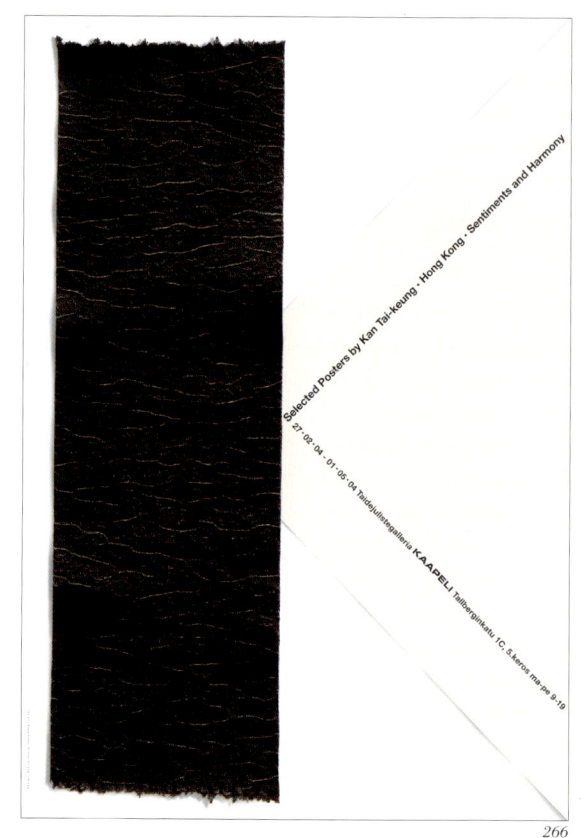

265_ *Cultural Promotion Poster*
t. Of Ink and Chairs
e. Kan & Lau Design Consultants
cd. ad. d. Kan Tai-keung
p. C.K. Wong
i. Kan Tai-keung, Freeman Lau, Benson Kwun
cl. DDD Gallery

266_ *Cultural Promotion Poster*
t. Kan's Helsinki Poster Exhibition
e. Kan & Lau Design Consultants
cd. ad. Kan Tai-keung
d. Kan Tai-keung, Justin Yu
cp. G.L. Graphic & Printing Ltd.
cl. Kaapeli Poster Art Gallery

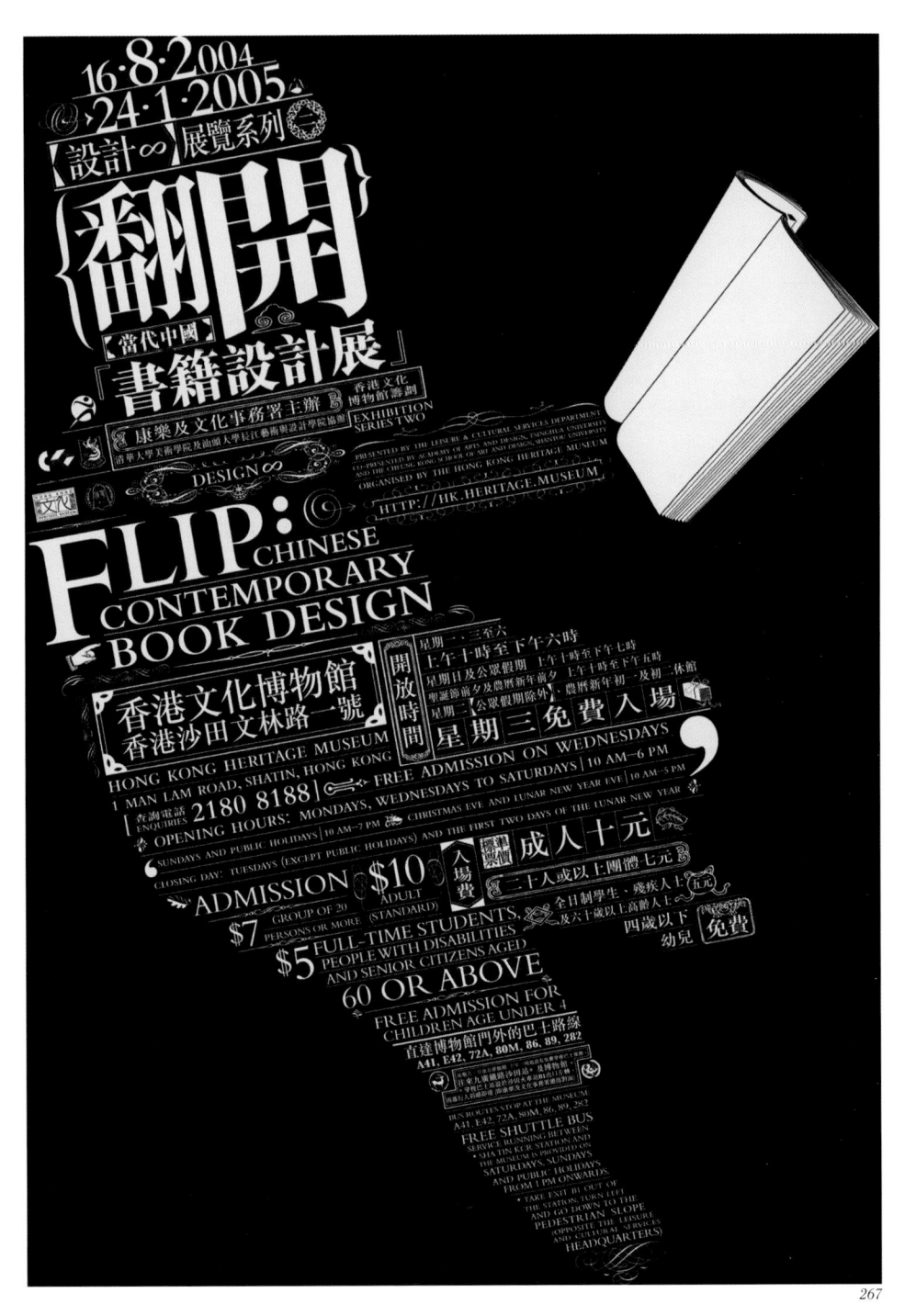

Excellent
267_ *Cultural Promotion Poster*
t. Flip: Chinese Contemporary Book Design
e. Kan & Lau Design Consultants
cd. ad. Freeman Lau Siu Hong
d. Freeman Lau Siu Hong, Ko Siu Hong
cl. Hong Kong Heritage Museum

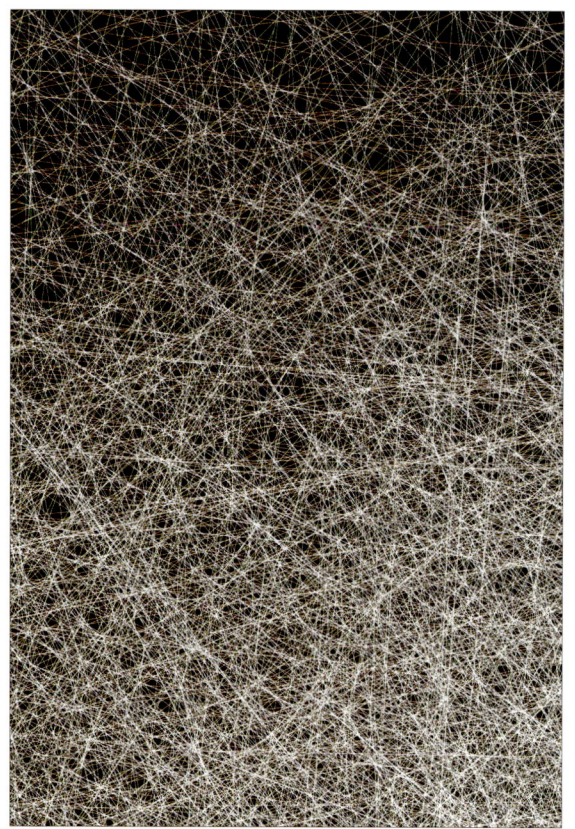

268

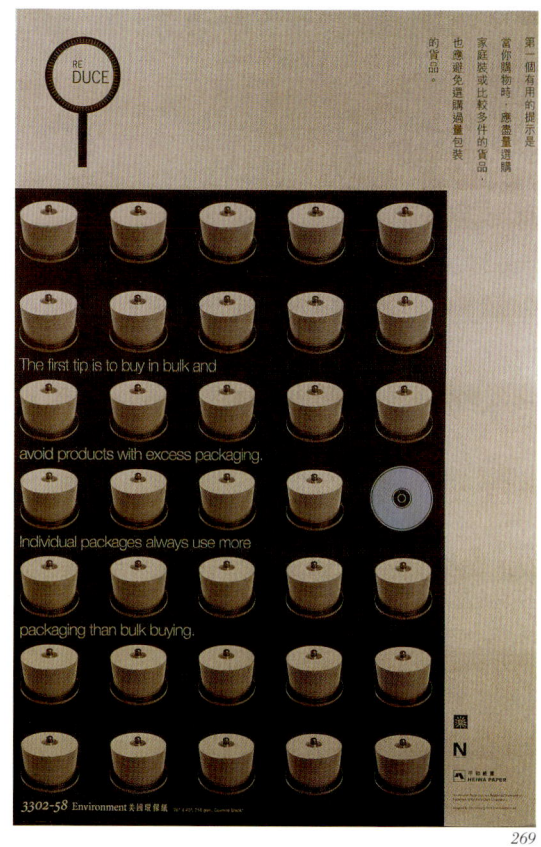

269

268_ Thematic Poster
t. Space
e. ad. d. Au Tak-shing, Benny
pt. Hin Lee Screen Printing Co., Ltd.
cl. Hong Kong Heritage Museum

Excellent
269_ Commercial Poster
t. Reduce, Reuse & Recycle
e. BrandsNation Ltd.
cd. dd. d. cw. Eric Cheung
p. Danny Chui
pt. Hoi Kwong Printing Ltd.
cl. Heiwa Paper Co Hong Kong Ltd.

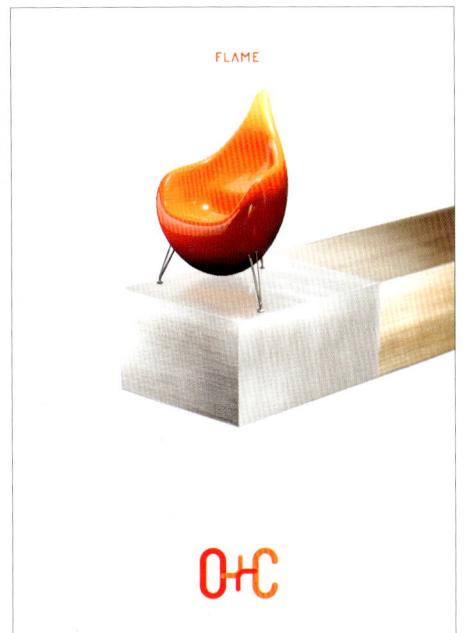

270_ *Commercial Poster*
t. 0 + C Furniture "Al Dente Chair"
e. Bliss Partners Int'l Ltd.
cd. Ivan Leung

271_ *Commercial Poster*
t. 0 + C Furniture "Flame Chair"
e. Bliss Partners Int'l Ltd.
cd. Ivan Leung

272_ *Commercial Poster*
t. Command G Show 01
e. dd. Cheng Kar Wai
cd. Cheng Kar Wai, Queen Chan
cl. Command G

273_ *Commercial Poster*
t. We're a notch higher
e. cd. d. Colan Ho
cl. Esperanto Design Workshop

274_ *Commercial Poster*
t. Cosmic Wind
e. cd. d. Colan Ho
cl. Esperanto Design Workshop

275_ *Commercial Poster*
t. CUBE Show
e. cd. dd. Cheng Kar Wai
cl. CO1 School of Visual Arts

276_ *Thematic Poster*
t. Hentaikana
e. cd. dd. ad. d. Michihito Sasaki
pp. Cybig, Co.
cl. Graves, Co.

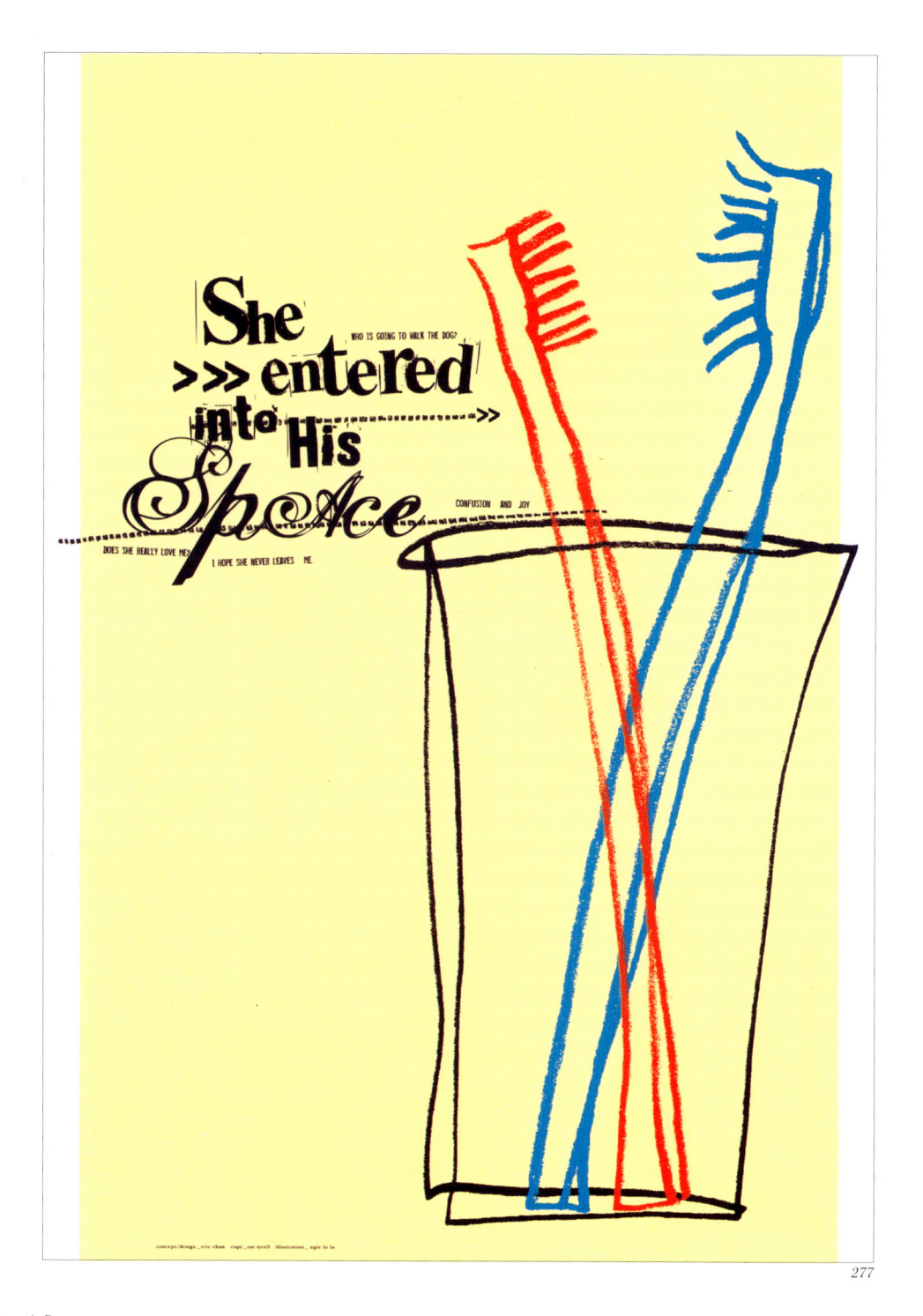

277_ Thematic Poster
t. She Entered into His Space
e. cd. Eric Chan
d. Eric Chan, Sindy Mok
i. Lu Lu Ngie
cl. Hong Kong Heritage Museum

278_ Thematic Poster
t. Space : Inside Out
e. Circle Design Ltd
cd. d. p. Clement Yick
cl. Inside Out 8 Designers Show

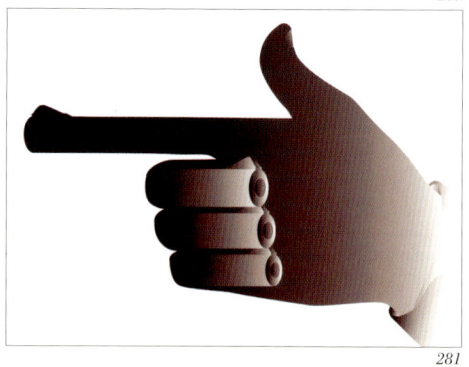

279_ *Thematic Poster*
t. Black is Me
e. CoDesign Ltd.
dd. d. p. Hung Lam
cl. 3rd International Poster Competition, Ningbo, China, 2004

280_ *Cultural Promotion Poster*
t. Waiting for Godot
e. Kan & Lau Design Consultants
cd. ad. Freeman Lau Siu Hong
d. Freeman Lau Siu Hong, Karen Li
p. Stanley Wong
cp. G.L. Graphic Co., Ltd.
cl. TNT Theatre

281_ *Thematic Poster*
t. 玩火自焚
e. cd. dd. ad. d. 密博

266

282_ *Thematic Poster*
t. Hong Kong Reload
e. Chan Yiu Tong, Sherman
cd. dd. ad. d. Alexander Cheung
pt. Suncolor Printing Co., Ltd.
cl. Hong Kong Chingying Institute of Visual Arts

283_ *Cultural Promotion Poster*
t. Poster Triennial 2004 - Call For Entry
e. cd. dd. ad. Angus Wong
d. Mark Ho-man
cl. Hong Kong Heritage Museum

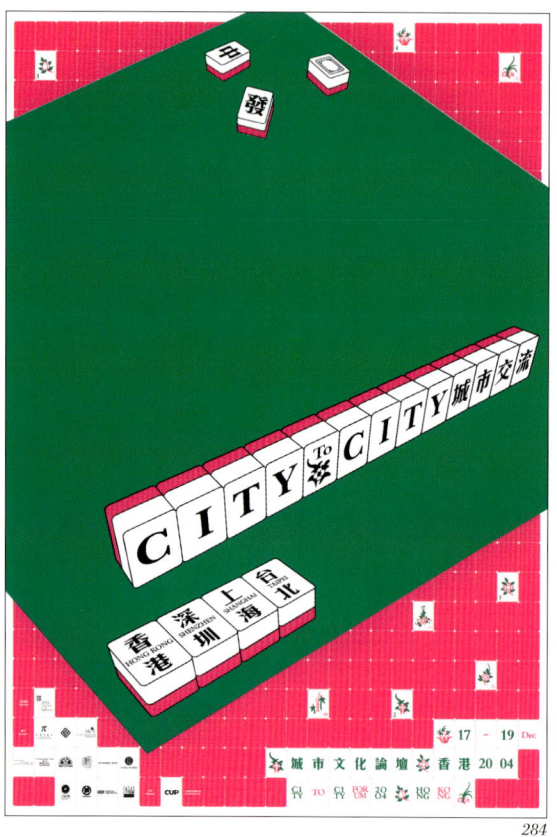

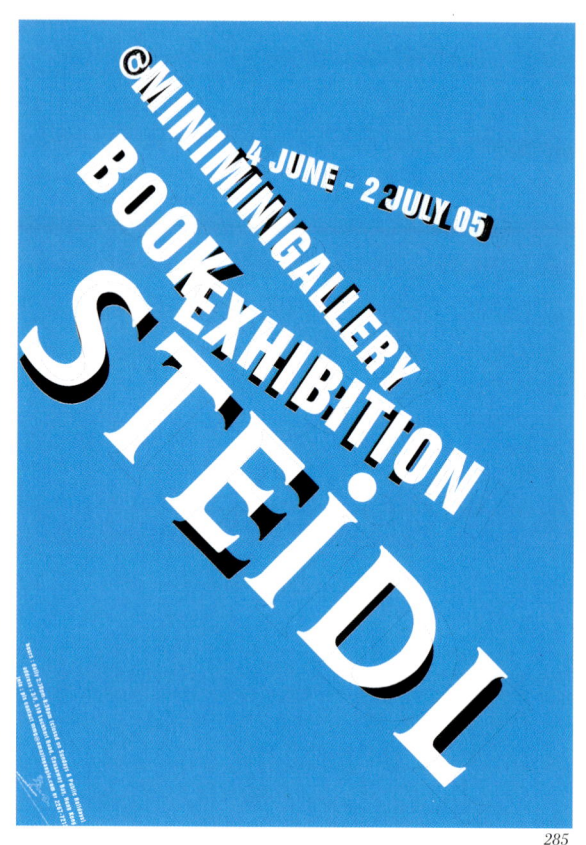

284_ Cultural Promotion Poster
t. City to City
e. Kan & Lau Design Consultants
cd. dd. ad. Freeman Lau Siu Hong
d. Freeman Lau Siu Hong,
   Margaret Chu
pt. Tom (Cup Magazine) Publishing Ltd.
cl. Hong Kong Institute of
   Contemporary Culture

Excellent
285_ Cultural Promotion Poster
t. STEiDL Book Exhibition
e. ad. d. Au Tak-shing, Benny
pt. Suncolor Printing Co., Ltd.
cl. miniminigallery

286_ Thematic Poster
  t. Inner Beauty
  e. FCB Shanghai
  cd. Poh Hwee Beng, Danny Chan, Cetric Leung
  dd. Cetric Leung
  ad. Poh Hwee Beng, Cetric Leung, Lee Pui Ho
  p. Sam Nugroho
  i. Lim Peng Yam, Lee Pui Ho
  cw. Danny Chan, Antonius Chen
  cs. Wilmin Ha
  pt. Lily Jin
  cl. Natural Beauty

Excellent
287_ Cultural Promotion Poster Illustration
  t. Foolish
  e. Choi Kim Hung
  cd. d. i. Choi Kim Hung, Tori Leung
  cl. CO1 School of Visual Arts

Excellent
288_ Cultural Promotion Poster
  t. 80th ADC. NY in China NYADC
  e. Kan & Lau Design Consultants
  cd. ad. d. p. Freeman Lau Siu Hong
  cp. G.L.Graphic Co., Ltd.
  cl. Capital Corporation Image Institution

289_ Thematic Poster
t. Chinese Traditional Symbol Exhibition
e. ad. d. i. Au Tak-shing, Benny
cl. Tsing Hua University, China

290_ Thematic Poster
t. Chingying 25th Anniversary
e. Acorn Design Ltd.
ad. d. Frank Chan Wah Hung
p. Oswald Cheung
cl. Chingying Institute of Visual Arts

291_ Thematic Poster
t. NO:2 Exciting Game
e. 共同品牌策略顧問共同包裝設計
cd. dd. ad. d. 馬深廣
p. 文建軍
i. 馬蘭
cl. 2003深圳反戰海報展

292_ Commercial Poster
t. 109 Birthday Fair
e. cd. dd. ad. Seichi Ohashi
d. Aiko Nakamura
p. Hisashi Yoshino
cw. Tatuhiro Yano
cl. TMD Corporation

293

294

293_ *Thematic Poster*
t. Berlin-Seen by AGI
e. Kan & Lau Design Consultants
cd. ad. Kan Tai-keung
d. Kan Tai-keung, Garfield Chan
cp. G.L. Graphic Co., Ltd.
cl. Kan & Lau Design Consultants

294_ *Cultural Promotion Poster*
t. The 27th Hong Kong International Film Festival
e. Kan & Lau Design Consultants
cd. ad. Freeman Lau Siu Hong
d. Freeman Lau Siu Hong, Justin Yu
cp. G.L. Graphic Co., Ltd.
cl. Hong Kong Arts Development Council

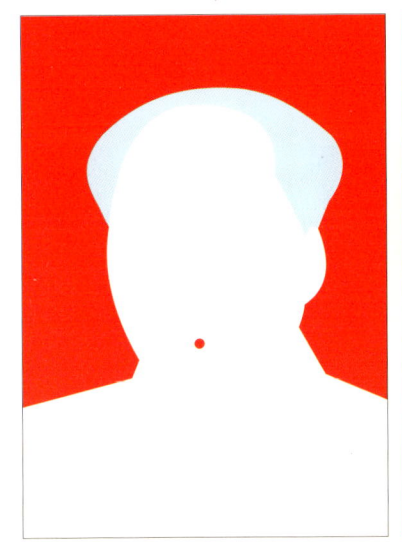

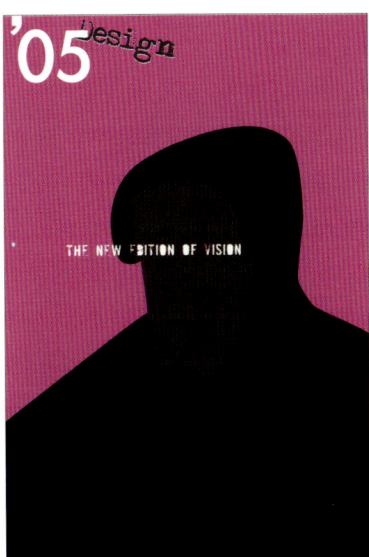

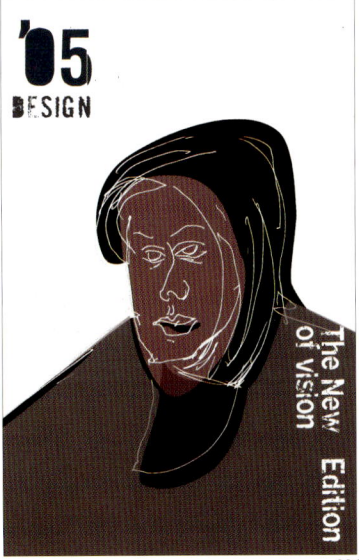

295_ *Thematic Poster*
t. Life Spot
e. ad. d. 肖偉棠
cl. International Design Center NAGOYA Inc.

296_ *Thematic Poster*
t. The New Edition of Vision Series
e. cd. dd. ad. d. Chen Ping Bo

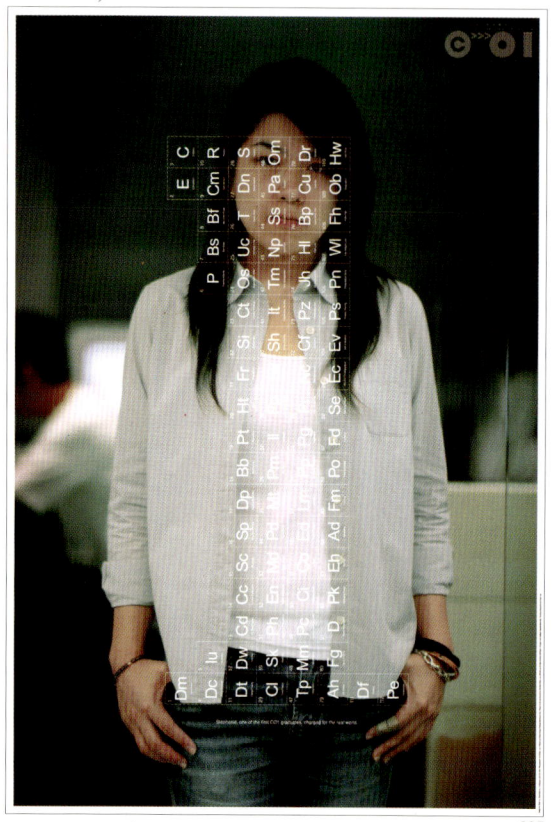

297_ Thematic Poster

t. C01 1st Anniversary
e. CoDesign Ltd.
dd. Eddy Yu
d. Eddy Yu, Stephanie Au
p. Bobby Lee
cw. Stephanie Au
cl. C01 School of Visual Arts

Excellent

298_ Thematic Poster

t. Reading is ...
e. cd. d. Eric Chan
p. Lau Kwok Tim of TIM Photography
cw. Steven Lee
cl. Joint Publishing (Hong Kong) Co., Ltd.

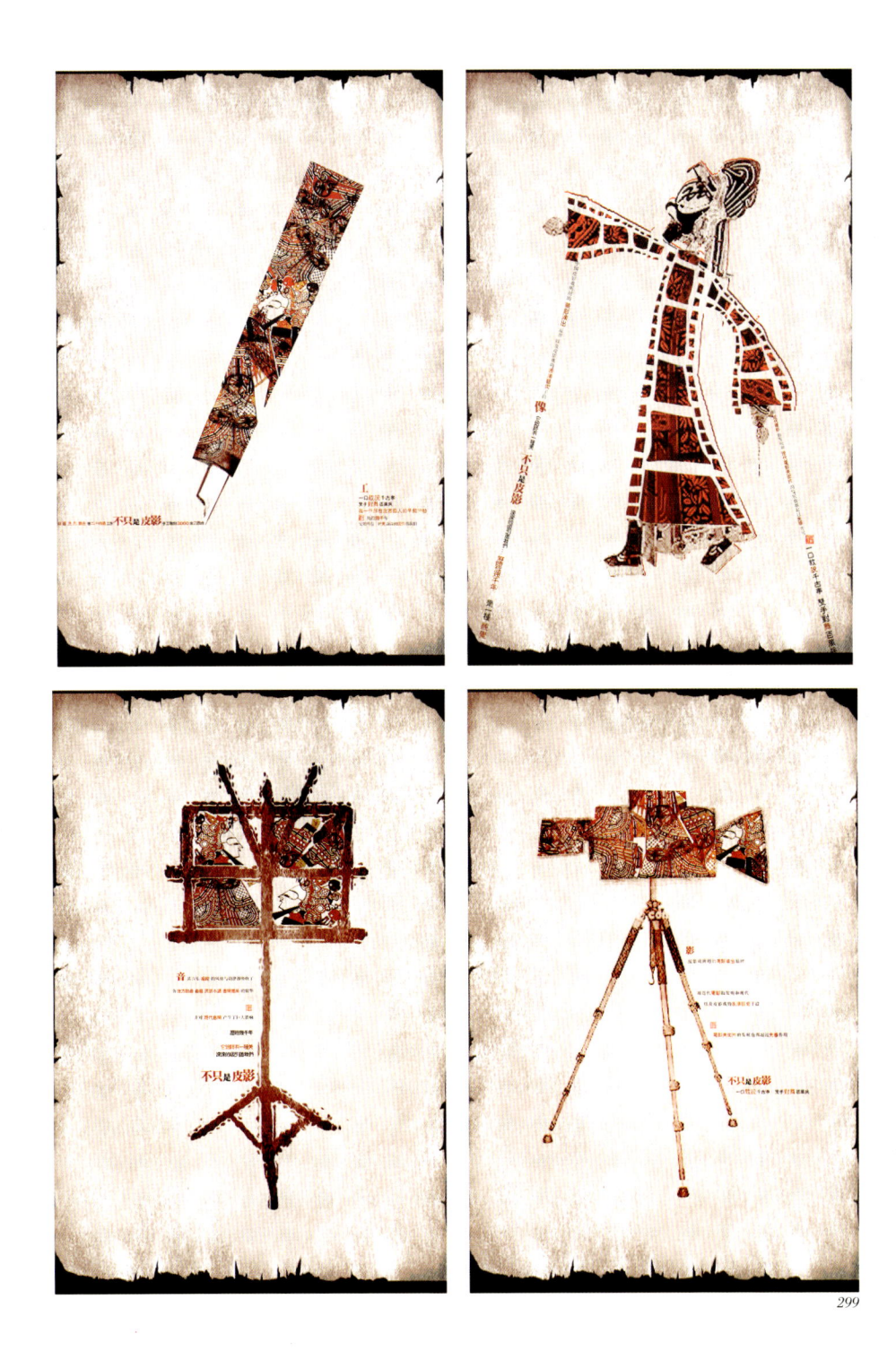

299_ Thematic Poster
t. 不只是皮影
e. cd. dd. ad. 李長春
d. 李長春, 趙國振

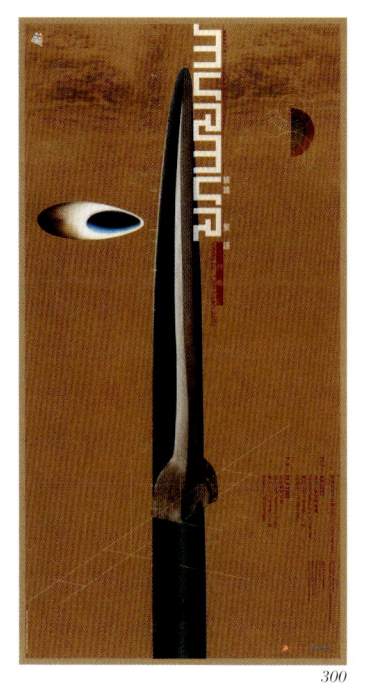

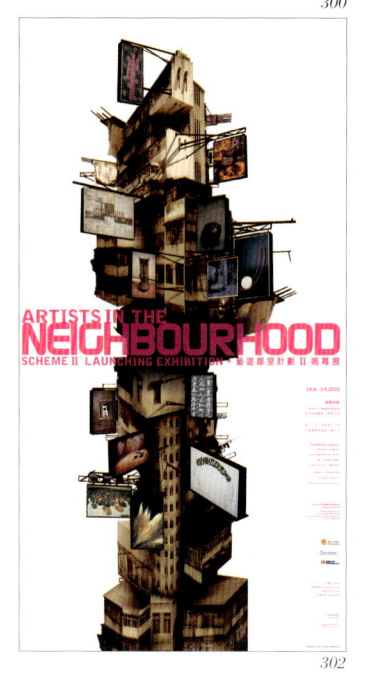

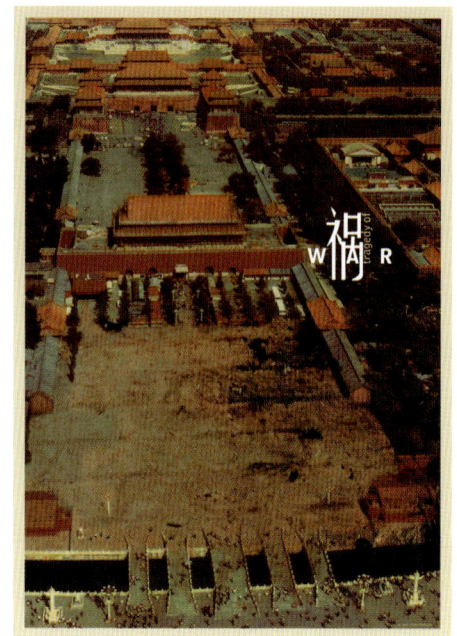

300_ Cultural Promotion Poster
- t. Murmur - Works by Lam Laam Jaffa
- e. Tommy Li Design Workshop Ltd.
- cd. Tommy Li
- d. Tami Leung
- cs. Lancy Chiu
- cl. Art Promotion Office

301_ Cultural Promotion Poster
- t. Sun
- e. Tsang Chi Ping
- cd. d. i. Tsang Chi Ping
- cl. CO1 School of Visual Arts

302_ Cultural Promotion Poster
- t. Artists in The Neighbourhood Scheme II Launching Exhibition
- e. Tommy Li Design Workshop Ltd.
- cd. Tommy Li
- d. Thomas Siu
- cs. Lancy Chiu
- cl. Art Promotion Office

Excellent
303_ Thematic Poster
- t. Tragedy of War
- e. Tommy Li Design Workshop Ltd.
- cd. Tommy Li
- d. Tami Leung
- cl. "No War" Poster Design Exhibition

276

304_ *Thematic Poster*
t. Thoughts about my little planet
e. Kan & Lau Design Consultants
cd. ad. Kan Tai-keung
d. Kan Tai-keung, Garfield Chan
p. C.K. Wong
cp. pt. G.L. Graphic Co., Ltd.
cl. ETAPES GRAPHIGUES

305_ *Commercial Poster*
t. Poster of TAMAKI
e. ad. Osamu Misawa
d. Satomi Kajitani
pp. Dai Nippon Printing Co., Ltd.
cl. TAMAKI

306_ Thematic Poster
t. Hong Kong Good Things
e. Circle Design Ltd.
cd. d. p. Clement Yick
cl. Hysan Development Ltd.

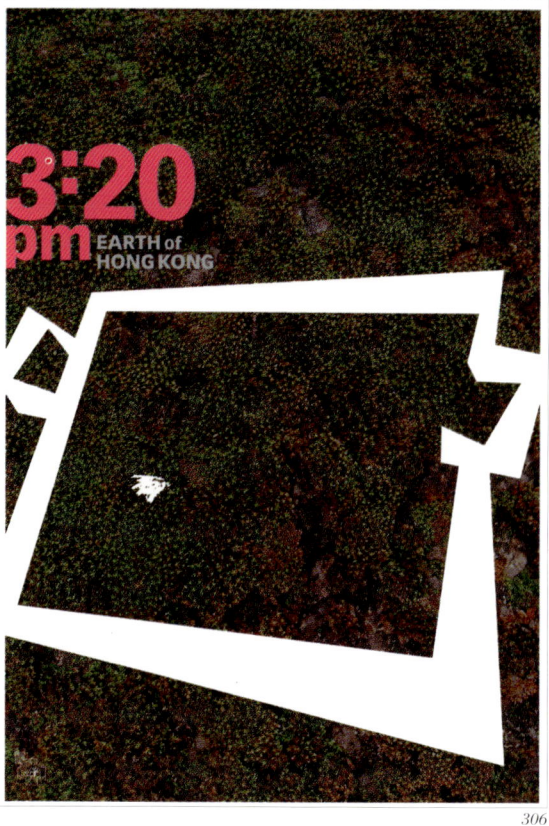

307_ Commercial Poster
t. CO1 Design 03 Show
e. Paul Lam Design Associates
cd. Paul Lam, Cheng Kar Wai
d. Cheng Kar Wai, Queenie Shek, Sindy Mok, Queen Chan, Landre Chiu
p. Danny Chiu
cp. Art Point Production
pt. Hoi Kwong Printing Co., Ltd.
cl. CO1 School of Visual Arts

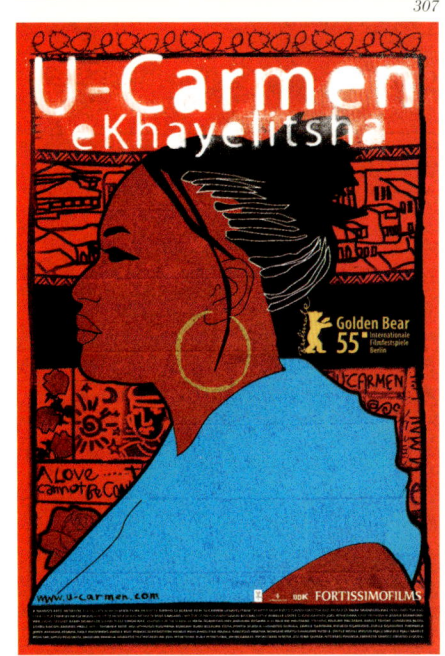

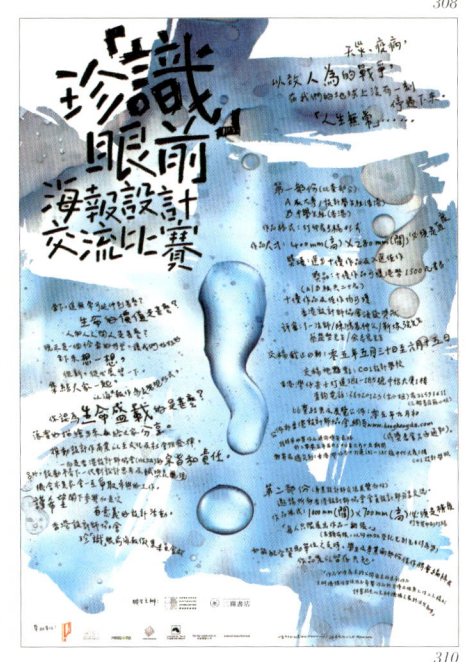

308_ Cultural Promotion Poster
t. Benny Au Talk To You
e. ad. d. i. Au Tak-shing, Benny
pt. Hoi Kwong Printing Co., Ltd.
cl. Polytrade Paper Co., Ltd.

309_ Commercial Poster
t. U - Carmen
e. Acorn Design Ltd.
ad. d. Frank Chan Wah Hung
i. Albert Leung Chi Yan,
   Frank Chan Wah Hung
cl. Fortissimo Films

310_ Thematic Poster
t. Tsunami Call for Entry Poster
e. cd. Eric Chan
d. Eric Chan, Iris Yu
p. Stephen Cheung Studio
i. Iris Yu
cl. Hong Kong Designers Association

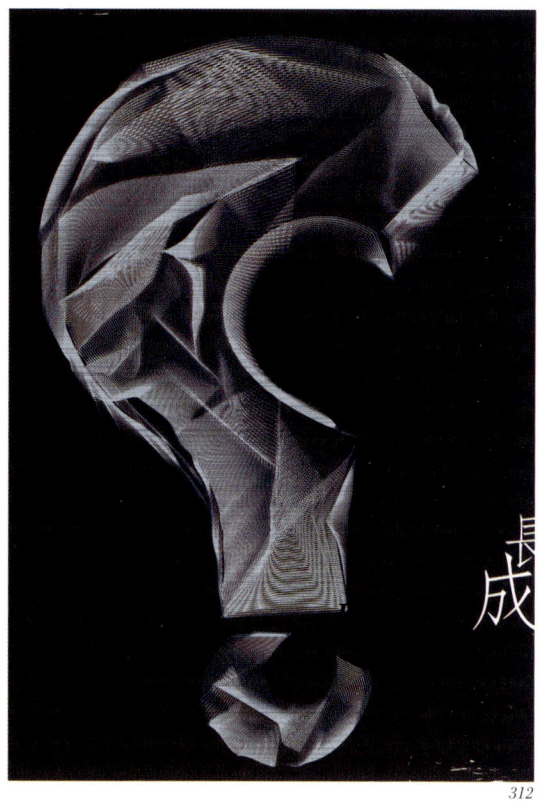

311_ Thematic Poster
t. Man, Cross, Wood
e. Ameba Design Ltd.
cd. dd. ad. d. Gideon Lai
cl. Tsinghua University - China
  Traditional Graphics & Contemporary Art

312_ Thematic Poster
t. 成長
e. dd. ad. d. i. 周強

280

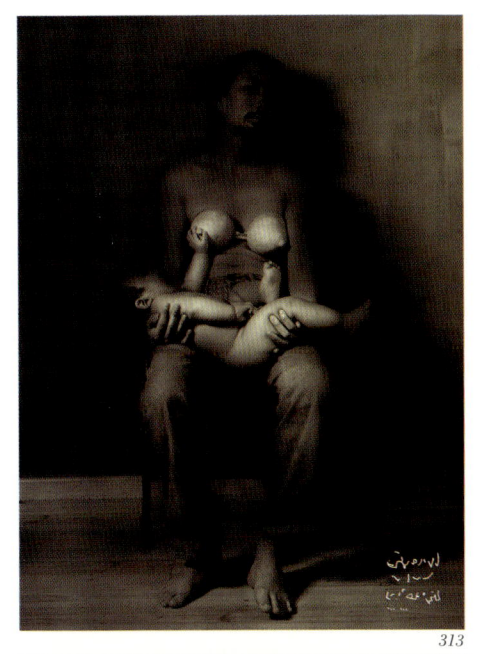

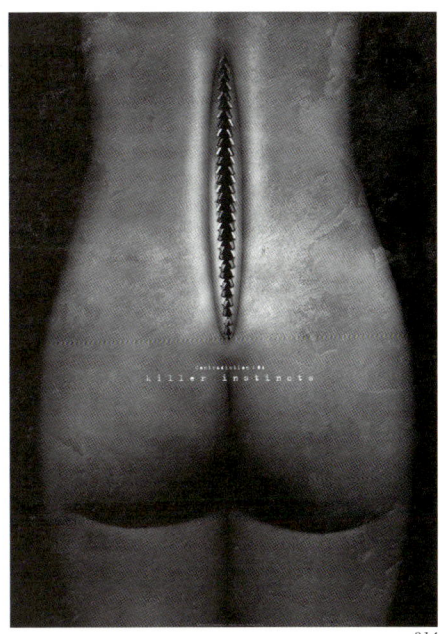

313_ Thematic Poster
t. Law Father
e. 索曼斯包裝設計公司
cd. dd. ad. d. i. cw. 于永芳
p. 李嘉賓, 黃思源
pt. 麗翔數碼輸出公司
cl. 民間社會文化社

314_ Thematic Poster
t. Superwoman
e. Tommy Li Design Workshop Ltd.
cd. Tommy Li
d. Kimmy Ng
p. Lester Lee
cw. Tommy Li, Mabel Leung
cl. Hong Kong Heritage Museum

315_ Thematic Poster
t. CO1
e. Circle Design Ltd.
cd. d. Clement Yick
p. C.K. Wong
cl. CO1 School of Visual Arts

316_ Thematic Poster
t. Evolution of Space
e. CoDesign Ltd.
dd. d. Eddy Yu
p. C.K. Wong
i. LuLu
cl. The 3rd International Poster Triennial, Heritage Museum

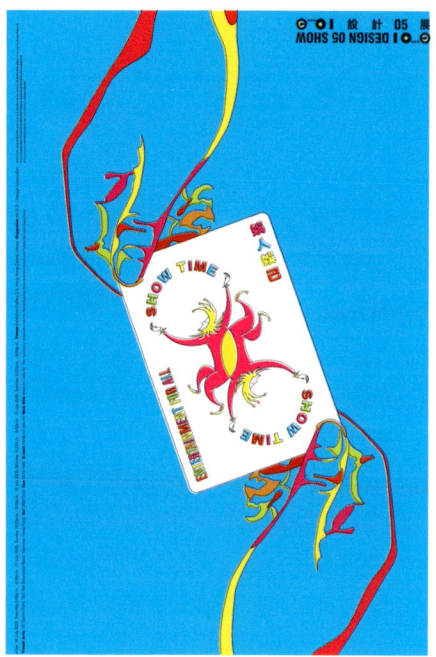

317_ *Thematic Poster*
t. Reading is ...
e. Acorn Design Ltd.
cd. ad. d. Frank Chan Wah Hung
p. Osward Cheung
cw. Sally Lim
cl. Joint Publishing (HK) Ltd.

318_ *Commercial Poster*
 Visual Identity Systems
t. CO1 Design 05 Show
e. Paul Lam Design Associates
cd. Paul Lam
d. Paul Lam, Cheng Kar Wai, Tequila Chan, Anissa Cheng, Patrick Chan, Queenie Shek
i. Patrick Chan
cp. Art Point Production
pt. Hoi Kwong Printing Co., Ltd.
cl. CO1 School of Visual Arts

319_ *Thematic Poster*
t. The System
e. cd. dd. ad. d. i. Michael Miller Yu
cl. CreationHouse

321

322  323

Excellent
321_ Thematic Poster
t. Private Space, Hong Kong 1-6
e. Sandy Choi Associates Ltd.
dd. Sandy Choi
d. Goldie Wong
p. Francis Chen, Alan Yu
pp. Art Factory
cl. Hong Kong Heritage Museum

320_ Commercial Poster
t. A Natural Sense of Acumen Paper
e. Acumen Paper
cd. dd. ad. d. Tin Li
cl. Acumen Paper

322_ Thematic Poster
t. 化煙氣為氧氣
e. cd. dd. ad. d.i. cw. 鄧遠健
cl. 廣東五葉神反煙害主題海報設計大賽

323_ Cultural Promotion Poster
t. Book Festival 2003
e. 28aDesign
cd. dd. ad. i. Leo Kwok
d. Kit Yeung
cw. Loretta Cheng @ BBlue Sky
cl. BBlue Sky

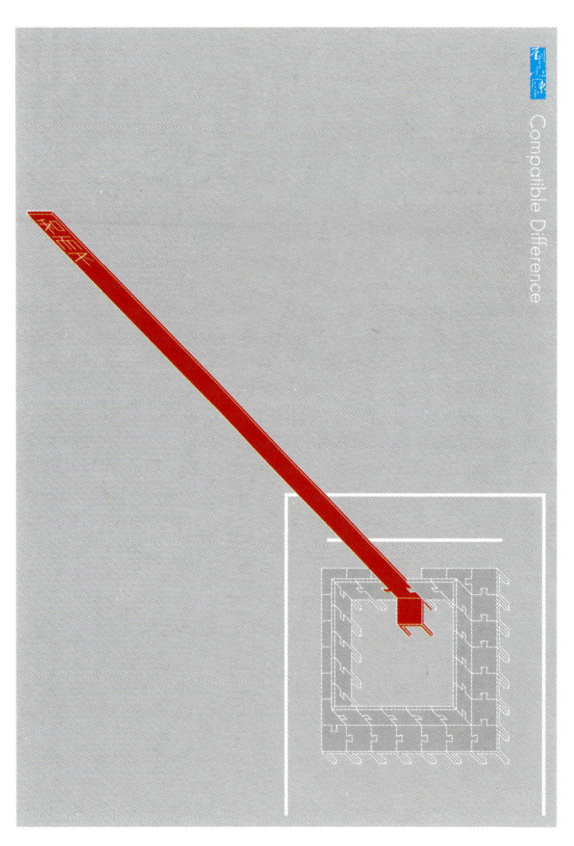

324_ Thematic Poster
t. Compatible Difference
e. Kan & Lau Design Consultants
cd. ad. d. Freeman Lau Siu Hong
cp. G.L. Graphic Co., Ltd.
cl. Kan & Lau Design Consultants

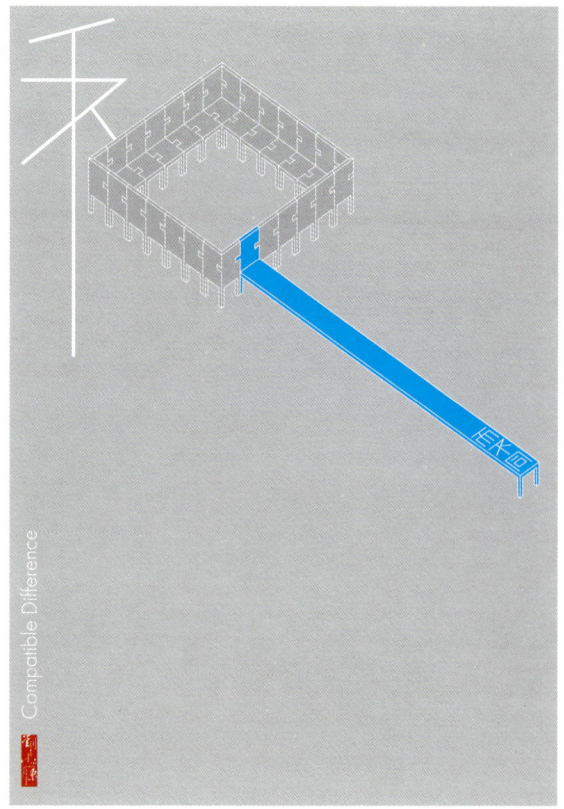

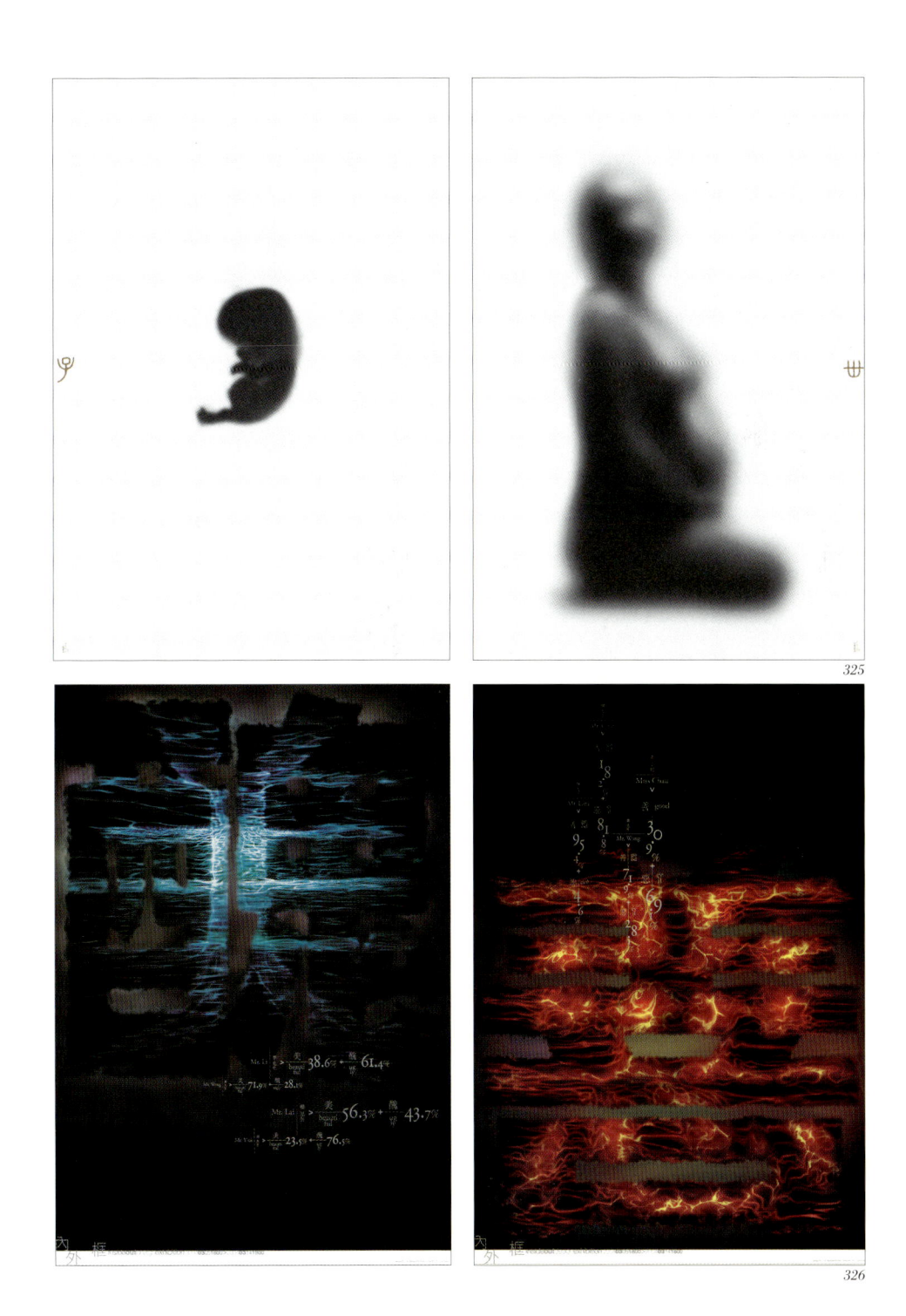

325_ *Thematic Poster*
t. Mother and Child
e. d. Imaya Wong
cp. Tye Cine Colour Separations
cl. Self promotion

326_ *Thematic Poster*
t. 2 Internal Values Series
e. cd. d. Eric Chan
i. Fei Wong of Fine Effort Illustration
cl. Insideout 8 Designers Show

327_ Thematic Poster
t. Reading is ...
e. cd. dd. ad. d. Michael Miller Yu
p. Baily Chan
i. Joe Yu
cs. Fiona Kwok
pt. The Joint Publishing (H.K.) Ltd.
cl. Hong Kong Designers Association

328_ Thematic Poster
t. Process
e. cd. dd. d. 畢學鋒

329_ Thematic Poster
t. Human Bomb
e. Eric Chan
cd. d. Michael Miller Yu, Eric Chan
dd. Eric Chan
p. Lester Lee Photo Workshop
cw. Cat Tyrell
cl. Hong Kong Heritage Museum

330_ Thematic Poster
t. 天蠶變
e. Charles Ng &
  Maxi Communication Ltd.
cd. cw. Charles Ng
dd. Sang Chan
d. Young Hoi Chun, Lukie Leung
p. Baily Chan
cl. 澳門設計師協會

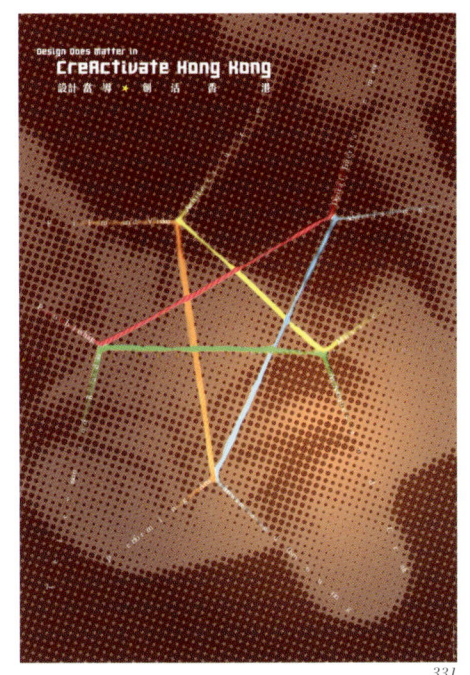

331

332

333

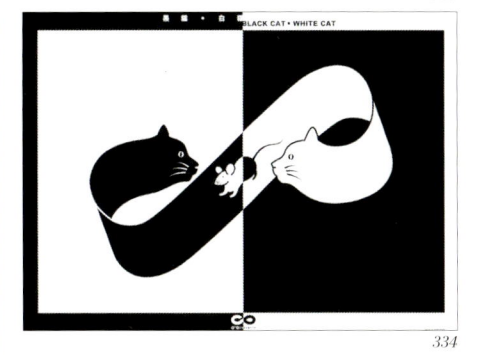

334

331_ Thematic Poster
t. CreActiveHongKong
e. Charles Ng & Maxi
   Communication Ltd.
cd. cw. Charles Ng
dd. Sang Chan
ad. Charles Ng, Sang Chan
d. Young Hoi Chun
p. Baily Chan
cp. Ricky Chu, Top's Creative Studio
cl. Centre for Cultural Policy Research

332_ Cultural Promotion Poster
t. CO1 School of Visual Arts
   Poster Exhibition (Cow)
e. cd. d. i. Eddy Chun
cl. CO1 School of Visual Arts

333_ Thematic Poster
t. CO1 1st Anniversary
e. cd. dd. ad. Angus Wong
d. Mark Ho Man
cl. CO1 School of Visual Arts

334_ Cultural Promotion Poster
t. Black Cat White Cat, Dog Eats
   Dog, Peace, War
e. Paul Lam Design Associates
cd. Paul Lam
ad. Anissa Cheng
d. Patrick Chan, Queenie Shek
i. Patrick Chan
cw. Maria Angela Lee
pt. Wide Ocean Printing Co., Ltd.
cl. CO1 INFINITY

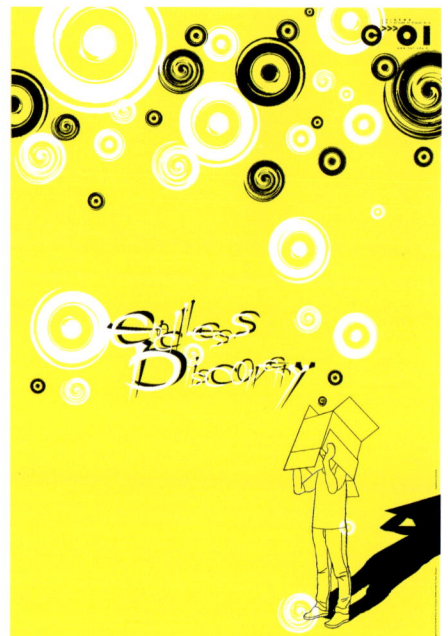

335_ *Cultural Promotion Poster*
t. CO1 School of Visual Arts
  Poster Exhibition (Keep Dreaming)
e. cd. d. i. cw. Law Tak Wah
cl. CO1 School of Visual Arts

336_ *Cultural Promotion Poster*
t. CO1 School of Visual Arts
  Poster Exhibition (Endless Discovery)
e. cd. d. i. Chan Wing Yan
cl. CO1 School of Visual Arts

337_ *Cultural Promotion Poster*
t. CO1 School of Visual Arts
  Poster Exhibition (Enter)
e. cd. d. Ng Ching Nam
cl. CO1 School of Visual Arts

338_ *Thematic Poster*
t. 無題
e. 共同品牌策略顧問共同包裝設計
cd. dd. ad. d. 馬深廣
i. 胡子
cl. 廣州平面社會

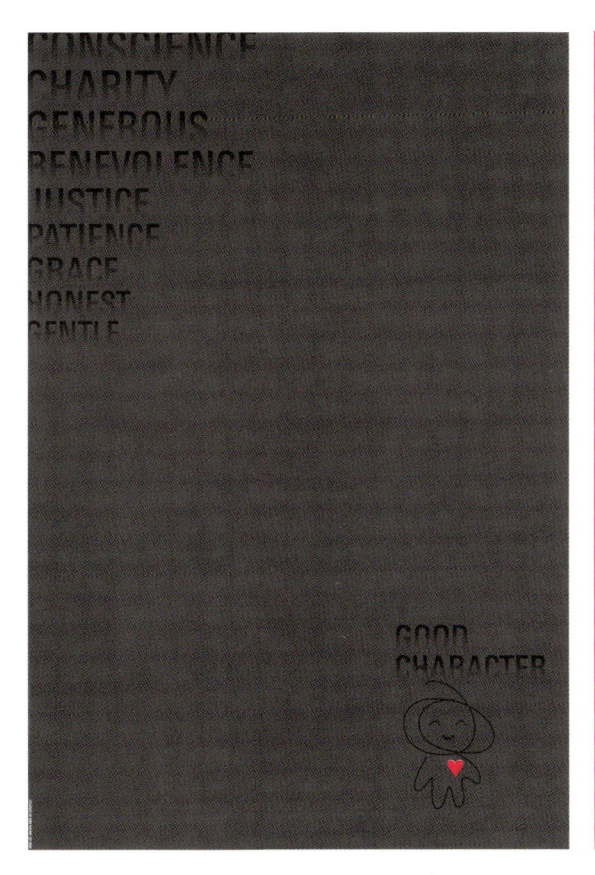

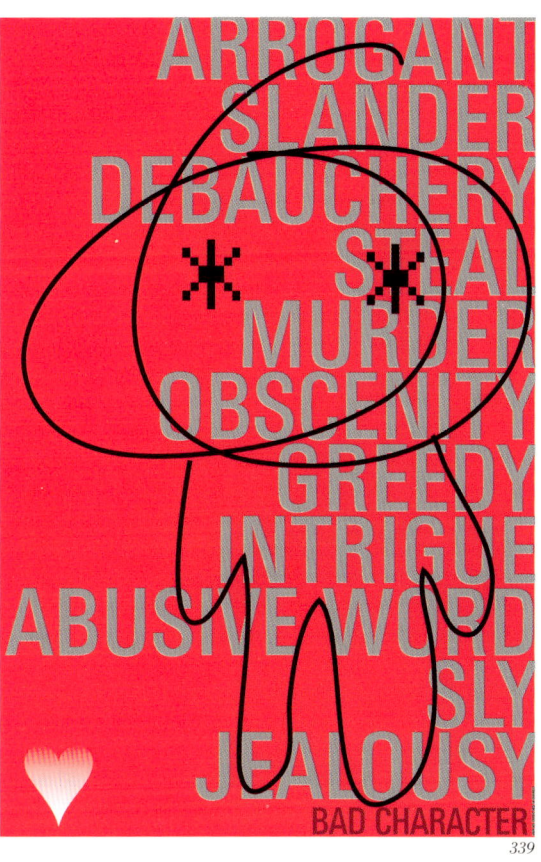

339_ Thematic Poster
t. Good Character and Bad Character
e. cd. ad. dd. d. i. Kirk Cheong Tak Wah

340_ *Thematic Poster*
t. Hong Kong Reload
e. CoDesign Ltd.
dd. d. Eddy Yu
cl. Hong Kong Chingying
 Institute of Visual Arts

341_ *Thematic Poster*
t. Water / Share
e. Circle Design Ltd.
cd. d. Clement Yick
p. C.K. Wong

Excellent
342_ *Thematic Poster*
t. Life-nature invites us to graphic art
e. I-Hsuan Cindy Wang
d. Cindy Wang

Excellent
343_ *Thematic Poster*
t. Poster of Wedding
e. ad. Osamu Misawa
d. Mamoru Takeuchi
pt. Dai Nippon Printing Co., Ltd.
cl. Tsuyoshi Horita

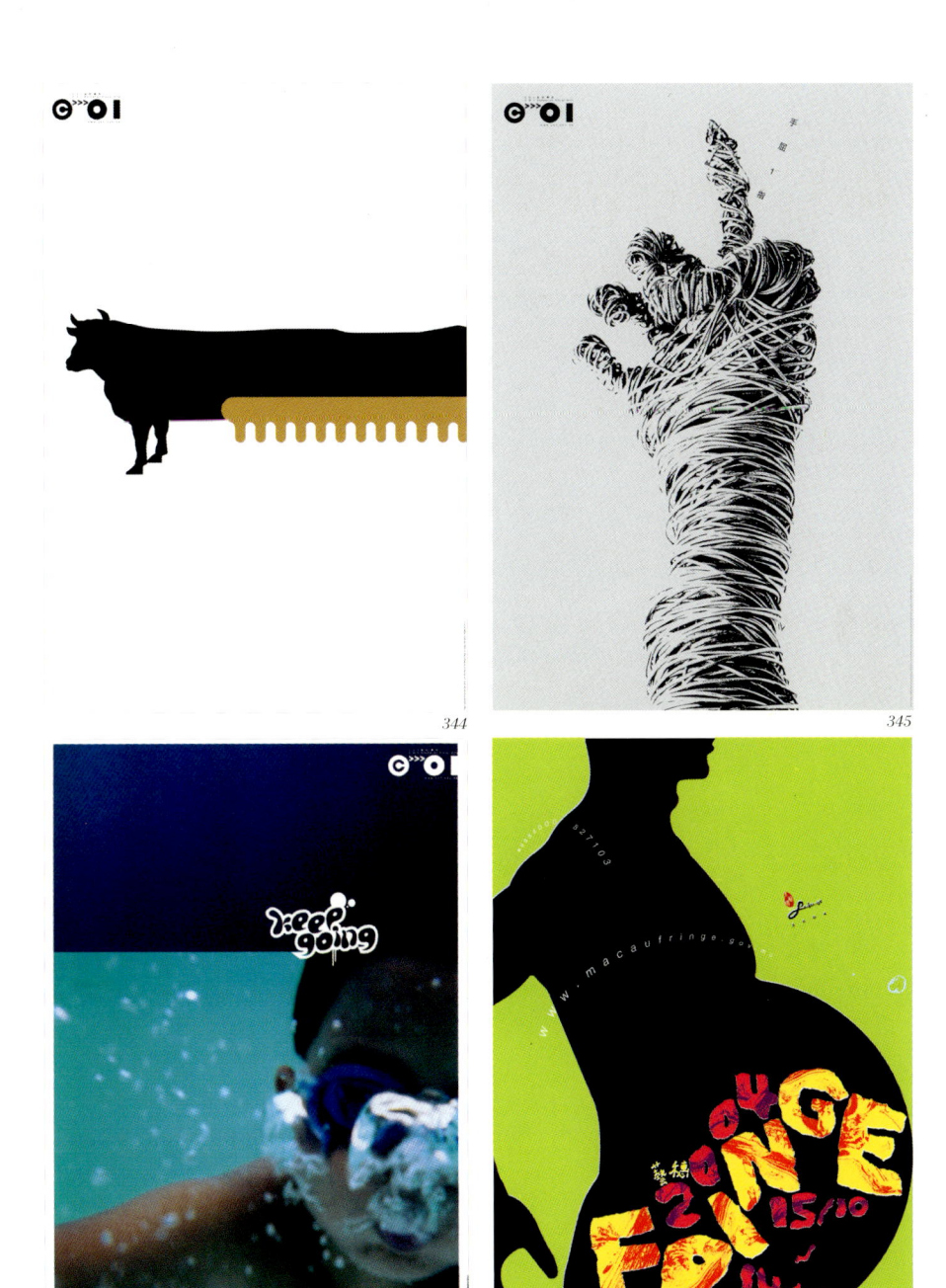

344_ Cultural Promotion Poster
t. C01 School of Visual Arts Poster
   Exhibition (Cow)
e. cd. d. i. Li Ying Ho
cl. C01 School of Visual Arts

345_ Cultural Promotion Poster
t. C01 School of Visual Arts Poster
   Exhibition (Second to None)
e. cd. d. i. Joe Wong
cl. C01 School of Visual Arts

346_ Cultural Promotion Poster
t. C01 School of Visual Arts
   Poster Exhibition (Keep Going)
e. cd. d. Thomas Siu
cl. C01 School of Visual Arts

347_ Cultural Promotion Poster
t. 澳門藝穗節 2004
e. d. i. 周小良
cd. ad. 朱焯信
cl. IACM

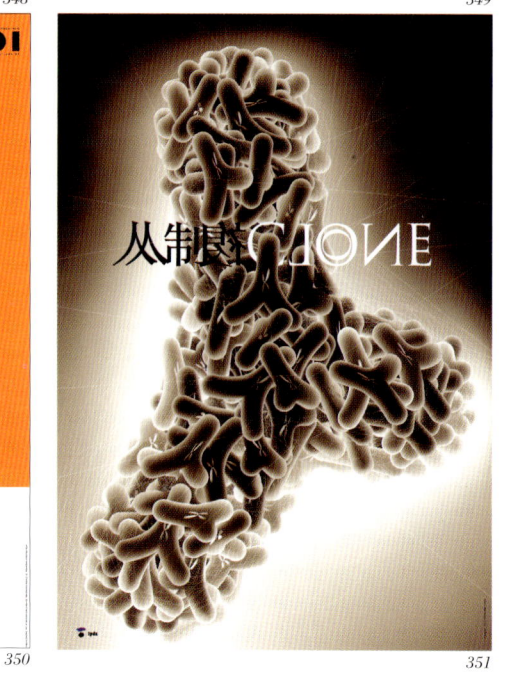

348_ *Thematic Poster*
t. C01 1st Anniversary (Apologize?)
e. Hippo Studio
dd. Chin-lee MA
ad. William S.C. HO
cl. C01 Shool of Visual Arts

349_ *Thematic Poster*
t. C01 1st Anniversary Poster
e. dd. ad. d. Eric Chan
i. Danny Ko
cl. C01 Shool of Visual Arts

350_ *Cultural Promotion Poster*
t. C01 School of Visual ArtsPoster
   Exhibition (The Road not Taken)
e. cd. d. Goldie Wong
cl. C01 School of Visual Art

351_ *Thematic Poster*
t. Cloned human (X/Y Chromosome)
e. cd. d. Chiu, Hsien-Nen
pp. Chart Design Ltd.
cl. TPDA

292

352_ Thematic Poster

t. Vanishing Animals
e. cd. d. Chiu, Hsien-Nen
pt. Chart Design Ltd.
cl. TPDA

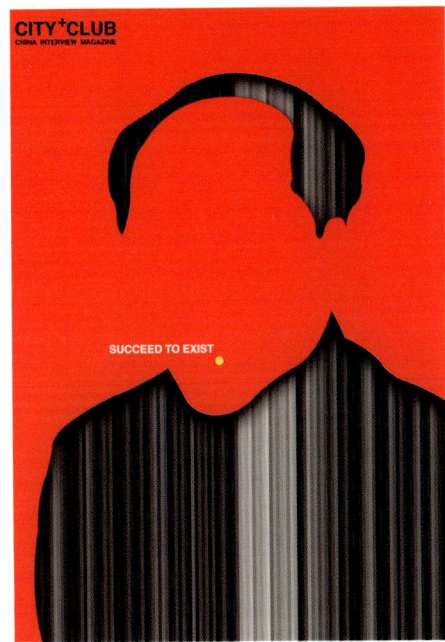

353_ Thematic Poster

t. Stop Starving
e. cd. ad. d. i. Michael Miller Yu
cs. Fiona Kwok
cl. The Chubu Creators Club, Japan

Excellent

354_ Commercial Poster

t. Succeed to Exist
e. Eric Cai Design Co.
cd. dd. ad. cw. Cai Shi Wei, Eric
d. Duan Lian, Zhang Xiao Ning
cl. City Club Magazine

VISUAL IDENTITY ビジュアル アイデンティティ 시각적 동일성 视觉形象系统

See the logo, identify the body - this section showcases exceptional visual identity systems and logos on stationery and other branded items.

Stationery
Visual Identity Systems
Logo

2004.12.3 fri -12.6 mon

6eauty of 6ooks
2004 · Beijing Book Designers Forum

6eauty of 6ooks
2004 · Beijing Book Designers Forum
The 6th Chinese Exhibition of Book Design

6eauty of 6ooks
2004 · Beijing Book Designers Forum
The 6th Chinese Exhibition of Book Design
2004.12.3 fri -12.6 mon
6eauty of 6ooks
2004 · Beijing Book Designers Forum
The 6th Chinese Exhibition of Book Design
2004.12.3 fri -12.6 mon

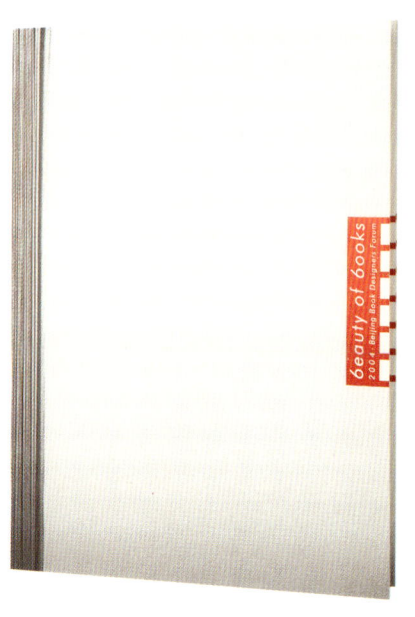

355

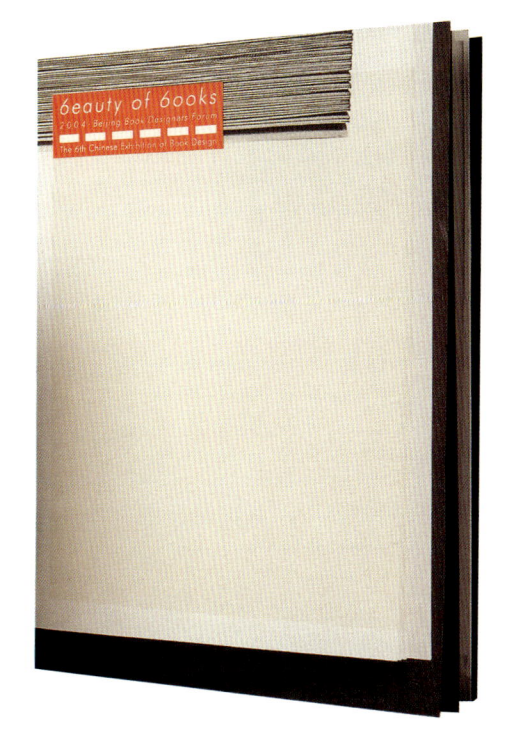

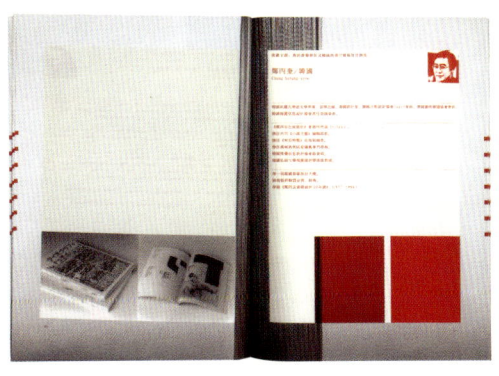

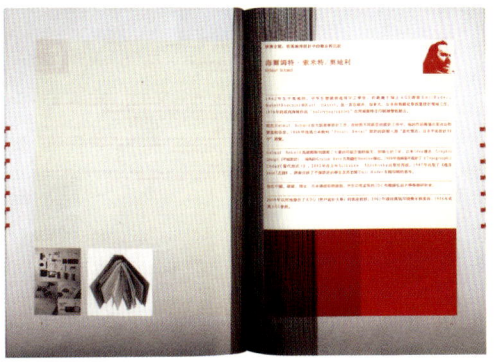

Silver

355_ Visual Identity Systems
t. Beauty of Books - 2004 Beijing Books Desingers Forum
e. cd. dd. ad. d. He Jun
cl. Organizing Committee of Beijing Books Desingers

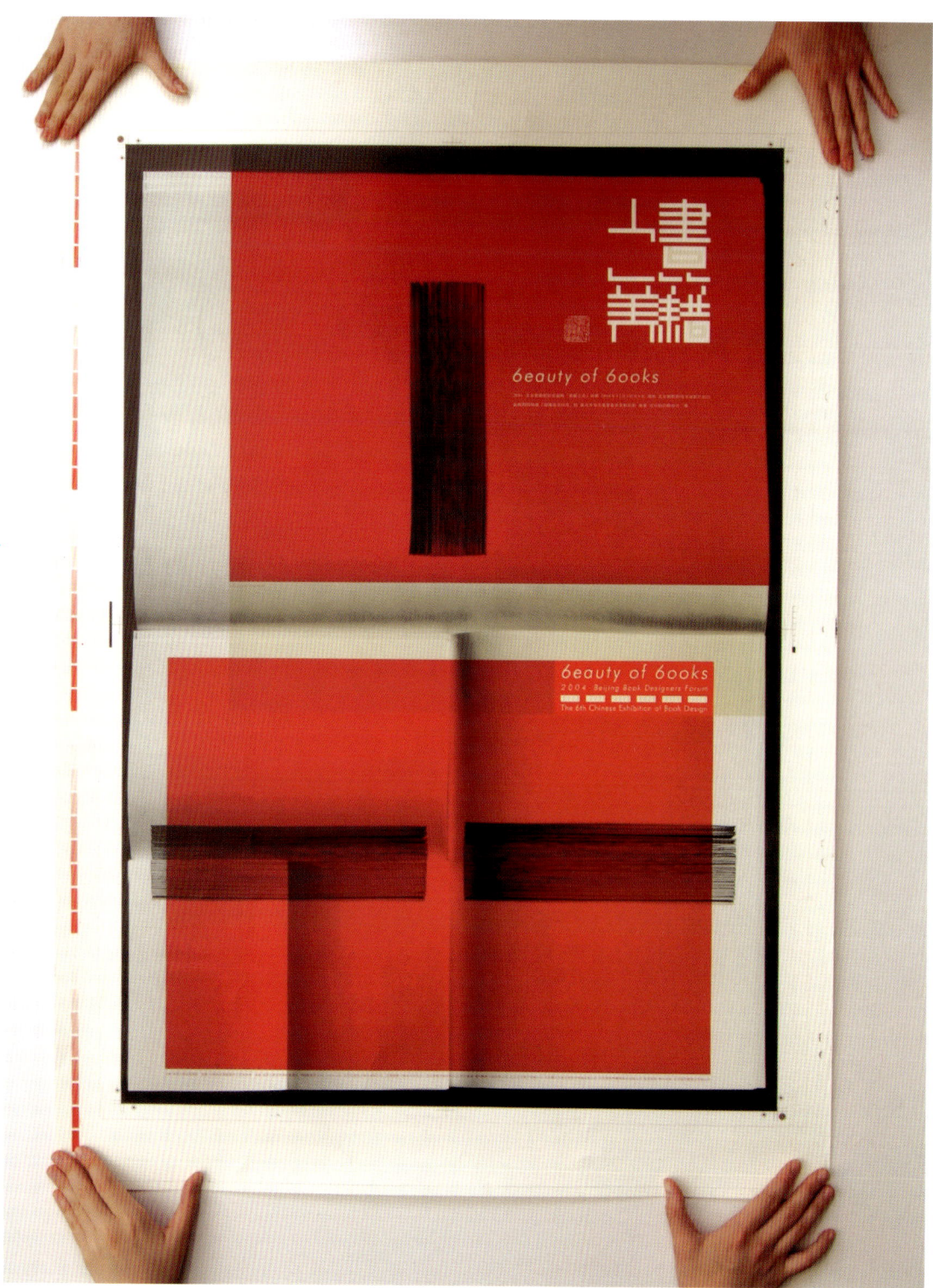

beauty of books

Bronze

356_ Visual Identity Systems
t. 2004 One Show China Festival Visual Design
e. Eric Cai Design Co.
cd. dd. Cai Shi Wei, Eric
ad. Ma Li Guo, Mike
d. Duan Lian, Zhang Xiao Ning
pt. JinGe Print Company
cl. One Show China

DD!

**Bravo
Hong Kong
Design**

Capturing New Business
for Hong Kong SMEs

好設計 展商機

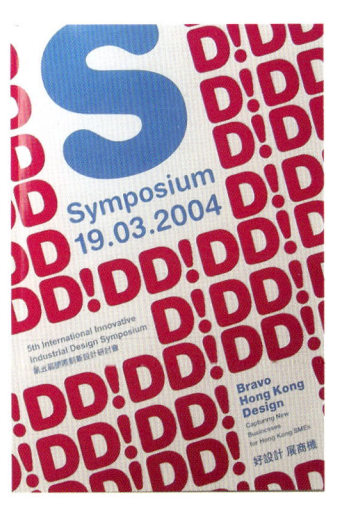

Bronze
357_ Visual Identity Systems
t. Bravo Hong Kong Design
e. CoDesign Ltd.
dd. Eddy Yu, Hung Lam
d. Teresa Hui
cl. Hong Kong Designers Association

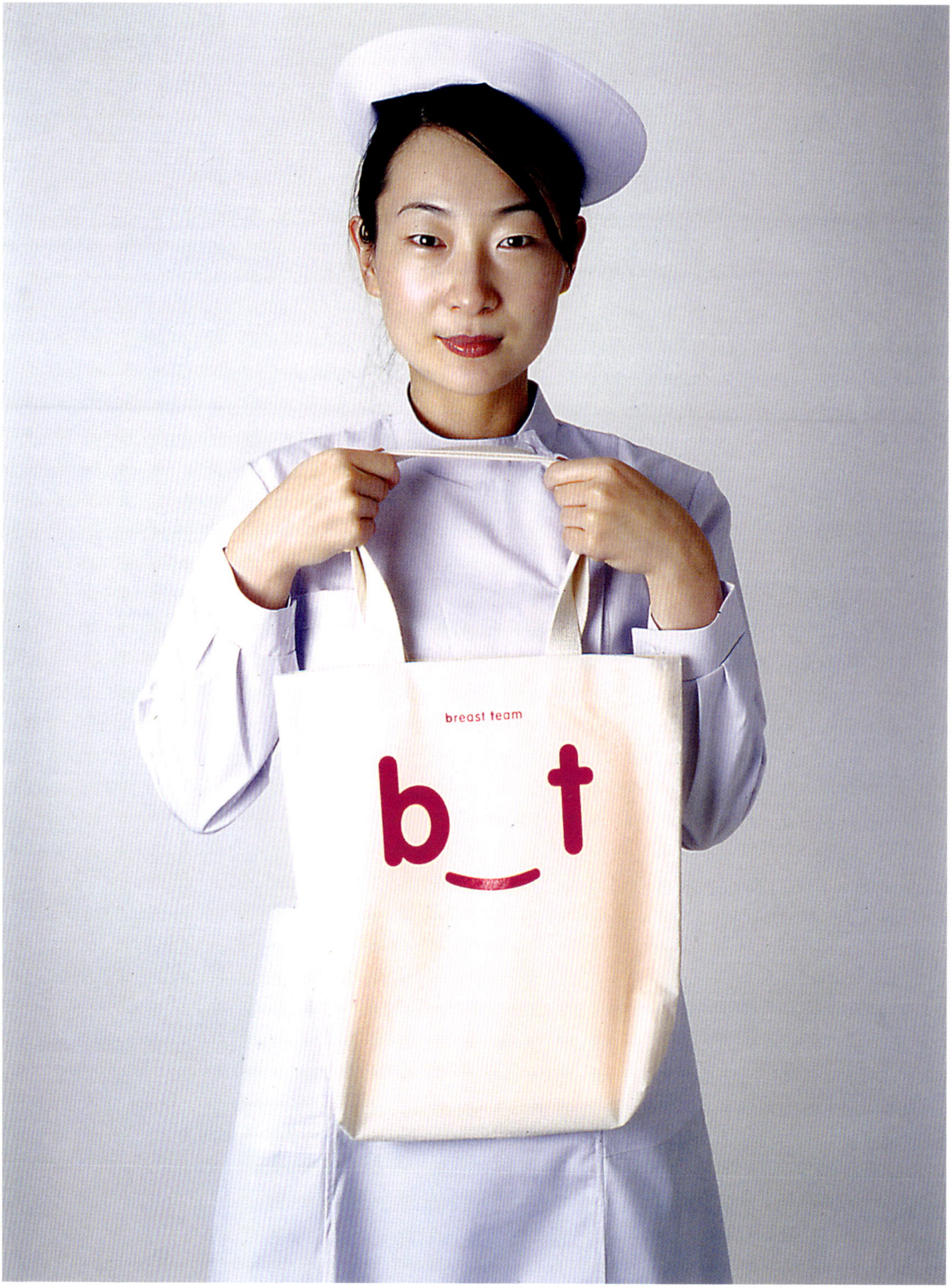
breast team
b_t

(b_t)

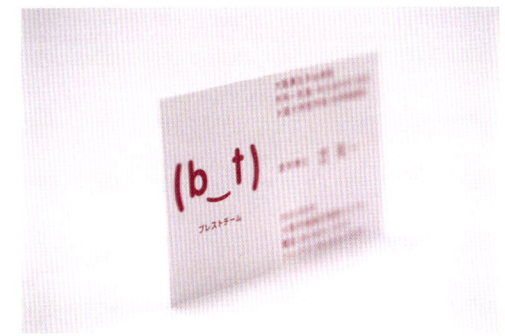

ブレストチーム

358

Bronze
358_ Visual Identity Systems
t. Breast Team
e. dd. ad. Shinnoske Sugisaki
cd. Reiko Kojima
d. Shinnoske Sugisaki, Okuno Chiaki
pt. Asahi Seihan Printing Co., Ltd.
cl. Osaka Welfare Pension Hospital

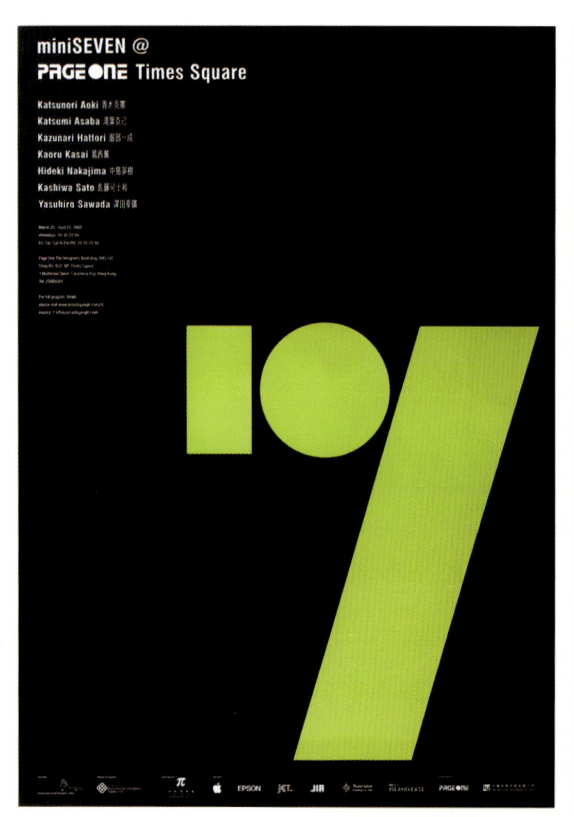

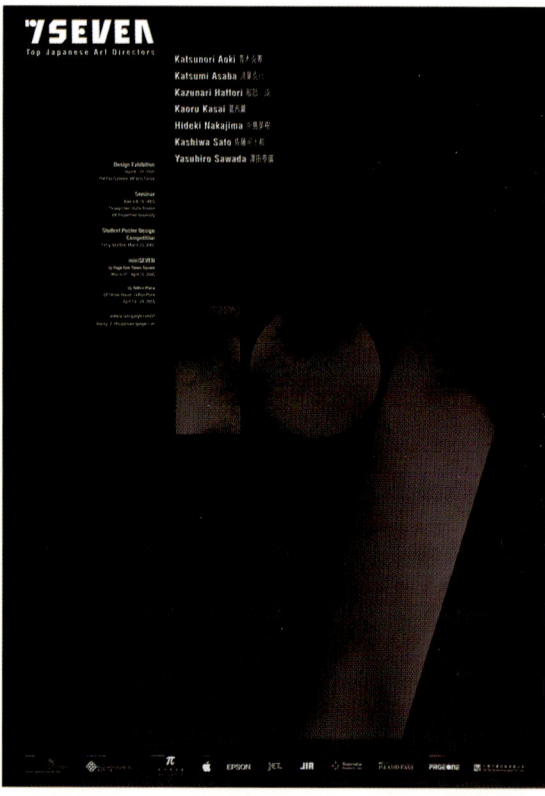

360

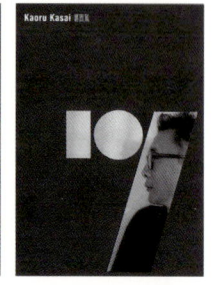

359

Bronze
359_ Visual Identity Systems
t. SEVEN
e. ad. d. Au Tak-shing, Benny
pt. Suncolor Printing Co., Ltd.
cl. Amazing Angle Design Consultants Ltd.

Excellent
360_ Logo
t. SEVEN
e. ad. d. Au Tak-shing, Benny
pt. Suncolor Printing Co., Ltd.
cl. Amazing Angle Design Consultants Ltd.

361_ Visual Identity Systems
t. Tiantu Sunny Advertising VI
e. cd. dd. ad. d. He Jun
p. Peng Yangjun
cl. Tiantu Sunny Advertising

362

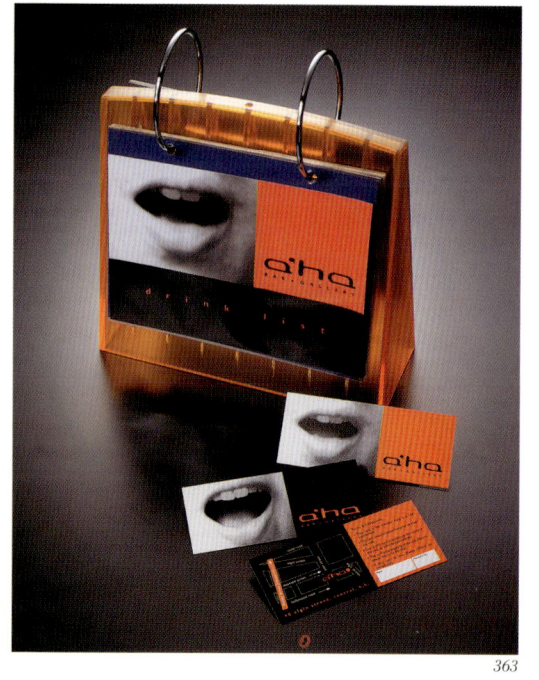

363

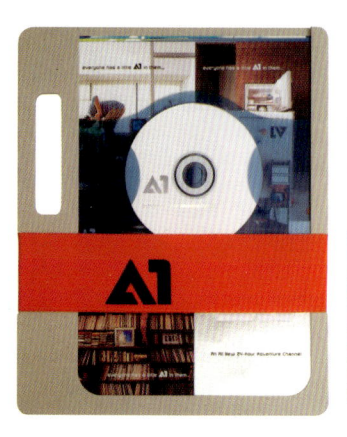

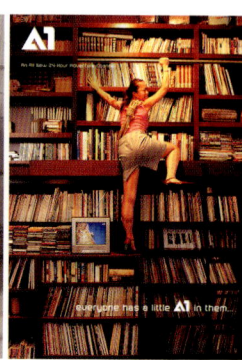

364

Excellent
364_ *Visual Identity Systems*
t. A1 Rebrand Campaign
e. STAR Group Ltd.
ad. Cat Lam Siu Hung
d. David Chan
p. Wher Law
pd. Koji Inamura
cl. National Geographic Channel - A1

362_ *Visual Identity Systems*
t. Phoenix New Programming 2004
e. STAR Group Ltd.
cd. Cat Lam Siu Hung
d. Cat Lam, Angel Tsang, Stephen So
pp. Winsome Ho
cl. Phoenix

363_ *Visual Identity Systems*
t. aha Bar & Gallery
e. aMaze Workshop
cd. Miranda Yiu
d. Franky Ng
p. Danny Chiu
cl. aha Bar & Gallery

365

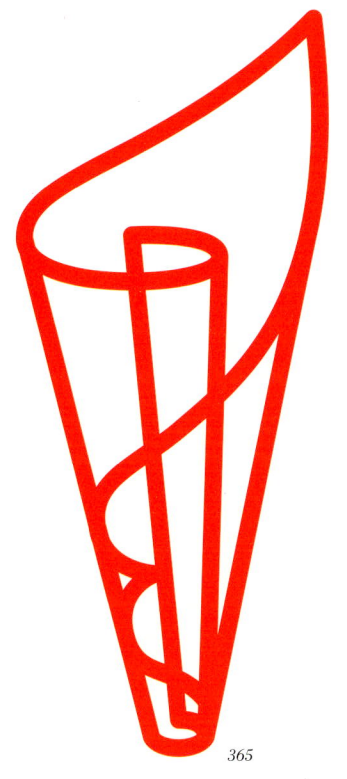

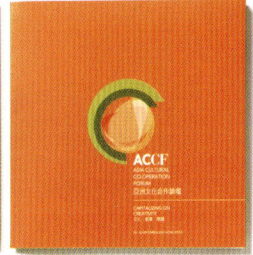

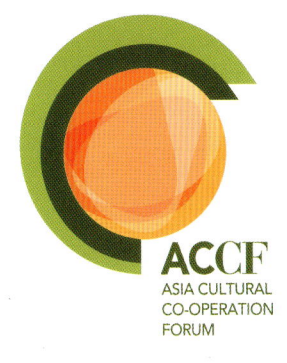

366

365_ Visual Identity Systems
t. Your Perfect Choice
e. Circle Design Ltd.
cd. Clement Yick
ad. d. Leung Wai Yin
p. CK Wong
cl. Polytrade Paper
  Corporation Ltd.

366_ Visual Identity Systems
t. Asia Cultural Co-operation Forum 2003
e. Tommy Li Design Workshop Ltd.
cd. Tommy Li
dd. Javin Mo
d. Thomas Siu, Tami Leung,
  Joshua Lau
cs. Lancy Chiu
cl. Home Affairs Department

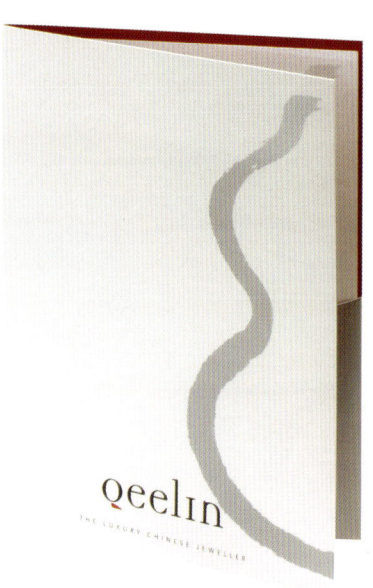

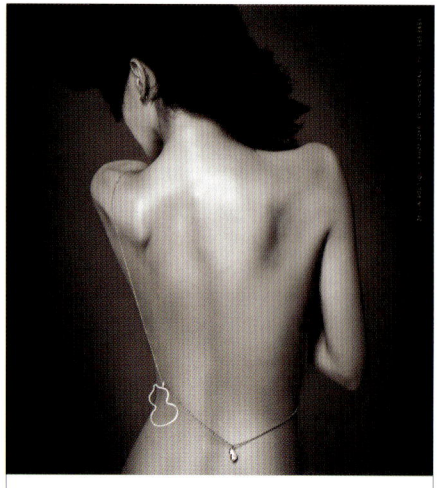

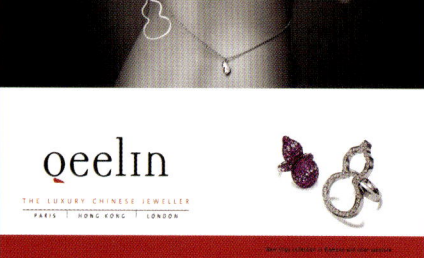

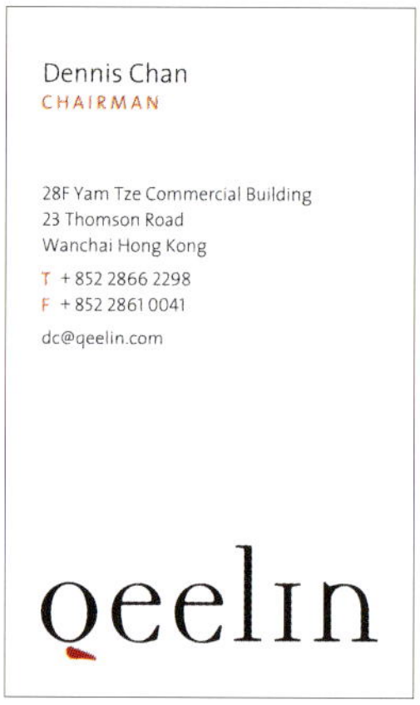

Excellent
367_ *Visual Identity Systems*
t. Qeelin
e. Alan Chan Design Company
dd. Alan Chan
d. Ting Man Yan
cs. Jessica Choi
cl. Qilin

东方 RED
方 MOON
亮

368_ *Visual Identity Systems*
t. Artists in the Neighbourhood Scheme III
e. ad. d. Au Tak-shing, Benny
pt. Suncolor Printing Co., Ltd.
cs. Candas Yeung
cl. Art Promotion Office

369_ *Visual Identity Systems*
t. Red Moon
e. Alan Chan Design Company
dd. Alan Chan
d. Peter Lo
cs. Candas Yeung
cl. Grand Hyatt Beijing, China

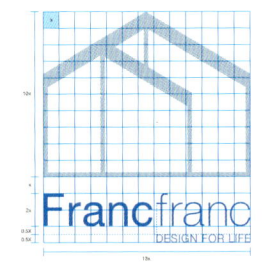

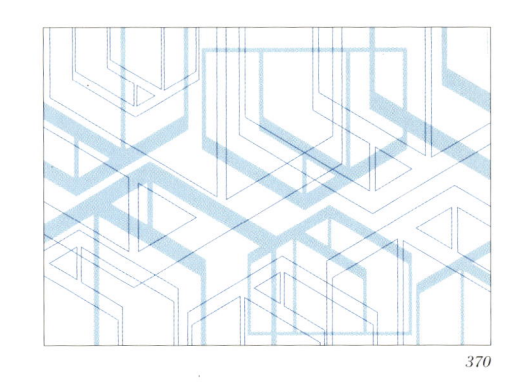

370_ Visual Identity Systems
t. Franc Franc
e. Alan Chan Design Company
dd. Alan Chan
d. Peter Lo, Ting Man Yan
cs. Jessica Choi
cl. BALS Hong Kong Ltd.

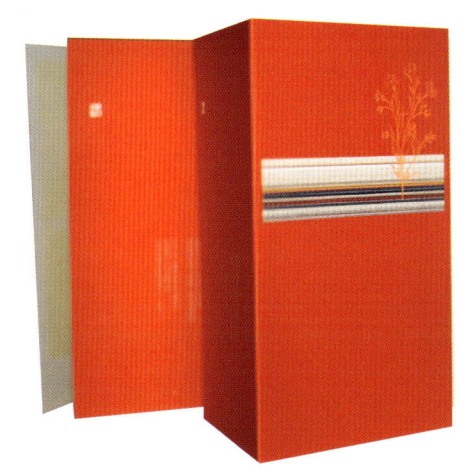

371_ Visual Identity Systems
t. Paper Living Show
e. ad. d. i. Au Tak-shing, Benny
p. Au Tak-shing, Benny
 Cheung Man-ho, Billy
pt. Suncolor Printing Co., Ltd.
cl. Tai Tak Takeo Fine Paper Co., Ltd.

PAGE ONE
BOOKSHOP @ TIMES SQUARE
EXPANSION
EYE ON NINE!
9/F PHASE TWO
NOW OPEN
Lane Crawford

9/F
EYE ON NINE!
PAGE ONE
TIMES SQUARE

EYE ON NINE!
PAGE ONE 9/F
BOOKSHOP @ TIMES SQUARE
11DEC2004 > GRAND OPENING
EYE ON NINE!

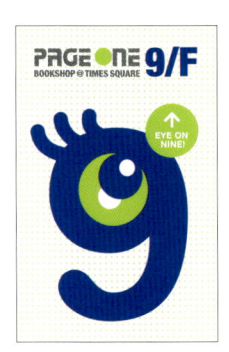

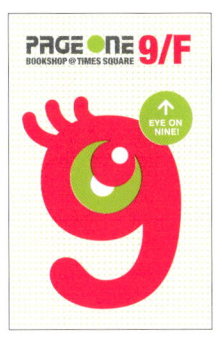

372_ Visual Identity Systems
t. Page One Designer Bookshop
Removal Promotion
e. CoDesign Ltd.
dd. Eddy Yu, Hung Lam
d. cw. Ken Lo
cl. Page One Designer Bookshop

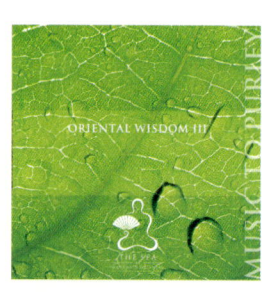

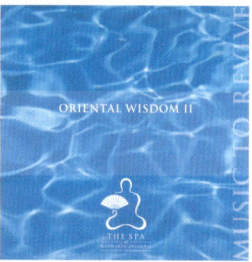

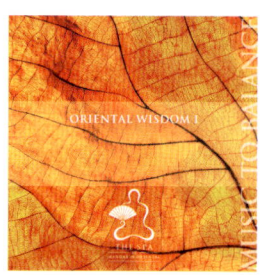

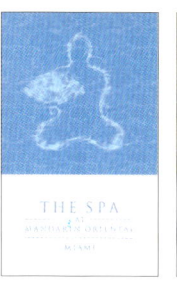

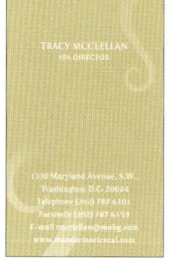

373_ *Visual Identity Systems*
t. The Spa at Mandarin Oriental
e. Alan Chan Design Company
dd. Alan Chan
d. Peter Lo, William Poon
cs. Jessica Choi
cl. Mandarin Oriental Hotel Group

374_ *Visual Identity Systems*
t. Aico
e. Kan & Lau Design Consultants
cd. Freeman Lau Siu Hong
ad. Freeman Lau Siu Hong, Ko Siu Hong
d. Freeman Lau Siu Hong, Ko Siu Hong, Garfield Chan
cl. Guangzhou Aico Baby & Kid Necessites Co., Ltd.

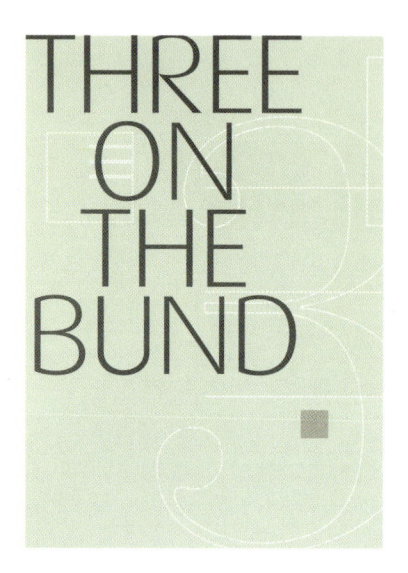

THREE ON THE BUND

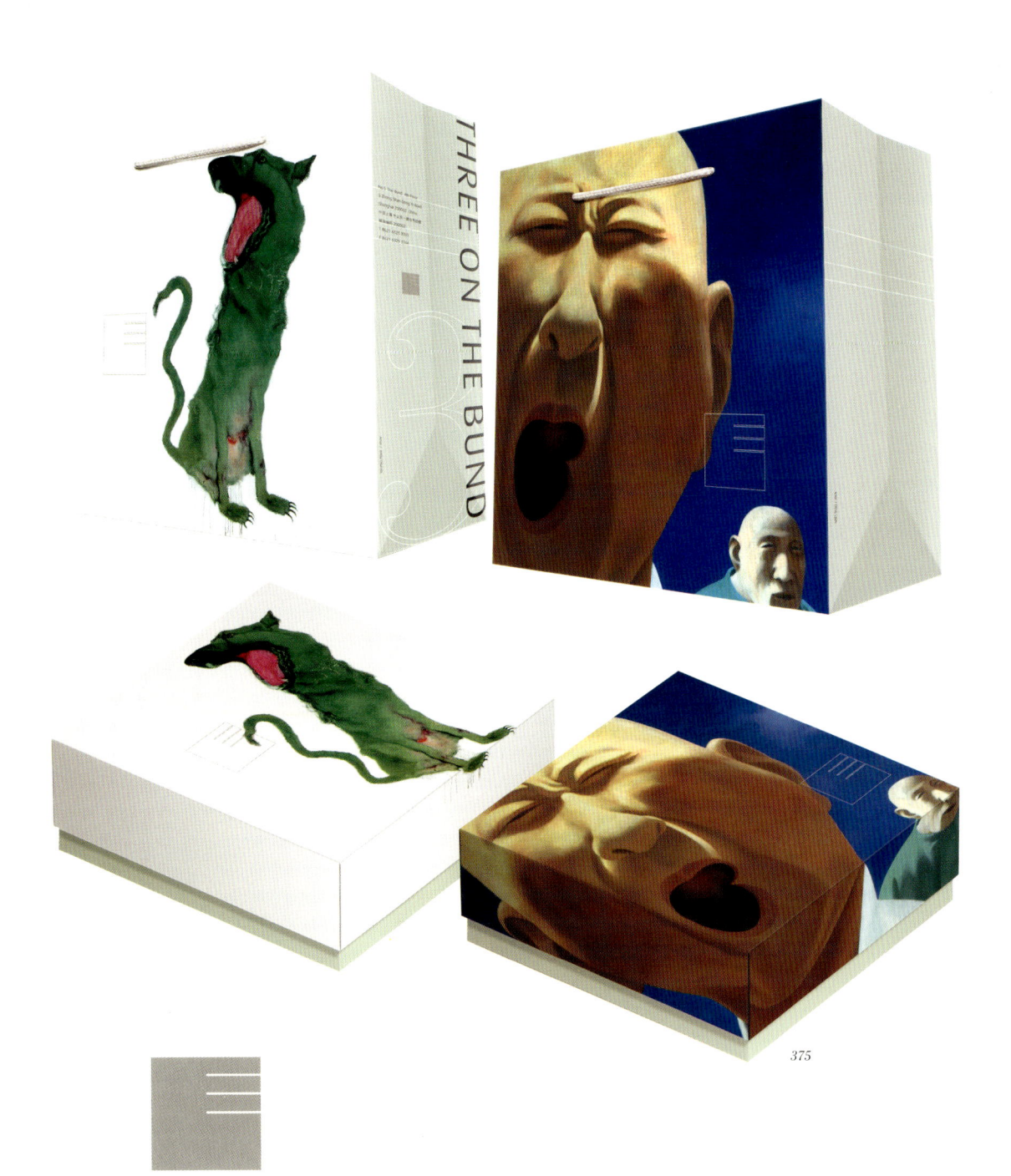

THREE ON THE BUND
外 | 滩 | 三 | 号

375_ *Visual Identity Systems*
t. Three on the Bund
e. Alan Chan Design Company
dd. Alan Chan
d. Peter Lo, Alvin Chan,
  Esther Ho, Winky Law
cs. Jessica Choi
cl. Shanghai GT Courtyard
  Cultural Investment Ltd.

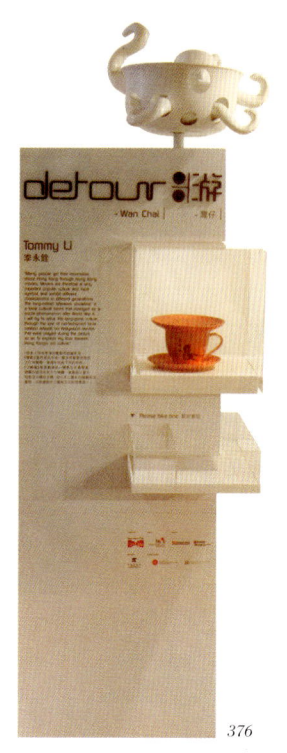

detour 设计游
- Wan Chai －灣仔

Excellent
376_ *Visual Identity Systems*
t. Detour - Wanchai
e. Tommy Li Design Workshop Ltd.
cd. Tommy Li
d. Joshua Lau
cs. Lancy Chiu
cl. Hong Kong Design Centre

377_ *Visual Identity Systems*
t. Fairwood
e. Alan Chan Design Company
dd. Alan Chan
d. Peter Lo
cs. Jessica Choi
cl. Fairwood Holdings Ltd, Hong Kong

simplybread
bread boutique

mixing   forming   tasting   bread boutique

378_ Packaging, Visual Identity Systems
t. Simplybread
e. Tommy Li Design Workshop Ltd.
cd. Tommy Li
d. Tami Leung
p. Larry Hou
cs. Lancy Chiu
cl. Maxim's Caterers Ltd.

380

379

Excellent
379_ Character Design
t. da dolce kid
e. Tommy Li Design Workshop Ltd.
cd. Tommy Li
dd. Choi Kim Hung
d. Tami Leung
cs. Lancy Chiu
cl. Fu Gar International Ltd.

380_ Visual Identity Systems
t. dadolce
e. Tommy Li Design Workshop Ltd.
cd. Tommy Li
dd. Choi Kim Hung
d. Tami Leung
p. Thomas Siu
cl. Fu Gar International Ltd.

381

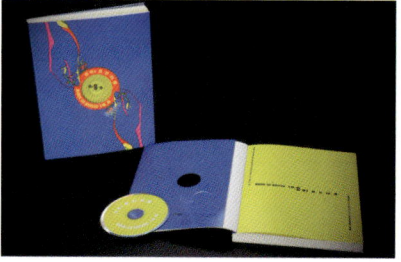

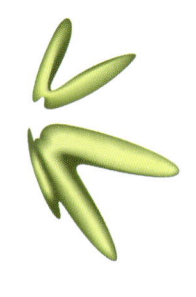

382  *383*

382_ *Visual Identity Systems*
t. CO1 Design 05 Show
   Visual Identity System
e. Paul Lam Design Associates
cd. Paul Lam
d. Cheng Kar Wai, Tequila Chan,
   Anissa Cheng, Patrick Chan,
   Queenie Shek, Wu Wai Hang
i. Patrick Chan
cp. Art Point Production
pt. Hoi Kwong Printing Co., Ltd.
cl. CO1 School of Visual Arts

383_ *Visual Identity Systems*
t. CO1 Design 04 Show
   Visual Identity System
e. Paul Lam Design Associates
cd. Paul Lam
d. Cheng Kar Wai, Tequila Chan,
   Anissa Cheng, Patrick Chan,
   Queenie Shek, Jacky Wan
i. Patrick Chan
cp. Art Point Production
pt. Hoi Kwong Printing Co., Ltd.
cl. CO1 School of Visual Arts

381_ *Visual Identity Systems*
t. Konew Financial Express
e. Tommy Li Design Workshop Ltd.
cd. Tommy Li
d. Thomas Siu, Choi Kim Hung,
   Joshua Lau
p. Danny Chiu
cs. Lancy Chiu
cl. Konew Financial Express

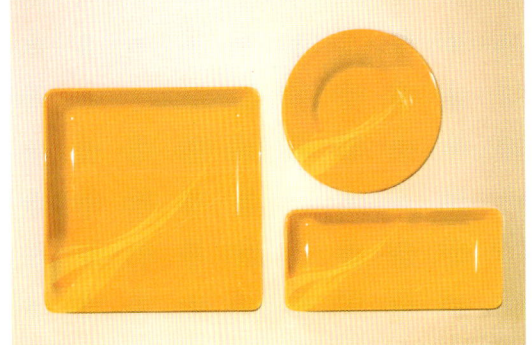

384_ *Visual Identity Systems*
t. 千燒百味
e. Tommy Li Design Workshop Ltd.
cd. Tommy Li
d. Joshua Lau, Thomas Siu
cs. Lancy Chiu
cl. Maxim's Caterers Ltd.

Bronze
385_ *Visual Identity Systems*
t. Arts Initiative Tokyo
e. ad. d. Masayoshi Kodaira
cl. Arts Initiative Tokyo

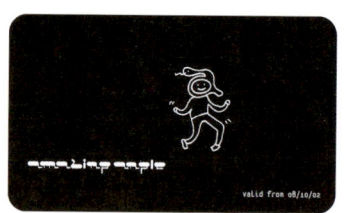

Excellent

386_ *Character Design*
t. Amazing Angle Design Consultants Ltd.
e. ad. d. i. Au Tak-shing, Benny
cl. Amazing Angle
  Design Consultants Ltd.

387_ *Character Design*
t. Amazing Angle Design Consultants Ltd.
e. ad. d. i. Au Tak-shing, Benny
cl. Amazing Angle
  Design Consultants Ltd.

Bronze

388_ *Stationery*
t. Amazing Angle Design Consultants Ltd.
e. ad. d. i. Au Tak-shing, Benny
pt. Suncolor Printing Ltd.
cl. Amazing Angle
  Design Consultants Ltd.

Excellent

389_ Stationery
- *t.* Hong Kong Designers Association Stationery
- *e. cd.* Eric Chan
- *d.* Eric Chan, Francis Lee
- *cl.* Hong Kong Designers Association

Excellent
390_ Stationery
t. Latentimage
e. d. Chung Man Wai
cl. Latentimage

391

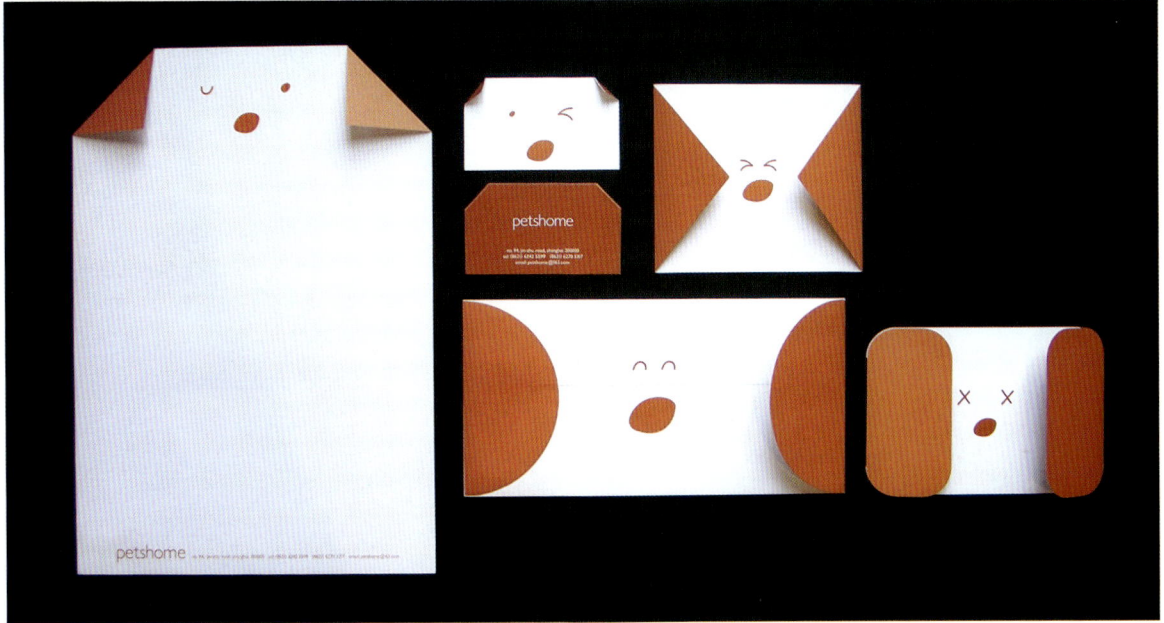

392

391_ Stationery

t. Egg Design
e. ad. d. i. Chung Chi Wing, Edward
cs. Chan Chi Ha, Grace
cl. Egg Design

392_ Stationery

t. Petshome Stationery
e. Leo Burnett Shanghai
cd. Ruth Lee, Dennis Ou
ad. d. Lemon Dao
cs. Eric Lee
pp. Jason Kong

393_ *Illustration, Logo, Packaging, Stationery,*
   Visual Identity Systems

t. Chi of Beauty
e. FCB Shanghai
cd. Poh Hwee Beng, Cetric Leung
dd. Cetric Leung
ad. *d*. *i*. Cetric Leung, Lee Pui Ho
cs. Wilmin Ha
pp. Lily Jin
cl. Natural Beauty

394_ Stationery
 t. Nex Branding design
 e. Nex Branding Design
 cd. Simon Siu
 ad. Simon Siu, Joseph Leung
 d. Joseph Leung
 cs. Fanny To, Cathy Cheung

395_ Stationery
 t. Personal Stationery
 e. SparKreative
 cd. Louis
 ad. Louis
 d. Louis, Rebecca
 i. cl. Loyiu

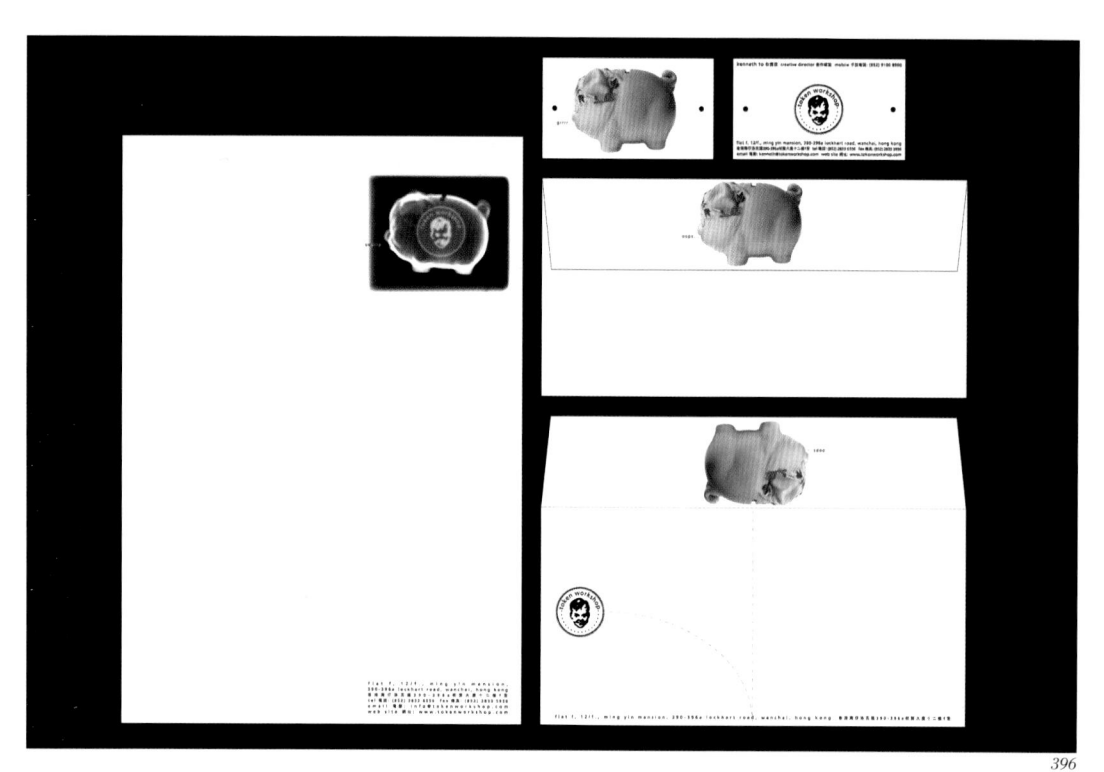

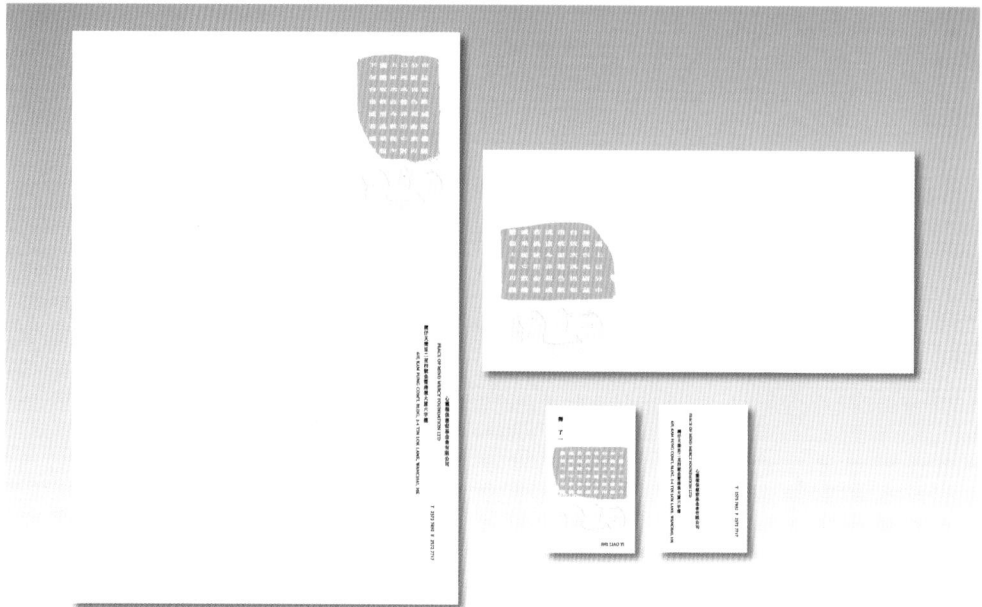

396_ Stationery
t. e. cl. Token Workshop
cd. ad. Kenneth To Po Keung
d. Danes Chong
p. Kwong Kwok Wing
cw. Stephinie Au
cp. Output Plus Workshop Ltd.
pt. Printhouse Workshop

397_ Stationery
t. Peace of Mind
  Mercy Foundation Ltd.
e. CoDesign Ltd.
dd. d. Hung Lam
pt. L. Force Printing Co., Ltd.
cl. Peace of Mind
  Mercy Foundation Ltd.

398_ Stationery

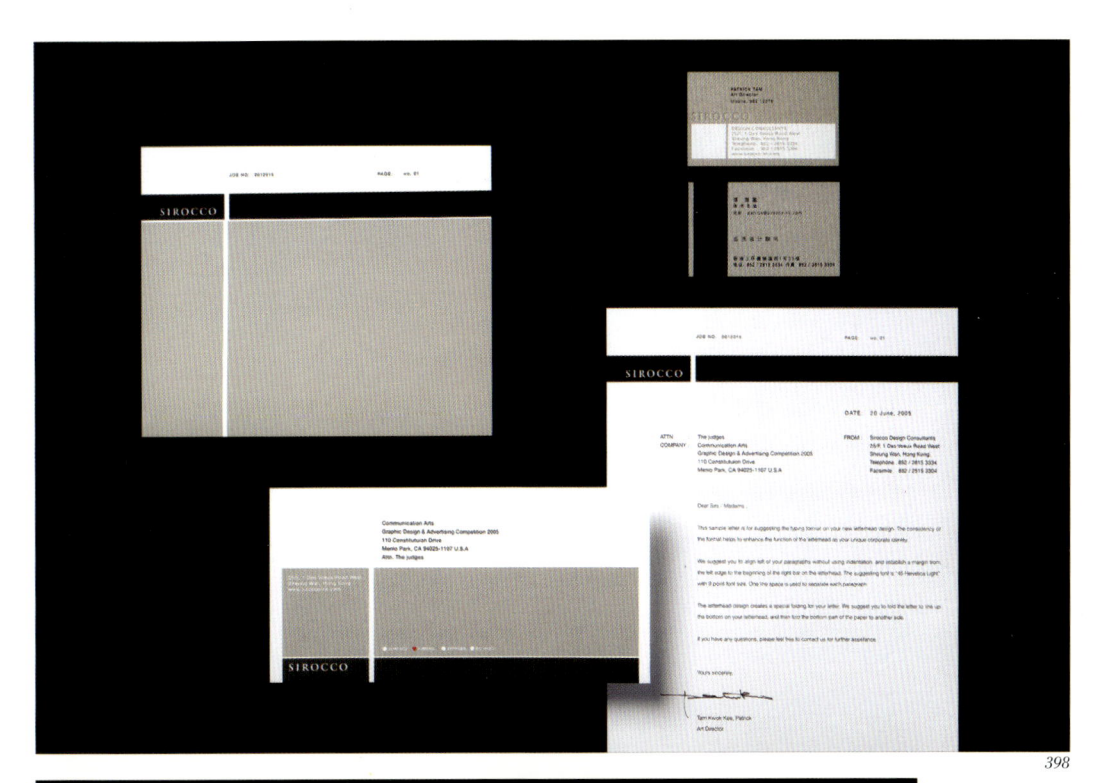

    t. Stationery
    e. Sirocco
    cd. ad. Patrick Tam Kwok Kee
    d. Ricky Lo
    pt. Suncolor Printing Co., Ltd.
    cl. Sirocco Design Consultants

399_ Stationery

    t. The Creative Cat
        Company Stationery
    e. ad. Eric Chan
    d. Francis Lee
    cl. The Creative Cat Company

401_ Stationery
t. Make-Up For Faces
e. Tommy Li Design Workshop Ltd.
cd. Tommy Li
d. Tami Leung
p. Danny Chiu
cs. Lancy Chiu
cl. Mae Von Makeup

400_ Stationery
t. Judy Mok
e. cd. ad. d. Hong Ko
cl. Judy Mok

*402_* Stationery

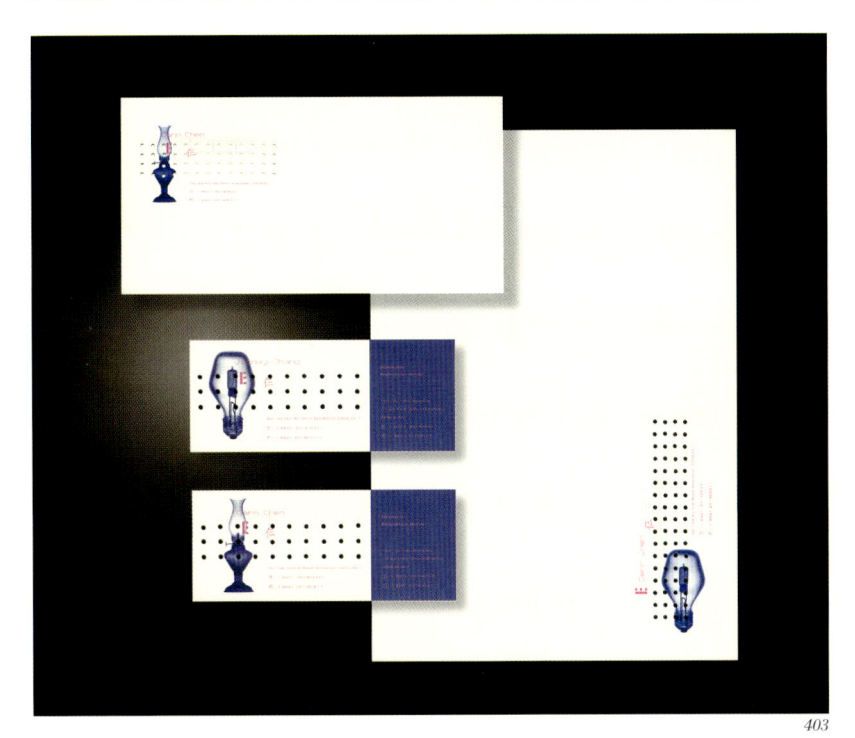

t. Sound and Pictures Ltd.
e. Sandy Choi Associates Ltd.
dd. Sandy Choi
d. Becky Yeung
cs. Angela Lee
pt. Strategic Press Company
cl. Sound and Pictures Ltd.

*403_* Stationery

t. E&E studio
e. cd. dd. ad. d. p. i. pp. Cann Chan
cw. Elrin
cl. E&E studio

404

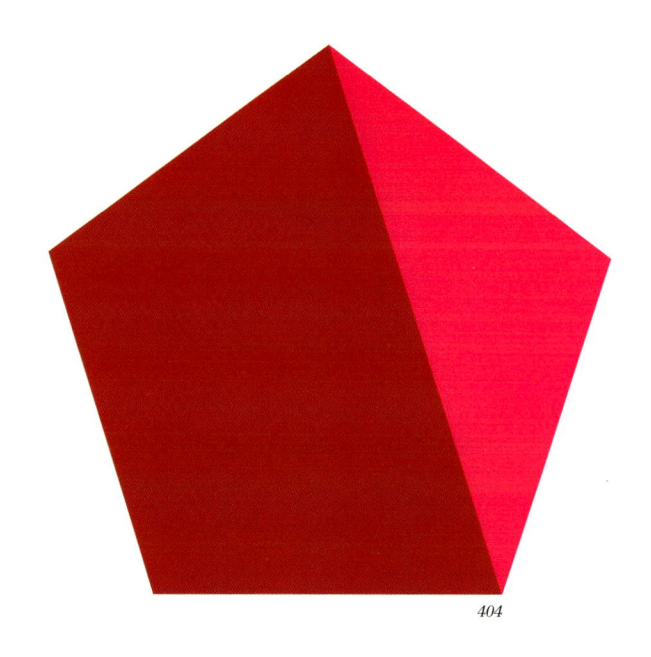

405

Bronze
404_ Logo
t. cl. 2D + 3D 視覺計畫所
e. cd. ad. d. 洪源

Excellent
405_ Logo
t. CS 24
e. 28aDesign
cd. dd. Leo Kwok
d. i. Si Keung
cl. CS 24

406_ Logo
t. Chair Play by Freeman Lau
e. cl. Kan & Lau Design Consultants
cd. ad. Freeman Lau Siu Hong
d. Freeman Lau Siu Hong, Vinci Fung

407_ Logo
t. Ulti
e. cl. Kan & Lau Design Consultants
cd. Freeman Lau Siu Hong
ad. Freeman Lau Siu Hong, Veronica Cheung
d. Freeman Lau Siu Hong, Wilson Heng
cl. Gold Peak Industries (Holdings) Ltd.

Excellent
408_ Logo
t. Y Angle
e. ad. d. Au Tak-shing, Benny
cl. Art Centre - Art School

Excellent
409_ Logo
t. Six Solo Shows
e. ad. d. Au Tak-shing, Benny
cl. miniminigallery

バウハウス

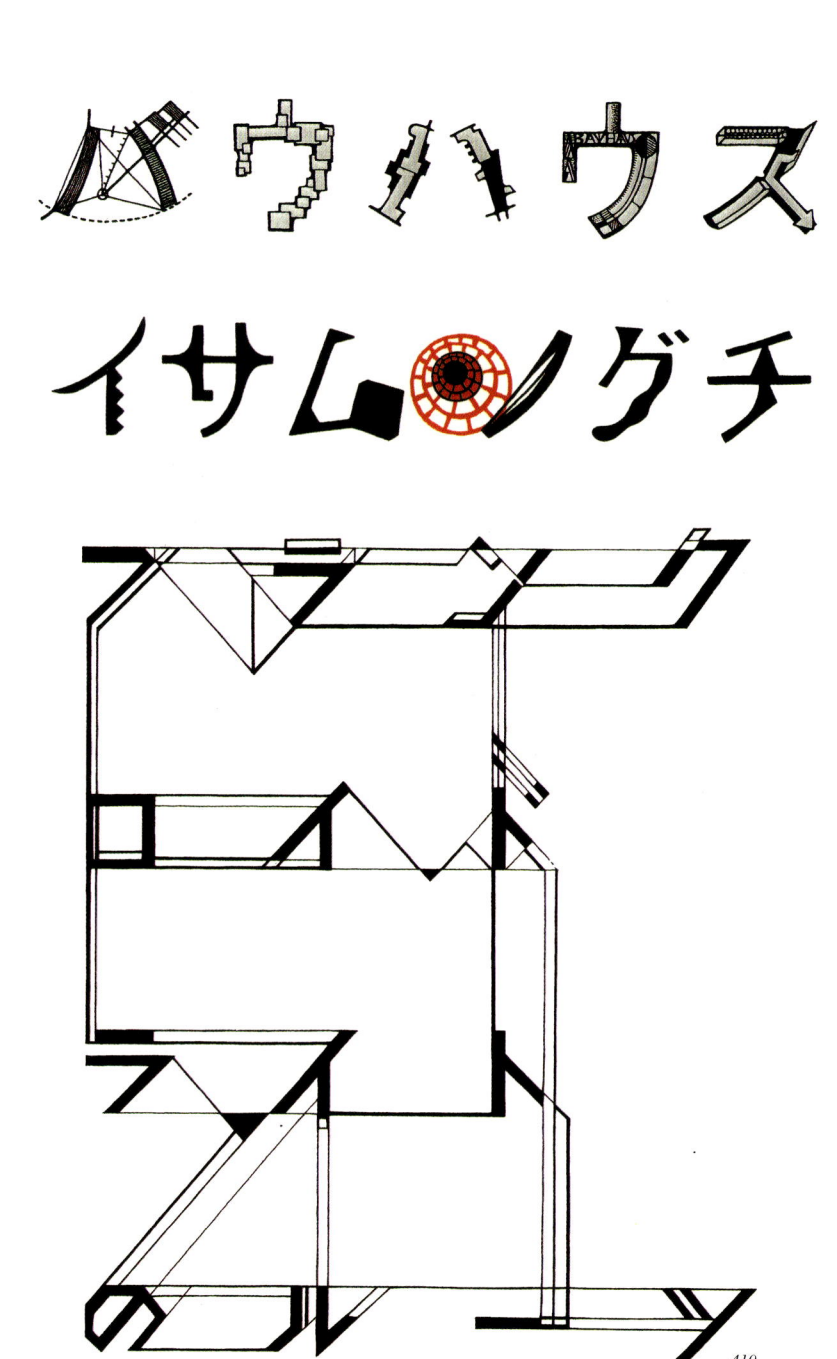

イサム・ノグチ

フランク・ロイド・ライトのグレーツ

410

411_ Logo
t. Huatai Insurance Co., Ltd.
e. Kan & Lau Design Consultants
cd. Freeman Lau Siu Hong
ad. d. Freeman Lau Siu Hong, Wilson Heng
cl. Burson-Marsteller

410_ Logo
t. X-Knowledge HOME
e. ad. d. Masayoshi Kodaira
i. Shigekiyuriko Yamane
cl. X-Knowledge Co., Ltd.

412_ Logo
t. Cattle Depot College
e. Kan & Lau Design Consultants
cd. ad. d. Freeman Lau Siu Hong
cl. Cattle Depot College

413_ Logo
t. HKDA Awards
e. cd. ad. Eric Chan
d. Eric Chan, Salie Lo
cl. Hong Kong Designers Association

414_ Logo
t. KCH
e. Nex Branding Design
dd. Joseph Leung
d. Joseph Leung, Fanny To
cs. Fanny To
cl. Kong Chung Hing Industrial Ltd.

415_ Logo
t. Too Art
e. ad. d. Heung Kin Fung, Alex
cl. Too Art

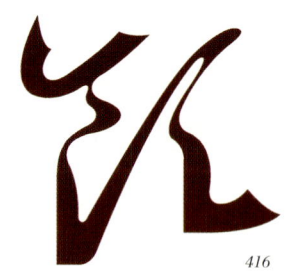

416_ Logo
t. Links Media Promotions
e. dd. ad. d. Lawrence Choy
cl. Links Media Promotions

417_ Logo
t. Ladybird Drama Club
e. cd. dd. ad. d.
Michael Miller Yu
cs. Fiona Kwok
cl. Ladybird Drama Club

418_ Logo
t. 中山市大涌紅木家具標誌
e. cd. dd. d. 洪衛

419_ Logo
t. CGST Logo
e. MI Design Ltd.
dd. ad. Kenneth Kwan
d. James Shum, Kenneth Kwan
cl. China Graduate School of Theology

420_ Logo
t. Hong Kong Tramways
   Centennial Celebration Logo
e. Step Design Consultants Ltd.
cd. Stephen Barry
ad. d. Eric Chan
cs. Sarina Ramjahn
cl. Hong Kong Tramways Ltd.

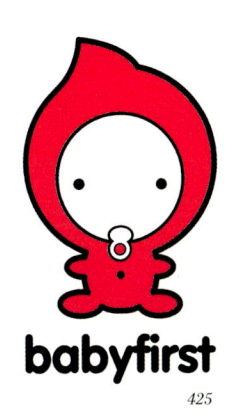

Excellent
421_ Logo
t. Superwoman Exhibition Logo
e. Sandy Choi Associates Ltd.
dd. Sandy Choi
d. Becky Yeung
cs. Angela Lee
cl. Hong Kong Poster League,
Hong Kong Heritage Museum

422_ Logo
Visual Identity Systems
t. R:fm2
e. Nex Branding Design
dd. d. Joseph Leung
cl. Welcome House

423_ Logo
t. Inspiration Global
e. Mad Studios
cd. dd. ad. d. Brian Lau
cl. Inspiration Global
SCM Consultants and Educators

424_ Logo
t. modelBASE
e. Ringo Hui
cd. dd. ad.
Ringo Hui, Ting Man Yan
d. cs. Ringo Hui
cl. modelBASE

425_ Logo
t. babyfirst
e. Mad Studios
cd. dd. Brian Lau
ad. d. Brian Lau,
Lilian Chan
cl. babyfirst

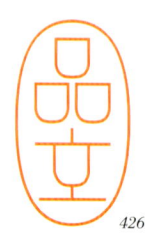

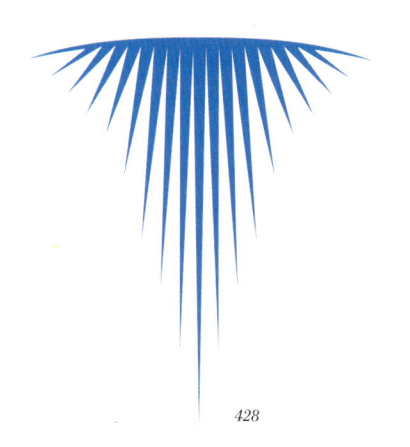

426_ Logo
t. BrandsNation
e. BrandsNation Limted
cd. dd. d. Eric Cheung
cl. BrandsNation Ltd.

427_ Logo
t. DOT
e. CoDesign Ltd.
dd. d. Eddy Yu
cl. Hoo Wah Co., Ltd.

428_ Logo
t. Guang Zhou Tian Xun
   Communication Equipment Co., Ltd.
e. CoDesign Ltd.
dd. Eddy Yu, Hung Lam
d. Teresa Hui
cl. Guang Zhou Tian Xun
    Communication Equipment Co., Ltd.

429_ Logo
t. FullStop
e. Marc & Chantal Design
cd. Chantal Rechaussat, Marc Cansier,
    Marc Brulhart
d. Esther Ho
cl. FullStop

340

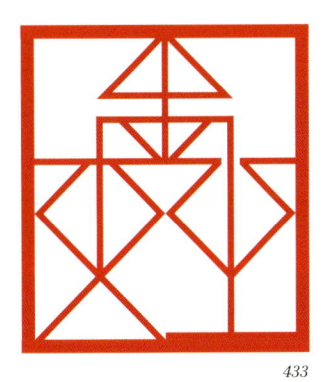

430_ Logo
t. 慧光科技股份有限公司
e. 袁世文

431_ Logos
t. 七聖公司
e. 袁世文

432_ Logos
t. 改變21服飾
e. cd. ad. d. 洪源
cl. 深圳東方新人商貿有限公司

433_ Logos
t. 金木水火土
e. Sirocco
cd. ad. Patrick Tam Kwok Kee
cl. Siu Lung & Co.

434_ Logo
t. Victor Onward
e. ingDesign
dd. ad. Chau So-hing
d. Kua Ling
cl. Victor Onward
　　Printing & Dyeing (HK) Co., Ltd.

435_ Logo
t. Hi!
e. Hippo Studio
dd. William SC Ho
ad. Chin-lee Ma
cs. Ivor Poon
cl. Polytrade Paper Corporation Ltd.

436_ Logo
t. Klong Bar & Grill
e. ingDesign
dd. ad. d. Chau So-hing
cl. Elite Concepts

437_ Logo
t. 5 + 2
e. Sirocco
cd. d. Patrick Tam, Kwok Kee
cl. 吳嘉兒福音工作坊

342

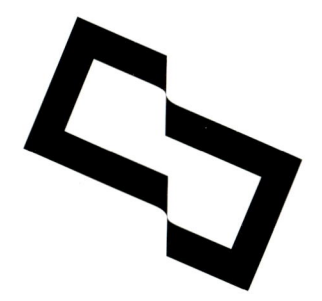

438_ Logo
t. LILLY
e. siDE Architects
cd. Colin Chan
dd. Pal Yu
d. Fung Chi Keung
i. Eric PT Lau
pp. siDE Architects
cl. Lilly Company Ltd.

439_ Logo
t. Lifestyle Asia 2004
e. Sandy Choi Associates Ltd.
dd. Sandy Choi
d. Goldie Wong, Lau Sui Wah
cs. Emma Chan
cl. Hong Kong Design Centre

440_ Logo
t. WEM Technology Ltd.
e. BrandsNation Limted
cd. dd. d. Eric Cheung
i. Roxy Lau
cl. WEM Technology Ltd.

441_ Logo
t. 玻璃公司標志
e. d. 杭春暉
cl. 北京漢頓玻璃有限公司

442_ Logo
t. O!
e. Token Workshop
cd. ad. d.
Kenneth To Po Keung
cl. Tai Loy Trading Company

443

444

445

443_ Logo
- *t.* MINDdesign Consultants Co., Ltd.
- *e. cd. dd. ad.* John Chui tak ming
- *d.* John Chui, Erik Yu
- *i. cw.* John Chui
- *cp.* High Qualitity Output Co.
- *cs. pp.cl.* MINDdesign Consultants Co., Ltd.

444_ Logo
- *t.* Longman Chinese Carnival Event Identity
- *e.* Charles Ng & Maxi Communications Ltd.
- *cd.* Charles Ng
- *dd.* Sang Chan
- *ad.* Charles Ng, Sang Chan
- *d.* Young Hoi Chun, Lukie Leung
- *cl.* Longman Hong Kong Education

445_ Logo
- *t.* Basheer Design Books Shop
- *e. ad.* Eric Chan
- *d.* Iris Yu
- *cl.* Basheer Design Books Shop

446_ Logo
t. Plastic Design Asia
e. cd. dd. ad. Angus Wong
d. Mark Ho-Man

447_ Logo
t. m-Finance
e. cd. ad. d. Hong Ko
d. Mark Ho-Man
cl. m - Finance Co., Ltd.

448_ Logo
t. MIIA
e. cd. ad. d. cw. John Chui, Tak Ming
i. Erik Yu
cs. pp. MINDdesign Consultants Co., Ltd.
cl. Macau Innovation & Invention Association

449_ Logo
t. Cheung Kong Graduate School
e. Alan Chan Design Company
dd. Alan Chan
d. Eddy Yu
cs. Candas Yeung
cl. Cheung Kong Graduates School

Bran**d****hild** *450*

Takahashi Design Hong Kong Limited *451*

Wah Man (HongKong) Publication Company
452

450_ Logo
t. Brandchild
e. cd. dd. ad. d. Michael Miller Yu
cl. Creation House Ltd.

451_ Logo
t. Takahashi Design
e. Takahashi Design Hong Kong Ltd.
ad. d. Shinnosuke Takahashi
cl. Takahashi Design Hong Kong Ltd.

452_ Logo
t. Wah Men (HongKong) Publication Company
e. cd. dd. ad. p. Shi Xiao Fan
cl. Wah Men (HongKong) Publication Company

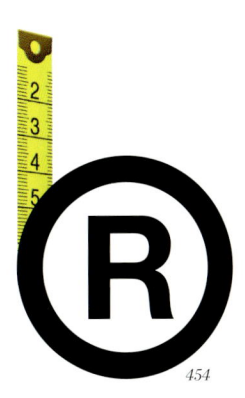

453_ Logo
t. 0 + C
e. Bliss Partners Int'l Ltd.
cd. Ivan Leung

454_ Logo
t. BrandTailor
e. cd. dd. ad. d. Michael Miller Yu
i. Henry Yu
cl. BrandTailor.com

455_ Logo
t. FAB
e. cd. dd. ad. MILKXHAKE.

456_ Logo
t. MILKXHAKE
e. ad. cl. MILKXHAKE

457_ Logo
t. Herpiin Space Plan & Design
e. 創型堂設計公司
cd. dd. ad. d. i. 林志嘉
cl. Herpiin Space Plan & Design

458_ Logo
t. 泳橡股份有限公司
e. cd. ad. d. 林宏澤

459_ Logo
t. PCCW CVG
e. Alan Chan Design Company
dd. Alan Chan
d. Karen Yeung
cs. Jessica Choi
cl. PCCW Ltd.

460_ Logo
t. World Source International Market Place Ltd.
e. cd. dd. ad. Angus Wong
d. Mark Ho-Man
cl. World Source International Market Place Ltd.

461_ Logo
t. SH2OP
e. cd. dd. ad. d. Michael Miller Yu
cs. Fiona Kwok
cl. Michaelsolve Ltd, Hong Kong

NEIGHBOR
CAFÉ
HOT TO GO
462

463

464

465

466

462_ *Logo*
t. Neighbor Café
e. cd. dd. 陳永基
ad. 陳永基，翁岱鍵
d. 翁岱鍵
cl. Neighbor Café

463_ *Logo*
t. Organic Certification
e. cd. Lau Siu Tsang
d. Irene, So Hoi-lam
cl. Hong Kong Organic
Resource Centre

464_ *Logo*
t. Young "揚"
e. cd. dd. ad. d. 郭宗軍
cl. Helena Yang

465_ *Logo*
t. 888 DATA.COM
e. cd. dd. ad. AngusWong
d. Mark Ho-Man
cl. 888 DATA.COM

466_ *Logo*
t. Wellness
e. Alan Chan Design Company
dd. Alan Chan
d. Peter Lo
cs. Candas Yeung
cl. Kolon Wellcare Co., Ltd.

467

468

469

470

471

467_ *Logo*

t. Bauhinia
e. Grey Wba HK Ltd.
cd. ad. David Lo
d. Liver Ng
cs. Kathy Wong
cl. The Hong Kong and China Gas Co., Ltd.

468_ *Logo*

t. DIVINE
e. cd. dd. ad. d. Michael Miller Yu
cl. Grasse Ltd., Paris

469_ *Logo*

t. Hong Kong : Hug & Kiss
e. ad. MILKXHAKE
cl. Hong Kong

470_ *Logo*

t. OLP Logo design
e. Ameba Design Ltd.
cd. dd. ad. d. Gideon Lai
cl. Sundar (H.K.) Ltd.

471_ *Logo*

t. PAO 80
e. Ameba Design Ltd.
cd. dd. ad. d. Gideon Lai
cl. The Association of Evangelical Free Churches of Hong Kong

472
473
474
475

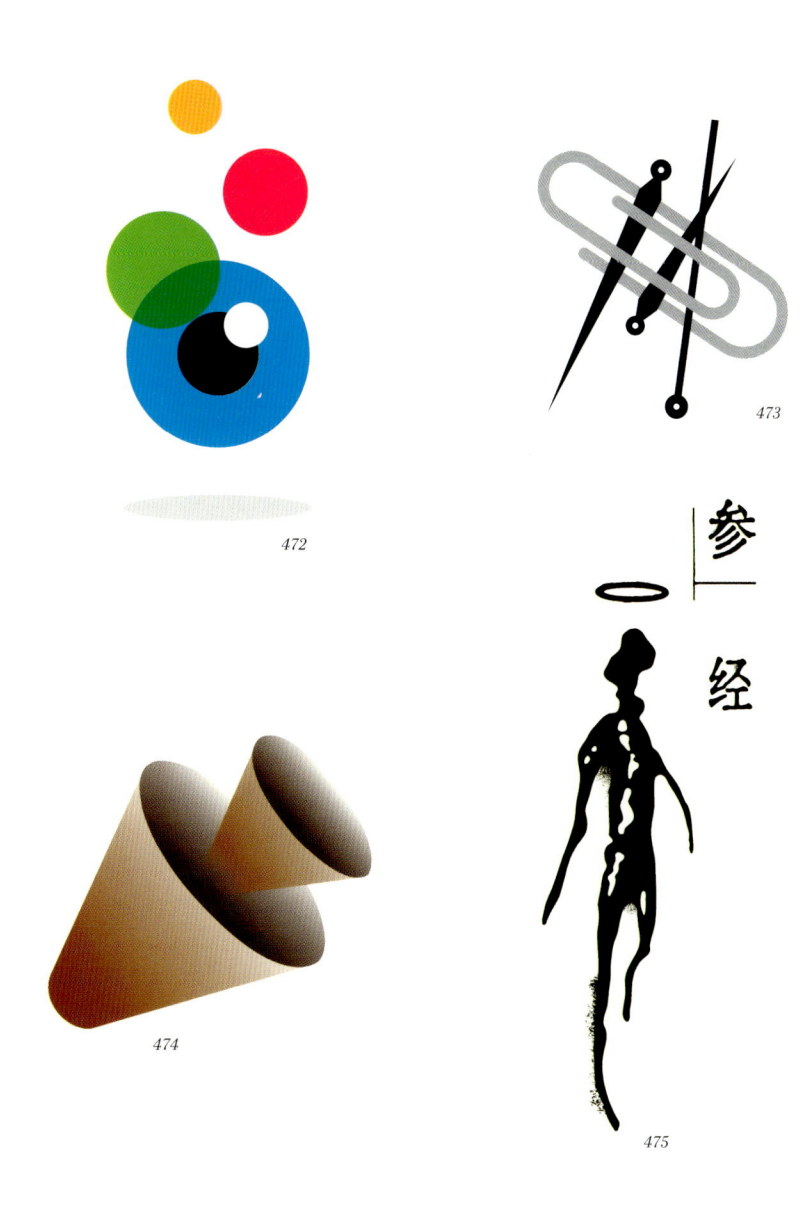

472_ Logo
t. Memento Workshop
e. d. Mark Ho Man
cl. Memento Production

473_ Logo
t. Memento Production
e. d. Mark Ho Man
cl. Memento Production

474_ Logo
t. Corporate Voice
e. Recipe
cd. dd. ad. Ben Lai
d. Ben Lai, Jennifer Deng, TS Chen
cl. Corporate Voice

475_ Logo
t. Saint Ginseng
e. Tommy Li Design Workshop Ltd.
cd. Tommy Li
d. Choi Kim Hung
cl. Saint Ginseng, Shanghai

ILLUSTRATION & PHOTOGRAPHY イラストと写真 도판과 사진 插图及摄影

Never underestimate the value of illustration and photography - this section highlights their outstanding role as fundamental elements of graphic design.

Illustration
Photography

Excellent
476_ Illustration
t. Finalazy Live
e. i. Michael Lau
cd. dd. d. Prodig
ad. Michael Lau, Prodig
pp. pt. Long Goal Company Ltd.
cl. Lazymuthafucka

finalazylive

presented by aroom production 2003

15/16 Aug 03

Painting by Michael Lau

atsui Branch 1-9 Cameron Lane Kowloon Tel : 2723 9932 /
el : 2519 0238 double - park Shop 37, LG/F Slivercord 30
useway Bay HK Tel: 2831 0890   Any patrons under 18 years old must be accompanied by an adult guardian 十八歲以下人仕需由成年人陪同方可進入

澳門賽馬會 MACAU JOCKEY CLUB double-park TOM LEE Music roxy PLAYFORD

Sound & Lighting by A.H.M. ENGINEERING CO., LTD   Produce by John Y   Painting by Michael Lau   crazysmiles co.

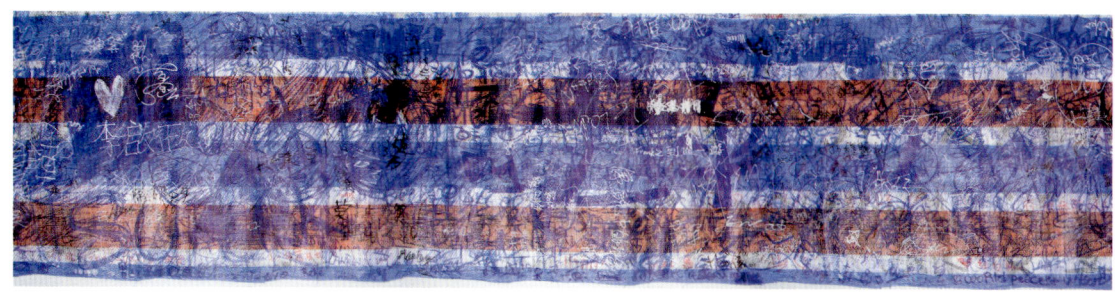

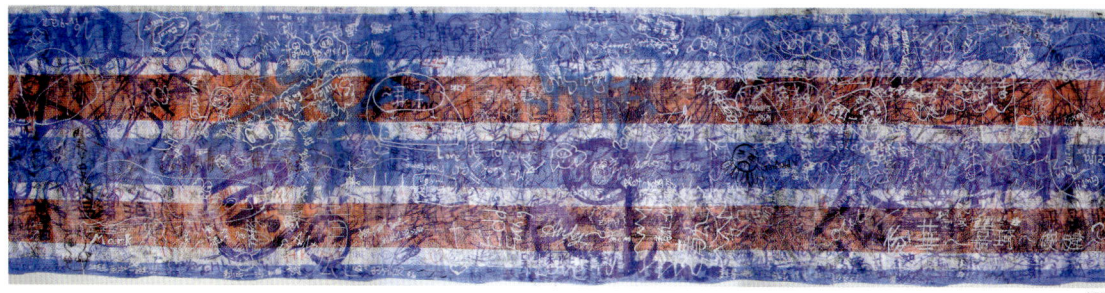

Bronze
477_ Illustration
t. R.W.B Exhibition - In Search of My Own Attitude
e. Kan & Lau Design Consultants
cd. ad. d. Kan Tai-keung
i. Kan Tai-keung, Thousands of Audience
cl. Hong Kong Heritage Museum

478

Excellent
478_ Illustration
t. Book Festival
e. Lau Siu Tsang
cd. d. i. Benny, Lau Siu-tsang
cl. Bbluesky

Excellent
479_ Illustration
t. Shanghai 1972
e. cd. i. Michael Kwong
cl. Spectrum

480_ Illustration
t. Socks Heaven
e. Lau Siu Tsang
cd. i. Benny, Lau Siu Tsang
cl. MCCM Creations

Excellent
481_ Illustration
t. Viva - Hong Kong
cd. ad. d. i. Sky Liu
cp. pp. dp. pt cl. Viva-Hong Kong Development Ltd.

482

482_ Editorial
- *t.* C01 Design 03 Show (C01 設計○三展)
- *e.* Paul Lam Design Associates
- *cd.* Paul Lam, Cheng Kar Wai
- *ad.* Cheng Kar Wai
- *d.* Cheng Kar Wai, Patrick Chan, Queenie Shek, B Wong, Landre Chiu
- *i.* Cheng Kar Wai, Patrick Chan, B Wong
- *cp.* Art Point Production
- *pt.* Hoi Kwong Printing Co., Ltd.
- *cl.* C01 School of Visual Arts

482_ Illustration
- *t.* C01 Design 03 Show
- *e. dd.* Cheng Kar Wai
- *cd.* Cheng Kar Wai, Paul Lam
- *i.* Cheng Kar Wai, Pui Chan, B Wong
- *cl.* C01 School of Visual Arts

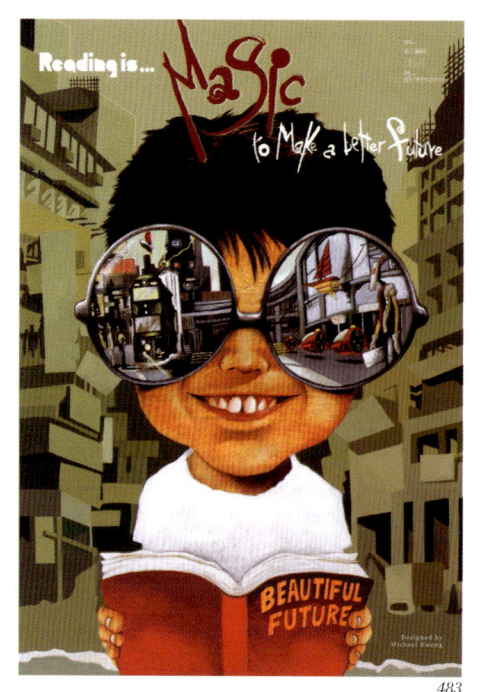

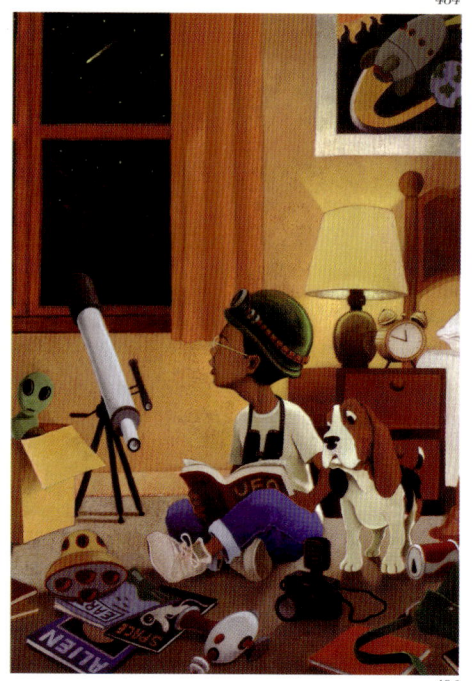

483_ Illustration
t. Reading is ...
e. cd. d. i. Michael Kwong
pp. Joint Publishing Co., Ltd.

484_ Illustration
t. Ganhdi
e. cd. i. Michael Kwong

485_ Illustration
t. 3p in Breakthrough
e. ad. d. i. Mok Wing Hung
cl. Breakthrough, U-plus

486_ Illustration
t. Wishing to the Star
e. cd. i. Michael Kwong

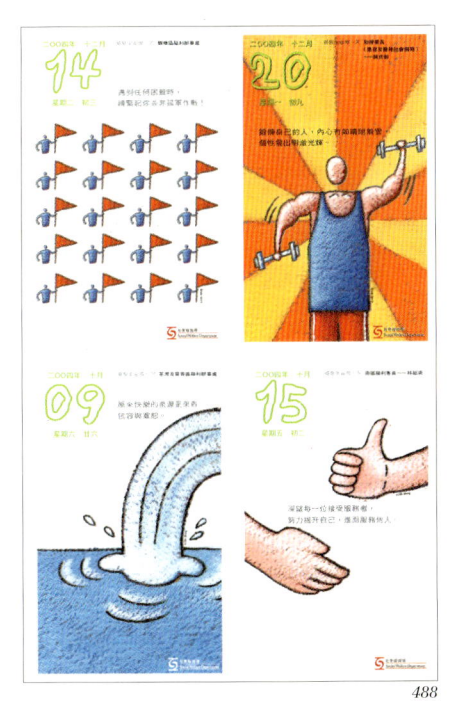

Excellent

487_ *Illustration*
t. 香料愛琴海
e. i. Wang Tsen
cp. 台灣彩色製版印刷公司
pp. 媽媽咪呀美食誌
pt. 紅藍彩藝印刷股份有限公司
cl. 時報週刊股份有限公司

488_ *Illustration*
t. 凝聚生命每一天
e. Bezalel Design Communication
ad. i. Ice Lam Siu Bing
cl. Social Welfare Department

489_ *Illustration*
t. Chinese Character
e. ad. i. Lawrence Choy
cl. Sharp & Fortune Management Co., Ltd.

Bronze
490_ Photography
t. Photographs Billy Cheung + Benny Au
e. Au Tak-shing, Benny
p. Billy Cheung, Benny Au
cl. miniminigallery

491

Bronze
491_ Photography
t. Paper Living Show
e. Au Tak-shing, Benny
p. Billy Cheung, Benny Au
cl. Tai Tak Takeo Fine Paper Co., Ltd.

493_ Photography
t. Supasoft
e. Lester Lee Photo Workshop
cd. Timothy Chan, Ming Chan
ad. Dennis Mak, Mandy Ng, Timothy Li
p. Lester Lee
i. Henry Chan
cw. Wilson Ang
cl. Freeway Communications Ltd.

494_ Photography
t. MYOB - Listen Immediately
e. Lau Kwok Tim
cd. Ming Sai
ad. Tony Mak
p. Lau Kwok Tim
cl. MK2 Communications Ltd.

495_ Photography
t. Visual Dynamic
e. Lester Lee Photo Workshop
d. Eric Chan
p. Lester Lee
pp. Gulliver White
cl. Hong Kong Heritage Museum

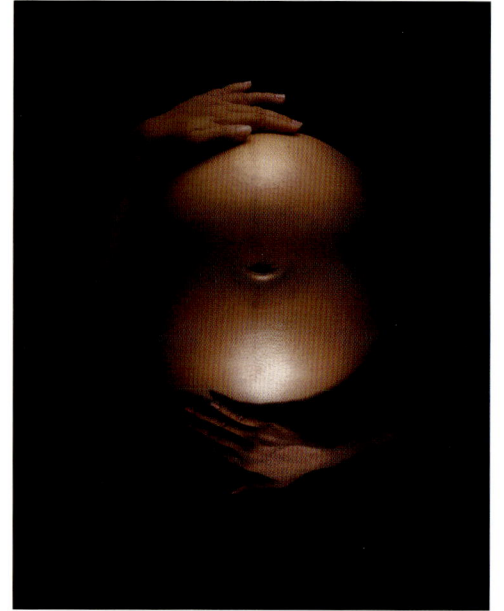

Excellent
492_ Photography
t. Moments In China - Market Hawker
e. ad. p. Lau Kwok Tim
cl. HKIPP

366

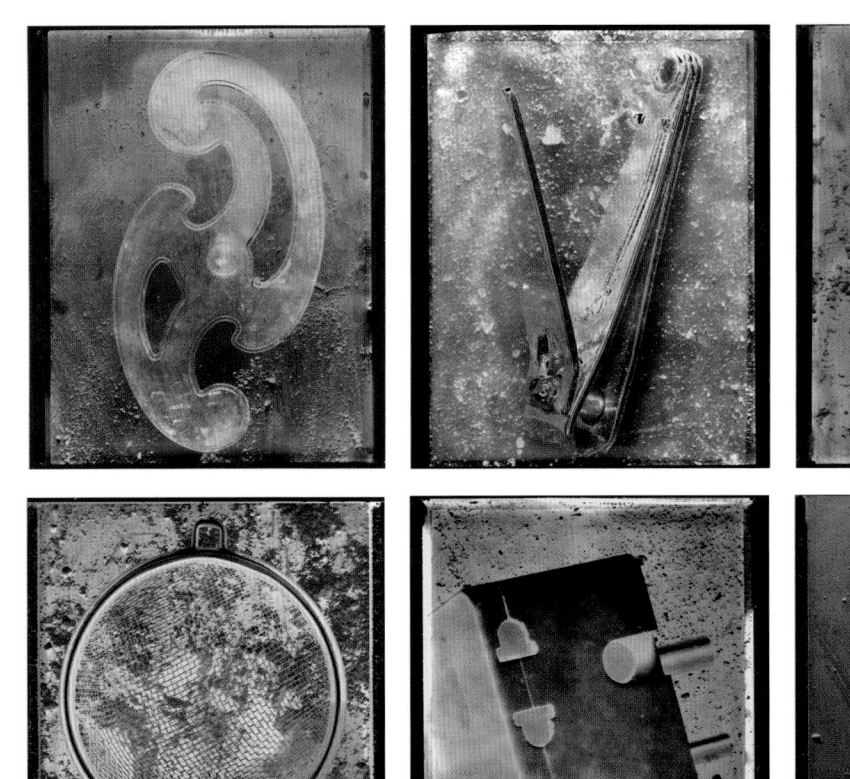

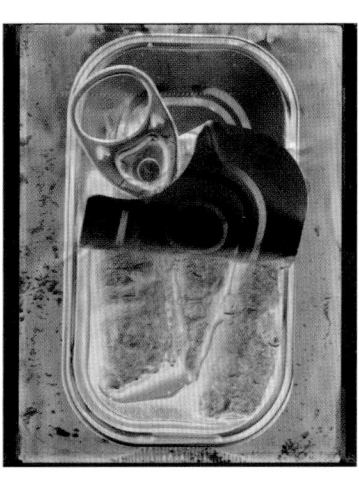

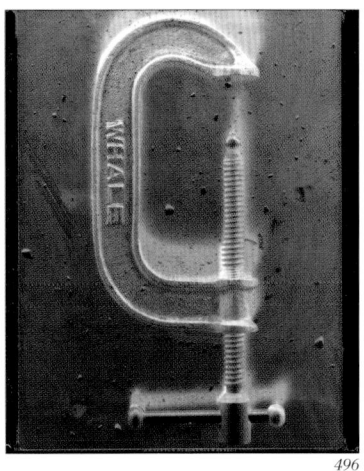

496_ *Photography*
t. Inside Out
e. cd. dd. ad. Angus Wong
d. Mark Ho-Man
p. Lester Lee

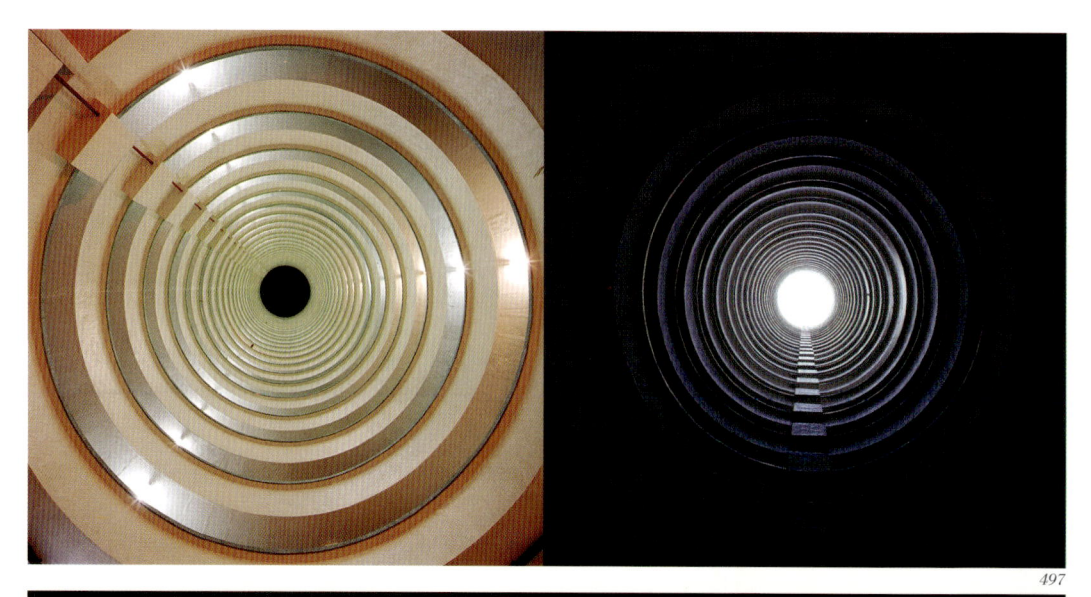

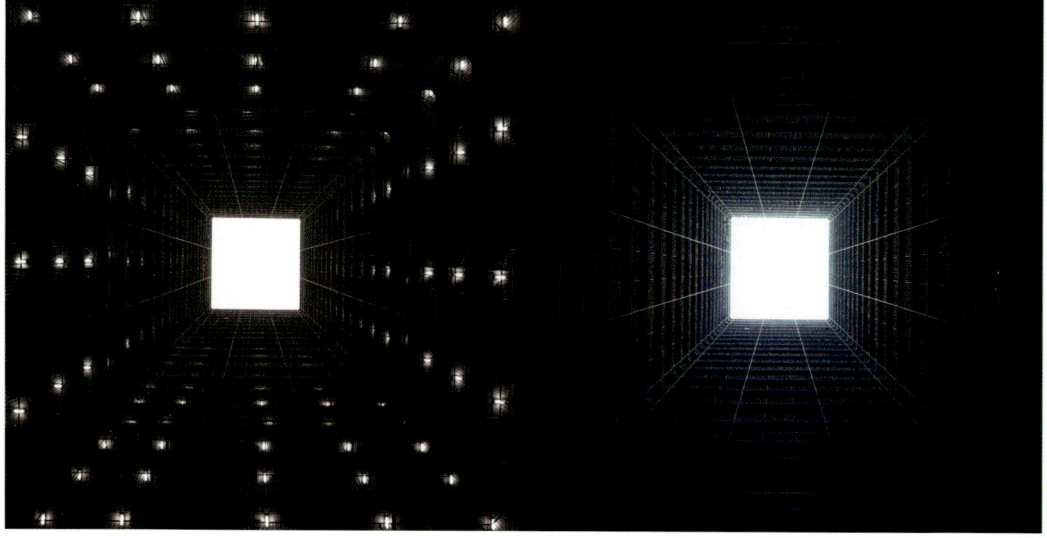

497_ Photography
t. Imperfect Matrix
e. Poon Chee Kin Albert

498_ Photography
t. From Dusk Till Dawn
e. Poon Chee Kin Albert

499

499_ Photography
t. Take A Break
e. Farm Design Consultant
ad. p. Siu Ming Fung

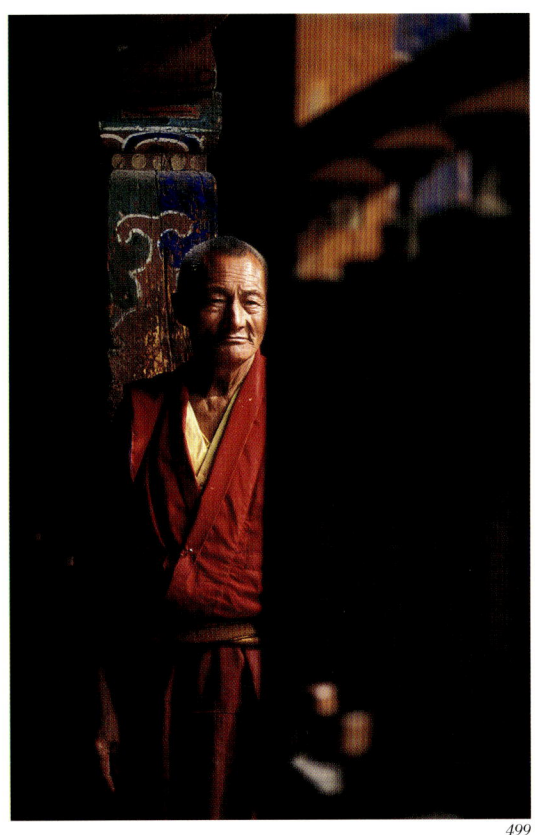

CHARACTER DESIGN フィギアとキャラクター
외모와 성격 模型人偶及造像

Characters personify the message, product or service; figurines give them a palpable form. This section exhibits the many expressive faces of character design.

Figure & Character

Bronze
500_ Character Design
t. Crazychildren Series 1
e. cd. dd. ad. d. Michael Lau
cl. Crazysmiles Co. Ltd.

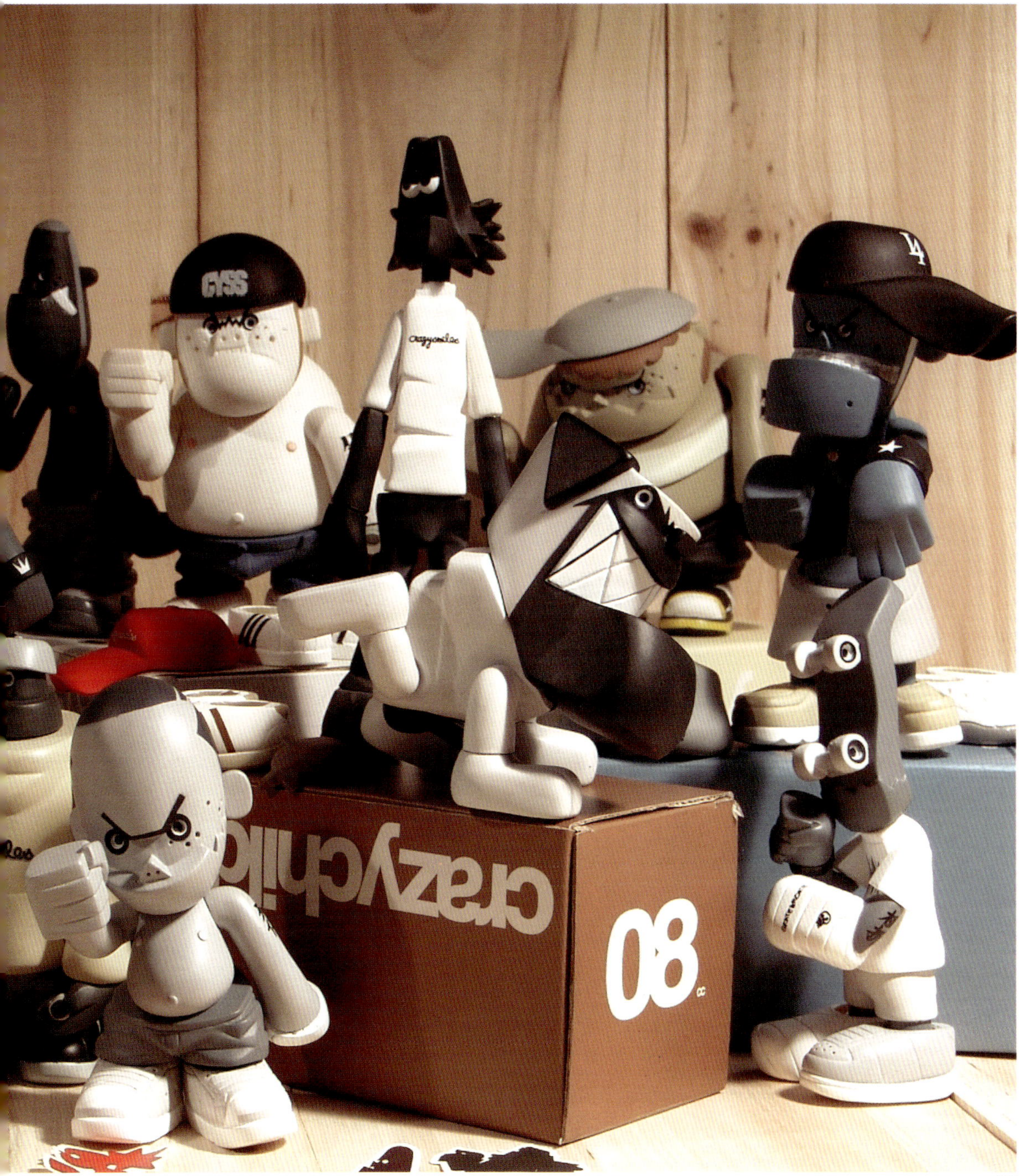

500

501

Excellent
501_ Character Design
t. S.F.C.C.
e. cd. dd. ad. d. Michael Lau
cl. Crazysmiles Co. Ltd.

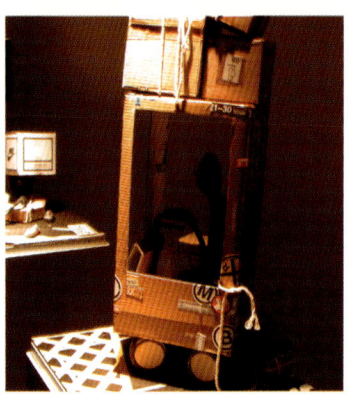

Bronze
502_ Character Design
t. Hong Kong Hero - China Tourist
e. Tommy Li Design Workshop Ltd.
cd. Tommy Li
d. Choi Kim Hung
p. Danny Chiu
cl. Tommy Li Solo Exhibition @ MTR ARTtube

Marstin#1

Bronze
503_ *Character Design*
t. Sed Unuz
e. ad. i. Benny Au Tak-shing
cl. Amazing Angle Design Consultants Limited

504_ *Character Design*
t. Spit Monster Character Design
e. Dennis Yuk Pui Wong
cd. Dennis Wong
dd. Dominic Kam
i. Ringo Lam
cl. Information Services Dapartment

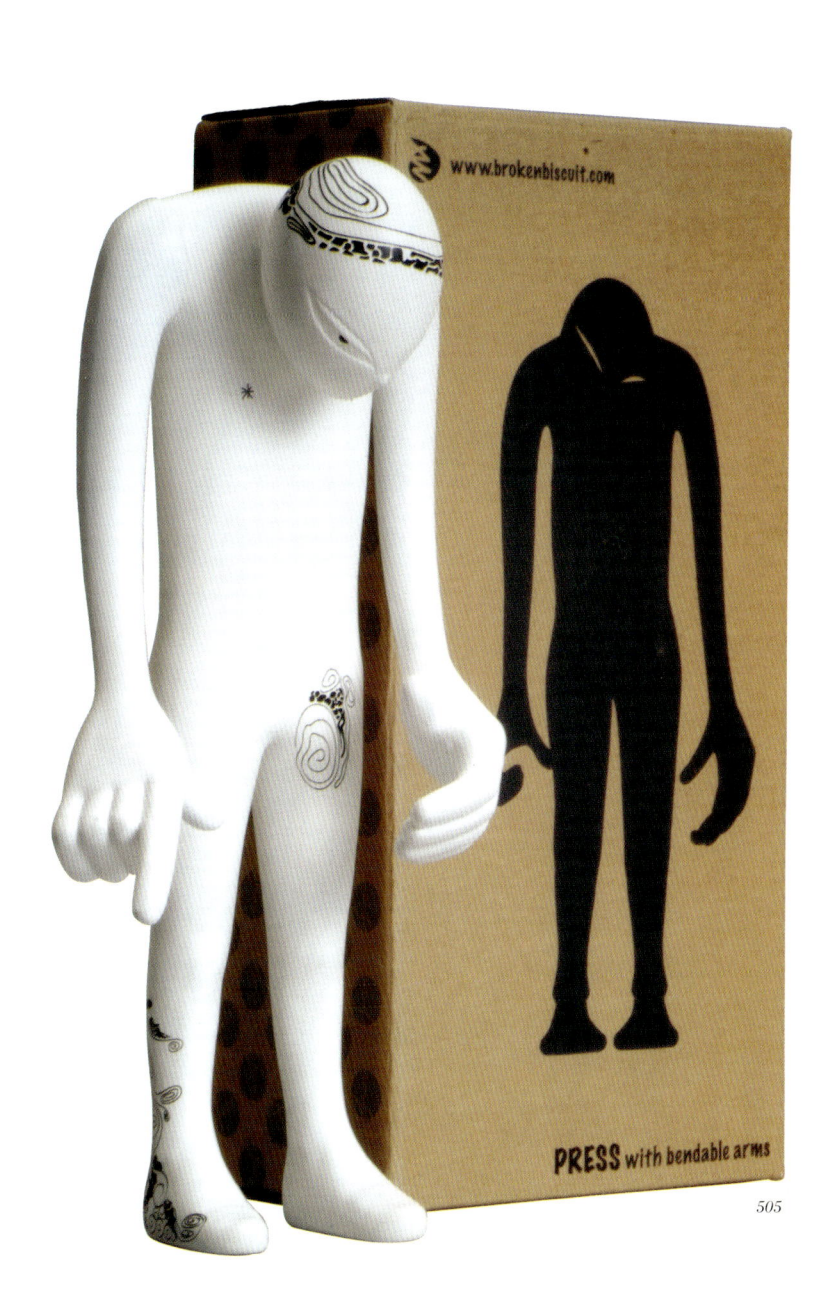

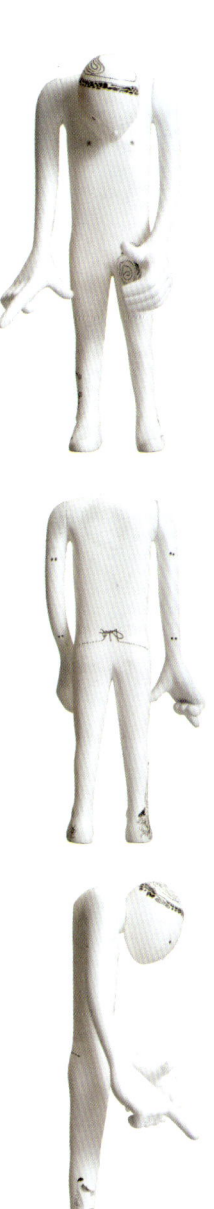

Excellent
505_ *Character Design*
t. p.r.e.s.s.
e. Broken Biscuit
cd. dd. ad. d. p. i. cw. Roy Man

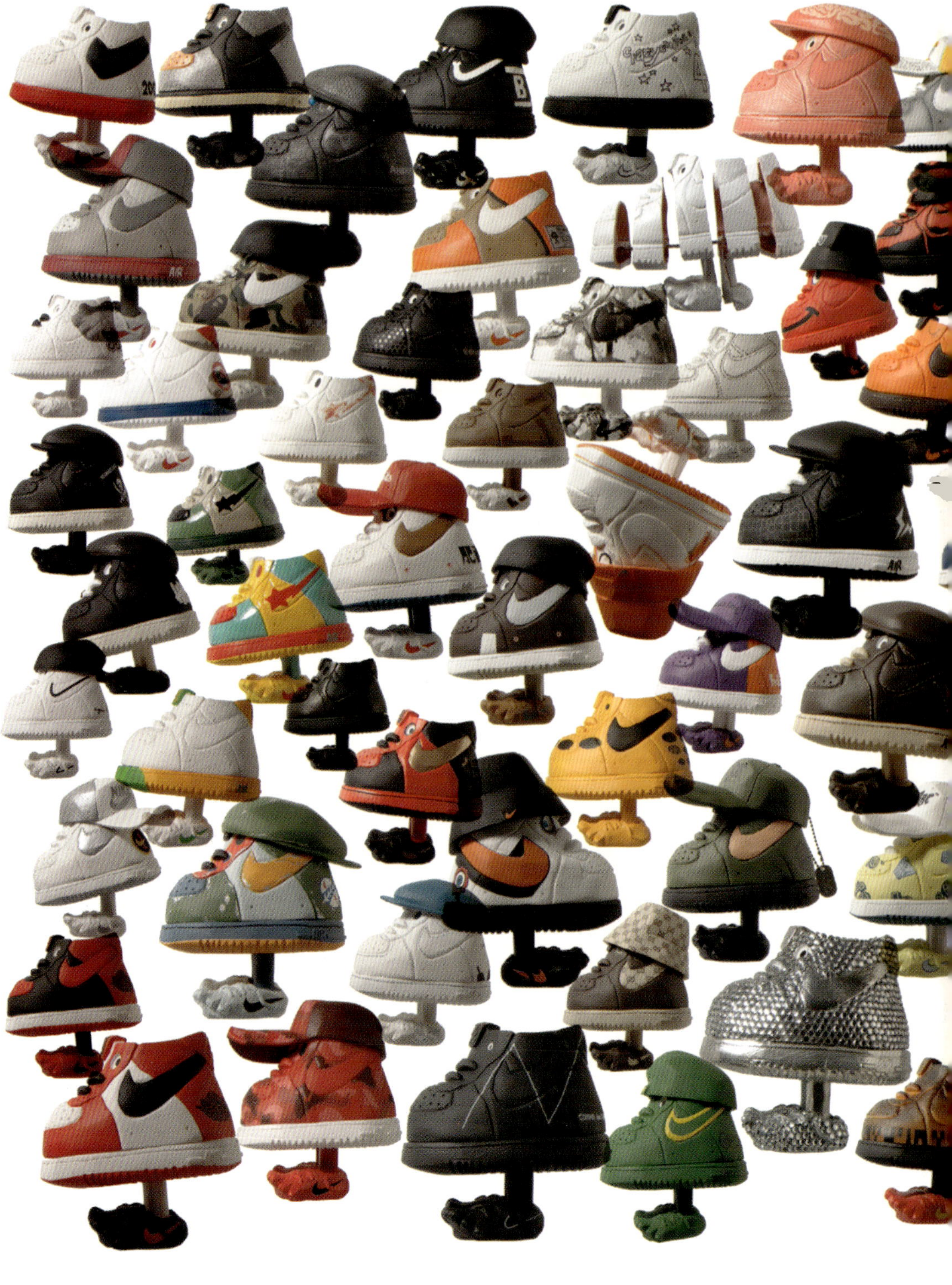

506_Character Design
t. Mr. Shoe (sample)
e. cd. dd. ad. d. Michael Lau
cl. Crazysmiles Co. Ltd., Nike

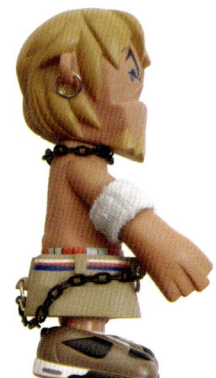

507_ *Character Design*
t. Gardenergala Book
e. cd. dd. ad. Michael Lau
d. Junkie Design
pp. pt. Dai Nippon Printing Co., Ltd.
cl. SMETV Inc.

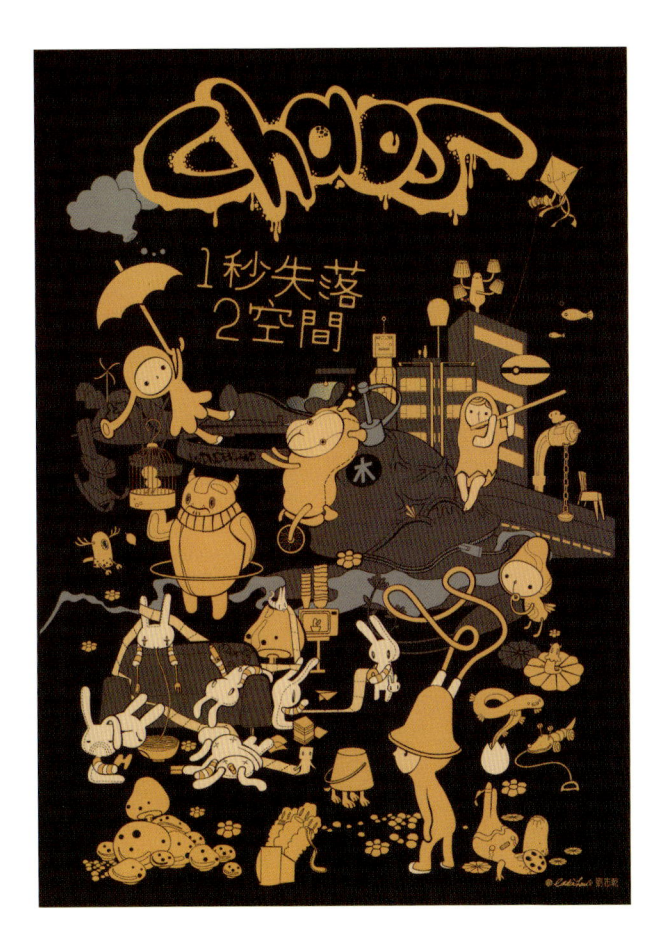

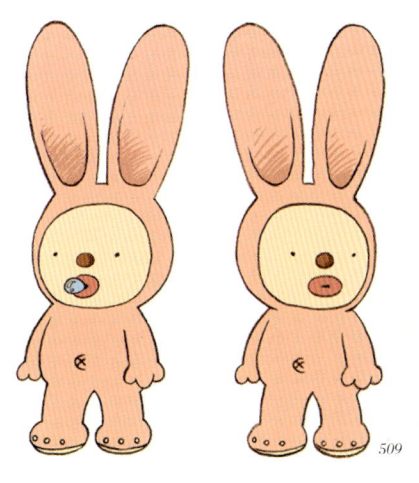

508_ Character Design
    t. LoLo Mascot
    e. Kan & Lau Design Consultants
    cd. ad. Freeman Lau Siu Hong
    d. i. Kong Khong Chang
    cl. World Wide Fund for Nature Hong Kong

509_ Character Design
    t. Clumsy Poppet
    e. cd. d. i. Michael Kwong
    cl. Locomotive Productions Limited

510_ Character Design
    t. Chaos
    e. Eddie, Lau Chi Kin
    cd. Les Suen
    i. Eddie Lau

ENVIRONMENTAL GRAPHIC 環境グラフィック
환경적 그래픽 环境图象

This is design you can alternatively look up to, sit on, or wipe the walls with - environment graphics look and feel as if they belong, without failing to catch our eye as we pass by.

Environmental Graphic

Silver
511_ Enviromental Graphic
t. The Gorgeous Charger
e. cd. ad. d. p. Hong Ko
pt. Acumen Production
mo. Vinci Fung

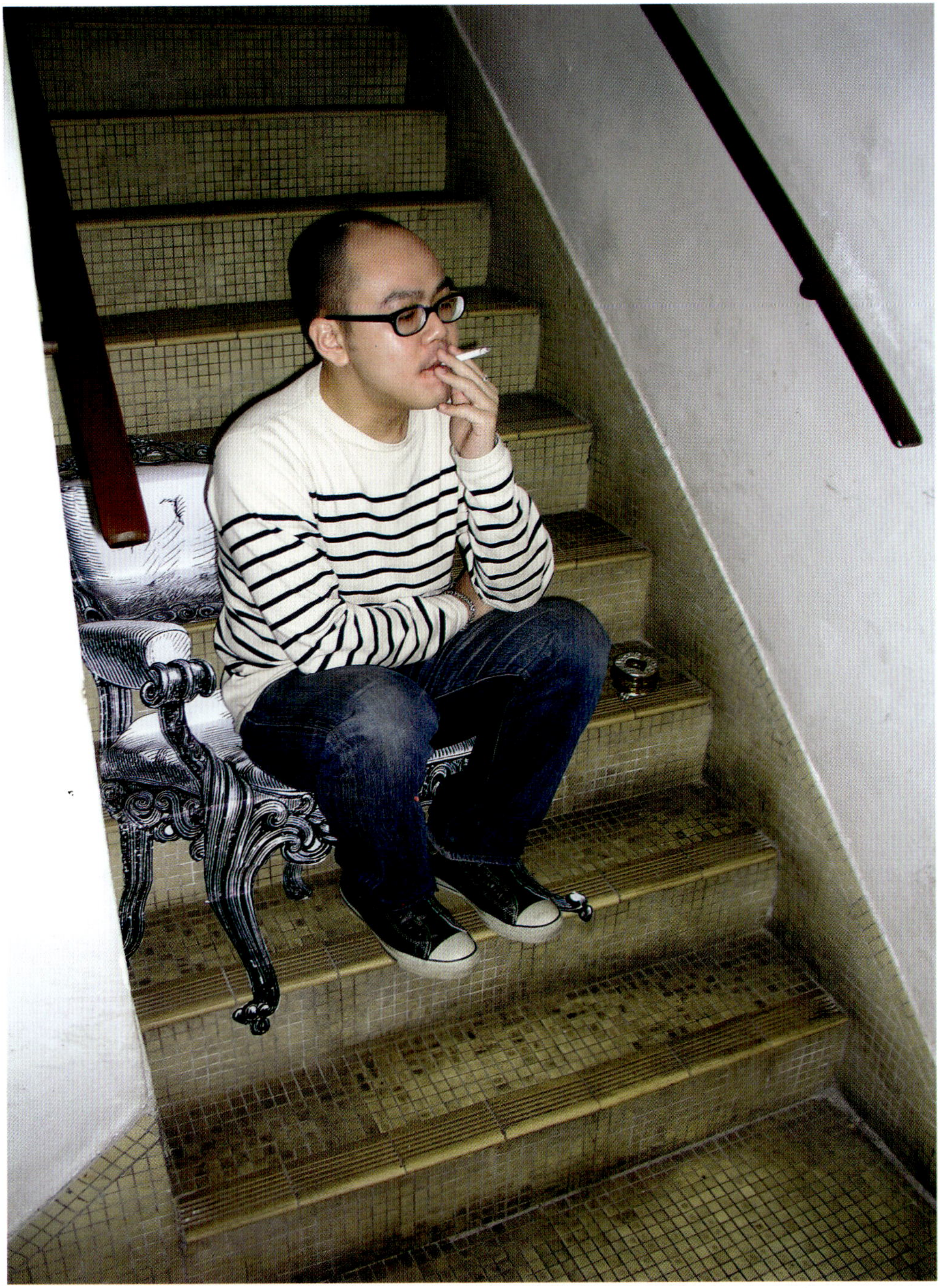

511

Bronze
512_ Environmental Graphic
t. Homage to IKKO TANAKA :
  with and without IKKO TANAKA
e. ad. d. Katsuhiro Kinoshita
p. Masataka Nakano
cl. Tokusyu paper Mfg. Co., Ltd.

387

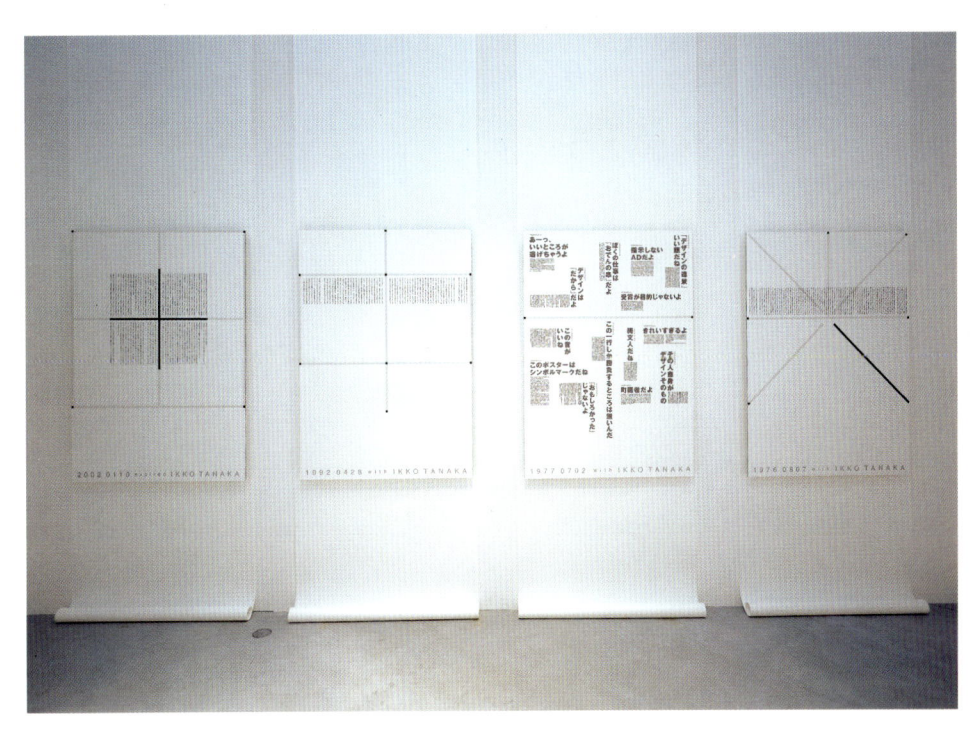

Bronze
513_ Evironmental Graphic
t. Tommy Li Solo Exhibition
  @ MTR ARTtube - "Black & White"
e. Tommy Li Design Workshop Ltd.
cd. Tommy Li
d. Choi Kim Hung, Joshua Lau
p. Danny Chiu
cs. Lancy Chiu
cl. MTR Corporation

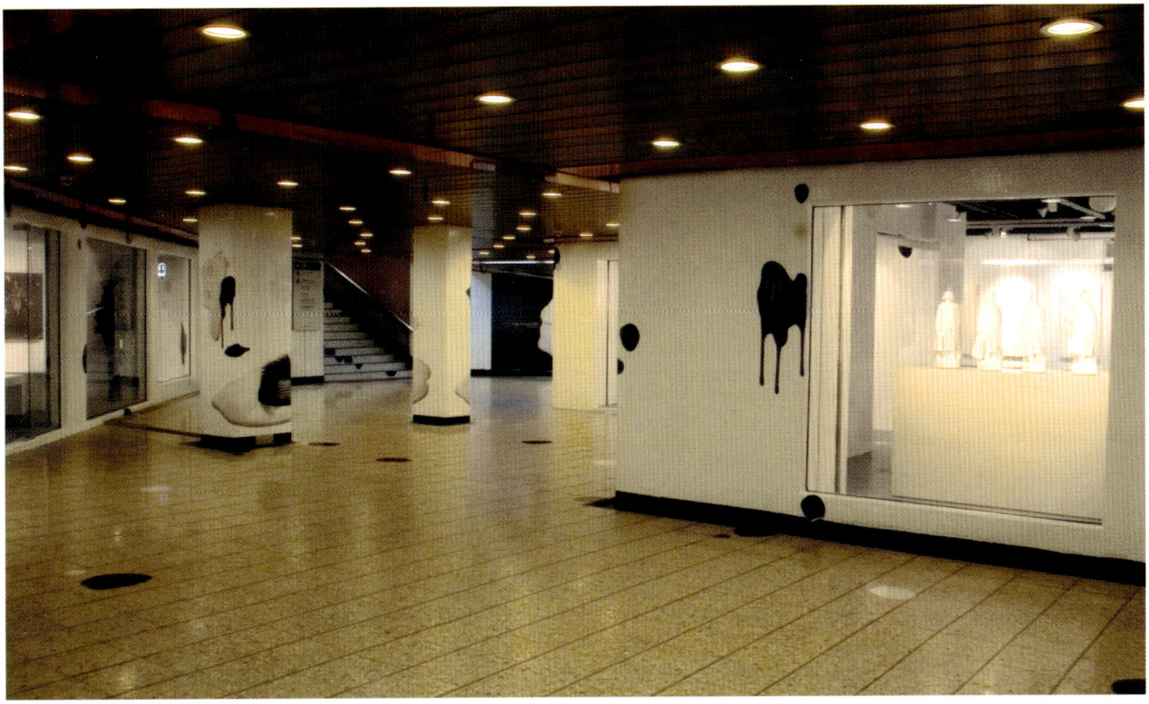

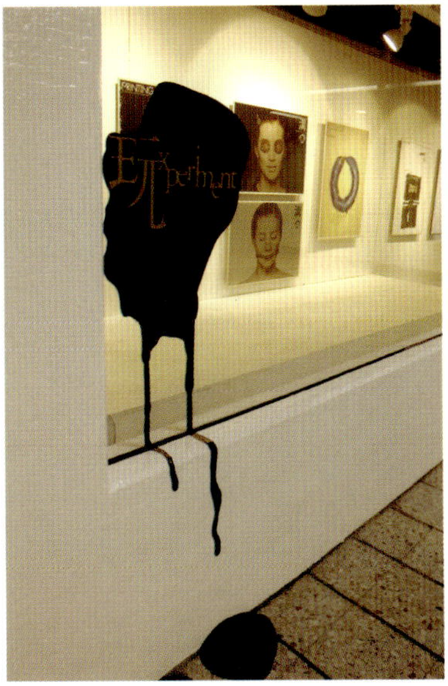

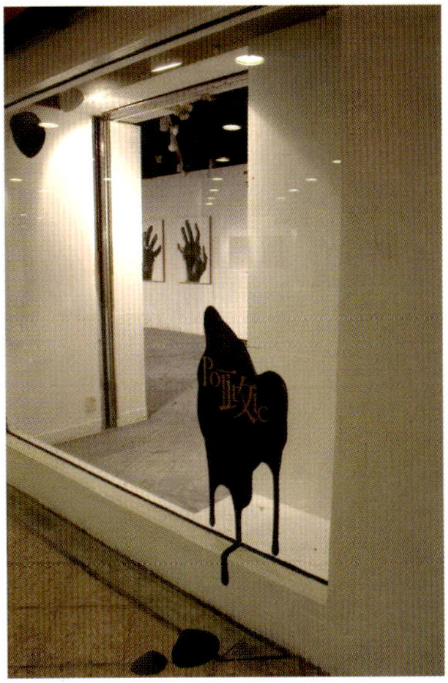

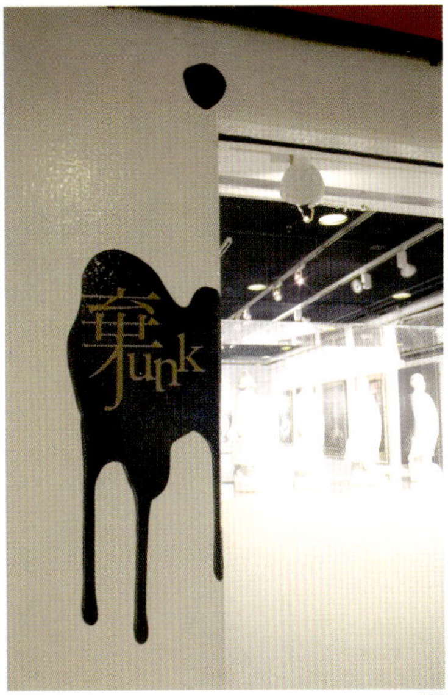

513

514_ *Environmental Graphic*
t. I Don't Mind, If You Forget Me.
e. ad. d. Masayoshi Kodaira
p. Mikiya Takimoto
cl. Organizing Committee for the Exhibition "Nara Yoshitomo" in Hirosaki

514

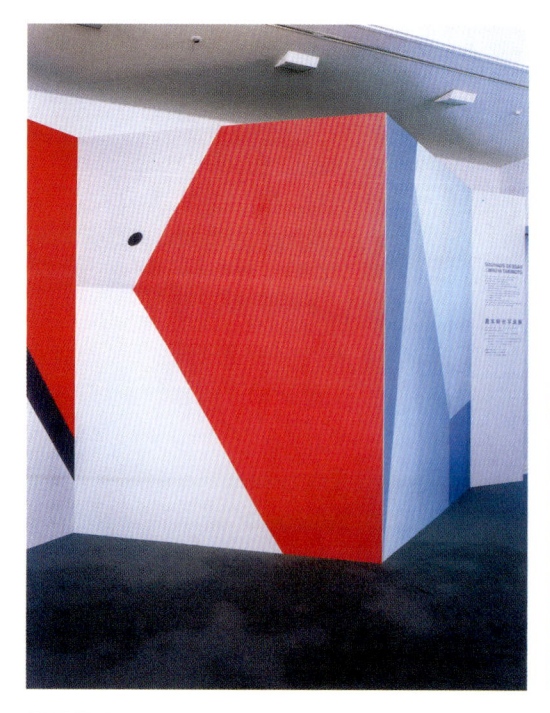

Excellent
515_ *Environmental Graphic*
t. Bauhaus Dessau, Mikiya Takimoto
e. ad. d. Masayoshi Kodaira
p. Mikiya Takimoto
cl. Organizing Committee for the Exhibition
  "Bauhaus Dessau, Mikiya Takimoto"

516_ Environmental Graphic
t. Hong Kong Police Headquarters - Library Feature Wall
e. Marc & Chantal Design
cd. Chantal Rechaussat, Marc Cansier, Marc Brulhart
d. Esther Ho
cl. Architectural Services Department

517_ Environmental Graphic
t. Hong Kong Police Headquarters - Auditorium Feature Wall
e. Marc & Chantal Design
cd. Chantal Rechaussat, Marc Cansier, Marc Brulhart
d. Agnes Wong
cl. Architectural Services Department

PRODUCT 製品
제품 产品设计

Well-designed objects can be functional, beautiful, playful, and often all of the above - see this showcase of domestic and fashion accessories, electronics and electrical appliances, furniture, time pieces, gifts, premiums and toys.

Domestic Accessory
Electronic & Electrical Appliance
Time Pieces, Gift & Premium
Fashion Accessory
Furniture
Toys

Silver
518_ Domestic Accessory
t. 飲食思源
e. dd. ad. d. 陳俊良
cl. Council for Cultural Affairs Executive Yuan

519

Bronze
519_ Domestic Accessory
t. "Well" tea set
e. m. Metier Atelier Co., Ltd.
d. What's That Product Development

Excellent
520_ Gift & Premium
t. Coaster Key
e. Zanif Advertising and Promotion Ltd.
dd. d. Winnif Pang Chi Kong
da. Frankie Fu

521_ Domestic Accessory
t. Magic Cup Cap
e. Zanif Advertising and Promotion Ltd.
dd. d. Winnif Pang Chi Kong
da. Kan Chau

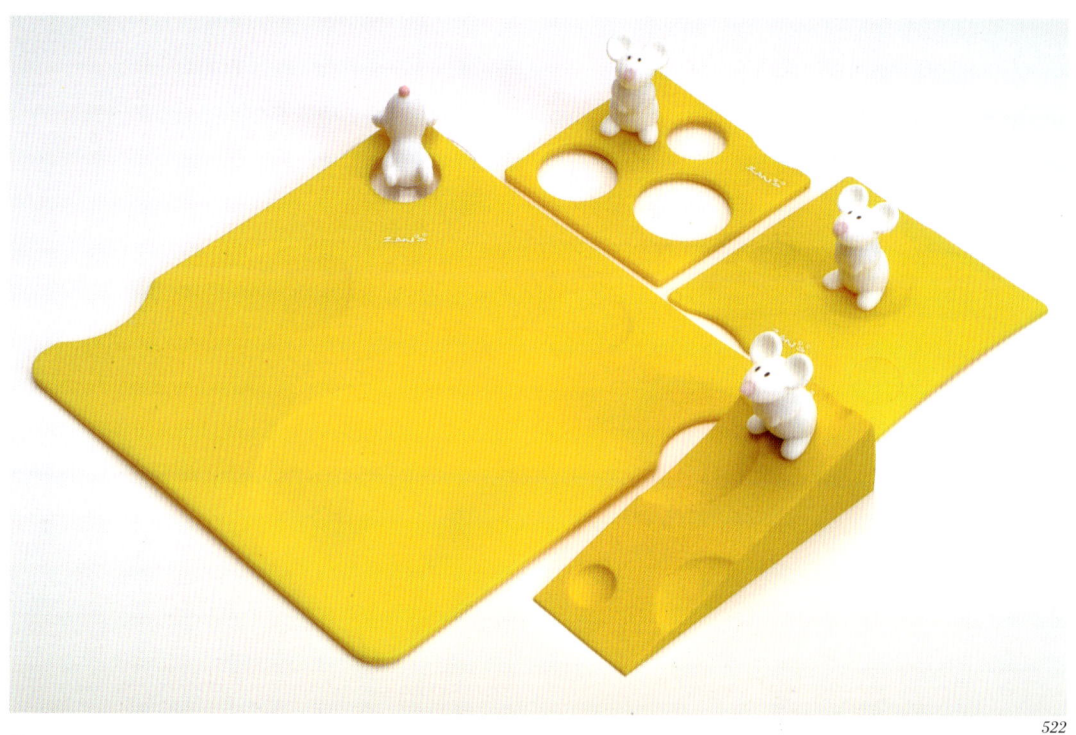

522_ *Domestic Accessory*
t. Mouse and Cheese Kitchen Product
e. Zanif Advertising and Promotion Ltd.
dd. Winnif Pang Chi Kong
d. Winnif Pang Chi Kong, J Ho

Silver
523_ *Domestic Accessory*
t. Hand Puppet Mitt
e. Zanif Advertising and Promotion Ltd.
dd. *d*. Winnif Pang Chi Kong

524_ *Gift & Premium*
t. Memo Loop Pen
e. Zanif Advertising and Promotion Ltd.
dd. *d*. Winnif Pang Chi Kong

398

525

526

527

528

Silver
527_ Domestic Accessory
t. T. Dog series
e. Semk Products Ltd.
dd. Eddie Hui
d. Eddie Hui, Julia Tam, Edna Tam, Heidi Chan, Wing Lam, Keung
m. Semk Products Ltd.
pt. Jerry Chan, Julia Tam, Edna Tam, Heidi Chan
cl. Sony, Nokia, Canon

Excellent
525_ Domestic Accessory
t. Spa Mood Light
e. Zanif Advertising and Promotion Ltd.
dd. d. Winnif Pang Chi Kong
da. Frankie Fuo

Silver
526_ Domestic Accessory
t. Ice Stirrer
e. Zanif Advertising and Promotion Ltd.
dd. d. Winnif Pang Chi Kong
da. J.Ho

Excellent
528_ Gift & Premium
t. Mini-mal Stationeries
e. Zanif Advertising and Promotion Ltd.
dd. Winnif Pang Chi Kong
ad. Winnif Pang Chi Kong, Mandy Li
d. Winnif Pang Chi Kong, Mandy Li, Kan Chau, Frankie Fu, J.Ho

Excellent
529_ Domestic Accessory
   t. Tommy Li Design Workshop Ltd.
     - "Evening Collection"
   e. Tommy Li Design Workshop Ltd.
   dd. Tommy Li
   d. Choi Kim Hung, Tami Leung
   cs. Lancy Chiu
   cl. Hong Kong Design Centre

529

400

530

531

532

533

530_ *Gift & Premium*
t. Spiral Luggage Tag
e. Zanif Advertising and Promotion Ltd.
dd. d. Winnif Pang Chi Kong

531_ *Gift & Premium*
t. Vida
e. Ikonee International Ltd.
dd. ad. Samuel Yeung
d. Jeff Lam
cl. Ikonee International Ltd.

532_ *Gift & Premium*
t. GOGO
e. m. Sunhing Millennium Ltd.
dd. d. Geckothinks

Excellent
533_ Electronic & Electrical Appliance
t. Baby bath thermometer - Angelfish
e. Eagletron Telcommunications Ltd.
dd. d. Amelia Cheung Kar Yee
m. Eagletron Telcommunications Ltd.

Bronze
534_ Toys
t. Magic Light 'n' Sounds
e. Talentoy Factory Ltd.
dd. Sherman Lo
ad. Angus Wong
d. Gary Kwok

Excellent
535_ Toys
t. Rc shark
e. Zanif Advertising and Promotion Ltd.
dd. Winnif Pang Chi Kong
d. Alan Cheung
m. cl. Super Grand Enterprise Ltd.

536_ Gift & Premium
t. Rolling
e. Winner Mfy. Ltd.
dd. Dick Chan
d. Selina Shum

Excellent
537_ Electrical Consumer Product
t. Ionic Hair Straightener HS543
e. m. Kenford Industrial Company Ltd.
d. Michael Keong Wai Ho

Bronze
538_ Gift & Premium
t. USB Storage Series
e. P.S.L.
d. Fai Leung
m. SWEDA Ltd.
cl. PSL Limited

402

540

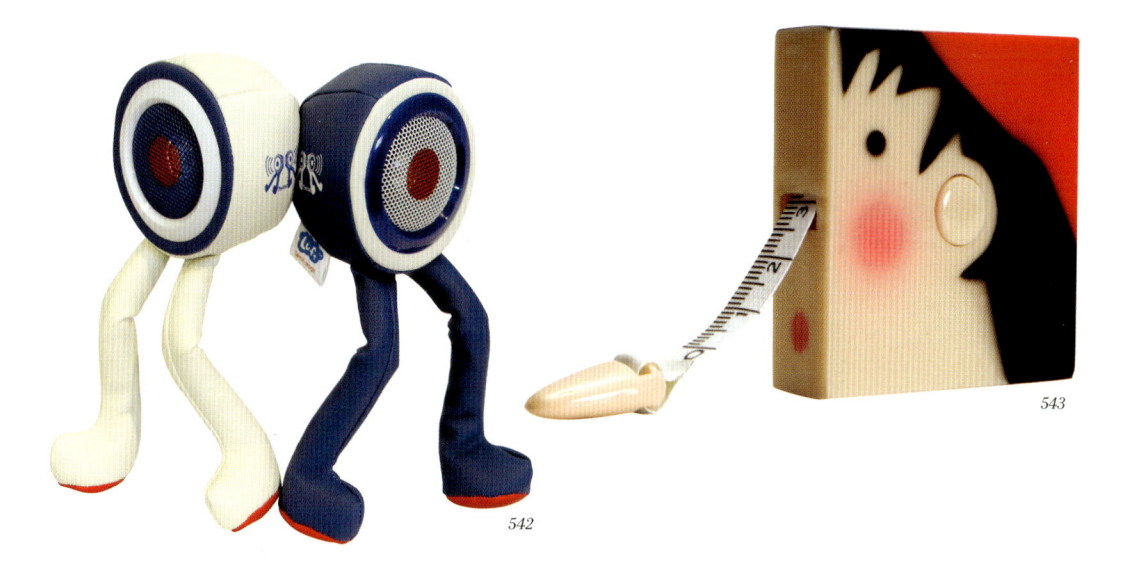

541

542

543

Bronze
539_ Electronic & Electrical Appliance
t. Cordless ThermoCeramic Straightener HS604
e. m. Kenford Industrial Company Ltd.
d. Kay Yu King Kuen
cl. Morphy Richards

Silver
540_ Electronic & Electrical Appliance
t. Crestbay Luminaire
e. Philips Electronics Hong Kong Ltd.
dd. Murray Camens, Sean Hughes
d. Ernest To
m. cl. Philips Lighting

541_ Gift and Premium
t. SCM Infernal Affairs Trilogy
e. STAR Group Limited
dd. Cat Lam Siu Hung
d. David Chan
cl. STAR Chinese Movies Channel

Excellent
542_ Gift & Premium
t. Mr. Leg Series
e. Semk Products Ltd.
dd. ad. Eddie Hui
d. Eddie Hui, Jerry Chan, Julia Tam
m. Semk Products Ltd.
cl. Nokia, Sony

543_ Gift & Premium
t. MB
e. Willtech Industrial Ltd.

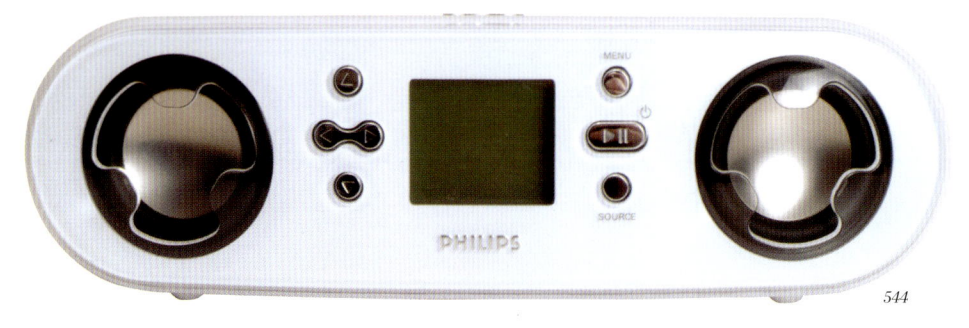

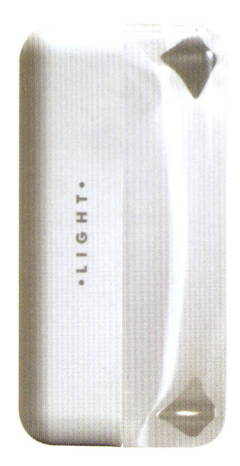

Silver
544_ Electronic & Electrical Appliance
t. Personal Sound System - PSS110
e. m. Philips Electronics Hong Kong Ltd.
dd. Murray Camens, Greg Foster
d. Jono Schultz
cl. Philips Electronics Hong Kong Ltd.
 -BG Mobile Infotainment

Bronze
545_ Gift & Premium
t. Mood Light AM/FM Radio
e. Man Nin Shing Co., Ltd.

546_ Electronic & Electrical Appliance
t. SM6 Slider Mobile Phone - 960
e. m. Philips Electronics Hong Kong Ltd.
dd. Murray Camens, Timothy Homewood
d. Wai Chung Lee, Rodney Loh
cl. Philips Electronics Hong Kong Ltd.
 - BG Mobile Infotainment

404

547_ *Electronic & Electrical Appliance*
t. Digital Audio Player - SA177
e. *m*. Philips Electronics Hong Kong Ltd.
dd. Murray Camens, Greg Foster
d. Greg Foster, Alvin Yuen
cl. Philips Electronics Hong Kong Ltd.
   - BG Mobile Infotainment

548_ *Electronic & Electrical Appliance*
t. EM3 Swivel Clamshell Mobile Phone - 868
e. *m*. Philips Electronics Hong Kong Ltd.
dd. Murray Camens, Timothy Homewood
d. Makorn Chaovanich, Kent Li
cl. Philips Electronics Hong Kong Ltd.
   - BG Mobile Infotainment

Bronze
549_ *Electronic & Electrical Appliance*
t. Nokia 6060
e. Nokia_6060
dd. William Yau
d. Chun-wei Su
cp. Yan- jiang Hou

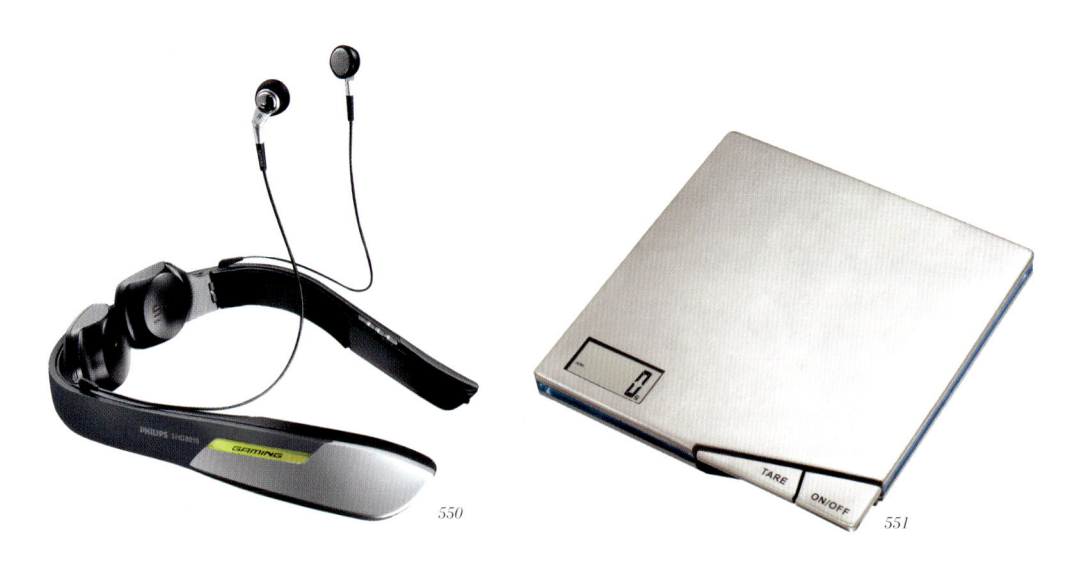

Silver
550_ *Electronic & Electrical Appliance*
t. In-ear Gaming Headphone
  - SHG8010
e. m. Philips Electronics Hong Kong Ltd.
dd. Murray Camens, Raymond Wong
d. Wai Chung Lee
cl. Philips Electronics Hong Kong Ltd.
  - Sound Accessories

Excellent
551_ *Electronic & Electrical Appliance*
t. Flat Stainless Steel Digital Scale
e. m. SWEDA Ltd.
d. Keith Mak

Bronze
552_ *Electronic & Electrical Appliance*
t. Palm Dryer HD576
e. m. Kenford Industrial Co., Ltd.
d. Michael Keong Wai Ho

Excellent
553_ *Electronic & Electrical Appliance*
t. DVD Portable Player - PET1000
e. m. Philips Electronics Hong Kong Ltd.
dd. Murray Camens, Greg Foster
d. Henry Law, Greg Foster
cl. Philips Electronics Hong Kong Ltd.
  - BG Mobile Infotainment

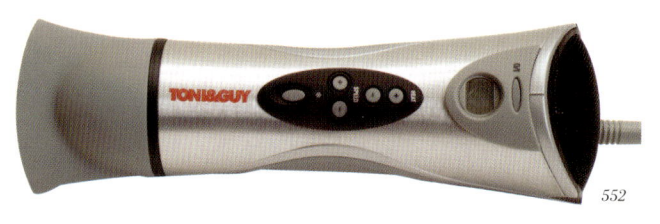

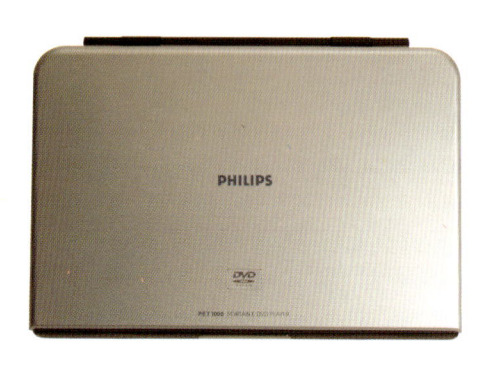

554

555

556

557

558

554_ Electronic & Electrical Appliance
t. Outdoor Corded Neckband Headphone
  - SHS850
e. m. Philips Electronics Hong Kong Ltd.
dd. Murray Camens, Raymond Wong
d. Laura Taylor
cl. Philips Electronics Hong Kong Ltd.
  - Sound Accessories

Excellent
556_ Electronic & Electrical Appliance
t. i.Tech Clip II
e. Chau Suk Man, Shirley
d. Shirley Chau
m. cl. i.Tech Dynamic Ltd.
p. i.Tech

557_ Electronic & Electrical Appliance
t. VTech Mini
e. VTech
dd. David Waterman
d. Philip Cheng
m. cl. VTech telecommunications Ltd.

555_ Electronic & Electrical Appliance
t. V-Mix Teen phone
e. VTech
dd. d. David Waterman
m. cl. VTech telecommunications Ltd.

Excellent
558_ Electronic & Electrical Appliance
t. Digital Ionic Professional
  Hairdryer HD608
e. m. Kenford Industrial Co., Ltd.
d. Kay Yu, Michael Koeng, Kwok Kin Sun

407

559

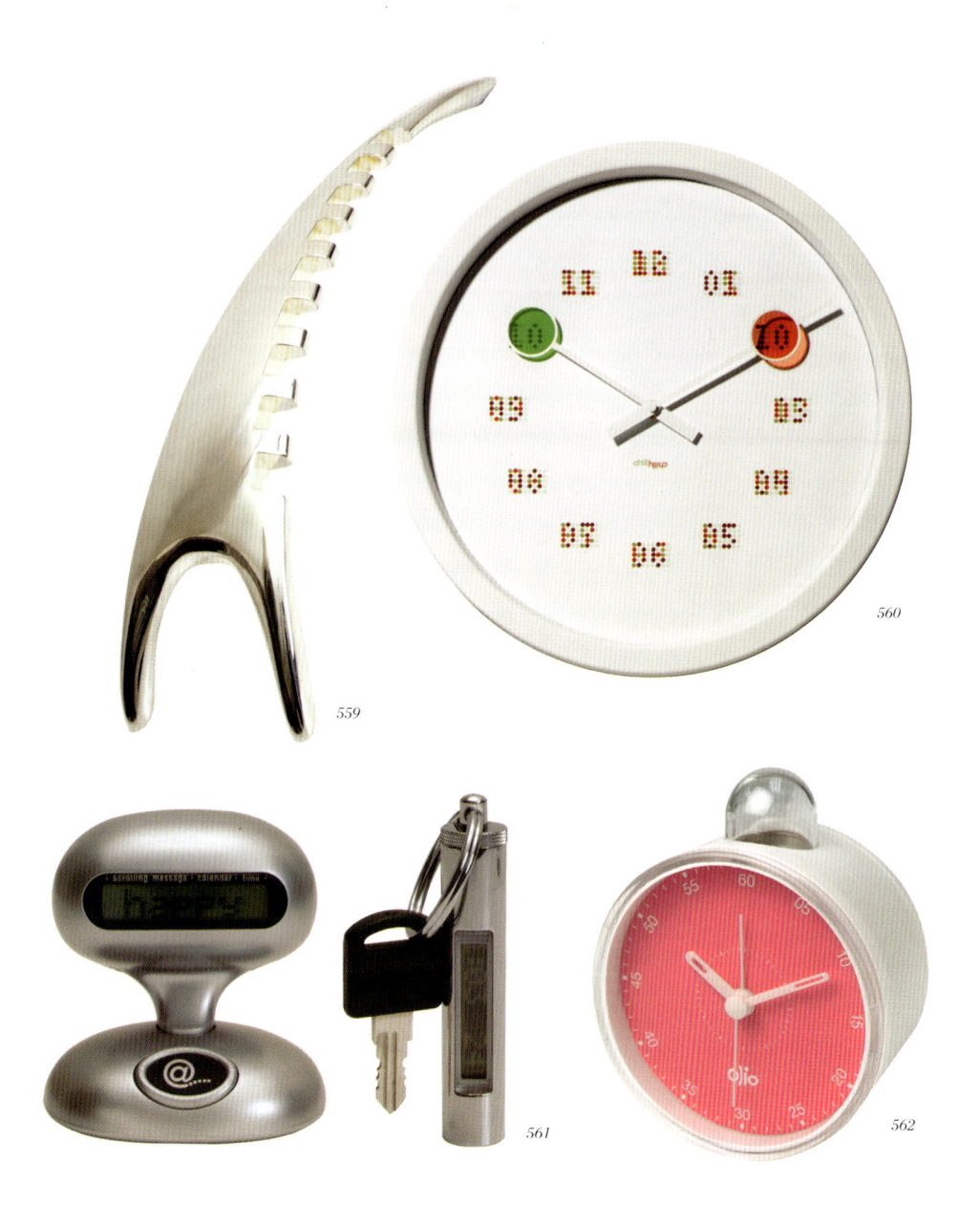

560

561

562

559_ *Domestic Accessory*
t. Streamlined CD Rack
e. m. Joyas Manufacturing Ltd.
d. Ho Sui Ling
d. Choi Kim Hung, Tami Leung

Silver
560_ *Time Pieces*
t. Seeing Doubles Clock
e. dd. Arthur Yung
ad. cs. Clement Cheung
m. Seedz Ltd.
cl. CHILLICHILLY by Seedz Ltd.

561_ *Time Pieces*
t. Scrolling Message Series
e. P.S.L.
dd. Jane Tang
d. Fai Leung, Hazel Wong
m. SWEDA Ltd.
cl. PSL Ltd.

562_ *Time Pieces*
t. Weeble Bomb Alarm Clock
e. Ikonee International Ltd.
dd. ad. d. Samuel Yeung
cl. Ikonee International Ltd.

408

Excellent

563_ *Fashion Accessory*
t. 十二金釵
e. Charles Ng &
   Maxi Communications Ltd.
cd. dd. d. Charles Ng, Eddie Cheung
ad. Charles Ng, Sang Chan,
   Eddie Cheung
cl. The Well Leatherware Mfy. Ltd.

564_ *Fashion Accessory*
t. 十二金釵手飾系列
e. Charles Ng &
   Maxi Communications Ltd.
dd. d. Charles Ng, Prudence Mak
ad. Charles Ng, Sang Chan,
   Eddie Cheung
cl. The Well Leatherware Mfy. Ltd.

Bronze

565_ *Fashion Accessory*
t. Nice Bags
e. dd. ad. d. Jack Chang
cs. Jack Chang Creative Lab
m. cl. Prinduct

Excellent

566_ *Fashion Accessory*
t. Ming Dynasty
e. Meh Meh Concept
dd. Juana Ho, Zita Tsang

Excellent

567_ *Fashion Accessory*
t. Qing Dynasty
e. Meh Meh Concept
dd. Juana Ho, Zita Tsang

Bronze
568_ Fashion Accessory
t. Jeans Shop Ginza
e. Alan Chan Design Company
cd. dd. d. Alan Chan
cl. Ginza Gallery, Ltd.

Bronze
569_ *Fashion Accessory*
t. Palace of the Moon
e. Stanley Lo Jewelry Designs
dd. Stanley Lo

Silver
570_ *Gift & Premium*
t. Phoenix Rice Bag
e. STAR Group Limited
dd. Cat Lam Siu Hung
d. Cat Lam, Stephen So
pm. Winsome Ho
cl. Phoenix

571_ *Fashion Accessory*
t. Folding Mistery
 - E/W collection
e. cd. dd. ad. Prudence Mak
d. Janice Liu
cs. Chocolate Rain Jewelery
 and Designs Co.
m. Chocolate Rain Jewelery
 and Designs Co., MAD Ltd.

Silver
572_ Furniture
t. light × table
e. dd. Bun Ho
m. Arcon International Ltd.

573_ Gift & Premium
t. Dream Garden
e. Milk Design

Excellent
574_ Furniture
t. Venus Chair
e. d. Hiroki Takada
m. Takada design

575

576

Silver
575_ Furniture

t. Donut
e. Draughtzman
dd. Ziggy Koo
ad. Alliot Cheng
d. Josephine Ching, Debby Cheng
m. Plan-in
cl. Sun Hung Kai Properties Ltd.

Bronze
576_ Furniture

t. Role Play
e. Kan & Lau Design Consultants
dd. ad. d. cl. Freeman Lau Siu Hong

577

Bronze
577_ Furniture
t. Goodss Contemporary
e. cl. Goodss Ltd.
dd. Gary Tam
d. Gary Tam, Keith Li
cl. Goodss Ltd.

578_ Furniture
t. IncreTable
e. Draughtzman
dd. Ziggy Koo
ad. Alliot Cheng
d. Ziggy Koo, Amornthep Tantikovit, Psyche Chiu, Janet Choy
m. Plan-in
cl. Sun Hung Kai Properties Ltd.

579_ Furniture
t. Script
e. Bliss Partners Int'l Ltd.
dd. Ivan Leung

580

581

Excellent
580_ Furniture
t. EXO Chaise
e. KplusK Associates
dd. Johnny Kember, Paul Kember
m. Arcon International Ltd.

Bronze
581_ Furniture
t. Goodss Fusion
e. cl. Goodss Ltd.
dd. Gary Tam
d. Gary Tam, Keith Li

582_ *Gift & Premium*
t. Mini Michael
e. dd. ad. d. Michael Lau
m. Long Goal Company Ltd.
cl. Crazysmiles Co., Ltd.

582

SPATIAL 空間的
공간 空间设计

These examples of exhibition scenography, window display and interior design (hospitality, entertainment, office, residential, retail) show how we best relate to the space around us.

Exhibition & Window Display
Hospitality & Entertainment
Office
Residential
Retail

Silver
583_ Exhibition
t. Lantern Wonderland
e. CL3 Architects Ltd.
dd. William Lim
d. Alvin Lee, Rain Ho, KK Kwok
p. Wu Kin Yat
cl. Hong Kong Tourism Board

583

584

585

Bronze
584_ Exhibition

t. China Hi-Tech Fair 2004 - Hong Kong Pavilion
e. d. Joey Ho
p. Aaron
cl. The Innovation and Technology Commission &
 Hong Kong Productivity Council

Bronze
585_ Exhibition

t. 'Superwoman' Poster Exhibition
e. Design Systems Ltd.
dd. Lam Wai Ming
d. Irene Ito, Fanny Leung,
 Esther Yeung, Helen Cheng
c. City Decoration Works Co., Ltd.
cl. Hong Kong Poster League

Bronze

586_ Exhibition
t. Style HK 2004
e. Draughtzman
dd. Ziggy Koo
ad. Alliot Cheng
d. Godwin Ko, Josephine Ching
cl. HKTDC

587_ Window Display
t. Yoho Town
e. dd. d. James Law
cl. Sun Hung Kai Properties Ltd.

588_ Window Display
t. Major Infrastructural Development in Hong Kong - Exhibition
e. Kan & Lau Design Consultants
ad. Freeman Lau Siu Hong
d. Freeman Lau Hong, Lam Wai Hung, Benson Kwun; Christopher Law, Sada, Cecil of The Oval Partnership Ltd.
cl. The Oval Partnership Ltd.

589_ Exhibition
t. Crystal World
e. Marc & Chantal Design
dd. Marc Brulhart, Marc Cansier, Chantal Rechaussat
d. Sandra Fay
cl. Swarovski

590_ Window Display
t. World Boutique 2003
e. Barrie Ho Architecture Interiors Ltd.

591_ Exhibition
t. 'City Heroes' Photographic Exhibition
e. p. Design Systems Ltd.
dd. Lam Wai Ming
d. Irene Ito, Fanny Leung, Esther Yeung, Ali Suryani
gd. Lilian Tang Design
c. Wing Dik Engineering Co., Ltd.
cl. Leong Ka Tai

592_ Window Display
- *t.* GE Silicones - Showroom
- *e.* Marc & Chantal Design
- *dd.* Marc Brulhart, Marc Cansier, Chantal Rechaussat
- *d.* Carol Li
- *cl.* General Electric

593_ Hospitality
- *t.* Decleor Spa, Beijing
- *e.* Joseph Sy & Associates
- *dd. ad. d. p.* Joseph Sy

594_ Exhibition
- *t.* apm Showsuite
- *e.* Draughtzman
- *dd.* Ziggy Koo
- *ad.* Alliot Cheng
- *d.* Godwin Ko, Josephine Ching
- *cl.* Sun Hung Kai Properties Ltd.

595_ Window Display
- t. Chinese New Year Decoration At Harbour City 2005
- e. Andy Tong Creations Co., Ltd.
- dd. Andy Tong
- d. Hei Chung
- p. Andy Tong, Garrige Ho
- cs. Carol Chan
- cl. Harbour City Estates Ltd.

596_ Exhibition
- t. Tao Heung Museum
- e. Draughtzman
- dd. Ziggy Koo
- ad. Alliot Cheng
- d. Josephine Ching
- cl. Tao Heung Holding Ltd.

Excellent
597_ Exhibition
- t. Chaneration
- e. dd. Alan Chan
- d. Alan Chan, Kent Lui, Stanley Wong
- cl. Hong Kong Heritage Museum

598

599

Bronze
598_ Hospitality

t. HKPA C&Y Service Centres
e. Laurence Liauw, Design Architect (PTEC)
dd. Laurence Liauw & Tony Leung (PTEC)
d. VC Lee (RDA Project Services M&E)
p. Roland Yeung
cl. Hong Kong Playground Association

Bronze
599_ Hospitality

t. Le Gallerie, Beijing
e. Joseph Sy & Associates
dd. ad. d. p. Joseph Sy

600

601

Bronze
600_ Hospitality
t. Mapping Ma On Shan - Ma On Shan Children's Public Library
e. ADO Design & Public Art Consultants (HK) Ltd.
dd. Yip Siu Ka
ad. p. Sik Lik Hoi
cl. Leisure & Cultural Services Department, HKSAR

Excellent
601_ Hospitality
t. Lei Garden Restaurant
e. Hashimoto & Sung
dd. Hashimoto Yukio, David Sung
p. Victor Lam
cl. Lei Garden

602

603

604

Excellent
602_ Hospitality
t. Nadaman Japanese Restaurant, Kowloon Shangri-la Hotel, Hong Kong
e. CL3 Architects Ltd.
dd. William Lim
d. Joey Wan, Karen Young, Morag Cameron
p. Wong Ho Yin
cl. Shangri-la Hotel & Resort

603_ Hospitality
t. MTM SPA
e. PAL Design Consultant Ltd.
dd. Patrick Leung
d. Gloria Au
p. Steve Mok
cl. Islington Asia Ltd.

Excellent
604_ Hospitality
t. Erba
e. KplusK Associates
dd. Paul Kember, Johnny Kember

Excellent

605_ Hospitality

t. Paradise Garden Restaurant
e. PAL Design Consultant Ltd.
dd. Patrick Leung
d. Sharon Sze
p. ZC Chai
cl. Jade Garden Shanghai Co., Ltd.

606_ Hospitality

t. Baishayuan
e. Alan Chan Design Company
dd. d. Alan Chan, CL3 Architects
cs. Candas Yeung
cl. Baisha Group, Hunan, China

607_ Hospitality

t. Evian Spa
e. CL3 Architects Ltd.
dd. William Lim, Alan Chan
d. Pan Mok
p. Steve Mok
cl. Three On The Bund

608

609

610

Bronze
608_ Hospitality
t. Fairwood Cafe
e. Steve Leung
dd. d. Steve Leung, Yasumichi Morita, Alan Chan
p. Steve Mok, Ulso Tsang
cl. Fairwood Holdings Ltd.

Excellent
609_ Hospitality
t. Ovolo
e. KplusK Associates
dd. Paul Kember, Johnny Kember
p. Graham Uden

Excellent
610_ Hospitality
t. Carpark, Repulse Bay
e. Joseph Sy & Associates
dd. ad. d. p. Joseph Sy

611

612

613

611_ Hospitality
t. Fitness Club TIPNESS ROPPONGI
e. Graphics & Designing Inc.
dd. ad. d. Masayuki Miyama
cl. Tipness Co., Ltd.

612_ Hospitality
t. Nadaman Japanese Restaurant,
   Island Shangri-la Hotel
e. CL3 Architects Ltd.
dd. William Lim
d. Joey Wan, Karen Young, Morag Cameron
p. Wong Ho Yin
cl. Shangri-la Hotel & Resort

613_ Hospitality
t. Evian Spa
e. Alan Chan
d. Alan Chan, CL3 Architects
cs. Jessica Choi
cl. Shanghai GT Courtyard
   Cultural Investment Ltd.

614

615

Silver
614_ Office
t. PMTD headquarters
e. p. Design Systems Ltd.
dd. Lam Wai Ming
d. Raymond Chan, Fanny Leung, Esther Yeung,
   Ali Suryani, Yau Tai Hing, Clara lai
c. City Decoration Works Co., Ltd., Wing Dik Engineering Co., Ltd.
cl. PMTD Ltd.

Silver
615_ Office
t. EDAW Office
e. CL3 Architects Ltd.
dd. William Lim
d. Karen Young, KK Kwok
p. Steve Mok, Wong Ho Yin
cl. EDAW

616

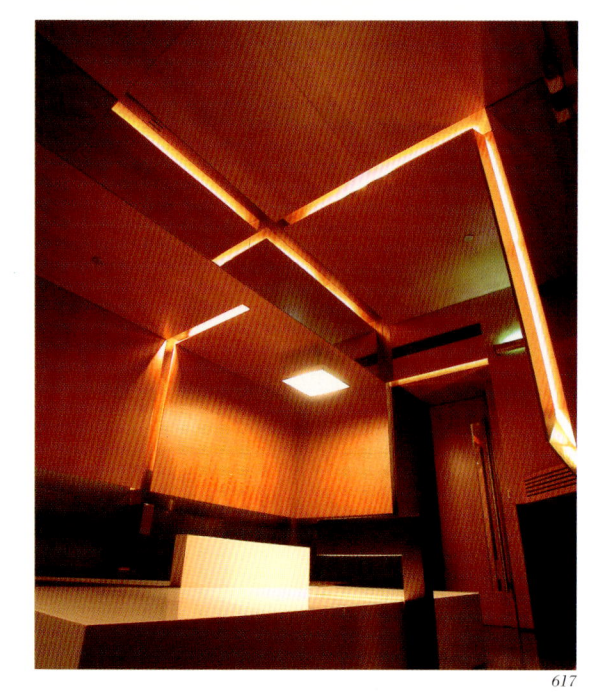

617

Bronze
616_ Office
t. Egana Goldpfeil (Holdings) Ltd.
 - Reception re-design
e. CC Plus Design Ltd.
dd. Crystalle Cheang
p. Marcel Lam Photography
cl. Egana Goldpfeil (Holdings) Ltd.

Bronze
617_ Office
t. IFC Entrance Lobby
e. Draughtzman
dd. Ziggy Koo
ad. Alliot Cheng
d. Godwin Ko, Josephine Ching, Debby Cheng
cl. Central Waterfront Property Project Management Co., Ltd.

618

619

620

Bronze
618_ Office
t. Office of Staccato, Hong Kong
e. Chan Sze Wah, Michael
dd. Michael Chan
d. Stanley Leung, Sharon Chan
p. Eric Tai
cl. Staccato Footwear Co., Ltd.

619_ Office
t. ZhongBao Logistics Headquarter
e. studioOFF
dd. Eddy Yip, Russell Law
d. Jerry Cheung, Timathy Cheng, Jo Cheng

Excellent
620_ Office
t. Hong Kong Police Headquarters - Public Lobby
e. Marc & Chantal Design
dd. Marc Brulhart, Marc Cansier,
    Chantal Rechaussat
cl. Architectural Services Department

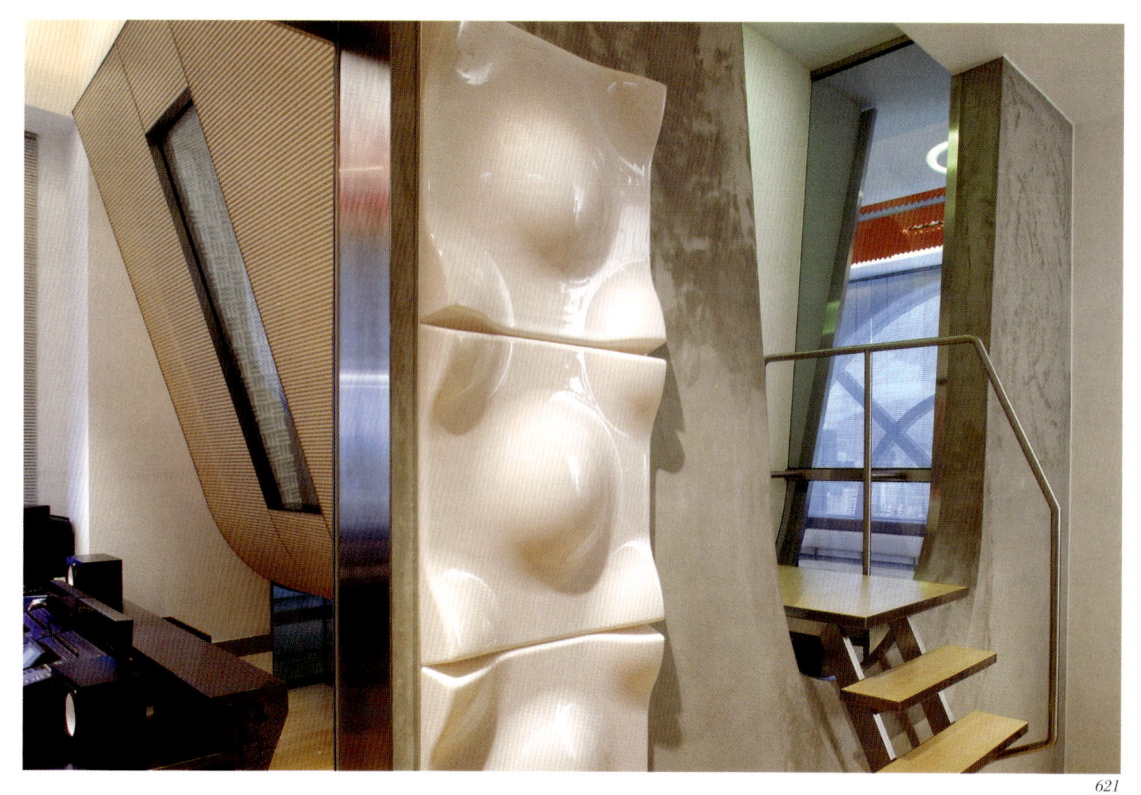

621_ Office
t. Drum Music Recording Studio
e. KplusK Associates
dd. Paul Kember, Johnny Kember
p. Graham Uden

Bronze
622_ Office
t. Green Food Center, Zhuhai
e. FRA Ltd.
dd. ad. Rose Poon, Francis Lee
d. Anna Li, Cosette Lai, Cyrana Mok
p. Hans Schlupp
cl. Green Food Center, Zhuhai

623_ Office
t. Star
e. Marc & Chantal Design
dd. Marc Brulhart, Marc Cansier, Chantal Rechaussat
d. Sandra Fay
cl. Star TV

624

625

624_ Office
t. Leo Burnett HQ - HK
e. KplusK Associates
dd. Paul Kember, Johnny Kember
p. Graham Uden

Bronze
625_ Office
t. SC Learning
e. Ptang Studio
d. Philip Tang

626

627

Bronze
626_ Residential
t. Chen's Residence
e. studioOFF
dd. Eddy Yip, Russell Law
d. Angel Ng, Jerry Cheung

Excellent
627_ Residential
t. Sorrento - Top of the town
e. dd. p. Steve Leung
d. Steve Leung, Alex Yim, Danny Chan
p. Steve Mok
cl. Wheelock Properties Ltd., The Wharf (Holdings) Ltd.

628

629

630

628_ Residential
t. LAX Apartment, Singapore
e. KplusK Associates
dd. Johnny Kember, Paul Kember
p. Graham Uden

629_ Residential
t. 117 Repulse Bay Road
e. dd. Steve Leung
d. Steve Leung, Alex Yim, Lam Cham Yuen
p. Ulso Tsang, Steve Mok
cl. Onshine Holdings Ltd.

630_ Residential
t. Garden House
e. d. Joey Ho
p. Dick
cl. Carol Chu

631_ Residential

t. Private resident
e. CC Plus Design Ltd.
dd. Crystalle Cheang
ad. Suzanne Wong
p. Marcel Lam Photography
cl. Mr. and Mrs. Huang

632_ Residential

t. Ray residence
e. dd. p. Bun Ho
cl. Raphael Wong

633_ Residential

t. The Upper East - Winter
e. dd. Steve Leung
d. Steve Leung, Alex Yim, Hsiao Yueh Min
p. Ulso Tsang
cl. Orient Overseas Project Management Ltd.

634

635

636

Excellent

635_ Residential
t. Shanghai Show House
e. CL3 Architects Ltd.
dd. William Lim
d. Pan Mok
p. Steve Mok
cl. Shanghai Delta Real Estate Co., Ltd.

634_ Residential
t. Living Proscenium
e. d. cl. Ida Sze, Billy Chan

636_ Residential
t. Habitat
e. dd. ad. d. p. Richy Ng
cl. Ronald Wong

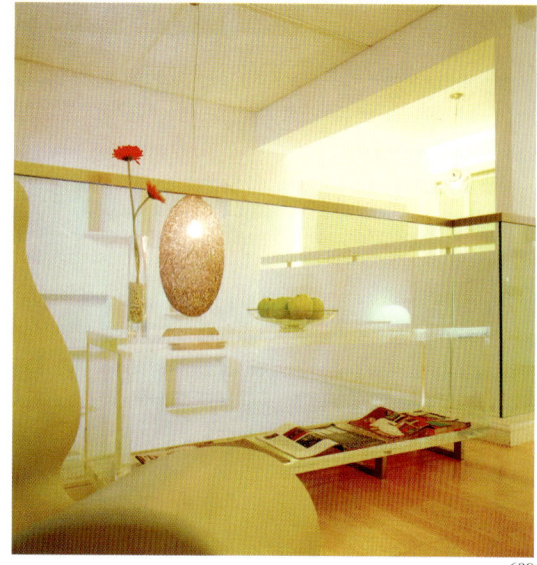

637_ Residential
t. The Refiguring Apartment
e. Wan Chuck Kwan Thomas
d. Wan Chuck Kwan Thomas, Esther Wong
p. Daniel Wong

638_ Residential
t. Wallace Residence
e. MAP Architecture & Planning Ltd.
dd. d. Edward Billson
p. John Butlin, Home Journal
cl. Craig Wallace

639_ Residential
t. Central Park Showflat
e. DPWT Design Ltd.
dd. Arthur Chan
p. Diamond Chan, Arthur Chan
cl. HongKong Land Ltd.

640_ Residential
t. 2WNT
e. cl. Draughtzman
d. Alliot Cheng, Ziggy Koo

641_ Residential
t. Green Apartment
e. Barrie Ho Architecture Interiors Ltd.

642_ Residential
t. Marbela Garden
e. dd. ad. p. Richy Ng
d. Eric Leung
cl. Belinda Wong

Silver
643_ Retail
t. Basheer Design Book Shop
e. d. Joey Ho
p. Hoi
cl. Basheer Design Books

Bronze
644_ Retail

t. America Eyes
e. Draughtzman
dd. Ziggy Koo
ad. Alliot Cheng
d. Josephine Ching, Janet Choy, Godwin Ko
cl. America Eyes

Bronze
645_ Retail

t. American Standard Flagship Store, Beijing
e. Marc & Chantal Design
dd. Marc Brulhart, Marc Cansier, Chantal Rechaussat
d. Karson Liu, Agnes Wong
cl. American Standard

Bronze
646_ Retail

t. MTM Facial Treatment Shop
e. PAL Design Consultant Ltd.
dd. Patrick Leung
d. Gloria Au
p. Steve Mok
cl. Islington Asia Ltd.

Bronze
647_ Retail
t. 2% Chain Store
e. Design Systems Ltd.
dd. Lam Wai Ming
ad. Volume 2 Ltd.
d. Fanny Leung, Esther Yeung, Ali Suryani, Rayomnd Chan, Christine Wong, Yau Tai Hing, Clara Lai
p. Design Systems Ltd.
cl. Two Percent Ltd.

Bronze
648_ Retail
t. Jade Art
e. Draughtzman
dd. Ziggy Koo
ad. Alliot cheng
d. Josephine Ching, Godwin Ko, Mervyn Lee
cl. China Resources

649_ Retail
t. Eu Yan Sang, Telford Garden Plaza
e. Joseph Sy & Associates
dd. ad. d. p. Joseph Sy
cl. China Resources

650_ Retail
t. Chin-Ma-Ya
e. Graphics & Designing Inc.
dd. Toshiro Miura
ad. Yoshimi Hara
d. Masato Aoki
p. Nacasa and Partners Inc
cl. Venture Link Co., Ltd.

651

652

653

654

651_ Retail
t. Louve Gallery, Ruttonjee Centre
e. Joseph Sy & Associates
dd. ad. d. p. Joseph Sy

652_ Retail
t. Mes Amis Bar
e. Chan Cheuk Pan
dd. Wilson Lee
d. p. Penny Chan
cl. Easiway Investment Ltd.

653_ Retail
t. O/3 Baby Collection
e. IDesign International Ltd.
dd. d. Kelvin Law
cl. Danny Yuen

654_ Retail
t. Mako
e. dd. ad. p. Richy Ng
d. Eric Leung
cl. Mako

NEW MEDIA ニューメディア
뉴 미디어 新媒体

As new media introduces new palettes of experimentation, this collection of CD/DVD-Rom and DVD graphics, online advertising, commercial and educational websites and more shows off new adventures in interactive screen design.

CD/DVD-Rom/DVD Graphic
Online Advertising
Business & Consumer Website
Educational Website
Other New Media Graphics

655

656

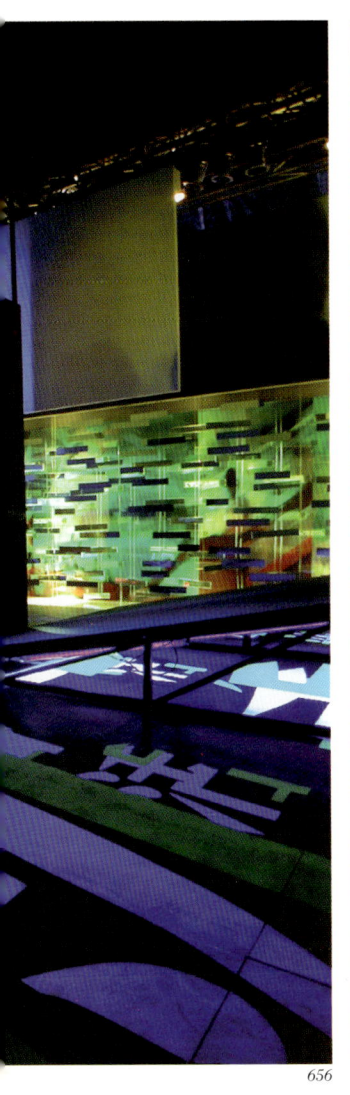

657

Bronze
655 _ *Other New Media Graphic*
t. Tao Heung Museum
e. Draughtzman
cd. *dd*. Ziggy Koo
ad. Alliot Cheng
d. Josephine Ching
a. Dino Technology
ap. NTlab
i. Draughtzman, NTlab
cl. Tao Heung Holding Ltd.

Bronze
656_ *Other New Media Graphic*
t. Style HK 2004
e. Draughtzman
cd. *dd*. Ziggy Koo
ad. Alliot Cheng
d. Godwin Ko, Josephine Ching
p. Kinetics
s. Wilson Tsang, Poon Tak Shu
a. Dino Technology
ap. NTlab
cl. HKTDC

Bronze
657_ *Other New Media Graphic*
t. apm Showsuite
e. Draughtzman
cd. *dd*. Ziggy Koo
ad. Alliot Cheng
d. Josephine Ching, Godwin Ko
p. *cw*. QiQihar
s. Wilson Tsang, Poon Tak Shu
a. *ap*. NTlab
sd. Draughtzman, NTlab, Dino Technology
ia. Draughtzman
i. Draughtzman, NTlab
cl. Sun Hung Kai Properties Ltd.

658

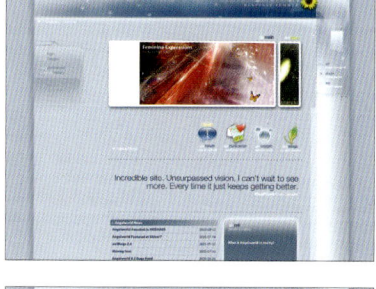

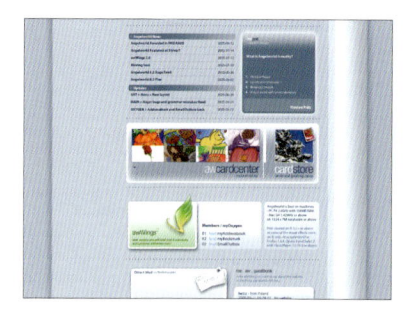

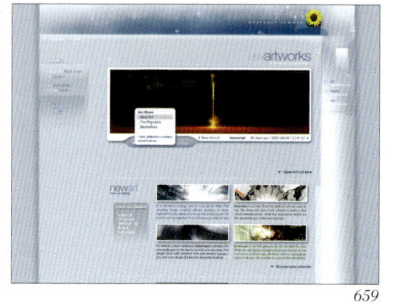

659

Silver
658_ CD Rom
t. Multi-media Game Design for Urban Renewal Authority
e. cd. Dennis Yuk Pui Wong
dd. ap. Jackson Choi
ad. Dominic Kam
d. Jack Lai
cl. Urban Renewal Authority

Silver
659_ Business & Consumer Website
t. Angelworld
e. Vincent Lai Wing Him
cd. dd. ad. d. p. a. i. Lai Wing Him Vincent
s. Kate

454

660

661

Silver
660_ *CD Rom*
  t. Hong Kong Arts Festival Society 05
     - Event Preview
  e. Edeas
  cd. Kelly Sze
  d. Carol Hui
  ap. Kenneth Ho
  cs. Vienna Leung
  cp. Wealthy Graphic Co., Ltd.
  pt. Printink Ltd.
  cl. Hong Kong Arts Festival Society Ltd.

Bronze
661_ *Online Advertising*
  t. Netvigator PSP offer
  e. Power Point Concepts Ltd.
  cd. Patrick Lam
  d. Derek Ng, Lee Man Wai
  cs. Anna Yuen
  cl. PCCW IMS Ltd.

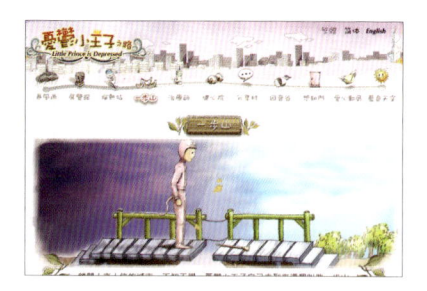

Bronze

662_ Educational Website

t. Website Development
e. Westcomzivo Ltd.
cd. Pasu Au Yeung, Jessie You
ad. Alex Cheng, Dido Chow
d. i. Dido Chow
cs. Jessie You
cl. The Hong Kong Jockey Club,
 Centre for Suicide Research and Prevention,
 The University of Hong Kong

Bronze

663_ Business & Consumer Website

t. Yugamama Website
e. pill & pillow
cd. ad. d. ap. Henry Chu
cw. Miriam Choi
cl. Harvest Loyal Development Ltd.

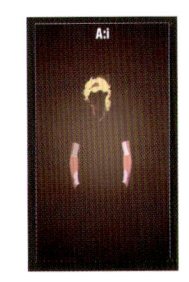

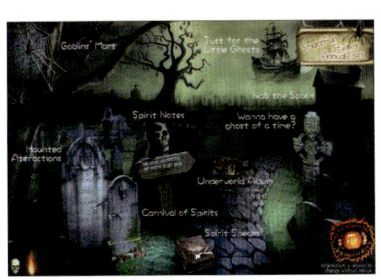

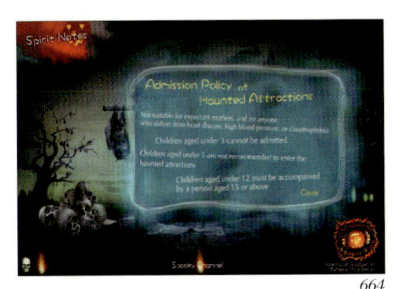

Excellent
664_ Online Advertising
t. Website Development
e. i Marketing Direct Ltd.
ad. Alex Cheng, Michael Cheung
d. Alex Cheng, Dido Chow, Don Li,
 Eric Wong, Kathy Chiu, Sarah Li
ap. Dido Chow
i. Alex Cheng, Dido Chow, Don Li,
 Eric Wong
cl. Ocean Park

Excellent
665_ Online Advertising
t. Viral Marketing Campaign
e. i Marketing Direct Ltd.
ad. Alex Cheng
d. Alex Cheng
ap. Kathy Chiu
i. Don Li
cl. Ocean Park

Excellent
666_ Online Advertising
t. a:i / 2004 interactive new year
e. archetype : interactive
cd. John Wu
ad. Benny Luk
ap. Titus Chan
cw. Cecilia Lau
cl. archetype interactive Ltd.

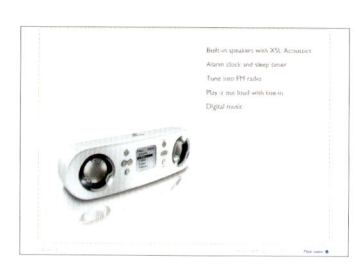

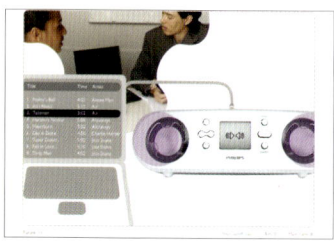

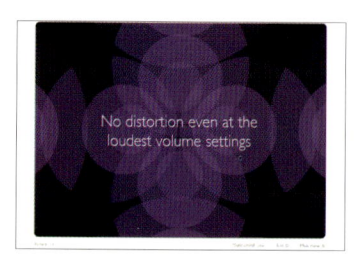

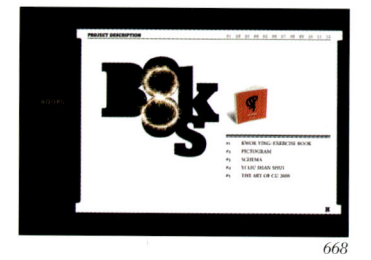

Excellent
667_ *Online Advertising*
t. Biotherm - Aquatrio
e. Media Explorer Ltd.
d. Gary Lui
ap. Henry Kwan
cl. L'Oreal Hong Kong Ltd.

Excellent
668_ *Online Advertising*
t. www.kosiuhong.com
e. cd. ad. d. cl. Hong Ko

Excellent
669_ *Other New Media Graphic*
t. Philips SHOQBOX product demo
e. Edeas
cd. Kelly Sze
d. Sharon Chan
s. Gary Sze
cs. Vienna Leung
cl. Philips Consumer Electronics

670

671

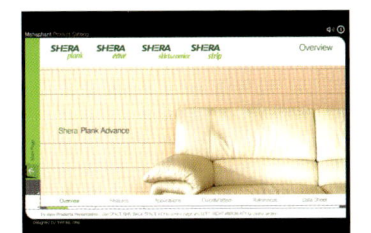

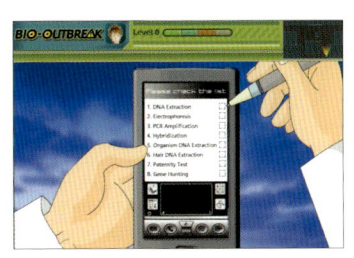

672

Excellent
670_ CD Rom

t. Mahaphant Product Catalog
e. Thomas Idea Co., Ltd.
cd. Araya Choutgrajank
d. Kietipoom Yuetreerak
cl. Mahaphant Group

Excellent
671_ CD Rom

t. Bio-Outbreak
e. Esthete Creative Consultants Ltd.
cd. Jacky Cheung
dd. Michael Tam
d. Natalie Wan, Carrie Lau
ap. Lam Pak Hong, Sam Lam
cl. Hybribio Ltd.

672_ CD Rom

t. Emotional Management
e. Zense Design Ltd.
cd. Garry Cheng
ad. Celina Chui
d. Eunice Chan, Gloria Ho
ap. Anthony Ho
cl. Hospital Authority

459

673

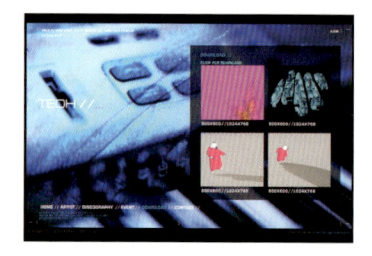

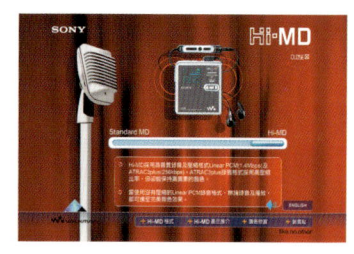

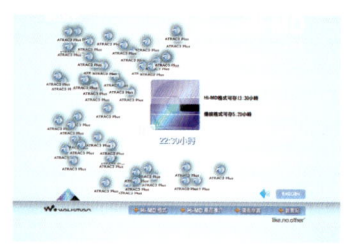

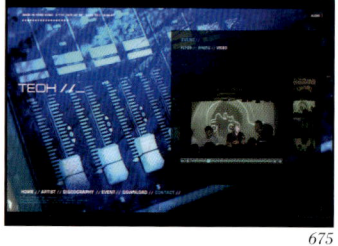

674

675

Excellent

673_ *Business & Consumer Website*

t. channel [v]
e. archetype : interactive
cd. John Wu
ad. Benny Luk, Kenji Wong
a. Ken Wu
ap. Henry Fu, Titus Chan
ia. Henry Fu, Kenji Wong
i. Benny Luk
cs. Cecilia Lau
cl. Channel V Music Networks
   Limited Partnership

Excellent

674_ *Business & Consumer Website*

t. Sony Hi-MD site - Leap into
   Boundless Music World
e. PacificLink iMedia Ltd.
cd. ad. Alex Lo
dd. Alex Lo, Lennon Ho
cs. Kristy Yeung
cl. Sony

Excellent

675_ *Business & Consumer Website*

t. mut a tech
e. archetype : interactive
cd. ia. John Wu
ad. Dick Po
d. ap. Yeson Ye
s. cw. cl. Anthony Teoh

460

676
677
678

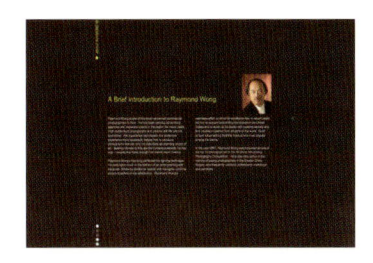

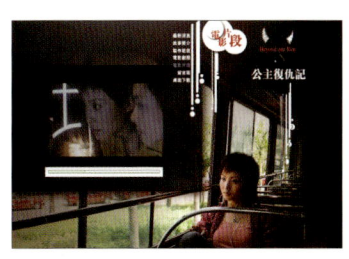

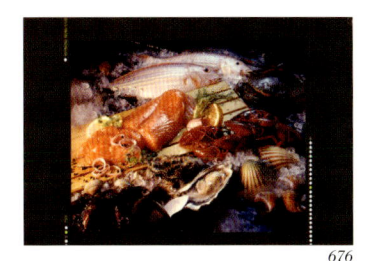

Excellent
676_ *Business & Consumer Website*
t. Raymond Wong Studio
e. pill & pillow
cd. d. ap. Henry Chu
cl. Raymond Wong

Excellent
677_ *Business & Consumer Website*
t. Mei Ah Entertainment Group Ltd. :
   Beyond Our Ken movie website
e. Eureka Group
cd. Louis Yang
cs. Fanny Lam

Excellent
678_ *Business & Consumer Website*
t. Aussie Planner
e. AGENDA (Hong Kong) Ltd.
cd. Clement Yip
dd. ia. Stanley Leung
d. Edwin Lo
ap. Ricky Wong
cw. Edwina Fung
cs. Yan Hui, Stanley Leung
cl. Tourism Australia

679

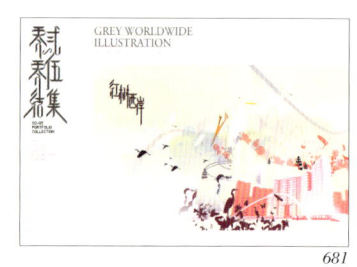

680

681

Excellent
679_ *Business & Consumer Website*
t. Garry Chan Studio
e. pill & pillow
cd. dd. d. ap. Henry Chu
cl. Garry Chan

Excellent
680_ *Business & Consumer Website*
t. Cool Distilled Water Website
e. Eureka Group
cd. Louis Yang
cs. Fanny Lam

Excellent
681_ *Business & Consumer Website*
t. Sixstation
e. ad. d. Benny Luk
ap. Wan Chun Hung

462

682

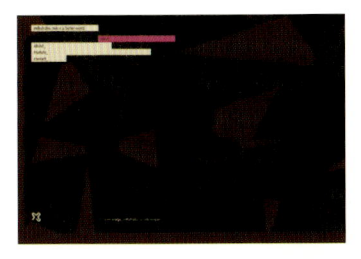

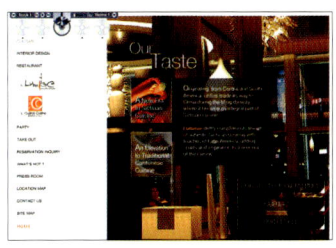

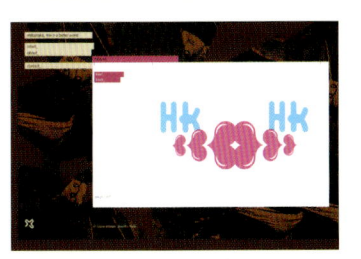

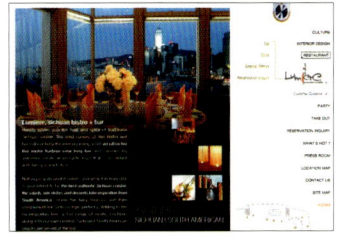

683

684

682_ Business & Consumer Website
t. MILKXHAKE
e. ad. cl. MILKXHAKE

683_ Business & Consumer Website
t. I LOVE ASIMO Cyber Community
e. Thomas Idea Co., Ltd.
cd. Araya Choutgrajank
pj. Uraiporn Cholsirirungskul
cl. Asian Honda Motor Co., Ltd.

684_ Business & Consumer Website
t. Lumiere | Cuisine Cuisine -
  A Tale of Two Cuisines
e. Esthete Creative Consultants Ltd.
cd. Jacky Cheung
dd. Michael Tam
d. Natalie Wan, Carrie Lau
ap. Lam Pak Hong, Sam Lam
cl. Miramar Hotel & Investment Co., Ltd.

APPENDIX 付録
부록 附录

Entries Statistics
Awardees' Statistics
Entrants Appendix
Members Appendix

Entries Statistics

Graphic

		No. of Entry	Awarded
1.01	Annual Report	59	13
1.02	Assorted Promotional Item	193	45
1.03	Book	133	39
1.04	Figure / Character	37	14
1.05	Editorial	62	19
1.06	Environmental Graphic	22	7
1.07	Illustration	48	16
1.08	Institutional / Marketing Literature	120	29
1.09	Logo	449	75
1.10	Packaging	127	32
1.11	Photography	44	12
1.12	Poster - Commercial	118	34
1.13	Poster - Cultural Promotional	140	42
1.14	Poster - Thematic	271	102
1.15	Stationary	68	17
1.16	Visual Identity Systems	125	31

New Media

		No. of Entry	Awarded
2.01	CD / DVD-Rom / DVD Graphic	13	5
2.02	Online Advertising	41	6
2.03	Website - Business & Consumer	100	14
2.04	Website - Educational	26	1
2.05	Other New Media Graphic	15	6

Product

		No. of Entry	Awarded
3.01	Domestic Accessory	29	10
3.02	Electronic & Electrical Appliance	42	20
3.03	Fashion Accessory	21	9
3.04	Furniture	25	10
3.05	Time Pieces, Gift and Premium	50	20
3.06	Toys	5	2

Spatial

		No. of Entry	Awarded
4.01	Exhibition / Window Display	58	14
4.02	Interior - Hospitality / Entertainment	54	17
4.03	Interior - Office	38	12
4.04	Interior - Residential	66	17
4.05	Interior - Retail	41	12

| **TOTAL** | | 2640 | 702 |

Awardees' Statistics

Entrant Name	Gold	Silver	Bronze	Excellent	Merit
Australia					
Eade + Evans	/	/	/	/	2
Tsen Wang 王蔘	/	/	/	1	/
Voice	/	/	1	/	/
China					
小馬哥 橙子	/	/	/	/	1
王剛	/	/	/	/	1
共同品牌策略顧問 共同包裝設計	/	/	1	/	8
肖偉棠	/	/	/	/	1
吳歆博	/	/	/	/	1
周強	/	/	/	/	1
洪衛	/	/	/	/	1
洪源	/	/	1	/	1
杭春暉	/	/	/	/	1
長江藝術與設計學	/	/	1	/	1
索曼斯包裝設計公司	/	/	/	/	1
密博	/	/	/	/	1
深圳朗圖公司	/	/	/	1	/
郭宗軍	/	/	/	/	1
Chen Hong 陳泓	/	/	/	/	1
陳康	/	/	/	/	1
彭克	/	/	/	/	1
畢學鋒	/	1	2	/	1
廣東天一文化有限公司	/	/	/	/	1
劉文	/	/	/	1	/
李長春	/	/	/	/	1
鄧遠健	/	/	/	/	1
Chenpingbo	/	/	/	/	1
Eric Cai Design Co.	/	/	2	/	1
FCB Shanghai	/	/	/	/	6
Han Jiaying	/	1	1	/	2
He Jun	/	1	1	1	1
Leo Burnett Shanghai	/	/	/	/	2
Nokia_6060	/	/	1	/	/
Shi Xiao Fan	/	/	/	/	2
Wu Yuan Min	/	/	/	/	1
Zhao Qing	/	/	/	1	/
Hong Kong					
28aDesign	/	/	/	2	1
Acorn Design Ltd.	/	/	/	/	5
Acumen Paper	/	/	/	/	3
Adjective	/	/	1	/	/
ADO Design & Public Art Consultants (HK) Ltd.	/	/	1	/	/
C01	/	/	/	1	12
AGENDA (Hong Kong) Ltd.	/	/	/	1	/
aMaze Workshop	/	/	/	/	1
Ameba Design Ltd.	/	/	/	/	7
Benny Au Tak-shing	/	1	9	6	17
archetype : interactive	/	/	/	3	/
Barrie Ho Architecture Interiors Ltd.	1	/	/	/	2
Bezalel Design Communication	/	/	/	/	1
Bliss Partners Int'l Ltd.	/	/	2	2	3
BrandsNation Ltd.	/	/	/	1	3
Broken Biscuit	/	/	/	1	/
Bun Ho	/	1	/	/	1
CC plus design Ltd.	/	/	1	/	1
Alan Chan	/	/	1	3	18
Chan Cheuk-pan	/	/	/	/	1
Michael Chan Sze-wah	/	/	1	/	/
Sherman Chan Yiu-tong	/	/	/	/	1
Chan Wing-yan 陳穎欣	/	/	/	/	1
Charles Ng & Maxi Communications Ltd.	/	/	/	1	5
Shirley Chau Suk-ma	/	/	/	1	/
Anissa Cheng 鄭亦芯	/	/	/	/	1
Cheng Kar Wai	/	/	/	/	3
Choi Kim Hung 蔡劍虹	/	/	/	1	/
John Chui Tak Ming	/	/	/	/	2
Edward Chung Chi-wing	/	/	/	/	1
Kirk Cheong	/	/	/	/	1
Chung Man-wai	/	/	/	1	/
Circle Design Ltd.	/	/	/	/	8
CL3 Architects Ltd.	/	2	/	2	2
CoDesign Ltd.	2	/	4	4	13
Creation Design	/	/	/	/	1
Design Systems Ltd.	/	1	2	/	1
DPWT Design Ltd.	/	/	/	/	1
Draughtzman	1	1	7	/	4
Eagletron Telecommunications Ltd.	/	/	/	1	/
Edeas	/	1	/	1	/
Eric Chan	/	/	/	3	14
Esthete Creative Consultants Ltd.	/	/	/	1	1
Eureka Group	/	/	/	2	/
Farm Design Consultant	/	/	/	/	1
FRA Ltd.	/	/	1	/	/
Eddy Chun 秦啓康	/	/	/	/	1
Genemix	/	/	/	/	2
Goodss Ltd.	/	/	2	/	/
Graphicat Ltd.	/	/	/	/	1
Grey Wba HK Ltd.	/	/	/	/	2
Hashimoto & Sung	/	/	/	1	/

Entrants Name	Gold	Silver	Bronze	Excellent	Merit
Alex Heung Kin Fung	/	/	/	/	1
Hippo Studio	/	/	/	/	2
Colan Ho	/	/	/	/	2
Joey Ho	/	1	1	0	1
Hong Kong Arts Centre	1	/	/	/	/
Ringo Hui	/	/	/	/	1
i Marketing Direct Ltd.	/	/	/	2	/
IDesign International Ltd.	/	/	/	/	1
IGOO	/	/	/	/	1
Ikonee International Ltd.	/	/	/	/	2
ingDesign	/	/	/	/	3
James	/	/	/	/	1
Joe Wong 黃桂源	/	/	/	/	1
Joseph Sy & Associates	/	/	1	1	3
Joyas Manufacturing Ltd.	/	/	/	/	1
Kan & Lau Design Consultants	1	/	5	5	23
Ken Lo	/	/	/	/	1
Kenford Industrial Company Ltd.	1	/	2	2	/
Hong Ko	/	1	/	1	3
KplusK Associates	/	/	/	3	3
Michael Kwong	/	/	/	1	5
Li Ying Ho 李英豪	/	/	/	/	1
Sky Liu	/	/	/	0	1
Lam Hon-hing 林漢興	/	/	/	/	1
Eddie, Lau Chi Kin	/	/	/	/	1
Michael Lau	1	/	1	2	5
Lau Kwok-tim	/	/	/	1	2
Lau Siu-tsang	/	/	/	1	3
Laurence Liauw Design Architect (PTEC)	/	/	1	/	/
Law Tak-wah 羅德華	/	/	/	/	1
Lawrence Choy	/	/	/	/	6
Steve Leung	/	/	1	1	2
Lester Lee Photo Workshop	/	/	/	/	2
Lo	/	/	/	/	1
Benny Luk	/	/	/	1	/
Ng Ching-nam 吳正楠	/	/	/	/	1
Mad Studios	/	/	/	/	2
Man Nin Shing Co.Ltd.	/	/	1	/	/
Prudence Mak	/	/	/	/	1
MAP Architecture & Planning Ltd.	/	/	/	/	1
Marc & Chantal Design	/	/	1	1	8
Mark Ho-man	/	/	/	/	2
Master Character Profile Company	/	/	/	/	1
Media Explorer Ltd.	/	/	/	1	/
Meh Meh Concept	/	/	/	2	/
Metier Atelier Company Ltd.	/	/	1	/	/
MI Design Ltd.	/	/	/	/	1
Milk Design	/	/	/	/	1
Milkxhake	1	/	1	1	7
Mok Wing-hung	/	/	/	/	1
Monopoly Design Ltd.	/	/	/	/	4
Nex Branding Design	/	/	/	/	4
P.S.L.	/	/	1	1	1
PacificLink iMedia Ltd.	/	/	/	1	/
PAL Design Consultant Ltd.	/	/	1	1	1
Paul Lam Design Associates	/	/	1	/	7
Philips Electronics Hong Kong Ltd. - Philips Design	/	3	/	1	4
Pill & Pillow	/	/	1	2	/
Albert Poon Chee Ki	/	/	/	/	2
Power Point Concepts Ltd.	/	/	1	/	/
Ptang Studio	/	/	1	/	/
RC Communications Ltd.	/	/	/	/	1
Recipe	/	/	/	/	1
Richy Ng	/	/	/	/	2
Sandy Choi Associates Ltd.	/	/	3	3	6
Semk Products Ltd.	/	1	/	1	/
Shellmoonsite	/	/	1	/	/
siDE Architects	/	/	/	/	1
Sirocco	/	/	/	/	3
SparKreative	/	/	/	/	1
Stanley Lo Jewelry Designs	/	1	/	/	/
STAR Group Ltd.	/	1	/	2	7
Step Design Consultants Ltd.	/	/	/	/	2
StudioOFF	/	/	1	0	1
Les Suen	1	/	0	1	1
Sunhing millennium Ltd.	/	/	/	/	1
SWEDA Ltd.	/	/	/	1	/
Ida Sze, Billy Chan	/	/	/	/	1
Takahashi Design Hong Kong Ltd.	/	/	/	/	1
Talentoy Factory Ltd.	/	/	1	/	/
Demo Tam Yu-hin	/	/	/	/	1
Tsang Chi-ping 曾子平	/	/	/	/	1
The Graphis Company Ltd.	/	/	/	/	2
Andy Tong	/	/	/	/	1
Token Workshop	/	/	/	/	5
Tommy Li Design Workshop Ltd.	0	1	2	7	14
Unioncult	/	/	/	1	1
VTech	1	0	/	/	2
Wan Chuck Kwan Thomas	/	/	/	/	1
Westcomzivo Ltd.	/	/	1	/	/
Willtech Industrial Ltd.	/	/	/	/	1
Winner Mfy. Ltd.	/	/	/	/	1
Goldie Wong 黃凱恩	/	/	/	/	1
Angus Wong	/	/	/	/	6
Woo Ka-yee	/	/	1	/	/
Yellow Creative (HK) Ltd.	/	/	/	/	3
Yip Yee-ki 葉綺琪	/	/	/	/	1

Entrants Name	Gold	Silver	Bronze	Excellent	Merit
Michael Miller Yu	/	/	/	/	8
Yuen Chun-kit 袁俊傑	/	/	/	/	1
Arthur Yung	1	1	/	/	/
Zanif Advertising and Promotion Ltd.	/	2	/	5	3
Zense Design Ltd.	/	/	/	/	1
Thomas Siu 蕭創英	/	/	/	/	1
Dennis Yuk Pui Wong	/	1	/	/	1
三聯書店（香港）有限公司	/	/	/	/	3

Japan

Entrants Name	Gold	Silver	Bronze	Excellent	Merit
Akihiko Tsukamoto	/	/	1	/	4
Daiko Advertising Inc.	/	/	1	/	2
Good morning Inc.	/	/	/	/	3
Graphics & Designing Inc.	/	/	/	/	2
Hiroki Takada	/	/	/	1	/
Katsuhiro Kinoshita	/	/	1	/	2
Kazuya Kondo	/	/	/	/	1
Keiko Yoshida	/	/	1	/	/
Masayoshi Kodaira	/	/	6	1	9
Michihito Sasaki	/	/	/	/	1
Norito Shinmura	/	/	1	2	/
Osamu Misawa	/	/	/	1	3
Seichi Ohashi	/	/	/	/	1
Setsue Shimizu	/	/	/	1	1
Shinnoske Sugisaki	/	/	1	1	/
Toshiyasu Nanbu	1	/	/	/	/
Yoshiteru Asai	/	/	/	/	1
Yukichi Takada	/	/	/	/	2

Macau

Entrants Name	Gold	Silver	Bronze	Excellent	Merit
周小良	/	/	/	/	1

Malaysia

Entrants Name	Gold	Silver	Bronze	Excellent	Merit
Imaya Wong	/	/	/	/	1
Joseph Foo	/	/	/	1	1

Singapore

Entrants Name	Gold	Silver	Bronze	Excellent	Merit
Epigram	/	/	/	/	2
Equus Design Consultants Pte. Ltd.	1	1	/	0	2

Taiwan

Entrants Name	Gold	Silver	Bronze	Excellent	Merit
I-Hsuan Cindy Wang	/	/	/	1	1
STONY	/	/	/	/	1

Entrants Name	Gold	Silver	Bronze	Excellent	Merit
李根在	/	1	1	2	/
林宏澤	/	/	/	/	1
知本設計廣告有限公司	/	/	/	/	1
邱顯能	/	/	/	/	3
紀健龍	/	/	/	/	1
袁世文	/	/	/	/	3
Jack Chang 張天捷	/	/	1	/	/
陳永基	/	/	1	/	3
陳俊良	/	1	1	3	3
創型堂設計公司 林志嘉	/	/	/	/	1

Thailand

Entrants Name	Gold	Silver	Bronze	Excellent	Merit
Thomas Idea Co., Ltd.	/	/	/	1	1

Entrants Appendix

c = contact
t = telephone number
f = fax number
e = email

Australia

Eade + Evans
c: Iain Evans
t: 61 3 9427 0266
f: 61 3 9427 9003
e: iain@eadeevans.com

Wang Tsen 王蔘
t: 61 414933691
e: jasonstyle0014@hotmail.com

Voice
t: 61 8 84108822
f: 61 8 84108933
e: anthony@voicedesign.net

China

Chen Hong 陳泓
t: 86 592 5989348
f: 86 592 5989348
e: yihong-design@sohu.com

Chen Pingbo
t: 86 755 82129341
f: 86 755 82129644
e: ivyfang19812004@hotmail.com

Eric Cai Design Co.
c: Shi Wei Cai
t: 86 10 65123888
e: 86 10 65138788
f: ecdesign@vip.sina.com

FCB Shanghai
t: 86 21 63609298
f: 86 21 63609208
e: jsheng@shanghai.fcb.com

Han Jiaying
c: Zhou Weifen
t: 86 755 83551760
f: 86 755 83551758
e: han@hanjiaying.com

He Jun
t: 86 10 64770095
f: 86 10 64770095
e: hejunnet@vip.sina.com

Leo Burnett Shanghai
c: Dennis Ou
t: 86 21 63352338
f: 86 21 6335 2308
e: dennis.ou@sh.leoburnett.com

Nokia_6060
c: Su/Chun-Wei
t: 86 13501267025
f: 86 1065393824
e: chunwei-sean.su@nokia.com

Shixiaofan
t: 86 755 83980938
f: 86 755 83980928
e: sxf@shixiaofan.com

Wu Yuan-Min 吳元敏
t: 86 571 85157799
f: 86 571 85157799 ext.111
e: wym9169@sina.com

Zhaoqing
t: 86 25 83192655
f: 86 25 83192469
e: raincolor0722@163.com

小馬哥 橙子
c: 馬惠敏
t: 86 13910637206
e: maggy2004@126.com

王剛
t: 86 0571 81883079
f: 86 571 81883079
e: wanggang310012@163.com

共同品牌策略顧問 共同包裝設計
c: 馬深廣
t: 86 755 25905039
f: 86 755 25905043
e: boss.cn@163.com

李長春
t: 86 371 63557180
e: lccbth@yahoo.com.cn

肖偉棠
t: 86 13822237171
e: markinchinacn@yahoo.com.cn

周強
t: 86 13915944100
e: zqfire@Yeah.net

洪衞
t: 86 760 8389079
f: 86 760 8389079
e: hwttxs@163.com

洪源
t: 86 13121023321
e: Woody-h@163.COM

吳軼博
t: 86 431 4644491
f: 86 431 444491
e: wybpc3392@sina.com

杭春暉
t: 86 10 64320544
e: hch586@yahoo.com.cn

長江藝術與設計學院
c: 崔德煒
t: 86 754 2903223
f: 86 754 2903226
e: ckad@stu.edu.cn

索曼斯包裝設計公司
c: 于永芳
t: 86 991 2835718
f: 86 991 2835718
e: sommese@163.com

密博
t: 86 13691049960
e: mibo2008@126.com

深圳朗圖公司
t: 86 755 83953387
f: 86 755 83953331
e: annie@rito.cn

郭宗軍
t: 86 21 63867358/
86 13916047629
f: 86 21 63867199
e: guogzj@sina.com

陳康
t: 86 21 13701749873
f: 86 21 63282583
e: cann66@21cn.com

彭克
t: 86 21 65922010 ext. 820
f: 86 21 65922010 ext.841
e: pink@pdesign.cn

畢學鋒
c: 劉亞敏
t: 86 755 83890788
f: 86 755 83890955
e: info@imagram.ocm

廣東天一文化有限公司
c: 黎春妍
t: 86 20 38860674
f: 86 20 38864449
e: market@tianyi.21cn.com

鄧遠健
t: 86 755 25910206
f: 86 755 25910213
e: yenken@163.com

劉文
t: 86 755 82307832
f: 86 755 25180164
e: leuwn@126.com

Hong Kong

28aDesign
c: Leo Kwok
t: 852 2915 6092
f: 852 2915 6096
e: leo.kwok@4apg.com

A

Acorn Design Ltd.
c: Frank Chan Wah Hung
t: 852 25910057
f: 852 25726920
e: acorndd@netvigator.com

Acumen Paper
c: Deris Ou
t: 852 28403116
f: 852 28403178
e: deris@acumenpaper.com

Adjective
c: Michael Fung
t: 852 91082934
f: 852 36902779
e: michael@adjective.com.hk

ADO Design & Public Art Consultants (HK) Ltd.
c: Annie Or
t: 852 26466381
f: 852 26346648
e: aor@ado-hk.com

Agenda (Hong Kong) Ltd.
c: Stanley Leung
t: 852 2298 3888
f: 852 2144 6332
e: stanley.leung@agenda-asia.com

Alan Chan Design Co.
c: Christine Lam
t: 852 25278228
f: 852 28656170
e: acdesign@alanchandesign.com

aMaze Workshop
c: Miranda Yiu
t: 852 25667113
f: 852 29795183
e: mirandayiu@a-maze.com.hk

Ameba Design Ltd.
c: Gideon Lai
t: 852 23896981
f: 852 27639800
e: DorcasW@AmebaDesign.com

archetype : interactive
c: John Wu
t: 852 25463918
f: 852 25463575
e: john@a-i.com.hk

B

Benny Au Tak-shing
t: 852 22677213
f: 852 22676482
e: benny@amazingangle.com

Barrie Ho Architecture Interiors Ltd.
c: Alan Lam
t: 852 21177662
f: 852 21177661
e: barrieho@barrieho.com

Bezalel Design Communication
c: Ice Lam Siu Bing
t: 852 93162814
e: icebing@bezalel-design.com

Bliss Partners Int'l Ltd.
c: Ivan Leung
t: 852 25206787
f: 852 25286182
e: ivanleung@bpl.cc

BrandsNation Ltd.
c: Eric Kai-wa Cheung
t: 852 25271303
f: 852 25271289
e: eric@brandsnation.com

Broken Biscuit
c: Roy Man
t: 852 92591694
e: info@brokenbiscuit.com

C

CC Plus Design Ltd.
c: Crystalle Cheang
t: 852 25239050
f: 852 25475307
e: design@ccplusdesign.com
   admin@ccplusdesign.com

Chan Cheuk-pan
t: 852 35792818
f: 852 35792788
e: pennychan@freeverse.com.hk

Eric Chan
t: 852 25277773
f: 852 28653929
e: ecdesign@netvigator.com

Michael Chan Sze-wah
t: 852 28870313
f: 852 28870451
e: info@edge-architects.com

Chan Wing-yan 陳穎欣
c: Paul Lam
t: 852 28920123
f: 852 25731992
e: info@co1.edu.hk

Sherman Chan Yiu-tong
t: 852 2591 4663
f: 852 2591 9062
e: sherman@chingying.edu.hk

Charles Ng & Maxi Communications Ltd.
c: Charles Ng
t: 852 28249328
f: 852 28249826
e: charles@maxicomm.com.hk

Shirley Chau Suk-man
t: 852 90134096
f: 852 24606832
e: shirleyc@hhr.com.hk

Anissa Cheng 鄭亦芯
c: Paul Lam
t: 852 28363368
f: 852 25731992
e: paul@paullamdesign.com.hk

Cheng Kar-wai
t: 852 28363368
f: 852 25731992
e: wai@monsterworkshop.com

Kirk Cheong
t: 86 10 13522921383
e: kirk10101@hotmail.com

Choi Kim-hung 蔡劍虹
c: Paul Lam
t: 852 28920123
f: 852 25731992
e: info@co1.edu.hk

Lawrence Choy
t: 852 3427-3273
f: 852 2806-8057
e: wychoy1111@netvigator.com

John Chui Tak-ming
t: 853 969191
f: 853 969292
e: jchuitsui@yahoo.com.hk

Eddy Chun 秦啟康
c: Paul Lam
t: 852 28920123
f: 852 25731992
e: info@co1.edu.hk

Edward Chung Chi-wing
t: 852 94873966
e: chiwing_edward@yahoo.com.hk

Chung Man-wai
t: 852 9302 1516
e: willwillchung@yahoo.com.hk

Circle Design Ltd.
c: Clement Yick
t: 852 28918007
f: 852 28912007
e: clement@circledesign.com

CL3 Architects Ltd.
c: William Lim
t: 852 2527 1931
f: 852 2529 8392
e: william@cl3.com

CoDesign Ltd.
c: Eddy Yu
t: 852 25108710
f: 852 25108711
e: eddy@codesign.com.hk

Creation Design
c: Tsun-Man Lok
t: 852 25619190
f: 852 25620463
e: man@creationdesign.com.hk

D

Design Systems Ltd.
c: Wai Ming Lam
t: 852 25276828
f: 852 25276801
e: lamwaiming@designsystems.com.hk

DPWT Design Ltd.
c: Arthur Chan
t: 852 28041683
f: 852 28041673
e: arthur@dp-wt.com

Draughtzman
c: Alliot Cheng
t: 852 2866 2112
f: 852 2861 2831
e: allyoop@netvigator.com

E

Eagletron Telecommunications Ltd.
c: Amelia Cheung
t: 852 26123023
f: 852 24089842
e: amelia@eagletron.com.hk

Edeas
c: Kelly Sze
t: 852 28824512
f: 852 28823943
e: kelly@edeas.hk

Esthete Creative Consultants Ltd.
c: Jacky Cheung
t: 852 25293711
f: 852 28667691
e: jacky@esthete.com.hk

Eureka Group
c: Louis Yang
t: 852 28828471
f: 852 28821173
e: louis@eureka-group.com

F

Farm Design Consultant
c: Maggie Woo
t: 852 93031874
e: maggiewoo@consultant.com

FRA Ltd.
c: Rose Poon
t: 852 25273088
f: 852 25273077
e: info@fragroup.com

G

Genemix
c: James Leung
t: 852 25041620
f: 852 25721210
e: james_leung@genemix.com

Goodss Ltd.
c: Fanny Chan
t: 852 28365218
f: 852 25738699
e: fanny@e-goodss.com

Graphicat Ltd.
c: Colin Tillyer/Ms. Law
t: 852 2838 8608
f: 852 2838 5285
e: design@graphicat.com

Grey Wba HK Ltd.
c: David Lo
t: 852 25106856
f: 852 28875186
e: dalo@wbahk.com

H

Hashimoto & Sung
c: David Sung
t: 852 28332111
f: 852 28332136
e: hashimotoddesign@yahoo.com.hk

Alex Heung Kin Fung
t: 852 25271778
f: 852 25272022
e: alex@designpartners.com.hk

Hippo Studio
c: Chin-lee Ma
t: 852 25296700
f: 852 25299269
e: design@hippostudio.com

Bun Ho
t: 852 91910554
f: 852 26758150
e: mingbunho@netvigator.com

Colan Ho
t: 852 23274008
f: 852 28574011
e: colan@esperantodesign.com

Joey Ho
t: 852 28508732
f: 852 28508972
e: enjoy@joeyhodesign.com

Hong Kong Arts Centre
t: 852 28245327
f: 852 28020798
e: clwong@hkac.org.hk

Ringo Hui
t: 852 6097 8273
f: 852 23240482
e: ringohuiwk@netvigator.com

I

i Marketing Direct Ltd.
c: Joey Pun
t: 852 25284046
f: 852 25270163
e: jpun@imd.com.hk

IDesign International Ltd.
c: Kelvin Law
t: 852 28816608
f: 852 28816658
e: info@ides1gn.com

IGOO
t: 852 28041678
f: 852 28918418
e: sally@igoo.com.hk

Ikonee International Ltd.
c: Samuel Yeung
t: 852 27972770
f: 852 24116563
e: samuel@ikonee.com.hk

ingDesign
t: 852 2234-0700
f: 852 2234-0720
e: info@ingdesign.com.hk

J

Joseph Sy & Associates
t: 852 28661333
f: 852 28661222
e: design@jsahk.com

Joyas Manufacturing Ltd.
c: Wincy Lam
t: 852 24080880
f: 852 24080906
e: info@joyas.com.hk

K

Kan & Lau Design Consultants
c: Biko So
t: 852 25748399
f: 852 25720199
e: biko@kanandlau.com

Kenford Industrial Company Ltd.
c: Michael Keong
t: 852 24228198
f: 852 24289819
e: michael@kenford.com.hk

KplusK Associates
c: Johnny Kember
t: 852 2541 6828
f: 852 2541 7885
e: johnnyk@kplusk.net

Hong Ko
t: 852 92176790
e: hong@kosiuhong.com

Michael Kwong
t: 852 97301374
f: 852 31182551
e: michael@locoism.com.hk

L

Lam Hon-hing 林漢興
c: Paul Lam
t: 852 28920123
f: 852 25731992
e: info@co1.edu.hk

Vincent Lai
t: 852 98695672
f: 852 23791280
e: niteangel@gmail.com

Benny Lau Siu Tsang
t: 852 28654240
e: benny@creativecafe.hk

Eddie Lau Chi Kin
t: 852 9582 4441
e: eddie@eddielau.net

Michael Lau
e: crazysmilesmail@yahoo.com

Lau Kwok-tim
t: 852 28660995
f: 852 28661954
e: timphotography@netvigator.com

James Law
t: 852 23819997
f: 852 23361385
e: james_law@jameslawcybertecture.com

Law Tak-wah 羅德華
c: Paul Lam
t: 852 28920123
f: 852 25731992
e: info@co1.edu.hk

Lester Lee Photo Workshop
c: Lester Lee
t: 852 28810336
f: 852 28335087
e: xlesterx@netvigator.com

Steve Leung
c: Joyce So
t: 852 25271600
f: 852 25272071
e: joyceso@steveleung.com.hk

Laurence Liauw Design Architect (PTEC)
t: 852 98488677
f: 852 27745067
e: sdliauw@polyu.edu.hk

Li Ying-ho 李英豪
c: Paul Lam
t: 852 28920123
f: 852 25731992
e: info@co1.edu.hk

Sky Liu
t: 852 34282584
f: 852 28978141
e: sky_liuszekeung@yahoo.com.hk

Jo Lo
t: 852 26094060
f: 852 26094050
e: zeroart@zeroartstudio.com

Ken Lo
t: 852 95297747
f: 852 23905546
e: hiutangabc@yahoo.com.hk

Benny Luk
t: 852 96394590
f: 852 23331440
e: benny@sixstation.com

M

Mad Studios
c: Brian Lau
t: 852 94143291
e: brian@mad-studios.com

Prudence Mak
c: Janice Liu
t: 852 94150039
f: 852 2975838
e: prudence@chocolaterain.com

Man Nin Shing Co., Ltd.
c: Karen Lau
t: 852 24816638
f: 852 24199329
e: karen@mns-hk.com

MAP Architecture & Planning Ltd.
c: Mandy Leung
t: 852 28779282
f: 852 28779283
e: map@maphk.com

Marc & Chantal Design
c: Marc Cansier
t: 852 2543774
f: 852 25437744
e: marc-c@marc-chantal.com

Mark Ho-man
t: 852 98858770
e: mark@shhhit.com

Master Character Profile Co.
c: Clarence Chiu
t: 852 91003361
f: 852 21782263
e: clarence_c@sinaman.com

Media Explorer Ltd.
c: Davy Ma
t: 852 25419978
f: 852 25410940
e: davy@me.com.hk

Meh Meh Concept
c: Juana Ho
t: 852 2528 3246
f: 852 2529 1701
e: juanaho@mehmeh.com

Metier Atelier Company Ltd.
c: Thera So
t: 852 2370 9887
f: 852 2370 8862
e: info@metier.com.hk

MI Design Ltd.
c: Helen Cheung
t: 852 25120702
f: 852 28071505
e: midesign@biznetvigator.com

Milk Design
c: Lee Chi-wing
t: 852 27978500
f: 852 27973335
e: wing@milkdesign.com.hk

Milkxhake
c: Javin Mo / Wilson Tang
t: 852 63369740
f: 852 30169245
e: javin@milkxhake.org

Mok Wing-hung
t: 852 2142 4507
f: 852 2142 4602
e: hung@deepworkshop.com

Monopoly Design Ltd.
c: Kevin Yuen
t: 852 25261656
f: 852 25259226
e: kevin@monopolydesign.com

N

Nex Branding Design
c: Joseph Leung
t: 852 28613809
f: 852 28650485
e: joseph@motakding.com

Ng Ching-nam 吳正楠
c: Paul Lam
t: 852 28920123
f: 852 25731992
e: info@co1.edu.hk

Richy Ng
t: 852 25733323
f: 852 25733998
e: richy@boxdesign.com.hk

P

P.S.L.
c: Fai Leung
t: 852 22607176
f: 852 27458511
e: fai@sweda.com.hk

PacificLink iMedia Ltd.
c: Kristy Yeung
t: 852 24890168
e: kristy.yeung@pacim.com

PAL Design Consultant Ltd.
c: Patrick Leung
t: 852 28771233
f: 852 28249275
e: email@paldesign.hk.com

Paul Lam Design Associates
c: Paul Lam
t: 852 28363368
f: 852 25731992
e: paul@paullamdesign.com.hk

Philips Electronics Hong Kong Limited - Philips Design
c: Rodney Loh / Amy Cheng
t: 852 24896797
f: 852 24892531
e: amy.sm.cheng@philips.com

Pill & Pillow
c: Henry Chu
t: 852 31193097
f: 852 31193097
e: henry@pillandpillow.com

Power Point Concepts Ltd.
c: Hyacinth Lam
t: 852 28931266
f: 852 28939731
e: hyacinthlam@power-point.com.hk

Ptang Studio
c: Philip Tang
t: 852 26691577
f: 852 26693577
e: office@ptangstudio.com

R

RC Communications Ltd.
c: Janet Chu
t: 852 31059567
f: 852 31052147
e: janet.chu@rc.com.hk

Recipe
c: Ben Lai
t: 852 6126 4688
e: ixxue@yahoo.com.hk

S

Sandy Choi Associates Ltd.
c: Sandy Choi
t: 852 2525 9577
f: 852 2525 9655
e: sc@sandychoi.com

Semk Products Ltd.
c: Eddie Hui
t: 852 24699599
f: 852 24562578
e: eddie@semk.net

Shellmoonsite
c: Lee Man-Chung
t: 852 94266377
e: info@shellmoonsite.com

siDE Architects
c: Colin Chan
t: 852 29155133
f: 852 29151773
e: colin@side.com.hk

Sirocco
c: Patrick Tam
t: 852 28153334
f: 852 28153304
e: patrick@sirocco-hk.com

Thomas Siu 蕭劍英
c: Paul Lam
t: 852 28920123
f: 852 25731992
e: info@co1.edu.hk

SparKreative
t: 852 25706036
f: 852 25704238
e: louis@sparkreative.com

Stanley Lo Jewelry Designs
c: Stanley Lo
t: 852 23120829
f: 852 22481140
e: info@stanleylojewelry.com

STAR Group Ltd.
c: Cat Lam
t: 852 26219107
f: 852 26219120
e: catlam@startv.com

Step Design Consultants Ltd.
c: Stephen Barry
t: 852 2581 4427
f: 852 2543 4269
e: stephen@step.com.hk

studioOFF
c: RussellLaw
t: 852 23900035
f: 852 23825728
e: studio_off@so-net.com.hk

Les Suen
t: 852 92152375
e: lesoles@netvigator.com

Sunhing Millennium Ltd.
c: Wai-Keung Chu
t: 852 27859446
f: 852 23750263
e: chuwaikeung@sunhing.com

Sweda Ltd.
c: Keith Mak
t: 852 22607171
f: 852 27458511
e: keithmak@sweda.com.hk

Ida Sze, Billy Chan
t: 852 92121804 / 852 9417 3968
e: idasze@yahoo.com

T

Takahashi Design Hong Kong Ltd.
c: Jolyne Chan
t: 852 2893-3706
f: 852 2893-3874
e: info@tdesign-hk.com

Talentoy Factory Ltd.
c: Gary Kwok
t: 852 35100035
f: 852 23116511
e: gary.kwok@talentoy.com.hk

Demo Tam Yu Hin
c: Democritus Tam
t: 852 93281597
e: demotam@gmail.com

The Graphis Company Ltd.
c: Bon Kwan
t: 852 25220973
f: 852 25220872
e: bon@thegraphis.com

Token Workshop
c: Kenneth, To Po Keung
t: 852 2833 6556
f: 852 2833 5956
e: info@tokenworkshop.com

Tommy Li Design Workshop Ltd.
c: Lancy Chiu
t: 852 28346312
f: 852 28347032
e: lancy@vqmagazine.com

Andy Tong
c: Carol
t: 852 28112881
f: 852 28811586
e: andy_tong@andycreations.com

Tsang Chi-ping 曾子平
c: Paul Lam
t: 852 28920123
f: 852 25731992
e: info@co1.edu.hk

U

Unioncult
c: Michael Cheung
t: 852 25109900
f: 852 25107755
e: michael@unioncult.com

V

VTech
c: David Waterman
t: 852 26801483
f: 852 26645521
e: david_waterman@vtech.com

W

Thomas Wan Chuck Kwan
t: 852 28673806
f: 852 21084629
e: wongesther@netvigator.com

Westcomzivo Ltd.
c: Joey Pun
t: 852 2285 6354
f: 852 2798 6997
e: joey.pun@westcomzivo.com

Willtech Industrial Ltd.
c: Sunny Lau
t: 852 2409 8408
f: 852 8343 8262
e: sunny@wthkg.com

Winner Mfy. Ltd.
c: Dick Chan, Selina Shum
t: 852 94265346
f: 852 82092003
e: mwdc02@hotmail.com

Woo Ka-yee
t: 852 61994862
e: dreamhouse1@i-cable.com

Angus Wong
852 28363328
852 29047947
angus@angusdesign.com.hk

Goldie Wong 黃凱恩
c: Paul Lam
t: 852 28920123
f: 852 25731992
e: info@co1.edu.hk

Joe Wong 黃桂源
c: Paul Lam
t: 852 28920123
f: 852 25731992
e: info@co1.edu.hk

Y

Yellow Creative (HK) Ltd.
c: Vicky Liu
t: 852 21277181
f: 852 21277112
e: yellow@yellowcreative.com

Yip Yee-ki 葉綺琪
c: Paul Lam
t: 852 28920123
f: 852 25731992
e: info@co1.edu.hk

Michael Miller Yu
t: 852 25729232
f: 852 28381375
e: Michael@Michaelsolve.com

Yuen Chun-kit 袁俊傑
c: Paul Lam
t: 852 28920123
f: 852 25731992
e: info@co1.edu.hk

Arthur Yung
t: 852 6200 8036
f: 86 755 8213 6629
e: arthur@seedz-design.com

Dennis Wong Yuk-pui
c: Edna Yeung
t: 852 2802-2033
f: 852 2511-2917
e: dennisw@oval-design.com

Z

Zanif Advertising and Promotion Ltd.
c: Winnif Pang
t: 852 24021289
f: 852 24021288
e: pang@zanif.com

Zense Design Ltd.
c: Garry Cheng
t: 852 28346163
f: 852 28365920
e: info@zensedesign.com

三聯書店（香港）有限公司
c: 李安
t: 852 93018399
f: 852 28455249
e: anne@jointpublishing.com

Japan

Akihiko Tsukamoto
t: 81 3 5411 1943
f: 81 3 5411 1810
e: zuan@big.or.jp

Daiko Advertising Inc.
c: Miwako Hamatake
t: 81 6392 8831
f: 81 6292 8198
e: miwako.hamatake@daiko.co.jp

Good Morning Inc.
c: Katsumi Tamura
t: 81 3 5421 1007
f: 81 3 5421 1009
e: tamura@goodmorning.co.jp

Graphics & Designing Inc.
c: Masato Shimazu
t: 81 3 3449 1550
f: 81 3 3449 1510
e: shimazu@quicheandtarte.com

Katsuhiro Kinoshita
t: 81 3 5952 7487
f: 81 3 5952 7489
e: jdd02134@nifty.ne.jp

Kazuya Kondo
t: 81 3 3423 7051
f: 81 3 3423 7052
e: info@kazuyakondo.com

Masayoshi Kodaira
c: Namiko Otsuka
t: 81 3 5469 5210
f: 81 3 5469 5217
e: otsuka@flameinc.jp

Osamu Misawa
c: Aika Hayashi
t: 81 3 5766 3410
f: 81 3 5766 3411
e: hayashi@omdr.co.jp

Toshiyasu Nanbu
t: 81 7 2824 5538
f: 81 7 2824 5583
e: tasteinc@osk.3web.ne.jp

Seichi Ohashi
c: Aiko Nakamura
t: 81 3 3407 1622
f: 81 3 3407 1019
e: nakamura@cc-lesmains.co.jp

Michihito Sasaki
t: 81 6 6772 7370
f: 81 6 6772 7370
e: sasaki@adseven.co.jp

Setsue Shimizu
c: Hideaki Mizutani
t: 81 3 3796 7544
f: 81 3 3796 7545
e: mizutani@c-dash.com

Norito Shinmura
t: 81 3 3572 5042
f: 81 3 3572 5045
e: ns@shinmura-d.co.jp

Shinnoske Sugisaki
t: 81 6 6943 9077
f: 81 6 6943 9078
e: shinn@shinn.co.jp

Hiroki Takada
t: 81 5 9386 2250
f: 81 5 9387 1203
e: hiroki@takadadesign.com

Yukichi Takada
t: 81 6 69490853
f: 81 6 69490854
e: cid-lab@gc4.so-net.ne.jp

Keiko Yoshida
t: 81 3 6216 7015
f: 81 3 6217 5671
e: gz1070@dentsu.co.jp

Yoshiteru Asai
t: 81 5 2761 1287
f: 81 5 2761 9519
e: chanploou@M_1.ktroad.ne.jp

Macau

周小良
t: 853 6282990
f: 853 839658
e: chaosiuleong@yahoo.com.hk

Malaysia

Joseph Foo
t: 603 7880 9477/9440
f: 603 7880 9441
e: joseph.foo@3nitydesign.com

Imaya Wong
t: 603 22836559
f: 603 22836512
e: imaya@chimera.com.my

Singapore

Epigram
c: Teresa Lim
t: 65 62924456
f: 65 62924414
e: zann@epigram.com.sg

Equus Design Consultants Pte. Ltd.
c: Alex Mucha
t: 65 63232996
f: 65 63232991
e: alex@equus-design.com

Taiwan

I-Hsuan Cindy Wang
c: Cindy Wang
t: 886 931987977
f: 886 62530793
e: wcindy210@yahoo.com.tw

Jack Chang 張天捷
t: 886 920 036676
e: mrjackchang@yahoo.com

Stony
t: 886 2 27790515
f: 886 2 27790519
e: stony@stony-image.com

林宏澤
t: 886 7 7116360
f: 886 7 7256601
e: jer@hugtop.com.tw

李根在
t: 886 2 28935236
p: 886 2 87803659
e: lkt111@pchome.com.tw

知本設計廣告有限公司
c: 胡松齡
t: 886 2 28331943
f: 886 2 28353948
e: proad.design@msa.hinet.net

邱顯能
t: 886 2 27185896
f: 886 2 27185894
e: chartcom@ms4.hinet.net

紀健龍
t: 886 2 87805935
f: 886 2 27204993
e: twoface@ms38.hinet.net

袁世文
t: 886 2 27455557
f: 886 2 27455423
e: onshow.mail@msa.hinet.net

陳永基
t: 886 2 25455435
f: 886 2 27151630
e: leslie@lcdesign.com.tw

陳俊良
c: 賴靜芬
t: 886 2 25770001
f: 886 2 25770002
aaron@freeimage.com.tw

創型堂設計公司
c: 林志嘉
t: 886 2 33221137
f: 886 2 23968700
e: sokedo@ms74.hinet.net

Thailand

Thomas Idea Co., Ltd.
c: Araya Choutgrajank
t: 66 27126365
f: 66 27127650
e: araya@thomasidea.com

Members Appendix

c = contact
t = telephone number
f = fax number
e = email

Fellow Members

John Au Yin-ho
c: John Au Design Associates
t: 852 2529 1133
f: 852 2529 1113

Alan Chan Yau-kin
Alan Chan Design Company
t: 852 2527 8228
f: 852 2865 6170
w: www.alanchandesign.com

Max Cheung Choi-lai
c: The Design Partners Ltd.
t: 852 2527 1778
f: 852 2527 2022

Choi Kai-yan
c: Choi Kai Yan
    Design Consultants Ltd.
t: 2711 3199
f: 2711 9277

Christopher Chow Chi-bor
t: 61 411 398292

Corazza Marshall
t: 649 530 8922

William Ho Chung-keung
c: William Ho Design Associates Ltd.
t: 852 2521 4278/281
f: 852 2840 1972

Ho Tao
c: Taoho Design Architects Ltd.
t: 852 2811 8780
f: 852 2811 0337

Hon Bing-wah
c: HS Art & Design
t: 852 2572 2275
f: 852 2572 9617

Kan Tai-keung
c: Kan & Lau Design Consultants
t: 852 2574 8399
f: 852 2572 0199
w: www.kanandlau.com

Ku Jennings
c: The Hongkong & Shanghai
    Banking Corporation Ltd.
t: 852 2822 4951
f: 852 2576 1155

Agnes Kwok Yuen-han
t: 852 28071125

Freeman Lau Siu-hong
c: Kan & Lau Design Consultants
t: 852 2574 8399
f: 852 2572 0199

Daniel Ng Man-bing
t: 612 9399 5029

Henry Steiner
c: STEINER&CO.
t: 852 2548 5548
f: 852 2858 2576
w: www.steiner.com.hk

Alan Zie Youngder
t: 2963 0205

Full Members

Elaine Ann
c: Kaizor Innovation
t: 852 2297 2311
f: 852 2297 0066
w: www.kaizor.com

Joe Au Chi-ming
c: Bmb Design Consultant Co., Ltd.
t: 852 2894 9227
f 852 2577 8755
w: www.bmbdes.com

Benny Au Tak-shing
c: Amazing Angle Design
    Consultants Ltd.
t: 852 2267 7213
f: 852 2267 6482
w: www.amazingangle.com

Roger Ball
c: The Hong Kong Polytechnic
    University
t: 852 2766 5444
f: 852 2774 5067

Nic Banks
c: Atelier Pacific Ltd.
t: 852 2869 8265
f: 852 2869 8251
w: www.atelierpacific.com.hk

Stephen Barry
c: Step Design Consultants Ltd.
t: 852 2581 4427
f: 852 2543 4269
w: www.step.com.hk

Virgile Simon Bertrand
c: Red Desert Ltd.
t: 852 2526 4465
f: 852 2900 0216
w: www.red-desert.com.hk

Oliver Breit
c: Format Industrial Design Co., Ltd.
t: 852 2957 8712
f: 852 2957 8713
w: www.formart.com.hk

David But Fuk-keung
c: D & R Design (H.K) Ltd.
t: 852 2887 1268
f: 852 2887 2219
w: www.dnrdesign.com

Eddie Chak Yiu-fai
c: Hong Kong Trade
    Development Council
t: 852 2584 4115
f: 852 2824 2285

Anson Chan Cheuk-pan
c: Point Architects Ltd.
t: 852 9191-3793
f: 852 2850-8972
w: www.pointarchitects.com.hk

Steven Chan Chin-pang
c: SLK Design Ltd.
t: 852 2116 2666
f: 852 2116 9884
w: www.slkdesign.com.hk

Eric Chan Chiu-wang
c: Eric Chan Design Co., Ltd.
t: 852 2527 7773
f: 852 2865 3929

John Chan Chun-ho
c: John Chan Design Ltd.
t: 852 2521 0050
f: 852 2526 7425

Zeus Chan Hing-fung
c: Giant Wireless Technology Ltd.
t: 852 9194 8979
f: 852 2425 3776

Arthur Chan Hin-ming
c: DPWT Design Ltd.
t: 852 2804 1683
f: 852 2804 1673
w: www.dp-wt.com

Chan Hung-ngan
c: Lingyi Xiaozu
t: 852 9198 0301

Matthew Chan Kai-cheong
t: 604 434 8923

Owen Chan Kin-hing
t: 852 2388 5391
f 8522388 5399

Arick Chan Koon-wick
c: Arick Chan Design Ltd.
t: 852 2896 3337
f: 852 2896 7898
w: www.arickchan.com.hk

Paul Chan Kwok-keung
c: Pauldesign Workshop
t: 852 8102 1610
f: 852 8102 1630

Daniel Chan Kwong-yiu
c: HK Institute of Vocational Eduction (Shatin)
t: 852 2256 7415
f: 852 2436 9564

Rosanne Chan Lai-heung
c: C A Design
t: 852 2865 6787
f: 852 2866 3429
w: www.cadesign.com.hk

Irene Chan Lai-ngar
c: Avantec Manufacturing Ltd.
t: 852 2763 0203
f: 852 2389 4089
w: www.avantec.com.hk

Mayer Chan
t: 852 2979 5369
f: 852 2979 5148

Circula Chan Sau-lin
c: HK Institute of Vocational Eduction (Shatin)
t: 852 2256 7410
f: 852 2436 9564

Chan Sau-ming
c: Top Idea Design & Production Co.
t: 852 2504 1330 / 2834 7268
f: 852 2504 1311

Ringo Chan Shan-hung
c: Fine Art Interior Design Ltd.
t: 852 2602 8811
f: 852 2792 6867

Dennis Chan Shui-lun
c: Longford Industrial Ltd.
t: 852 2866 2298
f: 852 2861 0041
w: www.longford.com.hk

Paul Chan Sui-kam
c: Dot Come Associates Ltd.
t: 852 2543 2856
f: 852 3007 2284
w: dot-come.com.hk

Ringo Chan Sze-chung
c: Mango Global
t: 852 2432 0163
f: 852 2432 0501
w: www.mangoglobal.com

Michael Chan Sze-wah
c: Edge Architects Ltd.
t: 852 2887-0313
f: 852 2887-0451
w: www.edge-architects.com

Dick Chan Tin-lok
c: Masterwin Group Building
t: 852 2493 0831
f: 852 2492 1715/ 2413 2272

Frank Chan Wah-hung
c: Acorn Design Ltd.
t: 852 2591 0057
f: 852 2572 6920

Judy Chan Wai-lan
c: Edwin Eddie Tommy Advertising Ltd.
t: 852 2833 6902
f: 852 2573 2291
w: www.eet.com.hk

Raphael Chan Wing-yik
c: R.C Interior Design Ltd.
t: 852 2881 0143
f: 852 2894 8970

Ringo Chan Yee
c: Leo Burnett
t: 852 9326 8365
f: 852 2569 3656

Sherman Chan Yiu-tong
c: Hong Kong Chingying Institute of Visual Arts
t: 852 2591 4663
f: 852 2591 9062
w: www.chingying.edu.hk

Andrew Chan Yu-chung
c: Horizon Creative Ltd.
t: 852 2882 2229
f: 852 2882 6900
w: www.horizonHK.com

Neville Chan Yuen-hung
c: Since Communications
t: 852 2838 8106
f: 852 2838 7433
w: www.sinceonline.com

Gary Chang Chee-keung
Edge Design Institute Ltd.
t: 852 2802 6212
f: 852 2802 6213
w: www.edge.hk.com

Cansier Chantal
Marc & Chantal Design
t: 852 2543 7744
f: 852 2544 9170
w: www.marc-chantal.com

Chau So-hing
c: Ing Design Consultants
t: 852 2234 0700
f: 852 2234 0720
w: www.ingdesign.com.hk

Alvin Cheang Che-kong
c: Avenue
t: 852 9700 7268

Crystalle Cheang Peng
c: CC Plus Design Ltd.
t: 852 2523 9050
t: 852 2547 5307
w: www.ccplusdesign.com

Cheng Kar-wai
Monster Workshop
t: 852 2836 3368
f: 852 2573 1992
w: www.monsterworkshop.com

Vivian Cheng Wai-kwan
c: HK Institute of Vocational Education (Shatin)
t: 852 2338 3611 ext. 736
f: 852 24369564

Kirk Cheong Tak-wah
c: Megacom Advertising Ltd.
t: 86 10 6597 8768
f: 86 10 6597 8782

Victor Cheong Wai-hong
c: The Design Associates Ltd.
t: 852 2522 2626
f: 852 2973 0883
w: www.tda.com.hk

Bill Cheung
Astone Innovation Ltd.
t: 852 2305 9568
f: 852 2756 7568
w: www.innovation.astone.com.hk

Morrissey Cheung Chak-man
c: Motiv8
t: 852 2836 8928
f: 852 2893 0320

Paul Cheung Chi-hoi
c: Group Art Development Ltd.
t: 852 2893 1936
f: 852 2575 3197

Joe Cheung Cho-leung
c: Legend Design Ltd.
t: 852 2542 2399
f: 852 2542 2878

Clement Cheung
c: Seedz Ltd.
t: 852 9022 5553
w: www.chillichilly.net

David Cheung Jr.
c: May Cheong Toy Products Fty. Ltd.
t: 852 2341 6321
f: 852 2341 9872

Max Cheung Fuk-fan
c: Three Plus Two Design Ltd.
t: 852 2544 1700
f: 852 2542 4875

Eric Cheung Kai-wa
c: Brandsnation Ltd.
t: 852 2527 1303
f: 852 2527 1289
w: www.brandsnation.com

Eddie Cheung Kam-wah
c: Edwin, Eddie, Tommy Advertising Ltd.
t: 2833 6902
f: 852 2838 1280

Frankie Cheung Kin-hung
c: Trend Design Ltd.
t: 852 2518 8861
f: 852 2518 8801
w: www.trendgroup.com

Eddie Cheung Kwok-kuen
c: Miclowood Interiors Ltd.
t: 852 2369 0104
f: 852 2311 8598

Eddy Cheung Kwong-hung
c: EC Communications
t: 852 2575 1702
f: 852 2575 4519

Michael Cheung
c: Union Cult Ltd.
t: 852 2832 7897
f: 852 2590 8598

Po Cheung
c: Futurebrand
t: 852 2501 7993
f: 852 2544 0600
w: www.futurebrand.com

Shirley Cheung
c: HK Insitute Of Vacational Education (Kwun Tong)
t: 852 2727 9579
f: 852 2638 3336

Cheung Tad-ki
c: Arc Hong Kong
t: 852 9773 1110
f: 852 2865 7237

Esther Cheung Yat-man
c: Mast Industry Ltd.
t: 852 9648 6180
f: 852 2730 4491

Franco Chiu Ka-kit
c: Design Media Interiors (HK) Ltd.
t: 852 2121 8081
f: 852 2121 8082

Candy Choi Lai-wah
c: Hong Kong Science Museum
t: 852 2732 3286
f: 852 2311 2248

Sandy Choi
c: Sandy Choi Associates Ltd.
t: 852 2525-9577
f: 852 2525-9655
w: www.sandychoi.com

Steven Chong Pui-yik
t: 852 2784 4722

Adam Chow
t: 852 6358 2803
w: www.adamchow.com

Chow Chi-chung
c: Evision Ltd.
t: 852 2881 6222
f: 852 2573 1698

Wayne Choy Wing-wai
c: Con-Tech Contracting Co.
t: 852 2893 8728
f: 852 2832 7137

Lawrence Choy Wing-yiu
c: Lawrence Choy Design Ltd.
t: 852 3427 3273
f: 852 2806 8057

Dennis Chu Sung-yau
t: 852 9278 1962

Cecilia Chu Wai-sim
t: 852 9277 3047
f: 852 2982 4012

Chu Wing-hong
c: HK Institute of Vocational Education (Shatin)
t: 852 2256 7425
f: 852 2727 8396

John Chui Tak-ming
c: Mindconcept Design / Minddesign Co.
t: 852 6508 3062
f: 852 2104 3137
w: www.mddesign@macau.ctm.net

Stephen Chung Kui-shing
t: 853-524355

Simon Chung Tak-wah
c: Creative Station
t: 852 2591 5562
f: 852 2891 7723
w: www.creativestation.com.hk

Gordon Chung Wing-kan
c: Information Services Department, HKSAR
t: 852 2842 8873

Constant Diu Fu-kwong
c: I&D Project Consultant Ltd.
t: 852 2581 9200
f: 852 2309 2400
w: www.ideashan.com

Patrick Fong Chun-wah
c: Archistar Design Ltd.
t: 852 2851 4818
f: 852 2579 0014

Alex Fung
c: The Hong Kong Polytechnic University
t: 852 2766 5469
f: 852 2774 5067
w: www.sd.polyu.edu.hk

Dixon Fung Tak-sang
Zwei Advertising Co., Ltd.
t: 852 2851 8713
f: 852 2851 8610

Victor Fung
t: 852 9752 5860
f: 852 2570 5968

Raymond Fung Wing-kee
c: Architectural Services Department
t: 852 2867 3969
f: 852 2524 8194

Wynne Fung
c: Winbox Company Ltd.
t: 852 2421 5281
f: 852 2420 4009
w: www.kolorkombi.com

Percy Fung Tze-cheong
c: Film Magic Ltd.
t: 852 2570 9016
f: 852 2807 3619 / 2512 2430
w: www.filmmagic.com.hk

Wilson Heng Aik-soon
t: 852 95171244

Patrick Heung Hon-keung
c: E-Link Design & CommunicationsLtd.
t: 852 2187 3933
f: 852 2187 3939
w: www.elinkinter.net

Alex Heung Kin-fung
The Design Partners Ltd.
t: 852 2527 1778
f: 852 2527 2022

Bun Ho
t: 852 9191 0554
f: 852 2675 8150

Barrie Ho Chow-lai
c: Barrie Ho Architecture Interiors Ltd.
t: 852 2117 7662
f: 852 2117 7661
w: www.barrieho.com

Colan Ho Ka-chiu
c: Esperanto Design Workshop
t: 852 2327 4008
f: 852 2857 4011

Marco Ho Kan-hung
c: Plugin Design
t: 852 2786 0116
f: 852 2744 5283
w: www.plugin-design.com

Vincent Ho Nai-yiu
c: Whim Advertising Ltd.
t: 852 2566 8613
f: 852 2570 5825
w: www.whimad.com

Juana Ho Yuen-ping
c: Wellfine Contracting Co., Ltd.
t: 852 2528 3246
f: 852 2529 1701

Joey Ho
c: Point Architects Ltd.
t: 852 2850 8732
f: 852 2850 8972
w: www.pointarchitects.com.hk

William Ho Siu-chuen
Hippo Studio
t: 852 2529 6700
f: 852 2529 9269
w: www.hippostudio.com

Allen Hong Siu-fan
c: Next Media
t: 852 2990 8110
f: 852 2744 0190

Hui Check-Wing
c: New Universal Jewelry Co.
t: 852 2525 2878
f: 852 2526 7733

Eddie Hui Ha-lam
c: Semk Products Ltd.
t: 852 2469 9599
f: 852 2456 2578
w: www.semk.net

Patrick Hui Wang-yip
c: Designext
t: 852 2591 6304
f: 852 2591 1686
w: www.designext.com.hk

Kelvin Hung Chung-meng
c: Tink Visual Communication
t: 852 2887 9628
f: 852 2887 9801

Anthony Ip Kui-chi
t: 852 9316 7253
f: 852 2573 0174

Ip Pui-ling
c: Jockey Club Ti-I College
t: 852 2691 7150
f: 852 2632 7763

Ip Wai-shan
c: Ideas / Shan Project Consultants Ltd.
t: 852 2518 8861
f: 852 2518 8801
w: www.ideashan.com

Trevor Iu Che-wai
c: Aedas Lpt
t: 852 2861 1728
f: 852 2529 6419

Anna Kan Mung-lai
c: Digital Magic Ltd.
t: 852 2570 9016
f: 852 2807 3619/ 2512 2430
w: www.digitalmagic.com.hk

Grace Kao
c: HK Institute of Vocational Education (Shatin)
t: 852 2256 7404
f: 852 2436 9564

John Robert Kember
c: K Plus K (Hk) International Ltd.
t: 852 2541 6828
f: 852 2541 7885
w: www.kplusk.net

Paul Anthony Kember
c: K Plus K (HK) International Ltd.
t: 852 2541 6828
f: 852 2541 7885
w: www.kplusk.net

Keith Ko Chi-wai
c: Azu Concept Ltd.
t: 852 2782 0017
f: 852 2782 1055
w: www.azuoo.com

Ko Shiu-wai
c: Shiuwai Ko Design Ltd.
t: 852 2810 0949
f: 852 2536 9803
w: www.shiuwaiko.com

Ko Siu-hong
c: Kan And Lau Design Consultants
t: 852 2574 8399
f: 852 2834 8213
w: www.kosiuhong.com

Joseph Kong Tin-chi
c: HK Institute of Vocational Education (Kwun Tong)
t: 852 2727 9469
f: 852 2727 9575

Victor Kong Che-wing
c: Sealco Atelier
t: 852 2570 2574

Kenneth Kwan Chan-chi
c: Mi Design Ltd.
f: 852 2512 0702
f: 852 2807 1505
w: www.midesign.com.hk

Winnie Kwan Wai-kan
c: Hong Kong Museum Of Art
t: 852 2734 2109
f: 852 2723 7666/ 2312 2752
w: www.lcsd.gov.hk/hkma

Bon Kwan Shun-kong
c: The Graphis Co., Ltd.
t: 852 2522 0973
f: 852 2522 0872
w: www.thegraphis.com

Kevin Kwok Chuen-leung
c: Epoch Associates
t: 852 2630 2165
f: 852 8343 8655
w: www.epochassociates.com.hk

John Kwok Kwai-sum
c: Leo Burnett Ltd.
t: 852 2884 6248
f: 852 2967 1767

Iris Kwok Suk-ling
c: Tupos Design Company
t: 852 2390 4668
f: 852 2396 1102

Michael Kwong Chi-man
c: Locomotive Productions Ltd.
t: 852 3118 2550
f: 852 3118 2551
w: www.locoism.com.hk

Kenneth Kwong Wing-tong
Oaki Design Company
t: 852 2121 1497
f: 852 2104 2690
w: www.opusdesign.com.hk

Lai Ben-gold
c: LSDS
t: 852 2522 6188
f: 852 2522 6198

Gideon Lai Wai-kwan
c: Ameba Design Ltd.
t: 852 2389 6981
f: 852 2763 9800
w: www.amebadesign.com

Calvin Lai Wang-yeh
c: Great Art Multi-Media
t: 852 2384 9528
f: 852 2385 4528
w: www.ga-media.com

David Lai Yuk-shing
Edwin Eddie Tommy Advertising Ltd.
t: 852 2833 6902
f: 852 2838 1280
w: www.eet.com.hk

Vic Lam Chi-pui
t: 852 2517 7373
f: 852 2553 0089

Yanta Lam H T
c: Hong Kong Polytechnic University
t: 852 2766 5480
f: 852 2774 5067
w: www.sd.polyu.edu.hk

Raymond Lam Kin-choi
c: Born Design
t: 852 2511 9972
f: 852 2542 2087

Mike Lam
c: The Hongkong & Shanghai Banking Corporation Ltd.
t: 852 2822 4954
f: 852 2914 2523

Catherine Lam Siu-hung
c: Star Group Ltd.
t: 852 2621 9107
f: 852 2621 9120

Stephen Lam
c: Design Pacific
t: 852 2836 3836
f: 852 2905 1668

Paul Lam Tik-bong
c: Paul Lam Design Associates / C01 School Of Visual Arts
t: 852 2836 3368
f: 852 2573 1992

Lam Wai-hung
c: Codesign Ltd.
t: 852 2510 8710
f: 852 2510 8711

Lam Yan-yan
c: HK Vocational Training Council
t: 852 2256 7430
f: 852 2256 7477

Peter Lam Yuk-yung
t: 852 2838 3103

Brian Lau
c: Mad Studios
t: 852 2291 4177
w: www.mad-studios.com

Ivan Lau Chun-man
t: 852 2707 9244

Lau Hing-pong
c: Hong Kong Developer Marketing Consultants Ltd.
t: 852 8203 3559
f: 8528303 3533
w: www.developer-adv.com

Michael Lau Kin-man
t: 852 9418 0724
f: 852 2571 2965

Grace Lau Kwan-bick
c: City Univeristy of Hong Kong
t: 852 2788 9681
f: 852 2788 9716

Lau Kwok-tim
c: Tim Photography Ltd.
t: 852 2866 0995
f: 852 2866 1954

Lau Man-chuen
c: Decomas
t: 852 2536 9258
f: 852 2522 6794

Lisa Lau Man-man
c: G.A.L Graphics & Consultants Ltd.
t: 852 2802 2798
f: 852 2824 9009
w: www.galgraphics.com

Benny Lau Siu-tsang
c: Creative Cafe
t: 852 2865 4240
f: 852 2865 2925
w: www.creativecafe.com.hk

Andrew Law
c: Salotto Ltd.
t: 852 2898-9777
f: 852 2898-9169
w: www.salotto.com.hk

Kelvin Law Kin-wai
c: Idesign International Ltd.
t: 852 2881 6608
f: 852 2881 6658
w: www.idesign1gn.com

Wing Law Wing-keung
c: La Cave
t: 852 6196 3193
f: 852 2570 6307
w: www.wing-lacave.com

Lee Chi-wing
c: Milk Design
t: 852 2797 8500
f: 852 2797 3335
w: www.milkdesign.com.hk

Savio Lee Hok-kai
c: Show Art Advertising & Decoration Co., Ltd.
t: 852 2889 3912
f: 852 2889 4432

Alex Lee Kin-ming
c: Alex Design
t: 852 2311 3856
f: 852 2311 3859

Lester Lee
c: Lester Lee Photoworkshop
t: 852 2881 0336
f: 852 2833 5087
w: www.lesterlee.com

Lee Sai-man
Infovision Design
t: 852 2887 2681
f: 852 2806 0322
w: www.ivdesigns.com

Stella Lee Suk-yee
R.C Interior Design Ltd.
t: 852 2526 3123
f: 852 2850 7072

Lee Tak-wai
c: HK Institute of Vocational Education (Tsing Yi)
t: 852 2436 8714
f: 852 2434 5695

Tommy Lee Tat-hong
c: Edwin Eddie Tommy Advertising Ltd.
t: 852 2833 6902
f: 852 2838 1280

Psyche Lee Tsing-wai
c: Egg Production Ltd. /Pm Kneativ
t: 852 2369 3633
f: 852 2205 1633
e: info@egg-group.com
w: www.egg-group.com

Alpha Lee Wai-keung
c: The Hong Kong Polytechnic University
t: 852 2766 4707
w: www.micn.polyu.edu.hk/~mcalpha

Patre Lee Wing-tak
c: Canal Design Centre International Ltd.
t: 852 2836 3323
f: 852 2836 3873

Denis Lee Yiu-chung
c: Media Explorer Ltd.
t: 852 2541 9978
f: 852 2541 0940
w: www.me.com.hk

Francis Lee York-wah
c: Francis Lee & Associates Ltd.
t: 852 2527 3088
f: 852 2527 3077
w: www.francislee.com

Leong Ding
c: Hong Kong Polytechnic University
t: 852 2766 5458
f: 852 2774 5067

Raymond Leung Cheuk-kwun
c: Greatart Multi-Media Company
t: 852 2384 9528
f: 852 2385 4528
w: www.ga-media.com

Leung Chi-sum
c: Pingkee Construction (HK) Co., Ltd.
t: 852 2605 1337
f: 852 2604 2989

Cetric Leung Chiu
c: Cetric Leung Design Company
t: 852 2520-0311
f: 852 2572-0310

Joseph Leung Chun-wai
c: Nex Branding Design
t: 852 2861 3809
f: 852 2865 0485
w: www.nexbd.com

Bosco Leung Fu
t: 852 8100 2850
w: www.conair.com

Man Leung Ho-man
c: Orient Overseas Containerline Ltd.
t: 852 2833 3308
f: 852 2531 8232
w: www.oocl.com

Setmund Leung Kam-biu
c: Setmund Leung Design & Planner
t: 852 9013 1868

Beam Leung Pak-yuen
c: HK Institute of Vocational Education (Shatin)
t: 852 2256 7408
f: 852 2623 0863 / 2436 9564

James Leung Wai-mo
c: Genemix Group
t: 852 2504 1620
f: 852 2572 1210
w: www.genemix.com

Ann Leung Yan-yan
c: The Hong Kong Polytechnic University
t: 852 2766 6286
f: 852 2333 8812
w: www.anstudio.com

Denzel Leung Yik-shan
c: Charmtop Consultants Ltd.
t: 852 2973 1800
f: 852 2850 7770

Ivan Leung Ip-tin
c: Bliss Partners Ltd.
t: 852 2520 6787
f: 852 2528 6182

Anna Li Chung-sum
t: 852 9688 6072

Alex Li Hong-shong
c: Moi Ltd.
t: 852 2816 2911
f: 852 2816 2910
w: www.moiltd.hk

Li Kai-Yip
c: Raymon De Sign
t: 852 6028 8983
f: 852 2968 1771

Ken Li Kam-fai
c: Designation Advertising Ltd.
t: 852 2598 8911
f: 852 2598 8920
w: www.designation.com.hk

David Li Kam-kuen
c: Hang Seng Real Estate
t: 852 2198-4185
f: 852 2877-0627
w: www.hengseng.com

Li Kin-nang
c: Li Design Associates Ltd.
t: 852 2893 2851
f: 852 2572 1846

Tim Li Man-Wai
t: 852 9250 3714

Li Min-wah
c: Zanif Advertising & Promotion Ltd.
t: 852 2402 1289
f: 852 2402 1288
w: www.zanif.com

Tommy Li Wing-chuen
c: Tommy Li Design Workshop Ltd.
t: 852 2834 6312
f: 852 2834 7032
w: www.tommylidesign.com

Li Yu-kwan
t: 852 9185 5419

Liang Zhi-ming
c: Liang Zhi Ming Interior Design Consultants Co.
t: 852 2464 9558
f: 852 2782-8188

William Lim
c: CL3 Architects Ltd.
t: 852 2527 1931
f: 852 2529 8392
w: www.cl3.com

Gloria Lin Sui-fong
Gloria & Associates
t: 852 9104 5816
f: 852 2551 1859

Esther Liu Kit-lin
c: Hong Kong Polytechnic University
t: 852 2766 5466
f: 852 2774 5067

David Lo Wing-keung
c: Whizzbangart Hong Kong Ltd.
t: 852 2510 6856
f: 852 2482 9213/ 2887 5186
w: www.wbahk.com

Jo Lo Yu-hin
c: Zeroart Studio
t: 852 2609 4060
f: 852 2609 4050
w: www.zeroartstudio.com

Alice Lo Choi Yuet-ngor
c: The Hong Kong Polytechnic Unversity
t: 852 2766 5465
f: 852 2774 5067

Bennie Lui Chi-leung
c: Reborn Image Consultants
t: 852 9808 6322
f: 852 2778 2440 / 3005 7233
w: www.bennielui.com

Kent Lui Man-chung
c: Tactics Kent Lui Ltd.
t: 852 9193 7170
t: 852 2591 6228

Henry Lui Po-man
Rainfield Design Ltd.
t: 852 2895 5898
f: 852 2577 5171

Joseph Lui Siu-yin
Signature Ltd.
t: 852 2191 2113
f: 852 2191 2110
w: www.signature-design.net

Frankie Lui Tat-man
c: Hok International
 (Asia/Pacific) Ltd.
t: 852 2534 0022
f: 852 2534 0099

Ma Chin-lee
c: Hippo Studio
t: 852 2529 6700
f: 852 2529 9269
w: www.hippostudio.com

Joseph Ma Chung-lee
c: Cymo International
t: 852 2317 1889
f: 852 2317 1188
w: www.cymo.com.hk

Kingsley Ma
c: The Chinese University of Press
t: 852 2609 6467
f: 852 2603 7355
w: www.chineseupress.com

Gerry Ma Kwai-yung
c: Colart Hong Kong Ltd.
t: 852 2872 6039
f: 852 2872 6029

Prudence Mak Ngar-tuen
c: Chocolate Rain
 Jewelry And Design
t: 852 2368 2407
w: www.chocolaterain.com

Wayne Man Wai-kin
c: Design Factory
f: 852 2693 6030
f: 852 2605 2235
w: www.designfactory.com.hk

Stephen Mao Kuan
c: I Group Ltd.
t: 852 2527 1028
f: 852 2527 8731
w: www.igroup.com.hk

Brulhart Marc
c: Marc & Chantal Design
t: 852 2543 7744
f: 852 2544 9170
w: www.marc-chantal.com

Cansier Marc
c: Marc & Chantal Design
t: 852 2543 7744
f: 852 2544 9170
w: www.marc-chantal.com

Christopher Mok Wai-keung
c: Spectrum Design &
 Associates (Asia)
t: 852 2646 3515
f: 852 2529 5560

Mok Wing-hung
t: 852 2142 4507
e: hung@deepworkshop.com

Leila Nachtigall
c: Tong / Mcknew & Nachtigall Ltd.
t: 852 2869 6966
f: 852 2869 6881

Hans Emil Neufeld
c: Ripples Total Communication
t: 852 2987 5718
f: 852 2987 5734
w: www.q2asolutions.com

Charles Ng
c: Maxi Communications Ltd.
t: 852 2824 9328
f: 852 2824 9826
w: www.maxicomm.com.hk

Frankie Ng
c: Hong Kong Polytechnic University
t: 852 2766 6462
f: 852 2773 1432
w: www.itc.polyu.edu.hk/staff/fng.htm

Bunny Ng Ka-wah
c: Bcs & Associates Ltd.
t: 852 2836 6118
f: 852 2836 6119
w: bcs.com.hk

Albert Ng Pun-tak
c: Organix Concept Ltd.
t: 852 2580 3677
f: 852 2580 1433
w: www.organix.com.hk

Keith Ng Shu-kei
c: Art Brochure International
 Enterprise
t: 852 2136 0287
f: 852 2136 0289
w: www.artbrochure.com

Mandy Ng Shun-chun
c: Iso-Production Ltd.
t: 852 2377 4842
f: 852 2377 4862
w: www.isoprodn.com

Ricky Ng Yuk-kwan
c: Norm Design & Associates
t: 852 9225 0247/ 9789 0015
f: 852 2640 3508

Alain Ng Yuk-lun
c: Tong / Mcknew Nachtigall Ltd.
t: 852 2281 7317

Kenneth Ngan Hou-nin
c: INT Ltd.
f: 852 2781 5561
f: 852 2385 2225

Norman de Brackinghe
t: 852 2813 1567
f: 852 2813 7092

Nurjannah Omer
c: Talent Team International Ltd.
t: 852 2890 5404
f: 852 3402 8944

David Robert Osborne
c: Graphia International Ltd.
t: 852 2511 1318
f: 852 2519 6955
w: www.graphiabrands.com

Horace Pan Hung-bing
c: Panorama International Ltd.
t: 852 2317 7850
f: 852 2317 7851

Grace Pan Nyun-ling
c: The Hong Kong Polytechnic
 University
t: 852 2766 4416

Winnif Pang Chi-kon
c: Zanif Advertising & Promotion Ltd.
f: 852 2402 1289
f: 852 2402 1288
w: www.zanif.com

Pal Pang
c: Another
t: 852 3156-1290
f: 852 3156-1291
w: www.another-design.com

Raymond Pang Tat-yin
t: 852 2256 7436
f: 852 2618 0694

Alexis Pepall
c: Pepall Design
t: 852 2425 6820
f: 852 2425 8510
w: www.pepall.com

Rose Poon Yuen-wah
c: Francis Lee & Assocaites Ltd.
t: 852 2527 3088
f: 852 2527 3077
w: www.francislee.com

Marc Aurel Schnabel
c: Department Of Architecture,
 The University of Hong Kong
t: 852 2241 5155
f: 852 2559 6484
w: www.arch.hku.hk/~marcaurel

Ana Shu
c: Expressions
t: 852 2517 8775
f: 852 2517 7222

Selina Shum Ching-wan
c: Secrets International Ltd.
t: 852 9233 2950

Walter Sin Wai-keung
c: Chinese University of
 Hong Kong
t: 852 2609 6546
w: www.watersin.com

Siu King-chung
c: Hong Kong Polytechnic University
t: 852 2766 5449
f: 852 2774 5067

Michael Siu Kin-wai
c: Hong Kong Polytechnic University
t: 852 2766 5455
f: 852 2774 5067

Norman Siu Wai-chung
c: Designopolis 21 Ltd.
t: 852 9306-8832

Victor Siu Yung-hung
c: VS Design
t: 852 2712 3392
f: 852 2768 9936

Donny So Ka-wai
c: Radica Games Ltd.
t: 852 2693 2238

Stephen So Kwan-ho
c: Yolkdesign Co., Ltd.
f: 852 2851 0150
f: 852 2850 4506
w: www.yolkdesign.com

So Man-yee
c: HS Art & Design
t: 852 2572 2275
f: 852 2572 9617
w: www.hsdesign.hk

Sun Terry
c: Positive Concepts Ltd.
t: 852 2368 2407
w: www.postiveconcepts.com.hk

Joseph Q. Sy
c: Joseph Sy & Associates
t: 852 2866 1333
f: 852 2866 1222
w: www.jsahk.com

Ida Sze
c: Architectural Services Department
t: 852 2867 3879
f: 852 2524 8194

Kelly Sze K.L.
c: Edeas Ltd.
t: 852 2882 4512
f: 852 2882 3943
w: www.edeas.hk

Elson Szeto Sing-ying
c: Hong Kong Institute of Education
t: 852 2948 7011
f: 852 2948 7046

Eric Tai Ka-man
c: Royal Cross Ltd.
t: 852 3151 7184
f: 852 2572 9538
w: www.royalcross.com.hk

Kelvin Tam Ka-fung
c: HKive (Shatin)
t: 852 2256 7412
f: 852 2436 9564

Gary Tam Ka-kwan
c: Teamwork Design Ltd.
t: 852 2897 4685
f: 852 2557 4742
w: www.teamworkdesign.com.hk

Patrick Tam Kwok-kee
c: Sirocco Design Consultants
t: 852 2815 3334
f: 852 2815 3304
w: www.sirocco-hk.com

Philips Tang Chi-ho
c: Ptang Studio Ltd.
t: 852 2669 1577
f: 852 2669 3577
w: www.ptangstudio.com

Lilian Tang Chiu-ying
c: Lilian Tang Design Ltd.
t: 852 2525 9515
f: 852 2525 7226

Eric Tang Chung-fat
c: Autosound
t: 852 2946 7012
f: 852 2345 8572
w: www.autosoundhk.com

Eric Tang Heung-sang
c: Elite Design Consultants Ltd.
t: 852 2369 9938
f: 852 2369 9819

Brian Tang Ming-fai
c: The Merz Design & Associates Ltd.
t: 852 2246 8281
f: 852 2246 8120
w: www.merz-design.com

Simon Tang Wai-hung
c: HK Institute of Vocational Education (Shatin)
t: 852 2256 7440
f: 852 2256 7477

Colin Tillyer
c: Graphicat Ltd.
t: 852 2838 8608
f: 852 2838 5285
w: www.graphicat.com

Kenneth To Po-keung
c: Token Workshop
t: 852 2833 6556
f: 852 2833 5956
w: www.tokenworkshop.com

Richard Tong Sing-lin
c: Life Is Good Ltd.
t: 852 2892 0083
f: 852 2892 0023
w: www.lifeisgood.com.hk

Andy Tong Siu-wing
c: Andy Tong Creations Company Ltd.
t: 852 2811 2881
f: 852 2881 1586
w: www.andycreations.com

Annie Tong Wung-wah
c: Watermark Associates Designers And Consultants Ltd.
t: 852 2892 0818
f: 852 2891 7027

Gabriel Tong Yui-lung
c: Totex International Ltd./ Totex Design Ltd.
t: 852 2309 2880
f: 852 2309 2680
w: www.totexdesign.com

Gabriel Tsang Hok-shing
c: Tupos Design Company
t: 852 2390 4668
f: 852 2396 1102
w: www.tupos.com

Tsang Kwong-ho
c: JTG Design Consultant Ltd.
t: 852 2559 9813
f: 852 2512 0389

Zita Tsang Man-sze
c: Cousin Ltd.
t: 852 3171 3028

Agatha Tsang Pui-lam
c: Bon Bone Design
t: 852 2508 0854
f: 852 2508 0864
w: www.bonbonedesign.com

Derek Tsang Yu-fung
c: The Merz Innovation Ltd.
t: 852 2559 1015
f: 852 2428 3599
w: www.tmi-designex.com

Chapman Tse
c: Yellow Atelier
t: 852 9834 2104
f: 852 2572 4998
w: www.yellowatelier.com

Andrew Tse Chung-shun
c: Kin Hung Watches Ltd.
t: 852 2489 9273
f: 852 2487 0209

Tse Wing-yee
c: Shelli & Company Ltd.
t: 852 2869 5628
f: 852 2526 9828
w: www.shelli.com.hk

Nancy Tsui
c: Derek Tsui Interior Design Ltd.
t: 852 2806 3962
f: 852 2887 6054

Christine Tsui Yee-man
t: 852 9831 1239

Victor Tung Lung-sang
c: Correctional Services Department
t: 852 2582 4086
f: 852 2802 4762

Wai Hon-wah
c: The Hong Kong Polytechnic University
t: 852 2766 4293
f: 852 3149 8148

Petet Wai
c: Ozure Design Ltd.
t: 852 2123 1400
f: 852 2104 2696
w: www.ozure.com

Bruce Wan Chi-kwong
t: 852 9529 6489
w: www.refink.net

David Waterman
c: Deep Blue Design Consultants
t: 852 3124 4214
f: 852 3124 4214
w: www.david-waterman.com

Wingate Geoffrey
t: 852 6185 0669

Florence Wong Cheuk-la
c: Zanif Advertising & Promotion Ltd.
t: 852 2402 1289
f: 852 2402 1288
w: www.zanif.com

Schwinger Wong Chi-kit
t: 852 2636 6323
f: 852 2636 0323
w: www.jccpahk.com

Joe Wong Chun-wai
c: Redwood Design & Production Co.
t: 852 2751 8830
f: 852 2631 2626
w: www.redwooddesign.com.hk

Johnney Wong Chun-wing
c: Creator Design & Production
t: 852 2332 0462 / 2332 0501
f: 2332 0466
w: www.creatordesign.net

Elaine Wong
c: Living Art Design
t: 852 2321 2992
f: 852 2321 2881

Wong Hoi-to
c: The Showcase Ltd.
t: 852 2598 6028
f: 852 2598 4009 / 2824 4699
w:www.showcasehk.com

Wong Ka-man
c: Vision Plus Co., Ltd.
t: 852 3110 1811
f: 852 3110 1800
w:www.visionplus.com.hk

Kacey Wong Kwok-choi
c: Object Factory
t: 852 9128 2270
f: 852 2808 2495
w:www.kaceywong.com

Wong Mei-fung
c: C & L Interior Design Co., Ltd.
t: 852 3107 1811
f: 852 3005 4604

Angus Wong On
c: Angus Wong Design Ltd.
t: 852 2836 3328
f: 852 2904 7947
w:www.angusdesign.com.hk

Stanley Wong Se-tang
c: Standesign
t: 852 2524 0302
f: 852 2524 0363
w:www.standesign.com

Yale Wong Siu-cheong
c: Designext
t: 852 2591 6304
f: 852 2591 1686
w:www.designext.com

Phoebe Wong Siu-yin
t: 852 6150 7885

Stanley Wong
c: Threetwoone Film Production Ltd.
t: 852 2887 1321
f: 852 2503 1321

Vincent Wong
c: Creative Premium Development Co., Ltd.
t: 852 2845 6393
f: 852 2845 2426
w:www.cpco.com

Benjamin Wong Wai-bun
c: Theo Texture
t: 852 2520 0720
f: 852 2520 0760

Deny Wong Wai-chung
c: Wiseman International Digitech Ltd.
t: 852 2797 2197
f: 852 2793 3357
w:www.wisemanhk.com

Stephen Wong Wai-kwong
t: 852 9782 0254
f: 852 2623 2694

Raymond Wong Wai-man
c: Hong Kong Christian Service Kwun Tong Vocational Training Centre
t: 852 2389 1238
f: 852 2346 7976

Wong Yuen-sun
c: Sunaqua Concepts Ltd.
t: 852 2833 5502
f: 852 3012 1760
w:www.sunaquahk.com

Dennis Wong Yuk-pui
c: Oval Design Ltd.
t: 852 2802 2033
f: 852 2511 2917
w:www.oval-design.com

May Wong May-yu
c: Gear Atelier Ltd.
t: 852 2845 7321
f: 852 2845 7334
w:www.livinggear.com

Yan Wood-choi
c: HK Institute of Vocational Education (Tsing Yi)
t: 852 2436 8714
f: 852 2434 5695

Raymond Yau Wai-man
c: HK Chingying Institute of Visual Arts
t: 852 2591 4663
f: 852 2591 9062
w:www.chingying.edu.hk

Ronald Yeung Wai-kai
RC Communications Ltd.
t: 852 3105 1787
f: 852 3105 9547
w:www.rc.com.hk

Joseph Yim Wai-man
c: Hong Kong Polytechnic University
t: 852 2766 4171

Andrew Yip Chiu-wing
c: Phace International Hong Kong
t: 852 2804 1328
f: 852 2866 7235

Alan Yip Chi-wing
c: Yip Design Ltd.
t: 852 2420 3288
f: 852 2420 2388
w:www.yipdesign.com

Bosco Yip Po-hoi
c: Hang Seng Bank Ltd.
t: 852 2198 4076
f: 852 2536 9793
w:www.hangseng.com

Yip Tin-sung
c: Postbox.Com Ltd.
t: 852 9400 1087
f: 852 2895 0695

Miranda Yiu Yuk-yee
c: A Maze Workshop
t: 852 2529 5343
f: 852 2979 5343
w:www.a-maze.com.hk

Eddy Yu Chi-Kong
c: Codesign
t: 852 2510 8710
f: 852 2510 8711

Edward Hardy Yu
c: Edward Hardy & Design Consultant
t: 852 8108 7507
f: 852 2388 5669

Joey Yu Kwong-cheung
c: Dog Dog Farm Ltd.
t: 852 9866 7317
f: 852 2602 6009
w:www.dogdogfarm.com

Michael Miller Yu
c: Creation House
t: 852 2572 9232
f: 852 2838 1375
w:creation house.com.hk

Alan, Yu Tat-ming
c: The Hong Kong Polytechnic University
t: 852 2766 4266
f: 852 2774 5067
w:www.tatmingphoto.com

Ted Yu
c: Conrad Design Ltd.
t: 852 9386 0087
f: 852 2801 7171
w:www.conradesign.com

Neville Yu Yuen-wah
c: Hong Kong Polytechnic University
t: 852 2766 6268
f: 852 2333 8812
w:www.polyu.edu.hk/mrs

Simon Yung Chee-mun
c: Channel 1 Workshop
t: 852 2521 5667
f: 852 2525 4593

Arthur Yung Ho-wai
c: Seedz Ltd.
t: 852 6200 8036
w:www.chillichilly.net

Jason Yung Kei-yau
c: Jason Caroline Design Ltd.
t: 852 2517 7510
f: 852 2893 4061
jason_kyy@hotmail.com

Clement Yick Tat-wa
c: Circle Design
t: 852 2891 8007
f: 852 2891 2007
w:www.circledesign.com.hk

Schupp Andreas
c: Philips Design
t: 852 2489 4428
f: 852 2480 5345

Paper Support:

Tai Tak Takeo Fine Paper Co., Ltd.
White Cover - Takeo Pulper White 198gsm PUL-170-1
Black Cover - Takeo Hammar Tone Black 198gsm HMT-170-4
White Box Paper - Mohawk Vellum Cool White 148gsm, MV-91-1

Luen Hing Paper Ltd.
Text (White Cover) - Cream Laid 100gsm 83-1012
Text (Black Cover) - Grey Laid 100gsm 83-1013

大德竹尾花紙有限公司
Tai Tak Takeo Fine Paper Co., Ltd.

Printing Support:

Vision and Mission Co. Ltd.

ARTECH GRAPHICS LTD.

Special Thanks:

Kelly Sze, Eddy Yu, Hung Lam, Sandy Choi, Stephanie Au, Michael Lau,
Antalis (Hong Kong) Ltd., Tai Tak Takeo Fine Paper Co., Ltd., David Lo,
Alex Yu, Kevin Tsang, Karen Tam/Harbour City, Young Kim,
Josephine Mun-Ying Kong, Jovy Tong, John Wu